What They <u>Didn't</u> Teach You About the Wild West

Other books by Mike Wright

What They <u>Didn't</u> Teach You About the Civil War

What They <u>Didn't</u> Teach You About World War II

What They <u>Didn't</u> Teach You About the American Revolution

What They <u>Didn't</u> Teach You About the Wild West

Mike Wright

PRESIDIO

Published by Presidio Press, Inc.
505 B San Marin Drive, Suite 160
Novato, CA 94945-1340

Library of Congress Cataloging-in-Publication Data

Wright, Mike, 1938–
    What they didn't teach you about the wild West / Mike Wright.
      p. cm.
    Includes bibliographical references (p. 353) and index.
    ISBN 0-89141-690-0
      1. West (U.S.)—History. 2. Frontier and pioneer life—West
(U.S.) 3. Overland journeys to the Pacific. I. Title.
F591 .W878 2000
978—dc21
                                        00-039142

Printed in the United States of America

To my brother, Richard Wright. We whooped and hollered through many Saturday-morning cowboy movies at the old Virginia Theater.

And always to my wife, Lin Drury, who understands my love of cowboy movies and my love of her.

"Only to the white man was nature a "wilderness" and only to him was the land "infested" with "wild" animals and "savage" people. To us it was tame. Earth was bountiful and we were surrounded with the blessings of the Great Mystery. Not until the hairy man from the east came and with brutal frenzy heaped injustices upon us and the families that we loved was it "wild" for us. When the very animals of the forest began fleeing from his approach, then it was that for us the "Wild West" began."

—Luther Standing Bear,
Chief of the Oglala Tribe of the Sioux Nation
Land of the Spotted Eagle, 1933

"Eastward I go only by force; but westward I go freely."
—Henry David Thoreau, *Walking*, 1862

Contents

Chronology

1000: Leif Eriksson sights Newfoundland.

1492: Christopher Columbus's first voyage to the New World. On November 11 he records natives' use of tobacco, the first recorded mention of the plant.

1541: Jacques Cartier conquers the native kingdom of Saguenay near Canada's St. Lawrence River.

1565: St. Augustine, Florida, founded by Spanish.

1587: Roanoke, North Carolina, founded by English.

1607: Jamestown, Virginia, founded by English.

1610: Santa Fe, New Mexico, founded by Spanish.

1619: Berkeley Plantation, Virginia: First Thanksgiving celebrated.

Jamestown, Virginia: First Africans brought to English America.

Jamestown, Virginia: First legislative body convenes in America (General Assembly).

1620: Plymouth, Massachusetts: *Mayflower* lands.

1622: Henrico, Virginia: First English college in America chartered.

1700: Population of English colonies in America at 250,000.

1754–1763: French and Indian (Seven Years') War.

1763: Proclamation of 1763 forbids English settlement west of Allegheny Mountains.

1775–1783: American Revolution.

1775: Daniel Boone cuts Wilderness Road to the mouth of the Kentucky River.

Battles of Lexington, Concord, and Bunker Hill in American Revolution.

1776: Declaration of Independence written.

Spanish establish mission San Francisco de Asís, known as Yerba Buena.

George Rogers Clark petitions Virginia to annex Kentucky as a county.

1777: Land west of Connecticut River declared independent of New York as New Connecticut, then renames itself Vermont.

In Treaty of DeWitts Corner, Cherokee Indians give up all South Carolina territory.

Treaty of Long Island: Overhill Cherokee Indians cede all western North Carolina east of the Blue Ridge Mountains and the Nolichucky River.

San Jose settled as first nonreligious community in California.

1778: Articles of Confederation written. It will be a year before some colonies endorse the document.

George Rogers Clark captures British garrisons at Kaskaskia, Illinois, and Vincennes, Indiana.

Shawnee Indians attempt unsuccessful siege of Boonesborough, Kentucky.

1779: Fort Nashborough founded on the Cumberland River, later renamed Nashville.

1780: Pennsylvania mandates gradual abolition of slavery within the state.

Benedict Arnold defects to Britain.

Congress urges states to cede their western territories to the Union.

1781: Rebellious slaves in Williamsburg, Virginia, set fire to capitol and several other buildings.

Washington defeats British at Battle of Yorktown, Virginia.

1782: Indian and Loyalist forces defeat a group of frontiersmen at Blue Licks, near present-day Lexington, Kentucky—then in Virginia's Fayette County.

1783: Treaty of Paris between the United States and Britain ends Revolutionary War.

The Society of the Cincinnati founded, the fraternal and hereditary order of Continental Army officers, with George Washington as its first president.

Massachusetts abolishes slavery in the commonwealth.

1784: The Tennessee Company organized by State of Georgia to grant lands to settlers in the Tennessee Valley region.

Virginia and North Carolina cede western lands to the United States.

Chronology

Congress narrowly defeats Thomas Jefferson's plan to ban slavery in the United States after 1800.

Spain closes the lower Mississippi River to American navigation.

Russia establishes permanent settlement on Kodiak Island at Three Saints Bay.

1785: Chippewa, Delaware, Ottawa, and Wyandotte Indians cede nearly all their land in present-day state of Ohio.

1787: U.S. Constitution written. It is ratified one year later.

1789: George Washington elected president.

1793: Eli Whitney invents the cotton gin.

1794: Whiskey Rebellion follows enactment of stiff excise tax on whiskey; President Washington declares the action of those protesting the tax to "amount to treason" and defeats opposition with thirteen-thousand-man militia army.

1803: President Jefferson concludes the Louisiana Purchase for fifteen million dollars, doubling the size of the United States.

1803–1806: Lewis and Clark Expedition to Louisiana Territory.

1806: Lieutenant Zebulon M. Pike discovers eighteen-thousand-foot peak in the Rocky Mountains of Colorado.

1809–1811: Shawnee chief Tecumseh campaigns to unite Native American nations west of the Mississippi River; defeated at the Battle of Tippecanoe, Indiana, by Gen. William Henry Harrison.

1811: National Road begun from Cumberland, Maryland, to Wheeling, West Virginia.

1812–1815: War of 1812.

1814: British burn Washington, D.C.

1816: The year without a summer, due to earlier volcanic eruption in Pacific Ocean.

1817–1818: General Andrew Jackson brutally removes Seminole Indians from Florida Territory.

1817–1819: Construction of Erie Canal.

1819: United States acquires Spanish Florida for five million dollars after General Jackson conquers Spanish settlements in the territory.

1820: Missouri Compromise.

1821: Santa Fe Trail opened.

1831: Virginia: Nat Turner slave rebellion.

1832: Congress declares all land west of the Mississippi River as Indian country.

1835: Samuel Colt of Hartford, Connecticut, patents pistol with revolving chambers.

Texas declares its independence from Mexico.

Battle of the Alamo.

1836: American Home Mission Society sends group of settlers to Oregon to convert Native Americans to Christianity.

Oceola and other Seminole Indians imprisoned after arriving in St. Augustine, Florida, under white flag.

1837: Panic of 1837.

1838: Trail of Tears, as more than eighteen thousand Cherokees are driven west of the Mississippi from their homelands in Georgia.

1842: Oregon Trail begun, two thousand miles from Independence, Missouri, to Pacific Northwest.

1844: Samuel F. B. Morse invents the telegraph.

1845: Editor John L. O'Sullivan formulates the idea of "Manifest Destiny."

United States annexes Texas.

1846–1848: United States declares war on Mexico; formal surrender includes land in Texas and California.

1846: Americans declare California an independent republic.

Mormon leaders Joseph and Hyrum Smith are murdered in Missouri. Under Brigham Young, Mormons begin trek from Nauvoo, Illinois to Salt Lake City, Utah.

Massachusetts General Hospital in Boston become the site of the first surgical operation in which ether is used to anesthetize a patient.

1848: Paris Commune.

Seneca Falls, New York, convention launches woman suffrage movement.

Gold discovered at Sutter's Mill, California.

1850: The United States of America now includes four states west of the Mississippi River: Arkansas, California, Iowa, and Texas. By the end of the century there will be seventeen.

1860–1861: Pony Express delivers mail from St. Joseph, Missouri, to Sacramento, California.

1860: Abraham Lincoln elected U.S. President.

1861–1865: Civil War between the North and the South.

1862: Homestead Act passed, offering 160-acre parcels of land for five years of improvement.

1865: Lincoln assassinated.

1866: Retaliating against the U.S. Army's trespass onto native lands, Chief Red Cloud ambushes and kills eighty soldiers near Fort Phil Kearny: the Fetterman Massacre.

1867: Great cattle drives begin from Texas to Abilene, a sleepy Kansas town bought by entrepreneur Joe McCoy.

1868: Red Cloud agrees to peace in exchange for U.S. Army's abandonment of forts along the Bozeman Trail in Wyoming.

Colonel George Armstrong Custer and his 7th Cavalry wipe out an entire Cheyenne village in what comes to be misnamed the Battle of the Washita.

1869: Union Pacific and Central Pacific Railroads meet, opening transcontinental travel.

1873: P. T. Barnum opens the New York Hippodrome, home of the "Greatest Show on Earth."

1876: Battle of the Little Big Horn, Montana.

Centennial exhibition held at Philadelphia.

James Butler "Wild Bill" Hickok shot in the head and killed during a poker game in Deadwood, South Dakota.

1877: After a thousand-mile flight to Canada and back, Chief Joseph of the Nez Percé surrenders, saying, "I will fight no more forever."

1881: Chief Sitting Bull surrenders to the U.S. Army.

Wyatt, Virgil, and Morgan Earp and Doc Holliday beat the Clanton family in the gunfight at the O.K. Corral.

Pat Garrett kills Billy the Kid near Fort Sumner, New Mexico.

1882: Bob Ford kills his cousin, Jesse James, and claims ten-thousand-dollar reward.

Buffalo Bill Cody begins the Wild West Show.

1886: Apache warrior Geronimo surrenders to U.S. Army general Nelson A. Miles.

Charleston, South Carolina, earthquake kills more than one hundred.

1888: Mary Ann Nichols murdered in London, the first victim of Jack the Ripper.

1889–1890: Ghost Dance sweeps northern Indian tribes, with dancers believing it will restore the earth to the days prior to the white man's coming.

1889: Moulin Rouge nightclub opens in Paris.

1890: Sitting Bull killed by Indian policemen.

Chief Big Foot tries to move 350 of his followers to Pine Ridge, South Dakota; at Wounded Knee Creek 500 members of the U.S. 7th Cavalry surround the band and, using Hotchkiss rapid-fire cannons, kill more than 200 Indians, including Big Foot; using clubs, the Indians kill 29 troopers. In 1927 poet Stephen Vincent Benét remembers the massacre in *American Names*—"Bury my heart at Wounded Knee"—and it's later the twentieth-century site of an Indian versus U.S. confrontation.

1892: Historian Frederick Jackson Turner declares that, after four hundred years, the American West is finally closed.

Introduction

West is both a location and a state of mind, and I often use this word to express both. There is no one Indian nation. Some historians have tried to count the number, and some may have been correct in listing the various tribes. Three hundred? Five hundred? And that's just in North America. Certainly, there is no single "Indian language." Native Americans are many people with many languages, most as different as, say, Spaniards from Scots. Or, the Scots from the Irish; now, there are two peoples who frequently don't get along but should.

As with others in this *What They Didn't Teach You* series, this is not meant to be a complete, definitive history of the West. Let's face it: No one will ever write a definitive history of the American West. Rather, this is intended to whet your appetite, if you will, for further research on your own.

The American West is perhaps the second most written about subject in American history—only the Civil War has more books and articles about it. The exploration and exploitation of that area generally west of the Mississippi truly makes for great human history. Often, however, authors try too hard, and thus insert themselves between the story and the reader. Sometimes historians forget that they are not doers but merely the recorders of great events. Usually it is best to let the story tell itself, and that is what I have tried to do in this and other books in this series. As historian David McCullough once said in a television interview, "There's no need to gussy it all up."

I try to keep in mind the perhaps apocryphal story of a young newspaper reporter sent to cover the 1889 Johnstown, Pennsylvania, flood. The flood was one of the worst tragedies in American history. An estimated five thousand people died and property damage totaled a figure nearly astronomical for the time, ten million dollars.

The story goes that when news of the flood first breaks, the only available reporter left to a major New York newspaper is an eager but inexperienced young man, a cub reporter—the term was then. Before he sends the fledgling journalist off to the hills of Pennsylvania, the newspaper's crotchety editor offers a few last-minute words of advice. "Whatever you do," says crotchety editor to cub reporter, "make the story live; make it colorful."

Off the fledgling reporter goes, repeating his editor's mantra: "Make it colorful, make it colorful."

Johnstown is about seventy-five miles from Pittsburgh, situated at the bottom of a gorge and at the junction of two rivers. At the top of the gorge, about sixteen miles from Johnstown, sat a manmade, dammed-up, privately owned lake, Lake Conemaugh. In 1852 a group of Pittsburgh industrialists bought the lake to use as a private fishing preserve. To assure that it was always deep enough for good fishing, they removed discharge pipes from the dam and partially blocked its spillways. Effectively, this left no way to relieve pressure on the dam, and the lake sometimes ran as deep as seventy feet.

On May 31 a heavy rainstorm hit the area, and in parts of Johnstown the water quickly rose ten feet or more. The locals were used to being flooded out and simply moved themselves and their belongings upstairs in their homes to wait out the flood.

Meanwhile, Lake Conemaugh was rising at a rate of six inches an hour.

Shortly after three in the afternoon the dam burst, spewing twenty million tons of water into the gorge and valley. Rushing water leveled small towns in its path and moved on to Johnstown.

A train engineer saw the torrent racing toward the town, and he frantically blew his whistle as a warning, but it did little good. The surge of water hit Johnstown, flattening the Cambria Iron Works and smashing through homes and farms and factories. It even smashed through that engineer's train. A survivor remembered how "an advancing rotary wave of black water, forty feet high," hit Johnstown. As often happens in floods, wreckage caught fire, and more than two hundred people who had sought refuge on a small island died in the flames. By the next day thousands of people were dead. Every family in Johnstown lost at least one member. In ninety-nine families there were no survivors.

By now our cub reporter has telegraphed his story back to his anxiously awaiting curmudgeon of an editor. Still repeating that "make it colorful, make it colorful" mantra, the reporter led his report: "God sat brooding on a mountaintop in Pennsylvania, while Johnstown lay flooded down below."

To which the editor quickly wired back: "Forget flood. Interview God."

In the essays that follow, I hope to remember both flood and God.

Acknowledgments

To those who aided and encouraged me in the research and writing of this book, my deep thanks. To everyone at Presidio Press—Bob Kane, Richard Kane, Robin Kane Vlassopoulos, Bob Nelson, and E. J. McCarthy—my continuing appreciation; this is the fourth in the What They Didn't Teach You . . . series, and it is a joy working with you—past, present, and future endeavors.
And especially my wife Lin. Saying "Thank you" isn't enough, but it is sincere.

CHAPTER ONE

When the East Was West:
Sunrise to Sunset

And where is the West? Who shall fix its limits? He who attempts it will soon learn that it is not a fixed, but a floating line.

Eleutheros Cooke, an address at Norwalk, Ohio, July 4, 1857

The frontier is the outer edge of the wave—the meeting point between savagery and civilization ... the line of most rapid and effective Americanization. The wilderness masters the colonist.

Frederick Jackson Turner, *The Significance of the Frontier in American History,* 1894

In its heyday the town of Two Guns, Arizona, had dozen of saloons and even more brothels. They're all gone now, but where they stood is symbolic of the West: something for everyone and a hard life for anyone who even thought about making the area home.

For more than fifty years, the high plains of northern Arizona were something of an American crossroads. Cowboys and outlaws, explorers and settlers, saints and sinners; they all struck out across the desert, inched their way down deep arroyos and wide canyons, struggled across the warm tan plains and under turquoise-blue skies. The distant San Francisco Mountains remind us of ancient volcanoes. Meteor Crater's 550-foot-deep, 4,150-foot-wide rim suggests a time when the earth was young. Potsherds recovered from around Two Guns date human settlement there to as early as A.D. 1050.

In the last quarter of the nineteenth century the area around Two Guns was primarily a military road, with U.S. cavalry troops keeping a wary eye out for emigrants headed for Prescott. In at least one incident the cavalry arrived too late. Pioneer families had been massacred and their corpses had been thrown into fires set by hostile Indians. All the troopers could do was to rake the would-be settlers' bones from the ashes and bury them in a common grave near the road.

About that same time members of the Church of Jesus Christ of Latter-day Saints, the Mormons, built Joseph City, Arizona, naming the town after their sect's founder, Joseph Smith. The Saints, as they designated themselves, had tried valiantly to establish farms in the area and, thanks to irrigation, had some brief success. Now, however, Joseph City's population of nine hundred is shrinking rapidly.

Settlers struggling westward through northern Arizona undoubtedly had thought more than once about turning back. Diablo Canyon at Two Guns likely was one of the reasons for such thinking. It's a sudden, deep gash in the earth's crust, several hundred feet wide and more than a hundred feet deep, too long to go around and too deep to drive a wagon down. A short distance away it's even deeper. Drivers had to unhitch their mules or oxen, carefully and laboriously lower their wagons down the canyon walls by block and tackle, then just as carefully and laboriously haul them up again on the other side. Mules, oxen, and humans suffered the same ignominious fate.

About 140 miles to the south of Two Guns rise the Superstition Mountains. Somewhere near an outcrop known as Weaver's Needle may lie the Lost Dutchman Gold Mine, once operated by "Dutch" Jacob Waltz, or Old Jake, as local Indians called him. Dutch died in 1891, and people have been looking for his supposedly rich mine ever since then, apparently with no success.

Two Guns was the site of one of the most bizarre incidents in the history of the West. But as bizarre as it was, it was perhaps typical of the time and place.

Actually, the trouble began about ten miles away, in Winslow, Arizona, which for a while was a center for nineteenth-century settlers and twentieth-century tourists. Why, the town even boasted the world's largest Navajo rug, twenty-one feet by thirty-seven feet, weighing 240 pounds.

The episode at hand began at the Wigwam Saloon on Second Street in Winslow. A local gambler named Frank Ketchum was running a dice game, and the kitty was up to over six hundred dollars. John Shaw and Bill Smith, a pair of young cowboys of the more avaricious persuasion, strolled into the Wigwam that day, looking for a quick drink. They ordered whiskey and waited for the bartender to serve them, looking around as they stood, each with a booted foot on the brass rail. Before they got their drinks, however, they spied Ketchum's stack of shiny silver dollars. For Shaw and Smith this was too good a chance. The boys drew their guns and ordered the poker players to hand over all of the money. They stuffed as much as they could into their pockets and backed out of the saloon to make their escape.

Quickly, the sheriff raised a posse, who rode off looking for the two cowpokes-turned-crooks. They cornered John Shaw and Bill Smith later that evening in a warehouse at Two Guns, near the Diablo Canyon Station. After a short but eventful shootout Shaw lay sprawled out dead and Smith was critically wounded.

The posse gave John Shaw a quick but presumably Christian burial in a shallow grave at Two Guns, then hopped the train to Winslow, where they put Bill Smith under a physician's care. With that the posse retired to the Wigwam Saloon to review the day's events and have a drink or three.

It wasn't long before someone remembered that Smith and Shaw originally had come to the Wigwam searching for a drink. However, the bartender had been slower than the boys, and the two cowboys never got their drinks. Fair is fair, a slightly inebriated posse member believed: Those fellas has got a drink comin' to them. With that a couple of dozen like-minded if besotted souls hopped the freight train headed back for Two Guns, taking with them a wide assortment of liquor to pass the time and a few borrowed shovels to do what they had in mind.

Which was to unearth Shaw's bullet-riddled body and set it up beside the man's barely cold grave. Just as the sun rose, they poured a shot of whiskey between his lifeless lips and they all cheered.

Legend has it that along with the Wigwam Saloon crowd that early morning was a photographer who snapped a picture of the scene. For many years, it's claimed, the photograph was proudly displayed in the Wigwam Saloon. Now, however, both Wigwam and photograph are gone.

Gone also are Two Guns's "Hell Street" saloons: the Colorado, the Texas, the Last Drink, the Road to Ruin, Bughouse Joe's, and Name Your Pizen. Gone are the gambling halls (called poker flats), the dance pavilions, and the whorehouses. In the 1920s and through the '50s, Route 66—that same route whereon songwriter Bobby Troop advised us all to get our kicks—carried travelers past Two Guns. That's when someone built a last-chance gas stop and a zoo featuring sad, caged mountain lions. Now the gas station, too, has closed its pumps and left its rusted sign to the wind. The zoo is a pile of rubble and the mountain lions are dead and gone.

Indians and cavalry. Cowboys, gamblers, gold miners, and thieves. Settlers. For reasons of geography they all converged on Two Guns, Arizona.

In the midday sun twentieth-century motorists speed past Two Guns. If you like, however, you can stop and walk a short stone bridge that crosses Diablo Canyon. Oh, how those emigrant setters would have loved that bridge. Today the roadway it carries seems to go nowhere.

Pick your way carefully, and scramble through the rubble of the Two Guns zoo; you might discover another gone-but-not-forgotten era. Stick around for nightfall. At twilight the turquoise sky turns scarlet with desert dust, offering some of the most beautiful sunsets you'll ever want to see.

Look away from the sunset—look eastward—and with your mind's eye you might see where the West began.

The first Europeans to reach America's East likely were sailors blown ashore in a strange, strange land. History does not list their names. It does list some of the latecomers.

Before Columbus, however, or Leif the Lucky, before Bjarni Herjolfsson or an Irish priest named Brendan, before the Scottish prince named Henry Sinclair, there were those who walked across a frozen strait from Russia to Alaska, searching for food and following game. There came a Welshman named Modoc, who apparently established a colony in America and even taught the natives to speak Welsh, a language seemingly devoid of vowels and thus virtually impossible for any non-Welshman to speak. An Oriental ship's bell was found off the coast of California, suggesting Asians sailed eastward at least as early as Europeans sailed westward.

Earlier, others sailed and floated to South America from both the East and West. Columbus named their descendants "Indians," because he believed he was in the East Indies—that is, Asia. He was wrong, of course. And, of course, the name stuck. Such are the ways of history.

The Spanish came to steal gold from the Indians in Mexico and South America; for several years they were wildly successful. Juan Ponce de León may have been the first European intentionally to set foot on what became the United States of America. He conquered Puerto Rico, then in 1513, at the ripe old age of fifty-three and feeling somewhat debilitated, Ponce de León went looking for the fabled fountain of youth, whose waters were said to restore vim and vigor to the elderly, and thus he launched this first senior citizen invasion. In the course of his search he explored—we don't know who actually discovered it—the area he named Florida. De León found the natives decidedly unfriendly to his search, and Spain lost a good number of men looking for de León's dream. Ponce never did find the fountain.

The French came to steal furs from Canadian natives but lost much of their territory to the British and Spanish after the international Seven Years' War, known in America as the French and Indian War.

The British came, not to steal gold or furs, but to steal the very land untold generations of Native Americans had called home.

The first generation of European explorers and settlers followed the sun as it sank in the western sky. Then came their children. From America's East the next generation also looked westward, and they too moved on.

Once Europeans decided there was something worthwhile on the western side of the Atlantic, they came in growing numbers. And although there are Scandinavian, Irish, Scottish, Welsh, French, and Portuguese advocates as to who came first, almost without doubt the first Europeans to come in any strength were the Spanish.

The only valuable commodity Columbus found in his four trips was a wood called "guaiacum," whose essence was supposed to cure another European blight upon the New World, syphilis. It didn't. For years it was believed that Columbus's sailors (maybe even Chris himself) were the first to infect the natives of Hispaniola with syphilis. Frequent European plagues of venereal disease, possibly a by-product of trade with Africa, occurred in Columbus's day. It's been reasoned, therefore, that the sailors of 1492 may have carried the disease with them. However, some recently exhumed pre-Columbian skeletons—that is, natives who died long before Columbus went looking for China and wound up sunning himself on the beaches of Santo Domingo—show signs of another form of syphilis. So the disease could have preceded Columbus. Then, too, European doctors often confused syphilis with Hansen's disease, more commonly known as leprosy. Maybe Columbus's sailors infected the natives with that disease. There's no doubt they carried disease and freely gave away germs.

While Europeans were infecting natives with everything from measles to smallpox, the natives were getting back. It turned out that the Europeans were vulnerable to yellow fever, that mosquito-carried virus that would rage unchecked up and down America's eastern seaboard for hundreds of years until the cause was discovered. "Yellow Jack," as it sometimes was called, was one of the things that delayed the building of the Panama Canal.

In any event, Europeans accustomed to milder weather deemed the American climate unhealthy. To take care of all their dirty work, the Spanish began importing black slaves into Hispaniola to replace Indians, many of whom had fallen ill to European diseases and old age.

The Spanish thought the local food was, at best, tasteless, unwholesome at worst, and some of the fish were downright poisonous. If it hadn't been for one commodity, they would have written off the whole New World: gold. Columbus had found gold in the islands. Not in any great quantity or in any mine or stream, but in the form of earrings worn by the natives. That was all, just enough to make Chris believe that the gold the natives wore was gold the natives had mined. It had come through trade, not overnight, but over a period of years, not from the Caribbean Islands but from that huge mainland off to the west somewhere.

In 1518 Hernán Cortés set out for Mexico looking for gold. "Looking for gold" did not mean "looking for places from which they could physically mine gold." Rather, it meant "looking for gold the natives had previously mined and which the Spanish could, with relative impunity, steal." Quite a different thing, indeed, especially if you are a native. It had taken the Aztecs and Mayans hundreds of years to acquire the golden earrings and other jewelry that so be-dazzled Columbus and company. Cortés and company either didn't realize this or didn't care; probably all they wanted was gold without too much work.

Thus began the "age of conquest," when, as historian Charles Gibson puts it, "a small band of amateur Spanish soldiers proceeded to march against and subdue the huge populations of the [American] mainland." From Hispaniola, Cortés took his troops on a tour of what he called "New Spain." The Spanish stormed ashore in the region of Vera Cruz—horses, armor, guns, and all splashing in the blue-green waves of the Gulf of Mexico's Bay of Campeche. The natives had been under Aztec control for only a few years, a fact that gave Cortés and his men a political foothold on the mainland; the natives weren't too happy under Montezuma's military and political thumb. So, as he moved inland, Hernán Cortés and his Spanish army attracted native allies, notably the Tlaxcala. With them at his side Cortés and his Conquistadors marched on the city of Tenochtitlán—present-day Mexico City—in the fall of 1519, where Montezuma greeted them and even invited Cortés in. Knowing a good, not to mention easy, thing when they saw it, the Spanish quickly took control of the capital. Montezuma's hospitality had turned against him. Cortés then used Montezuma as a puppet and stole all the gold he could lay his Conquistadorian hands on.

The next year, while Cortés himself was temporarily out of town, the natives rose up in rebellion. In what is called the Noche Triste, the Melancholy Night, the natives beat back the Spanish. Montezuma was killed (the circumstances remain mysterious, and his own men may have had something to do with it), but instead of his death benefiting the Spanish, it worked against them. Cortés no longer had a puppet through whom he could rule Tenochtitlán, and the natives once more drove the Spanish out of the city.

The now-conquered conquerors spent the next year with their native allies in Tlaxcala province, preparing for a rematch. When they assaulted Tenochtitlán in 1521, they did it with ships on the lake and men on the causeway. And with a small unseen ally: smallpox. By the time Cortés and his war-weary men reached Tenochtitlán, smallpox had killed most of the defenders, and the rest of the native soldiers were too ill to put up much of a fight. Like most Native Americans of the time the Aztecs had little immunity to outside diseases, certainly not to smallpox. Using a form of biological warfare, you might say, the Spanish won and the day of the Aztec was over.

The Spanish conquest wasn't confined to Cuba, Florida, and Mexico. They had an almost consuming desire to find what were called the "Seven Cities of Cíbola" or the "Seven Cities of Gold," a fable more alluring than the fountain of youth. That desire led the Conquistadors to march over half of North America looking for towns that were claimed to be built of solid gold. Francisco Vásquez de Coronado, the young governor of the western province of Nueva Galicia on the western coast of Mexico, heard the legend of Cíbola from a visitor and decided it called for a full-blown expedition. He took his search as far as modern Kansas.

For part of his push northward Coronado used what came to be called El Camino Real, the "royal road," which ran from Mexico City to Santa Fe, New Mexico, and which was a principal trade route for generations. Along the way, and for years to come, Coronado rode roughshod over the Pueblo Indians. It took more than a hundred years—not until the Pueblo Revolt of 1680—for the Indians to gather enough forces to fight back.

About the time of the New Mexico Pueblo Indian revolution, King Louis XIV strutted and postured around the French countryside, while missionary-explorer René La Salle sailed down the Mississippi River and claimed Louisiana—all of it, from Canada to the Gulf of Mexico—for the Sun King. La Salle didn't do this out of the goodness of his heart or his love for France, mind you. Louis had given him a monopoly on the fur trade and permission to build forts.

The modern saying is that if it seems too good to be true, it is. Those Seven Cities of Gold Coronado searched for didn't exist, not really. The cities were there, but as it turned out, the "gold" likely was the reflection of sunlight coming off the straw used in building adobe huts in Zuni pueblos in New Mexico. Still, the Spanish more readily believed the idea of the Seven Cities of Gold than they did the reality of buffalo. Coronado, for one, couldn't get over the sight of the buffalo, the American bison. "I reached some plains so vast," he wrote, that I did not find their limit anywhere that I went, although I traveled over them for more than 300 leagues. And I found such a quantity of cows [the buffalo] . . . that it is impossible to number them, for while I was journeying through the plains, until I returned to where I first found them, there was not a day that I lost sight of them.

For two years Coronado explored the American southwest, from 1540 to 1542, and while he never found one, much less seven, cities of gold, he discovered the Grand Canyon. Meaning, again, that he was the first European to make a written report of discovering some New World location.

Bedded inside Spain's colonial conscience lay the conviction that the land Isabella and Ferdinand called home had been chosen by God to convert New World heathens. No matter that these "heathens" had their own religions; it wasn't the religion of Spain and Rome.

Back in the Middle Ages, Christian knights struggled to free their Iberian homeland from the African Moors of Islamic faith. In doing so Spanish Catholicism became militant to a degree not previously known in Europe. Priests and soldiers worked hand in hand. The Church raised money to drive the infidel back across the Strait of Gibraltar and even furnished a noble reason for fighting. This collaboration gave us the image of armored conquistador and robed priest marching boot by saddle across the New World. In most cases this just didn't happen, certainly not in the early years of the Spanish conquest of America. Priests went their own way, conquered on their own, and to a certain degree ruled on their own. No help from the military was wanted or needed.

Take the case of Fray Agustín Rodríguez. In 1580 he was busy saving the souls of the Conchos Indians in southern Chihuahua, when he heard reports of an advanced agricultural people living to the north. Rodríguez and two other Franciscans, along with nine soldier volunteers and some faithful Indian servants (perhaps not so faithful; perhaps they didn't volunteer), pushed off down the Conchos River to its junction with the Rio Grande, then up into the Pueblo Indian villages of New Mexico. Here, Rodríguez discovered a potentially large harvest of converts—clean, handsome, and industrious natives. The only thing that kept the good friars from converting everybody in sight was that the priests didn't know the local language and hadn't brought along an interpreter. They continued onward and northward, "probing the secrets of this strange country," historian Marc Simmons writes, "visiting Taos in the far north, the buffalo range beyond the Pecos River, and the western homes of the Acoma and Zuni."

Native Americans never were totally docile; after all, someone was coming in to steal their land, and the number of whites seemed always to increase. When one of Rodríguez's fellow friars, Father Juan de Santa María, set off on his own to take a report back to Mexico, Pueblo warriors followed him. Believing he was going to fetch more soldiers, and perhaps remembering what Coronado and his men had done two decades earlier, they captured the priest and killed him.

When Hernando de Soto and his men marched ashore, they had with them, for food, more than a dozen hogs from the Canary Islands. De Soto enslaved natives to herd the pigs behind his men as they marched along looking for gold.

Sows being sows and boars being boars, shoats rapidly became shoats-a-plenty. That is, porkers of the female persuasion and porkers of the male persuasion produced porkers of the piglet persuasion in great numbers. The thirteen pigs de Soto started out with soon numbered three hundred; six months later the Conquistador's corps of pigs numbered more than five hundred. De Soto's trip took more than two years, and by the end (end of the trip and his personal end, since he died before reaching home), his own share of the pig herd numbered seven hundred animals.

The Spanish procession had to have been both noisy and noisome. At the head of the column rode de Soto; then his armored cavalry, followed by the infantry; followed by wagon after wagon of baggage with baggage handlers, male and female. Finally, the growing herd of pigs, all rumbling, grunting, squealing, and sweating along behind the invaders. Noise, dust, dirt, and diseases on hoof.

Toward the end of his journey Hernando de Soto and his band were desperate. They'd been lost for days in a forest of tall pines, scrub palms, magnolias, and live oak trees. Hundreds of soldiers and servants and priests were running out of food. Except for their herd of hogs. The Conquistadors constantly fought local natives who hid in the piney woods wilderness, waiting to ambush them with razor-sharp arrows. The Spanish swatted mosquitoes and faced disease in the canebrakes. They wanted to go home, to get away from the snakes and bears and panthers. Oh, my.

Forget those paintings of de Soto and his troop wearing brightly polished armor as they discovered the mighty Mississippi River. By the time Hernando and his men hit the river they'd tossed away their armor, and most of their clothing had been ripped and torn by bushes and trees along the way. Second, someone else had gotten there before them and named the river. The Chippewas called it Mis-cisibi, "Big River." De Soto saw the Mississippi for the first time on May 21, 1541. The next time was exactly one year later, and he had other things on his mind than who had first discovered it.

By this time twenty percent of his men had died on the trail. He'd hoped to find an empire in the north equal to that of the Aztecs and Incas in the south; he found nothing like that. For two years he wandered from Florida to Georgia, through Tennessee, Alabama, and Mississippi, and still he saw no sign of his hoped-for northern empire. Soon de Soto lay dying. Cause of death: unknown. Possibly poison, possibly brought on by depression; no one knows for certain.

In desperation de Soto ordered an unprovoked attack on a nearby village. He wanted to scare them, make them afraid to come near him. It wasn't an attack, more like a massacre, and the Spanish enjoyed it.

Too late for de Soto. He died there, somewhere along the Mississippi. A few days later his men stuffed his rotting carcass inside a hollow log, took it to the middle of the big river, and tossed it overboard.

Luis de Moscoso took over leadership and dragged the men and their herd of hogs into Texas, stopping near the Trinity River where they built boats to take them back to the more civilized land of New Spain. There was no northern El Dorado.

They realized they couldn't take their herd of hogs with them in their small, hastily built boats, so there, along the banks of the Mississippi River, before sailing off for Mexico, the defeated would-be conquerors held a pig roast, the first of many southern pig roasts to come.

Not all of de Soto's pigs became barbecue*—a word, incidentally, we get from the Haitians; a *barbacoa* was a "rude framework used in America for sleeping on, and for smoking or drying meat over a fire." One can only imagine the "used for sleeping on" part, but the whole thing becomes more interesting when the *Oxford Universal Dictionary* adds, "An open-air social entertainment."

Often, while slaves set to watch the Spanish porkers looked elsewhere, some of the pigs escaped. When you have a herd of seven hundred pigs in the middle of an alligator-infested swamp, you don't go looking for a few strays. As more and more pigs escaped, some of the local residents caught them and even went on to supply pork to other invading Europeans.

All up and down the Conquistador route pigs escaped, which is why some regions of Arkansas and Georgia today still are noted for their wild pigs. In the Okefenokee Swamp they're known as "piney woods rooters," and they're big and mean and savage and are still hunted and eaten by the locals.

Before the Spanish came with their squealing swine herds, the natives had never seen such creatures. They learned fast, almost as fast as they died. With the runaway hogs came runaway influenza and other diseases humans could contract from the pigs.

For years, first migratory animals—deer and buffalo—then Native Americans traveled a path through the Appalachians. The animals went looking for food and the Indians went looking for the animals. Later, as well as hunting animals, Indians from one side of the mountains went hunting Indians on the other side. This cross-mountain path from the Ohio to the Potomac Rivers became known as the "Warrior's Path," a trail of both trade and war for Native Americans, Siouan- and Algonquian-speaking tribes living to the east and Iroquois to the west. The area west of the mountains became known as

---

*Barbecue up North is a verb. Down South it's a noun. Northerners barbecue food. Southerners eat barbecue.

the "Dark and Bloody Ground," a name given it by Cherokee Chief Dragging Canoe.* Except for Indians and, in the 1600s, a handful of unknown Europeans who went exploring, the area was untouched.

In the mid-sixteenth century France made a couple of halfhearted attempts to colonize America. Jacques Cartier conquered the native kingdom of Saguenay near Canada's St. Lawrence River and shipped home what he thought were tons of gold and diamonds, but which turned out to be worthless fool's gold and quartz.

In April 1562 Jean Ribault took 150 Protestant prospects to South Carolina, where they set up a colony they named Port Royal. Ribault disbanded the colony two years later when a supply ship failed to arrive. It became a Spanish outpost named Santa Elena. Later it became Parris Island, home to a U.S. Marine base.

Not until 1608 would the French, under Samuel de Champlain, found the colony of Quebec. They turned to fur trading across the wide expanse of Canada—the new Port Royal, Montreal, Trois Rivières, and on to the Pacific Ocean. Earlier, the French had tried building a colony at Fort Caroline near modern Jacksonville in northeastern Florida, but the possibility disturbed the Spanish, who didn't take kindly to other nations horning in on their "discovery." Considering everything along North America's coastline, and particularly the area from the Chesapeake Bay southward, to be Spanish, they drove out the French and built forts along the Carolina coast.

About the only permanent result of the French attempt to colonize Florida was their introduction into European society of a product noted by Columbus and used by the local natives. John Hawkins of Plymouth, England, described it as follows:

> The Floridians have a kind of herb dried, who with a cane and an earthen cup on the end, with fire,—doe suck through the cane the smoke thereof, which smoke satisfieth their hunger.

*In 1768 Dragging Canoe warned North Carolina speculators, who had come to buy his tribal land, that "we have given you a fine land, brother, but you will find it under a cloud, a dark and bloody ground."

It was tobacco, and it would eventually be both the salvation of the Virginia colony (at one point so many people grew so much tobacco, they even planted the weed in the streets of Jamestown) and a scourge on human life.

After running out the French in 1565, the Spanish set up a colony of their own on the Florida coast, St. Augustine. It became the first permanent colony in what would, more than two hundred years later, be known as the United States of America.

Over the next decade Spanish Jesuits sent a mission to Chesapeake Bay, hoping to convert the natives to Catholicism. The natives, however, had other ideas and massacred the priests. That got rid of the Spanish and gave the locals a reputation for being brutal, warlike, and totally lacking in hospitality.

Ninety-two years after Johnny-come-lately Chris Columbus accidentally landed on a Caribbean island, and nineteen years after the Spanish intentionally settled at St. Augustine, it was England's turn. But the English had heard of the warlike nature of the Chesapeake natives and decided to set up a colony farther south. Not too much farther south—they wanted to be distant enough from Florida that the Spanish would ignore them.

England's first attempt to establish a colony along the North Carolina coast became, literally, lost to history. The area around Croatan Sound, North Carolina, was nearly perfect, according to Sir Walter Raleigh's man in America, Sir Humphrey Gilbert. Even the local natives were perfect—"most gentle, loving, and faithful, void of all guile and treason, and such as live after their manner of the golden age."

For two years, however, war between England and Spain prevented the English from resupplying their outpost at Roanoke Island. By mid-August 1588, when the English were finally able to send out another group of colonists, it was too late for the small group that had been left at what they called the "City of Raleigh in Virginia." When Governor John White returned to the colony, it was a mess. Huts were wrecked; the colonists had hidden boxes and trunks, but they'd been discovered and rifled. Maps, papers, and clothing had been dug up, torn up, and thrown out to rot. Discarded armor was rusted, and palisades built around the town were grass-grown and tumbling down. On a nearby tree—perhaps as some kind of message—White found the word *Croatan,* the name natives gave to the island on which present-day Cape Hatteras is situated, about a hundred miles southeast of Roanoke. That may be where the remnants of the Roanoke colony had gone, but Governor White couldn't get his sailors to sail to Hatteras Island, and the deserted City of Raleigh was too depressing to call home. So, the relief expedition returned to England.

Theories abound as to what happened to the "Lost Colony." The Croatan Indians (now called the Lumbee) believe that the blood of the Roanoke colony's survivors runs in their veins, and for years there were tales of blue-eyed Indians in the Lumbee tribe.

In 1607 the Virginia Company of London established the first permanent English colony in America. Earlier the site, an island in the James River, had been a village of Algonquian-speaking natives who called it Paspahegh. The English named it Jamestown, after King James. For the next sixty-two years, despite a 1622 attempt by Native Americans to end once and for all the white invasion, colonists slowly spread westward from Jamestown.

John Smith, who was among the first to come ashore at Jamestown in 1607, went looking for a way west later that same year, but he likely didn't find what he was after. Thirty-nine years later, Abraham Wood, who had come to the New World as an indentured servant, also tried. He led an exploring party westward from the upper James River, hoping to verify an Indian account of a way over the mountains: "Within five days' journey to the westward and by south, there is a great high mountain, and at the foot thereof, great rivers that run into a great sea; and . . . there are men that come thither in ships . . . and have reed caps on their heads, and ride on beasts like horses, but have much longer ears." The Indian wasn't talking about Smith and the other Englishmen, but about the Spanish who had come to the North American shore earlier. Either way, Wood didn't find the way to the West.

Which is not to say he gave up, because he didn't. In 1671, when he was an old man, Abraham Wood sent woodsmen westward, "for the finding out the ebbing and flowing of the waters on the other side of the mountain in order to discover the South Sea." Still, no luck.

It was then that Virginia governor Sir William Berkeley sent John Lederer (described as a "German scholar" or physician) to explore the colony's Blue Ridge Mountains. On March 18 Lederer became the first white man to reach the ridgetop. It's more likely that Lederer simply was the first white man to leave a written record of his trip; trappers and traders probably silently preceded him over the mountains. Lederer reported seeing wolves, beavers, "great herds of red and fallow deer feeding, and on the hill-sides bear crashing mast [acorns and chestnuts] like swine."

Lederer mistakenly believed that he saw the ocean—"I had a beautiful prospect of the Atlantick Ocean washing the Virginia shore." Sorry, not an ocean; it was haze in the valley below. It would be nearly a hundred years before any European would truly find a way to the West.

Lederer's journey didn't do what Governor Berkeley had hoped. It didn't encourage colonists to settle in the western lands. It did, however, begin to worry the French, who didn't want the English trampling on what they believed to be their territory, because by now the French had moved south from Canada.

As late as 1700 little was known of the country west of the Appalachian fall line. English settlement was still mainly confined to the coastal regions, but there was growing pressure to expand cultivated lands. In 1714, when a group of German and Swiss miners and artisans came to America, the Virginia colony settled them in land owned by Governor Alexander Spotswood. The area became known as Germanna, "on the south bank of the Rapidan [River] in a big horseshoe bend of the river, about twelve miles above its confluence with the Rappahannock." It was from Germanna that began the first major crossing of the mountain chain, when Governor Spotswood led a party to Virginia's Shenandoah River in 1716.

There were sixty-three members of the party, including the governor himself, two companies of "rangers" (each made up of six men and an officer), a number of "gentlemen" (one of whom would be the ancestor of two U.S. presidents—James Madison and Zachary Taylor), their servants, and guides. One member of the party was a recent Huguenot immigrant, Ens. John Fontaine, who had served in the British army and who kept a diary of the crossing.

We had a rugged way; we passed over a great many small runs of water, some of which were very deep, and others very miry. Several of our company were dismounted, some were down with their horses, others under their horses, and some thrown off.

Seventy-four horses and several hunting dogs were needed to make the trip, and for the most part the party had a party. In the evening the servants pitched tents near some clear mountain stream, then roasted whatever game had been unlucky enough to stumble in front of the group during the day. The gentlemen sat around the campfires toasting their good health and discussing their great adventure. Three days from Germanna, Fontaine wrote that they saw the "only notable depression or 'notch' visible in this long reach." Then, on September 5, Spotswood and his party reached the summit of the Blue Ridge, whereupon they drank more toasts: "King George's health, and the Royal Family's." To reach the western slope they followed a trail blazed on trees, which is a pretty good indication that they weren't the first to make the transmontane journey. They continued on for about seven miles until they reached the Shenandoah River, where they spent the night and proceeded to get something close to roaring drunk. Writes Fontaine,

> We crossed the river, which we call Euphrates [the Shenandoah?]. It is very deep; the main course of the water is north; it is fourscore yards wide in the narrowest part. We drank some healths on the other side, and returned; after which we went a swimming in it.

To the higher of two peaks guarding the pass they'd traveled through, they gave the name Mount George (after the king) and the lower peak they called Mount Alexander or Mount Spotswood (after the governor). Over the years the names of the peaks changed. Now they (or at least the peaks assumed to be those sighted by Spotswood and company) are called more simply "High Top" and "Saddleback." "Respectively," as one writer puts it, "if not respectfully."

The company spent the next week celebrating and exploring, fishing, and hunting. Apparently a good time was had by all. As the saying goes, they drank to the king's health so many times they damn near ruined their own.

Finally, while the rangers continued their explorations on the western side of the mountains, Spotswood and his gentlemen friends headed back east to Williamsburg, which, according to Fontaine, was about 219 miles away. In other words, a roughly 438-mile round-trip over the rivers and through the streams.

Out of this westward trek came one of the most romantic episodes in colonial American history. The land around Williamsburg, and indeed in much of Virginia, is sandy loam. Horseshoes normally aren't needed. Going over the mountains, however, horseshoes were called for to protect the beasts' hooves. To commemorate this "first" over-mountain journey, Governor Spotswood presented to each gentleman member of the party a golden horseshoe, "some of which," historian Hugh Jones declared a decade later, "I have seen studded with valuable stones resembling the heads of nails." On one side the golden horseshoes were inscribed: *Sic juvat transcendere montes.* On the other side: *Transmontane Order.* The members of the party—"any gentleman being entitled to wear this golden shoe that can prove his having drank his Majesty's health, upon Mount George," writes Reverend Jones—came to be called "Knights of the Golden Horseshoe."

Over the years some of the golden horseshoes themselves became family heirlooms. To the sorrow of today's historians and antiquers, however, none of the golden horseshoes can be located.

Exactly where the Knights of the Golden Horseshoe crossed the mountains isn't certain. For years it was assumed to have been at Swift Run Gap, and today monuments to that effect mark the spot. Now, however, it's believed the Spotswood group crossed at the same place as John Lederer had decades earlier, Milam Gap.

Lederer's crossing of the mountains didn't draw much attention. Spotswood and the Knights of the Golden Horseshoe did. Large landholders moved in, taking the choice spots of the Shenandoah Valley. Soon this and other valleys began to fill up with others: Germans (sometimes known as the "Pennsylvania Dutch"), Scottish and

Scotch-Irish families, and redemptioners—indentured servants whose time had expired and who, under law, were entitled to land grants that might include land on the western side of the mountains. Over time the valleys became virtual roadways north and south for settlers. Many Scots, for instance, entered America at modern-day Wilmington, North Carolina, traveled northwestward up the Cape Fear River, then spread out north and south once they reached the valleys around the Blue Ridge and Smoky Mountains.

Geologically, from East to West, there is the coastal plain, which Virginia settlers called "Tidewater"—the region east of Richmond still bears the name—and which South Carolinians refer to as the "low country."* Then comes the hilly midland called the "pied-mont"—the foot of the mountains—and, upward, to the Appalachians. South Carolinians referred to the area past the piedmont as the "upcountry." Virginians called it simply the "back country." It developed into a buffer between European settlers and the Indians that they'd pushed westward.

From the middle colonies, primarily Pennsylvania, land-based trade developed with the South along the "Great Philadelphia Wagon Road." Over the years it saw settlers travel, traders swap goods, and "colonies" become "states."

Between the haze-dotted Blue Ridge and the more westward hills—that is, between "Old Appalachia" and "New Appalachia"—lies a land of red clay soil and towering trees, oak and maple and chestnut and hickory, whose bright red leafage in fall dazzled even the most hard-bitten early settler. The woods provided logs for cabins and rails and fences. From the bark, primarily from chestnuts, came tannic acid for tanning, dyeing, and medicine. It is a land known even today as the "Trail of the Lonesome Pine"—longleaf pines towering a hundred feet above the mountains' rocky peaks. Great trees and sparkling rivers, a land abounding in game and birds. Flocks of wood pigeons so endless that they darkened the sky. Wolves and

---

*Notice that we do not mention North Carolina. Even today the whole of North Carolina is referred to as "a valley of humility between two mountains of conceit."

screech owls. And Indians imitating their sounds. Buffalo and deer, ducks, geese, and brant (a species of small wild geese).

The American bison seen earlier by Spanish explorers in the Southwest were larger than their eastern cousins, the woods buffalo. Like the western bison, however, the woods buffalo didn't last long after the white man came ashore. By 1794 Virginians had hunted it to extinction.

This fertile area—Virginia's Shenandoah Valley back country—was the first American West. Here, English settlers fought the French; then, after the Revolution, the settlers, who had become "Americans," fought the English. With the Shenandoah Valley opened up to settlers, easterners (as they were then) began looking to the West, beyond the Alleghenies.

For example, in 1749 young George Washington, his older half-brother, and a group of like-minded Virginia and Maryland landowners organized the Ohio Company, obtaining a patent to five hundred thousand acres along the Ohio River. About a year later George helped survey land owned by Lord Thomas Fairfax. Records of the Fairfax holdings apparently were somewhat in disarray, and Lord Fairfax wanted to find out just what he owned. George and Fairfax's nephew, George William, checked it out and came back with the information that, Good Lord, Fairfax! You own six million acres of land! From this one holding would come more than a dozen counties in Virginia and West Virginia.

In about 1750 Dr. Thomas Walker of the Loyal Land Company led a surveying party over the mountains, looking for a gap, a notch in the Great Mountains, as they were called. Either on his own, or shown the way by local natives, Walker followed the Clinch River in Southwestern Virginia until he reached the headwaters of the Cumberland River. He named the notch "Cumberland Gap," after England's duke of Cumberland, the son of King George II.* Walker

---

*The duke of Cumberland, Frederick Louis, was supposed to have been King George III. However, he died nine years before his father, George II, succumbed to a heart attack on October 24, 1760, while walking in his garden. Frederick Louis's son was crowned George III.

himself never got to the land the Indians called "Can-tuc-kee." It would be two years before legendary Pennsylvania hunter, adventurer, woodsman, and trader John Finley found the Kentucky region, and then he didn't exactly do the job himself. He was canoeing down the Ohio River when a band of Shawnee Indians captured him and took him to their camp in the Kentucky lowlands.

Finley escaped and told of a land filled with strawberries so high a horse would stain its knees red with juice just tramping through them, grapevines a foot thick and the way to harvest them was to chop down the trees. Of pigeons roosting by the thousands in trees, wild turkeys so fat that when you shot 'em, they fell to the ground an' their skins jest burst open. Deer, elk, and buffalo by the thousands crowded around licks, salt-impregnated rocks and dirt around saline springs. Why, so many animals swarmed around so many licks, they'd scraped trenches into the ground deeper than the animals' backs. Bears grew fat and sassy.

This truly was a land of milk and honey. If wild animals could satisfy their salt lust at the licks, farmers could use that same salt to preserve meat and tan hides. If buffalo could grow big on the tall grass in lands beyond the mountains, so, too, could domestic cattle. If bears could fatten on nuts from so many trees, so, too, could domestic pigs. Finley's tales might have been the start of migration west had it not been for the French and Indian War.

When the fighting ended, another problem arose: King George III's Proclamation of 1763 had laid down strict rules on the fur trade with the Indians and the purchase of Indian lands by private citizens. It forbade colonization west of the Alleghenies until a settlement could be reached with the Indians. Daniel Boone and others found a way around the proclamation. They ignored it.

In 1775 land speculator Richard Henderson headed up a group called the Transylvania Company, named after the European area inhabited by one Vlad the Impaler, better known to romantic if gory fiction as Count Dracula. Henderson hired Boone to explore the area. The young woodsman took about thirty other pioneers with him through the Cumberland Gap to the Kentucky River and on into the bluegrass country. Boone left the others building a fort at what he called Boonesborough (later, Boonesboro), Kentucky, and re-

21

turned to North Carolina to get his family and more men for the town. Along the way he blazed a trail, which at first wasn't large enough even for two horses to pass side by side, much less a wagon. Over time the trail widened and came to be known under several names: Boone's Trace, the Virginia Road, the "Road to Caintuck," and the Wilderness Road. Of course, only the last name stuck. The Transylvania area, Boonesborough, and the Wilderness Road grew and soon were crowded with travelers—on foot, horseback, and covered wagons—the first great migration westward over the mountains.

The abundance of land was one of the big draws of settlers to the New World, and now, with the exception of New England Puritans, who were afraid of the wilderness—they somehow equated the wilderness with the easy life, which would have surprised the hell out of later emigrants!—nearly everyone in the East looked to the West. Which worried the French, who still thought it was all theirs.

With a growing English interest in the Ohio Valley, in 1754 Virginia governor Dinwiddie sent George Washington, an officer in the Virginia militia, to warn the French not to bother the English settlers. There followed a confrontation in which Washington led a raid on a French encampment, killing a French diplomat, which led to French retaliation, which led to the Battle of Fort Necessity, which Washington lost—first battle, first defeat—which led directly to the French and Indian War, which led directly to Britain's King George III's Proclamation of 1763, which forbade the general settlement west of the Appalachian Mountains, which everybody ignored during the most notable consequence of the Washington-French skirmish: the American Revolution.

Despite the Proclamation of 1763 more and more settlers slipped westward—over the mountains, along the valleys, through wild passes, and across the ranges. It was there that settlers ran across one of the mid-1700s most colorful characters: British Army lieutenant colonel Henry Hamilton, known to both friend and enemy as "Henry the Hair Buyer." As commanding officer of the British post at Detroit, Hamilton gave the Indians arms, ammunition, rum, blankets, and trade trinkets. In return, Indians scalped the British-American settlers. During the Revolution the Continental Congress tried to mount several expeditions against the Detroit garrison, reasoning that if this source of Indian munitions were stopped, the western peril would end, allowing more American settlers to retain their hair. When that happened, Americans would be able to give their full attention to the war in the East.

In steps another colorful character, a big, rough, red-haired, Virginia-born surveyor who tried to reason out ways and means of controlling Indian raids in the land west of the Alleghenies. The man: George Rogers Clark.

In 1764 a French trader named Pierre Laclède Liguest established a settlement on the west bank of the Mississippi River, just south of where the Missouri River flowed into the larger stream, about one hundred fifty miles above where the Ohio River flows into the Mississippi. Liguest named his settlement St. Louis in honor of France's King Louis IX. By the end of the eighteenth century St. Louis had a population of about a thousand people and was becoming a major crossroads for settlers heading west. When Spain took control of the Mississippi River, St. Louis went with it.

George Rogers Clark hoped to control the Indians in the St. Louis area by hitting the British in the "Illinois country," the area bounded by the Wabash and Miami Rivers on the east, the Illinois on the north, the Mississippi on the west, and the Ohio River on the south. Among the main settlements of the time were Kaskaskia, where the Kaskaskia and Mississippi Rivers meet about fifty miles south of St. Louis; Prairie du Rocher, about seventeen miles north of Kaskaskia; and, closer still to St. Louis, Cahokia, the site of one of the earliest known major civilizations in the present-day United States.

One year after young and overeager George Washington inadvertently began the French and Indian War, British general Edward Braddock led his troops into a trap near Fort Duquesne, the modern-day Pittsburgh. In the ensuing debacle Washington escaped unharmed along with two mule skinners who would go on to greater fame: Daniel Morgan (in the American Revolution he led Continental troops to victory over the British at the Battle of Cowpens, South Carolina) and Morgan's cousin, young Daniel Boone.

Morgan was a six-foot, two-hundred-pounder who came to be known as "Old Wagoner," because of his mule-skinning days. Cousin Daniel, although he "appeared gigantic," was described by artist

John James Audubon, who knew him, as "rather low," between five feet eight inches and five feet nine. Boone's head, however, was large, and his blue eyes were overshadowed by heavy blond eyebrows. By all accounts Boone was brave, tough, and an outstanding woodsman, which sounds an awful lot like something out of a Hollywood script.

Daniel's father was an impatient man, who lived in southern Pennsylvania, near Reading. He wanted more land, but the Allegheny Mountains blocked him from an easy way to the West. So Squire Boone took his wife, six of their eight children (one of whom was Daniel), and a handful of grandchildren southward, first into Virginia's Shenandoah Valley, and then into the mountains of western North Carolina, near Yadkin, a town now called Booneville. The Boones were part of a growing trickle of rawboned "movers" who traveled along the mountain base, looking to better themselves.

Indians in the Old Northwest—the area now making up Ohio, Indiana, Michigan, and Illinois—hoped to keep the Ohio River the boundary between the races. They formed a confederacy to stop white migration along a line similar to the one that, in 1763, Britain ordered American settlers not to cross. In 1790 the United States government under the Articles of Confederation approved the Treaty of New York, a precarious formal peace with Indians in the area south of the Ohio River.

Still, settlers pushed westward despite the Proclamation of 1763, despite attacks by Indians, despite the American Revolution. From London, to give aid and comfort to restless and wary Indians, during the Revolution, King George III sent munitions and other manufactured goods.

The Reverend Manasseh Cutler of Ipswich, Massachusetts, possessed a bottomless appetite for food and wine. He had an encyclopedic mind and received a picayune salary as a minister of God. "Purchasing land in a new country," he wrote, "appeared to be ye only thing I could do to secure a living to myself and family." The upshot was the formation of a company to buy up depreciated continental certificates, a form of paper money that gave veterans of the Revolution the right to settle land in the Northwest. Cutler's Ohio Company of Associates was only one of several such ventures over the years.

As the company's negotiator, Cutler appeared before the Continental Congress in July 1787, seemingly at a bad time—down the street at what is now called Independence Hall, the United States was in the midst of revising itself with a new constitution—and at first the legislators paid the financially minded minister little attention. Until he was approached by William Duer, secretary of the Confederation's Board of Treasury. Several "principal men," Duer told Cutler, wanted to buy western lands. They couldn't do it themselves because of their positions in government—one of them was Arthur St. Clair, who at the time was president of Congress—and they wanted Cutler's aid in incorporating their venture, the Scioto Company, with Cutler's Ohio Company of Associates.

Cutler would front for the Scioto Company in an appeal for five million acres of land, and Duer and his friends would push through Congress legislation in which the United States overlooked its own requirements about price, public auction, and payment in full at the time of sale for all land deals. In return, Duer and friends would lend the Ohio adventurers money for a down payment on 1,781,760 acres of western land for it own use—five hundred thousand dollars down and five hundred thousand dollars when a survey of the land was completed. The money would be paid in government securities worth about twelve cents on the dollar.

The plan went through Congress with barely a ripple, and lawmakers went on to write a turgid but important piece of legislation called the Ordinance of 1787. Although it insisted on property qualifications for voting, and neglected the Indian problems, the Ordinance of 1787 became the basis for developing the West; as populations increased, settlements could become free and independent territories and, eventually, achieve statehood.

The same year the American colonies proclaimed their independence from Britain, England sent out two ships, *Resolution* and *Discovery*, with orders to search for the elusive Northwest Passage that many in the world believed would link the Atlantic and Pacific Oceans. Britain wanted a water route from Montreal to the Lake Athabaska fur trading region of Canada. England's greatest explorer of the day, Captain James Cook, led this latest search—one of three trips he made in this part of the world in 1768 and 1779.

He never did find the Northwest Passage, because it simply doesn't exist, at least not the way everyone envisioned it. Cook, however, penetrated the Northwest as far as Nootka Sound on the western side of what later was named Vancouver Island. This gave England a stake in the whole Northwest—land, furs, minerals, trade with the natives, you name it. Later Captain Cook sailed on to the Sandwich Islands (we now call them the Hawaiian Islands), where he was killed by natives unhappy with his earlier discovery of them.

Britain then sent Scottish fur trader Alexander Mackenzie on yet another search mission for the Northwest Passage. He headed westward from Montreal, and became the first white man known to cross the Rockies. He didn't make it to the Pacific Ocean; instead, he reached the Arctic Ocean, a slight miscalculation. Fittingly, the river he'd followed for much of the way he named the River of Disappointment. Four years later Mackenzie reached the Pacific mainly by walking, not by boat. The rivers, he discovered, were too swift and too turbulent to carry canoes, which carried voyageurs, who carried furs between the West and the East.

The American Philosophical Society got in on the search for the Northwest Passage, backing a proposal made by French-American André Michaux. He vowed to cross the North American continent, on foot if necessary, "to find the shortest & most convenient route of communications between the U.S. & the Pacific Ocean." Of particular interest to him were two rivers—the Missouri, and one farther west called "Oregon." Benevolent group that it was, the society blessed Michaux with funds totaling $128.25—of which $25 came from one George Washington; Alexander Hamilton and Thomas Jefferson each contributed $12.50.

All of this—the expeditions of Captain Cook, Alexander MacKenzie, and André Michaux—had American leaders looking to the Northwest. Thomas Jefferson took a tentative step toward Pacific Coast exploration by casually asking Revolutionary War hero George Rogers Clark to lead an expedition to the Northwest. Just as casually, Clark declined.

By the late 1700s once-powerful Spain was weak; even the new United States of America could bully the Spanish. As long as Spain owned New Orleans, sailing down the river and into the Caribbean presented only minor problems; however, a secret treaty in 1800 gave the Louisiana Territory back to France. In the fall of 1802 the Spanish intendant, or administrator, in New Orleans suddenly withdrew the duty-free rights of Americans to conduct business along the Mississippi River. This outraged frontiersmen along the Ohio River, and Washington sent American troops to Kentucky to prevent an armed expedition of Americans from sailing out of New Orleans and taking on Spanish authorities. The government of Madrid backed down, quickly disavowing their intendant's actions; all was calm again on the Mississippi.

Except, of course, by then Spain had returned to French control that tract of land north and west of New Orleans. Spain may have been weak; but France was anything but, and the new French emperor—a short, squat man named Napoleon Bonaparte—dreamed of a world empire that would stretch into the Caribbean and include parts of mainland America.

With the French in charge of Mississippi water traffic, alarm bells went off in the new American government; America might even have to ally itself with the British fleet, which in this case meant they'd have to beg for assistance. "Nothing since the Revolutionary War has produced such uneasy sensations through the body of the nation," President Jefferson wrote in April 1803. After all, through New Orleans "the produce of three-eighths of our territory must pass to market."

Secretary of State James Madison agreed, calling the Mississippi "the Hudson, the Delaware, the Potomac, and all the navigable rivers of the United States formed into one stream." With France controlling the mouth of the Mississippi, "worst events" were to be anticipated. Hoping to forestall those "worst events," Jefferson sent diplomats to Paris to test the waters. Would Bonaparte, Jefferson wanted to know, be willing to sell the port of New Orleans for, say, ten million dollars?

Among the diplomats Jefferson sent was his onetime coauthor of the Declaration of Independence, Robert Livingston, the new American minister to France. Livingston sent messages to French Foreign Minister Talleyrand, hoping to get through to Bonaparte. Were the Floridas (modern-day Florida was known as East Florida, with the strip of land that included parts of Mississippi, Alabama, and Georgia being known as West Florida) included in the Spain-to-France transfer? Talleyrand wasn't sure, but he'd check on it for Livingston.

Unlike Thomas Jefferson, Robert Livingston was no Francophile. In fact, he would much have preferred Great Britain as holder of the Mississippi. Napoleon also frustrated Livingston. "One man is everything," he wrote James Madison in 1802. "He seldom asks advice, and never hears it unasked."

In 1803 Jefferson sent James Monroe to Paris as American minister plenipotentiary. Along with Livingston he'd try to buy New Orleans from France and assure American merchants' safety at the mouth of the Mississippi River. He was hopeful, yes, but Jefferson was anything but certain his men in Paris could pull it off. "I am not sanguine," he wrote, "in obtaining a cession of New Orleans for money." However, as things sometimes do in history, the situation changed rapidly. By the time Monroe arrived in Paris, France had suffered heavy losses in a Haitian slave revolt, ending Napoleon's dream of a New World empire. This also left France facing yet another war with England. Rather than a strong Britain, Napoleon preferred a weak but friendly United States in control of the Mississippi waterway. And, too, he saw America as a cash cow. French Foreign Minister Talleyrand couldn't wait to milk her. In April 1803, Talleyrand agreed to sell New Orleans to the United States. New Orleans AND all of Louisiana AND the entire Mississippi Valley. Although Jefferson had been prepared to offer up to ten million for New Orleans alone, Bonaparte wanted just *fifteen million dollars* for the whole deal, cash down: $11,250,000 for the territory, with the remaining $3,750,000 to cover debts owed by France to American citizens. Such a deal! America got another 828,000 square miles between the Mississippi and the Rockies. With additional charges and interest, cost of the land came to about four cents an acre.

As soon as he heard about Napoleon's counterproposal, Jefferson went to the banks to get the money for the purchase. He hated banks in general and now he went tricorn hat in hand to rival Alexander Hamilton's favorite institution. Eventually the deal was done, signed, according to legend, while Napoleon Bonaparte sat soaking in a bathtub. Jefferson announced the purchase to a startled nation on July 4, 1803, the twenty-sixth anniversary of the passing of the Declaration of Independence.

It outraged Jefferson's political opponents, who said the Louisiana Purchase deal would bankrupt America. More land? Surely, we already had enough land. "I would rather," said former congressman Harrison Gray Otis of Massachusetts, "the Mississippi were a running stream of burning lava over which no human being could pass, than that the treaty should be ratified."

And, too, there was a constitutional question about the Louisiana Purchase, which shows both confusion and pragmatism on Jefferson's part. He was a strict constructionist and believed a president could do only what the Constitution said he could or should do. The Constitution said nothing about this. Some American politicians claimed that, since the Constitution said nothing about America buying foreign land, the deal should be canceled.

Perhaps not unexpectedly, those who wanted to call off the deal were Tom Jefferson's political enemies, the Federalists. At the time the Federalists were more the big-government-oriented political party, which under normal (whatever that means in politics) circumstances would have meant they'd favor expanding the country. In the way politics and politicians have of reversing themselves, however, this time they opposed the idea. Privately, even Jefferson admitted he probably was breaking the Constitution, but in the flip-flop of politics, he preached that the means justified the ends.* Jefferson wrote Senator John Breckinridge of Kentucky, saying that if France retained control of the Mississippi River—and remember, Jefferson was pro-France and anti-Britain—America would have to "marry ourselves to the British fleet and nation," something he wanted no part of:

> I would not give one inch of the Mississippi to any nation, but I see in a light very important to our peace the exclusive right to its navigation.... [The] Constitution has made no provision for our holding foreign territory, still less for incorporating foreign nations into our Union. The Executive, in seizing the fugitive occurrence which so much advances the good of their

---

*George Washington's family motto was *Exitus acta probat,* meaning, "The end justifies the means."

country, have done an act beyond the Constitution. The Legislature, in casting behind them metaphysical subtleties, and showing themselves like faithful servants, must ratify and pay for it, and throw themselves on their country in doing for them unauthorized what we know they would have done for themselves had they been in a situation to do it. It is the case of a guardian, investing the money of his ward in purchasing an important adjacent territory; & saying to him when of age, I did this for your good. . . .

In other words, Jefferson was enough of an opportunist to take advantage of a good deal when he saw it. On October 20, 1803, by a vote of twenty-four to seven, the U.S. Senate approved the sale.

When Congress approved the Louisiana Purchase, the original thirteen states had expanded to number seventeen. Over the years, thirteen more states would be formed out of that single fifteeen-million-dollar, bargain-basement land deal: Arkansas, Colorado, Iowa, Kansas, Louisiana, Minnesota, Missouri, Montana, Nebraska, North Dakota, Oklahoma, South Dakota, and Wyoming. Such a deal indeed!

Neither France nor America knew just how good a deal the Louisiana Purchase was, because neither nation knew how big the territory was. The Mississippi River and the Gulf of Mexico were set as the eastern and southern boundaries of the purchase, but the status of West Florida and Texas remained unclear. When Robert Livingston asked Talleyrand about the boundaries, the French minister told him, "I can give you no direction. You have made a noble bargain for yourselves and I suppose you will make the most of it." Thomas Jefferson set the boundaries as "the high lands inclosing all the waters which run into the Missisipi [*sic*] or Missouri directly or indirectly." Well, maybe. Maybe Jefferson exaggerated a bit. The president continued, "It therefore becomes interesting to fix with precision by celestial observations the longitude & latitude of the sources of those rivers."

It was up to Americans to determine where the boundaries were, and the simple way to do that was to go take a look. Well, not so simple, after all. That's where Meriwether Lewis and fellow Virginian

William Clark (George Rogers Clark's younger brother) came into the picture.

The primary purpose of the Lewis and Clark Expedition was imperial: find out was out there and how much there was of it. They were to observe and record the flora and fauna and to take note of the people they met along the way. Plainly put, however, the expedition amounted to a group of American citizens setting out to see just what their money had bought.

Jefferson chose Lewis to lead the Corps of Discovery, and, in turn, Lewis picked Clark, his former army commander. For all practical purposes it was a joint command, with the two men issuing joint orders whenever they were together. As historian Stephen Ambrose puts it, many Americans virtually think of them as one person and spin the names together into "Lewisandclark."

They were a remarkable pair. For example, there's no record of the two men ever disagreeing. On anything. At any time. Extraordinary. Lewis would sign all correspondence with his military rank: "Captain, 1st Infantry." Lewis, although ostensibly the expedition leader, had been an army lieutenant, serving *under* Clark; now he became captain of the Corps of Discovery or Captain of an "Expedition for N.W. Discovery." When it was all over, and the government decided to reward the two men with land grants, Congress first gave Lewis, as leader, a larger portion of land than Clark. Lewis insisted their grants be equal.

They would ascend the Missouri River to its source, wherever that might be, cross the "Highlands," as the Rocky Mountains were called, and follow "the best water-communication which offered itself from thence to the Pacific Ocean." Obviously planning ahead, two months before Napoleon agreed to the big land deal, Jefferson browbeat Congress into coming up with the money to send out an expedition. The amount originally appropriated was $2,500, but in the end it cost much more than that—exactly $38,722.25.

By July 1803 Lewis and Clark had left Washington City bound for Pittsburgh. The U.S. Senate wouldn't approve the Louisiana Purchase for another three months, and by then they were well on their way. By fifty-five-foot keelboat, first on the Ohio River, then on the Mississippi, they slipped over to St. Louis. During the next two weeks they enlisted members of the expedition, the two captains sizing up the candidates, making judgments as to their character, physical strength, and general hardiness, and testing their marksmanship. Initially, nine men were sworn into the army, with General George Rogers Clark on hand to make their enlistments official. Two others were on the original roster: a locally renowned woodsman named George Drouillard and William Clark's slave, York, described as big, very dark, strong, agile, and a natural athlete. Drouillard would go to Tennessee, pick up other soldiers who had signed on for the trip, and see that they got to the party's winter quarters on the east bank of the Mississippi, near St. Louis.

Their fleet now consisting of the keelboat and two pirogues, they were ready for the first leg of the trip, what you might call a preexpedition expedition. On November 11 the small party arrived at Fort Massac—where George Rogers Clark had routed a small British garrison during the Revolutionary War—in southern Illinois, along the Ohio River.

Immediately Meriwether Lewis began "shooting" the sun at noon, trying to determine their latitude. The job requires an accurate chronometer—determine the exact time where you are against the exact time in Greenwich, England, consult a handy table, and you'll know your latitude. Problem was, clocks then often weren't precise, and that was the case with the one Lewis had bought in Philadelphia to take along on the expedition. Still, given the liability the numbers Lewis and Clark came up with were remarkably accurate.

Another method of determining latitude involves identifying certain stars, measuring the moon's easterly motion as it orbits the earth, and then consulting yet another handy table.

Problem with both methods was that the "handy tables" were contained in not so handy books, volumes so heavy it was decided Lewis and Clark would not take them along. Instead, they would record the numbers in journals, and once they got back home where they'd left their handy tables, they'd determine just where they'd been at a given moment. In other words, they might not know where they were, but later they'd know where they had been.

In November they reached the army post at Kaskaskia, on the Illinois side of the river. They were almost ready to go.

Not if Spain had anything to say about it, however. St. Louis was still in Spanish hands; Spain would turn it over to France, and then France would turn it over to the United States. It would be December 20 before the United States officially would take possession of the Louisiana Territory.

Even then Spanish officials delayed in handing over St. Louis. In part, Madrid's opposition was directed by a man historian Ambrose calls "a fabulous if despicable character": former American Revolutionary War officer James Wilkinson. He'd been part of the Conway Cabal that unsuccessfully tried to oust George Washington as commander of the Continental Army. Along with Vice President Aaron Burr, Wilkinson would try to break off part of the Louisiana Purchase territory into a separate nation.

At the time Lewis and Clark made their cross-country trek, Wilkinson was the commander of America's small army. He was also a spy for Spain with a code name: "Agent 13." A man who never met a conspiracy he didn't like, James Wilkinson was charming, amoral, shrewd, and a survivor. He also was a double agent who'd sworn to Spain that he'd work for secession of the western part of America.

Madrid apparently was afraid America would set up Pacific seaports and steal its gold and silver mines in the Southwest. The Spanish governor of modern-day New Mexico sent at least four armed parties out from Santa Fe searching for the Lewis and Clark Expedition. None would succeed.

Colonel Carlos Dehault Delassus, the Spanish lieutenant governor of Upper Louisiana, denied the expedition permission to go up the Missouri until the official transfer of sovereignty—Spain to France to the United States—took place in St. Louis. Meriwether Lewis didn't see much sense in arguing. After all, it was too late in the season to head upriver.

In the meantime Lewis and Clark drilled their recruits in the techniques of frontiering. On May 14, 1804, William Clark wrote in his journal:

I set out at 4 o'clock, P.M., in the presence of many of the neighboring inhabitants and proceeded under a gentle breeze up the

Missouri to the upper point of the first island, 4 miles, and camped on the island.

The Corps of Discovery, as Thomas Jefferson called it, was on its way, the adventure of their—or almost anybody else's—life: twenty-seven expedition members (all unmarried), Lewis and Clark, woodsman George Drouillard, and York, the slave Clark had inherited from his father. They were undermanned and would need more muscle power to get them upstream to the Continental Divide, which they believed was somewhere in the Rockies, but they weren't sure just where.

From Wood River, Illinois (upstream from St. Louis and directly opposite the mouth of the Missouri), to Ecola Creek, Oregon, and back, the trip would total some 7,689 miles. The corps slowly moved up the Missouri, the "Big Muddy," riding, paddling, and walking their way into history.

Members of the corps—the average GIs of the time, if you will—were remarkable in many ways, and in just as many ways they've been forgotten by history. It was they, of course, who did most of the work but who got little recognition. Without them Meriwether Lewis and William Clark couldn't have succeeded.

Despite rumors spread by opponents back East, the Lewis and Clark expedition had few personnel problems. One man, Sgt. Charles Floyd, died, presumably of a burst appendix, which Lewis diagnosed as "Bilose Chorlick" (bilious colic?). Early-nineteenth-century medicine being what it was, if Floyd *did* suffer a burst appendix—peritonitis resulting from a ruptured or perforated, then infected, appendix—it's likely he'd have died no matter if he was in New York, London, Paris, or, as it was, on an island in the middle of the Louisiana Territory. When Floyd died on August 20, 1804, he had the dubious honor of being the first U.S. soldier to die west of the Mississippi River.

"We buried him," William Clark recorded in his journal, "on the top of the bluff a half mile below a small river to which we gave his name." The Missouri River later cut into the bank where Floyd had been buried and exposed his bones. Charles Floyd then was reburied along the Missouri River at Sioux City, Iowa. The site of his new grave and monument are believed to be as close as possible to the location of his original grave, the original site now being under the river itself.

The expedition court-martialed one member for desertion and theft, and they disciplined another for "mutinous expression." Private Moses Reed deserted and was brought back to camp under guard. Reed had claimed he'd left his knife back at an earlier campsite and was allowed to return to find the knife. After three days Reed hadn't returned, so Clark sent five other men "back after the deserter . . . with [an] order [that] if he did not give up peaceably to put him to death."

It took the searchers several days, but on August 17, they brought Reed back to the main camp. At his court-martial Reed

> confessed that he "deserted and stole a public rifle, shot-pouch, powder, and ball," and requested that we would be as favorable with him as we could, consistently with our oaths, which we were, and only sentenced him to run the gantlet [gauntlet] four times through the party, and that each man with 9 switches should punish him and for not to be considered in future as one of the party.

Lewis and Clark dismissed Reed in disgrace. The man had been a first-class grouser who'd tried to poison the minds of several expedition members. He succeeded with Private Newman, who lashed out verbally against Lewis and Clark and the expedition in general. Reed no longer was in the military; however, Newman was and they "confined [him] for mutinous expression," and Lewis and Clark set up a court-martial to try him. It consisted of "9 of his peers," Clark recorded. Newman had:

> uttered repeated expressions of a highly criminal and mutinous nature; the same having a tendency not only to distroy [sic] every principle of military discipline, but also to alienate the affections of the individuals composing this Detachment to their officers, and disaffect them to the service for which they have been so sacredly and solemnly engaged.

Finding Newman guilty, "They did 'sentence him 75 lashes and disbanded from the party.'" Even though he'd been "disbanded from the party"—in other words, dismissed—Lewis and Clark had to take him along or he likely would have died or been killed by the Indians. The corps "attached [him] to the mess and crew of the red pirogue as a laboring hand . . . and that he be deprived of his arms and accouterments and not be permitted the honor of mounting guard till further orders."

The next day they began Newman's punishment—those seventy-five lashes—and it caused some consternation among the Arikara Indians with whom the Corps of Discovery was visiting at the time. The Arikara chief was in camp when the lashing was carried out; it "allarmed verry much" the chief who "cried aloud, or he affected to cry." The Indians weren't used to corporal punishment. Clark says he spoke to the chief and "explained the punishment and the necessity of it. He [the chief] also thought examples were necessary." The chief's people "never whipped even the children," and under Indian law Newman would not have been flogged. Instead, the chief simply would have killed the malcontent Newman. Death, the chief felt, was the only sure cure for insubordination.

By late autumn Lewis and Clark had reached the Mandan Indian villages in North Dakota. They didn't know it, but at the time they were about seven hundred miles east of the Continental Divide.

They built a log village they called "Fort Mandan" and went into winter quarters. By all accounts the Mandan Indians saved the corps. They helped them through the winter, helped feed them, and when the ice began to melt the following spring, they sent along with the Lewis and Clark expedition three new members: a fur trapper named Toussaint Charbonneau, who was to act as their translator, and one of his wives, a sixteen-year-old Shoshone Indian who'd been captured by the Hidatsa* as a child and then sold to Charbonneau.

---

*Pronounced Hee-DAT-sa, the band lived in what is now North Dakota, in permanent villages composed of countless dome-shaped earth lodges. Mainly the Hidatsa were vegetarians who raised various crops; however, they supplemented their diet with that staple of the Indians' diet, buffalo.

Her name: Sacagawea, whom Lewis and Clark nicknamed "Janey." With them also was her newborn son, Jean-Baptiste.

Jean-Baptiste Charbonneau was born while Lewis and Clark wintered at the Mandan village. To ease her labor Lewis had given Sacagawea some crushed rattlesnake rattles in a little water. When the child was born, Clark fell in love with the squalling infant and nicknamed him "Pomp," which means "chief" in Shoshone. Clark described the child as "a butifull promising Child." William Clark dandled Pomp, tickled him, and in general spoiled him. After they reached the Pacific and turned back, Clark dandled, tickled, and spoiled him some more. He even wanted to adopt the boy, raising him as if he'd been his natural child; Sacagawea held Clark off by saying, maybe next year, after "Pomp" had been weaned.

On July 25, 1806, Clark named a rock tower on the south of the Yellowstone River after Pomp. He described "Pomp's Pillar" as being "two hundred feet high and four hundred paces in circumference." It's about thirty-five miles southwest of Custer, Montana. William Clark chiseled his signature on the rock, and it's still legible. Over the years editors of the Lewis and Clark journals frequently misread the phrase *Pomp's Pillar*. They apparently believed that Clark had named the tower after "Pompey's Pillar" in Egypt, so they changed the explorer's spelling, and therefore its meaning and dedication. It was Pomp, not Pompey, after whom William Clark named the pillar of rock. Aside from its original distinction, Pomp's Pillar played another role in history as the site of a pre–Little Big Horn battle between George Armstrong Custer and Sitting Bull.

By all accounts, if it hadn't been for Sacagawea, Lewis and Clark might have failed. With her they met, conversed with, and settled differences with several Native American tribes, which paradoxically led to trouble.

Along with the flora and fauna of the land they traveled, the Corps of Discovery discovered something else: Sexual customs practiced by some Native American tribes allowed frequent encounters between the outside men and Indian women. Apparently, most of the members didn't totally abstain from sex during the trip, and that may have included Lewis and Clark themselves.

Meriwether Lewis wrote about what may now be considered the open marriages of some Native American tribes. A Shoshone warrior, he wrote, "will for a trifle barter the companion of his bead [*sic*] for a night or longer if he conceives the reward adequate." However, the Sioux, Lewis added, were even more likely to offer up their bedmates. Lewis and Clark apparently didn't try to keep their men and the native women separate. "To prevent this mutual exchange of good offices altogether," Lewis wrote, "I know it impossible to effect, particularly on the part of our young men whom some months abstinence have made very polite to those tawney damsels."

Frequent sexual relations often had the foreseeable outcomes— mixed-breed children and venereal disease. At one point, March 15, 1806,

> we were visited this afternoon, in a canoe by Delashelwilt, a Chinook chief, his wife, and six women of his nation, which the Old Bawd, his wife brought for market. This was the same party which had communicated the venereal [disease] to several of our party in November last, and of which they have fully recovered. I therefore gave the men a particular charge with respect to them, which they promised me to observe.

At least two members of the Corps of Discovery contracted venereal disease. Private George Gibson contracted syphilis, and in January 1804 Lewis tried treating him with mercury, the remedy of choice among physicians of the period. If he followed the procedure of the time, Gibson spent many hours rubbing mercury directly onto his skin or swallowing a derivative in pill form. Mercury, we now know, is a poison, so the adage of the nineteenth century is more real than people of the time could have known: A night with Venus, a lifetime with Mercury. That lifetime with Mercury likely would have been short and deadly.

As for mercury's curative powers, they weren't nearly as strong as Meriwether Lewis believed. In 1805 he wrote of using mercury to cure Pvt. Silas Goodrich. "Goodrich," he claimed, "has recovered from the Louis veneri"—that is to say, syphilis—"which he contracted from an amorous contact with a Chinook woman." Lewis added that "I cured him as I did [Private] Gibson last winter with the uce [*sic*] of mercury." Six months later, however, Goodrich again showed the symptoms of syphilis.

On April 26, 1805, the Corps of Discovery reached the Yellowstone River. On June 13, they camped at the Great Falls of the Missouri River. "I hurried down the hill," Lewis wrote, "which was about 200 feet high and difficult of access, to gaze on this sublimely grand spectacle."

By August 11 they'd found a river "about 12 yards wide and barred in several places entirely across by beaver dams." Lewis and three others (Drouillard, Hugh McNeal, and John Shields), who were alone at the time, noticed an Indian "on horseback about two miles distant, coming down the plain toward us." By the way he was dressed, Lewis believed, the rider was a Shoshone—"His arms were a bow and a quiver of arrows, and he was mounted on an elegant horse without a saddle, and a small string which was attached to the under jaw of the horse which answered as a bridle." When they were about a mile apart, Lewis "made him a signal of friendship known to the Indians of the Rocky Mountains." The signal, however, "had not the desired effect." Lewis removed "some beads, a looking glass, and a few trinkets" from his baggage to give him as a peace offering. Leaving his companions and his musket behind, Lewis moved toward the Indian. When they were about two hundred yards apart, "I now called to him in as loud a voice as I could command, repeating the word *tab-ba-bone,* which in their language, signifies 'white man.'"

Well, not exactly. At that stage of the game it's unlikely the Shoshone *had* a word for *white man,* whom they rarely if ever saw. Back at the Mandan camp, Lewis had asked Sacagawea how to say "white man." She asked her French-Indian husband, Charbonneau, who gave her his version: *tab-ba-bone,* which *can* mean "white man," but it also means "stranger" or "enemy," which may have been the same thing at the time.

Lewis goes rushing forward, yelling at the top of his voice, *tab-ba-bone, tab-ba-bone, tab-ba-bone!* "Enemy, enemy, enemy!" The Indian did just what you'd expect; he got the hell out of there, galloping back to camp to spread the alarm Paul Revere–style, crying out, "The enemy is coming, the enemy is coming!"

By following the Indian's tracks Lewis hoped to find a village. By nightfall they hadn't located it, so they set up camp. Lewis didn't want a repeat of natives riding off in fear, so "I fixed a small flag of the U.S. to a pole which I made McNeal carry, and planted in the ground where we halted or camped." Sure, that should do it: a strange man who goes around shouting, "Enemy!" and who plants a flag it's unlikely anyone within a hundred miles has ever seen. Luckily, none of the natives came calling that night.

The next day they found the track the mysterious Indian had taken, along what Lewis described as "a large and plain Indian road." "At the distance of 4 miles," Lewis recorded, "the road took us to a most distant fountain of the waters of the mighty Missouri, in search of which we have spent so many toilsome days and restless nights." He drank "pure and ice-cold water which comes from the base of a low mountain." Later, they

> proceeded on to the top of the dividing ridge, from which I discovered immense ranges of high mountains to the west of us, with their tops partially covered with snow. I now descended the mountain about ¾ of a mile, which I found steeper than on the opposite side, to a handsome bold running creek of cold, clear water. Here I tasted the water of the great Columbia River.

He was wrong about the river. The water actually came from the Lemhi River, a tributary of a tributary (the Salmon River) of a tributary (the Snake River) of the Columbia River. What Lewis was drinking, of course, was water that, if he hadn't deprived the stream of it, eventually would have flowed into the Columbia and on into the Pacific Ocean.

Meriwether Lewis, however, had done something important. He'd reached the Continental Divide, and it was all downhill—literally, downhill—from there.

On November 7 Lewis and Clark saw something they'd been working a year and a half for:

> Great joy in camp. We are in view of the ocean, this great Pacific Ocean which we have been so long anxious to see, and the

roaring or noise made by the waves breaking on the rocky shores (as I suppose) may be heard distinctly.

Well, maybe not. What they probably saw was an inlet or an estuary. Most likely they were about fifteen miles from the Pacific. No matter. They thought they were there, and despite being tired and often hungry, their clothing by now in tatters, the end was in sight. On November 22, 1805,

Captain Lewis branded a tree with his name, date, &c. I marked my name, the day and year, on an alder tree. The party all cut the first letters of their names on different trees in the bottom. Our hunters killed 3 bucks, 4 brant, and 3 ducks today.

The hunt was not always so successful. On the return trip, while out looking for a wounded elk he shot, Meriwether Lewis was shot himself—"across the hinder part of the right thye," he recorded. No dummy he, Meriwether

instantly supposed that his hunting companion, Private Pierre [Cruzatte] had shot me in mistake for an elk, as I was dressed in brown leather and he cannot see very well. Under this impression I called out to him, "Damn you, you have shot me."

Lewis called out to Cruzatte, but the private didn't answer. Aha, Meriwether Lewis believed, it must have been Indians. Later, when the party located Cruzatte, the private swore he'd never heard Captain Lewis calling and, no, he hadn't shot Meriwether, or at least "declared if he had shot me it was not his intention." The spent shot had lodged in Lewis's leather breeches, and when he examined it, "I knew it to be the ball of the short rifles such as that he had"—a .54-caliber ball, from a U.S. Army Model 1803, not a weapon any local Indian was likely to have. Meriwether didn't believe Pierre had shot him intentionally, but he also didn't believe the private was entirely innocent either. As for Private Cruzatte not seeing "very well," Pierre had only one eye, and he was nearsighted in that one.

At any rate, Sgt. Patrick Gass helped clean the wound, "introducing tents of patent lint into the ball holes" to let new tissue grow from the inside. With that the party returned to their pirogue and proceeded downriver, Meriwether Lewis lying on his stomach to protect his wounded ass.

With the exception of a day's rest now and then, the Corps of Discovery trudged continuously. Finally, on September 23, 1806, Meriwether Lewis and William Clark completed their epic trek across the West. When they returned to St. Louis, their tales of a successful expedition fired the imagination of the new nation. They had proved the feasibility of an overland route to the West. Soon thousands of settlers and adventurers headed that way.

The same year Lewis and Clark returned to St. Louis, Congress authorized funds to construct a road from Cumberland, Maryland (not far from Fort Necessity, the scene of Washington's defeat by the French in 1754), to the village of Zanesburg, Virginia (now Wheeling, West Virginia), on the Ohio River. It was America's first federally funded public highway. From 1822 until 1838 the federal government funded the road, relinquishing each section to the states as it was completed.

It became known as the National Road. It's been realigned somewhat and resurfaced, but for the most part U.S. Route 40 follows the same route as the National Road, which itself pretty much followed a trail George Washington hacked out in 1754. It dipped southward about the point where General Braddock was buried after he fell into that French and Indian trap, and then headed for Zanesburg before finally aiming for Vandalia, Illinois, where it ended. In 1817 pioneer Morris Birkbeck wrote, "Old America seems to be breaking up and moving westward. We are seldom out of sight, as we travel on this grand track towards Ohio."

From the time that Daniel Boone first opened the Wilderness Road until about 1819, it had been the settlers' gateway to the West. Beginning in the 1820s the National Road took over from the Wilderness Road as the main route west for thousands of settlers. However, just as it earlier had replaced the Wilderness Road as America's way west, today's Route 40 has been supplanted in the traveler's favor by interstate roads. Such is fame. Such is history; one generation of people and roads giving way for the next.

Travelers, then as now, left their marks along the way, marks that weren't always straight A's. Today's travelers leave cans, bottles, and plastic wrappers in something of an unintentional and regrettable trail of breadcrumbs others can follow; so, too, did our ancestors. Eighteenth-century tourists complained of pollution. Spring water, they said, often was fouled with ashes, sweepings, putrid flesh, dead dogs, and horse excrement. Both travelers and settlers used the local water for soaking deer hides, washing clothes, and drinking.

It's a wonder anybody survived the East to die out West.

For several years theory had it that humans came to the Western Hemisphere by way of a land bridge from Siberia to Alaska and then southward. The earliest known site was Clovis, New Mexico, dated about 13,000 years ago. Now comes a new theory: it wasn't Asians who came east but, rather, Europeans who came west. Artifacts discovered in the area of southeastern Virginia known as Cactus Hill may have been settled as early at 23,000 years ago. And, chemical tests indicate they came from Eurpoe—Spain amd Ireland. Scientists are testing artifacts—like Clovis, no human remains have been found, so DNA testing can't be used—that indicate the inhabitants of Cactus Hill came from Europe by following the coast of Europe northward, then westward along an effective land bridge across the North Atlantic. So, instead of the earlist Americans moving West to East, they may have gone East to West. Just the way thousands of others did thousands of years later.

CHAPTER TWO

The Cowboys:
Making the Wild West Wild, Part One

Mammas, don't let your babies grow up to be cowboys.
Song title, Ed Bruce and Patsy Bruce

To mount a horse and gallop over prairies, completely losing one's self in vast and illimitable space, as silent as lonely, is to leave every petty care. In these grand wastes, one is truly alone with God. Oh, how I love the West!
Mrs. Orsemus Boyd, army wife

Lady Rose Pender of England traveled through Montana in 1883, and apparently she enjoyed the scenery. However, she called the American cowboy "a strange creature, unlike any other of his fellow men, and all he does must be done with swagger and noise." Lady Rose added that "I did not like the cowboys; they impressed me as brutal and cowardly, besides being utterly devoid of manners or good feeling."

She wasn't alone in her dislike for cowboys. Laramie, Wyoming, newspaper writer Edgar Nye once described cowboys as "dry land pirates . . . under the black flag." Nye claimed that the cowboy was "generally a youth who thinks he will not earn his twenty-five dollars per month if he does not yell and whoop and shoot, and scare little girls into St. Vitus's dance."

For much of the rest of the world, however, cowboys were heroes.

The years from 1865 to 1899 were the days of the trail driver, the homesteader, the Indian fighter, and the railroad builder. But most of all, they were the days of the cowboy, and it's often hard to determine where fact leaves off and fantasy picks up. Still, some things about them are certain.

They worked hard and played hard. They got roostered (the cowboy word for "drunk") and they gambled—one cowboy gambled away a whole herd of cattle. A typical cowboy was a young man between the ages of seventeen and twenty-eight. Teddy Blue Abbott, who was a cowboy himself, put the average age at twenty-three or twenty-four. Most were lightly built; big men, Abbott said, were just too hard on the horses. So much for big John Wayne and equally large James Arness, Matt Dillon of television's long-running *Gunsmoke.*

To borrow from a twentieth-century saying about airplane pilots: There were old cowboys and bold cowboys, but there were no old, bold cowboys. Not many, anyway. They started young and they died young. The *Galveston News* noted:

> The little children, as early as they can walk, pilfer their mother's tape [measure] and make lassos to rope the kittens and the ducks. The boys, as soon as they can climb on a pony, are off to the prairie to drive stock. As they advance toward manhood, their highest ambition is to conquer a pitching mustang or throw a wild bull by the tail.

Among stunts used by cowboys, along with roping and hog-tying young beeves for branding, was riding alongside a full-size animal, reaching down, and jerking and pulling the critter's tail until they tipped over the poor beast. Today's rodeo has banned tail pulling, at least publicly.

About the time the railroads came along, men who used a long stick to push or poke or prod cattle into rail cars got the nickname "cowpuncher" or "cowpoke." For a while, real cowboys hated the name; after all, cowpunchers weren't the ones out on the trail herding recalcitrant cattle. Finally, however, they accepted the terms.

Cowboys often had their own way of speaking. A balding cook "ain't got any hair 'tween him and heaven." Another cowboy might be so crooked that he "could swallow nails an' spit out corkscrews." And a no-good cowboy "wasn't worth a barrel of shucks," referring to corn shucks, for which there was little use at the time except as quick-burning torches, when a fast-moving cowboy would "light a shuck."

Cowboys went by names such as Pinnacle Jake and Mesquite Bill and Bronco Jim. Sometimes they had nicknames based on characteristics or looks or habits: Gloomy Thompson, Sudden Lucas,

Horseface Bill, Fatty Hamilton, Lazy Dick, Itchy Jake, or Vinegar Hall. They were Buckskin Joe and Wyoming Pete and, even, Teddy Blue, whose real name was Edward Charles Abbott. Teddy Blue Abbott became one of the most famous real-life cowboys. He got his nickname one night in 1881, Abbott remembered, at Turner's Theatre in Miles City, Montana:

> I went in there that night, and one of these box rustlers came up to me. You know in that kind of theatres [*sic*] they used to have curtained boxes running all around inside, and the box rustlers was what they called the girls that worked them. So this girl came up to me and she had on a little skirt, like a circus girl, and tights that looked like she had been melted and run into them. And first she invited me upstairs to buy wine—at five dollars a bottle. I said nothing doing to that. And then she told me she had a room back there and invited me to go with her. That sounded better to me and I was going to go. But there was a dark hall that ran around behind the stage, and as we started along it I remembered that I had seven hundred dollars on me, in my six-shooter belt. . . . And I thought there might be some kind of a deadfall back there—I was a wise guy. I'd heard stories.
>
> So I turned around, and . . . my spur catched on a carpet and I fell through a thin partition onto the stage. Well, I thought, If you're before an audience you've got to do something, so I grabbed a chair from one of the musicians and straddled it and bucked it all around the stage, yelling, "Whoa, Blue! Whoa, Blue!"—which was a cowpuncher expression at that time. Before they even got me off the stage, it had started. The manager yelled, "Hey, Blue, come out of there," and the audience was yelling with laughter and they took it up. And when I went out of that theatre that night I was Blue, and Teddy Blue I have been for fifty-five years.

Teddy Blue also remembered first taking to cowboying:

> I had a new white Stetson hat that I paid ten dollars for and new pants that cost twelve dollars, and a good shirt and fancy

boots. They had colored tops, red and blue, with a half-moon and star on them. Lord, I was proud of these clothes! They were the kind of clothes top hands wore, and I thought I was dressed right for the first time in my life.

Teddy Blue wasn't alone in how he dressed. The cowboy's life was rough and tough, but the man himself often was gaudy and pretentious. They wore sombreros and Stetsons, slouch hats, and high hats, had their photographs taken while wearing top hats or bowlers. Butch Cassidy, the Sundance Kid, and the Wild Bunch were pictured wearing bowlers, a fact the Bunch regretted after the law got hold of the picture and recognized the boys. Despite a late-twentieth-century saying, both good and bad guys wore black hats; light-colored planter's hats were left over from the pre–Civil War South but weren't too popular in the West. Sombreros originated in Mexico and had high curved edges on wide brims, sometimes with a regular mountain peak of a sugarloaf crown, dented into a blunt point, a *barbiquejo*—a chin strap, dangling long and loose beneath the cowboy's jaw. Old West farmers wore undented wool hats with narrow curled brims with tall, chimney-pot crowns. They cost about $1.50.

In 1862, while the East was at war, a man named John B. Stetson set out to hunt for gold in Colorado. He'd been born in New Jersey and became an apprentice milliner, but that seemed kinda dull to John. He also did a bit of trapping, and it was while working as a trapper that he invented the hat that made his name.

He sewed scraps of beaver pelts together to produce a large, vaquero-style, wide-brimmed hat that would keep the sun off his face on a hot day and serve as a bowl for water if need be. Others liked his hat, and John B. made a few more.

In 1871, with an investment of a hundred dollars, Stetson launched his world-famous hatmaking firm, not in the West, but way back East in Philadelphia. He almost went broke; in his first year he sold only a dozen hats. But then business got better, and the term for his hat—the *John B.* or *Boss of the Plains*—took its place with *Colt* and *Winchester.* By the time John B. Stetson died in 1906, the company he had founded was selling two million hats a year, all over the world. Made from beaver, nutria, or coney fur, a John B. cost you ten to twenty dollars, sometimes more, and this when a top hand's pay was thirty dollars a month.

Your pants looked baggy, and you were proud of it—like elephant's legs, because you purposely took the crease out of them. A crease would mark a man as a "cheap John," wearing ready-made pants off the stack in some frontier shop.

You'd pay as much as twenty-five dollars for handmade boots, but you could get a shirt for just a dollar and a suit might cost only ten—a price that would have been pretty darn good even back East.

Your shirt might be linen if you were dressed to go visiting, cotton or wool if you were working the trail. Likely, it pulled over your head, with lots of tail but no pockets. Pockets were taken care of by your vest. Maybe a coat of broadcloth and, if you could afford it, a heavy gold watch chain hooked into a buttonhole. Your watch might be an "American Horologe," made in Waltham, Massachusetts, or one from the National Watch Company, later the Elgin National Watch Company. Most cowboys didn't have watches, having been taught at an early age to tell time by the sun and stars. Riding night herd, they might count time by cigarettes, the distance a man could ride while rolling and smoking a cigarette: so many cigarettes east, so many north.

In your vest or coat pocket you might have a match case and some matches. Along with them you might carry a twisted bit of tobacco sometimes called a "stogie," because it was the kind Conestoga wagon drivers often smoked. About the time of the Civil War, cigars were being turned out by the millions by Connecticut Valley manufacturers. Called "long nines," they were the thin panatella type and were packed several thousand at a time in barrels. Sometimes long twists of tobacco, called "supers," would be aged in rum before being smoked. Shorter cigars, appropriately called "short sixes," often were handed out free by saloonkeepers or sold for two for a penny; it was these short sixes that are frequently remembered because of their dreadful smell. It was possible, but not likely, that cowboys might come across the better, higher priced, Cuban cigar, which would wholesale for $15 to $17 a thousand, compared to the $4 a thousand for domestic brands.

The Cowboys

In those pre-cancer-conscious days of the Wild West, cowboys chewed tobacco and dipped snuff and smoked pipes. In fact, just about anything you could do with tobacco, they did. Like the cowboys who posed for twentieth-century cigarette ads, they often died from their habits.

The Civil War brought on a tremendous increase in the use of tobacco. It often was the one item Confederates had to barter with Union troops. General Ulysses S. Grant once paid for a load of Virginia tobacco, even though the load had been burned during a Federal bombing. The Rebels, he said, had done their part by providing the tobacco; it wasn't their fault it was destroyed. Grant, of course, was a longtime cigar smoker, and he died of throat cancer.

After the Civil War, ex-Confederate John Ruffin Green began marketing granulated tobacco in small muslin sacks with a round tag dangling on the sack's drawstring. At one time the sack of tobacco carried a packet of brown "roll your own" papers attached. John Green lived near Durham's Station, North Carolina, but took his trademark bull picture from England's Durham's mustard.* Later, Green sold out to a onetime partner, William Blackwell, who reputedly paid just five hundred dollars for the Bull Durham trademark. The product continues as Bull Durham today, although the full-view, anatomically correct picture of the bull is no longer around to shock puritanical ladies as it did in the days of the Wild West.

So-called tailor-made cigarettes—that is, ready-made prerolled ones—were available even before the Civil War, but more so than the roll-your-own variety, they were considered wicked. Certainly, sissified and unmanly. It wasn't until the Philadelphia Centennial Exposition of 1876, where they were extravagantly displayed and promoted, that ready-made cigarettes really got going in America.

In a pinch, in place of cigarette papers, a farmer or cowboy could

---

*Prepared mustard was available beginning in the 1860s, as were such products as Lea & Perrins sauce. Noted British chemists John Lea and his partner William Perrins opened the first chain of drugstores in England in the early 1800s. They took a sauce popular in Bengal, India, analyzed and tasted it, and found out it was horrible. They put it aside and forgot it for two years. The next time they tried it, the sauce had changed its flavor. It had aged. They made up a big batch and began selling it in Europe and America as Worcestershire sauce.

use corn shucks to roll his own. After all, Indians and Mexicans had used this method for generations. One problem was, however, you had to hold the corn-shuck cigarette together. You just couldn't lick it to make it stay together. Which brings up the question of just how do you "roll your own"? There likely are several techniques, but one involves careful, two-handed, hand-to-eye coordination. You'd unfold the cigarette paper, hold it between three fingers with the center finger slightly denting the paper; with your teeth, you'd open the bag of Bull Durham (or that of a competitor—Pride of Durham, Duke of Durham, or Ridgewood), spill a small amount of tobacco onto the paper, reclose the tobacco bag with your teeth, and stuff it back in your vest pocket. Roll the tobacco-filled paper into a cylindrical appearance, and dampen one edge of the paper with your tongue. Twist the two ends of your completed cigarette and light up. As they say on television, Don't try this at home, kiddies.

In your vest or coat pocket you might also carry a lead pencil, that is, a wooden pencil with a graphite "lead," but you didn't have a fountain pen, since workable ones didn't appear until the 1880s. If you were really fancy, you might carry a pen case containing a penholder and steel points.*

Early on, you might tuck away in your pocket a "shin plaster," paper money in denominations of three, five, ten, twenty-five, and fifty cents. By the middle of the Civil War small metallic coins had practically disappeared, and Congress authorized the printing of "greenbacks," so called because of the color of the money. Beginning in 1875, metal coins replaced both greenbacks and shin plasters. All along, however, Spanish coins were readily available in the Wild West. There were the Spanish-colonial milled dollars, which were often cut up into "pieces of eight." "Two bits, four bits, six bits, a dollar," the old high school and college cheer went, but in the Wild West cutting Spanish coins into bits gave rise to "bit houses," where

---

*Until the mid-1940s elementary schools often insisted youngsters equip themselves with penholders and steel points; glass inkwells fitted into desks would regularly be filled by the teacher. Into such inkwells unruly boys often tried dipping vulnerable girls' pigtails.

everything cost one bit, and "two-bit" houses, where everything cost a quarter. The latter also gave rise to the phrase *two-bit whore,* for which you can use your imagination. Mexican pesos were available, the so-called "'dobe dollar," as were California gold pieces—made by private mints on the West Coast, they went all the way up to fifty-dollar pieces, many of them eight-sided instead of round—and, later on, U.S. cartwheels.

Cowboys came from all parts of the world, all parts of life. They'd been Europe's moneyed patricians and penniless immigrants, they'd been drifters, and even a future president of the United States would call himself a cowboy—Teddy Roosevelt. They'd be men on the dodge from the law one day and the next they might wear a sheriff or marshal's star. Cowboys were not born special; they made themselves that way.

Former Union and Confederate soldiers went west after the Civil War. Probably more rebels than bluebellies, if the truth be known, because Confederates, more so than their northern former enemies, needed new stakes and maybe even some fast action to work out their frustrations.

Some cowboys were former sailors, and they took with them some of their favorite songs, including a chantey that went:

O, bury me not in the deep, deep sea,
Where the dark blue waves will roll over me.

Out West they changed the words, but kept the flavor:

O, bury me not on the lone prairie,
Where the wild coyotes will howl over me.

Teddy Blue Abbott claimed that it was a "great song for a while, but . . . they sung it to death." There was, he claimed, "a saying on the range that even the horses nickered it and the coyotes howled it; it got so they'd throw you in the creek if you sang it."

As they sang to the cattle, cowboys recalled times probably not as good as they remembered, but times they wanted to have been good nonetheless.

Remember the Red River Valley
And the cowboy that loves you so true.

Sometimes, they sang with sheer joy:

As I was a-walking one morning for pleasure,
I spied a cowpuncher a-riding along. . . .
Whoopee ti yi yo, git along, little dogies,
It's your misfortune and none of my own,
Whoopee ti yi yo, git along, little dogies,
For you know Wyoming will be your new home.

They rode around the night-bedded herd, singing of the land they lived in—a song written by Brewster Higley in 1873 and still popular today:

Oh, give me a home where the buffalo roam,
Where the deer and the antelope play,
Where seldom is heard a discouraging word
And the skies are not cloudy all day.

And possibly the most mournful of all, "The Cowboy's Lament":

As I walked out in the streets of Laredo,
As I walked out in Laredo one day,
I spied a poor cowboy wrapped up in white linen . . .

Oh, bang the drum slowly* and play the fife lowly,
Play the Dead March as you carry me along;
Take me to the green valley, there lay the sod o'er me,
For I'm a young cowboy and I know I've done wrong.

Some of the most eccentric people of all time lived in Texas in the early years. George Webb Slaughter, for instance, had an outfit on the Brazos River, where he had a herd of fifteen hundred cattle.

---

*Also as "*beat the drum slowly.*"

Occasionally George would take a shot at a wandering Indian, and come Sunday, he'd rest his rifle against the pulpit when he served as an ordained Baptist preacher.

There's the story of a letter written by a cowhand out West and sent to the absentee owner back East. For all the punctuation it lacks, it clearly shows the harshness of a cowboy's life,

> Deer sur. We have brand 800 caves this roundup we
> have made some hay potatoes is a fare crop. That Inglishman
> yu lef in charge at the other camp got to fresh and we had to
> kill the son of a bitch. Nothing much has hapened sence yu
> lef. Yurs truely, Jim.

G. R. "Bob" Fudge was born in Lampasas County, Texas, in 1862, and when he was just ten years old, his father, mother, sister, and two brothers, along with two aunts and uncles, headed for California with a thousand head of cattle and two hundred horses. As the family passed through New Mexico, Comanches killed one of the uncles and ran off with all of the cattle and all but four of the horses. Then the group was hit by smallpox, which killed everybody except Fudge, his mother, and brothers. The four of them returned to Texas, where two years later Bob Fudge hired out with a local rancher. By the time he was nineteen, Bob was the exception to Teddy Blue Abbott's rule: a 250-pound, experienced cowboy. Once he drove a herd of eight hundred horses from Texas to Wyoming. Bob Fudge, as the saying goes, spent his life in the saddle.

Edgar Beecher Bronson was an easterner who went west, took up a life of boots and spurs, and even won the respect of those born to the saddle. Things didn't start out too well, however. Bronson went to Wyoming in 1872, with a letter of introduction to N. R. Davis from Davis's partner, Clarence King. When Bronson arrived in Cheyenne, he carried with him a "cowboy" outfit he'd bought in the East—laced boots, leggings, short hunting spurs, heavy leather chaps, and a Colt .45. Davis ordered him to get rid of everything except the Colt and his underwear, and they started all over—forty-pound saddle and bridle, rawhide lariat, California spurs with two-inch rowels, high-heeled boots, heavy leather chaps, and a big hat to shade Bronson from the Big Sky Country sun. Heading to the ranch, Davis told Bronson that he'd have to "take his medicine" with one of the orneriest trail bosses in the West, Con Humphrey. "He's about as tough a rawhide as ever led a circle," Davis said, "but he always gets there, and that's the only reason I keep him." Then he told the easterner, "Lay close to Con's flank, kid, and keep your end up or turn in your string of horses."

The American Wild West, like just about every other place in the nineteenth century, was sexist. The head of the house was a man; this job (name your choice of occupations) wasn't meant for a woman; barefoot, naked, and pregnant—to use a few of the more obvious and crude examples of the way male society hoped to keep women. That especially was true out on the prairie. It was a man's world.

About the only known salaried cowgirl was Middy Morgan, an Irish immigrant who wandered to Montana. She impressed a local rancher to hire her as a hand; later they became partners in the ranch. Later still, Middy Morgan became advisor to several British ranchers.

There were other women cowpunchers, of course, but apparently they were female relatives of the ranch owner and helped out on the family spread. Sometimes when their husbands died, these women took over the ranch. One such was Mrs. E. J. Guerin. When her husband died, Mrs. Guerin passed as a man in order to support herself and her child. She called herself "Mountain Charlie" and once drove a herd of cattle to California.

Teddy Blue Abbott wrote that cowboys were accustomed to hardship, even joked and laughed about the danger, but above all they were loyal, "intensely loyal to the outfit they were working for." They would "fight to the death for it."

They would follow their wagon boss through hell and never complain. I have seen them ride into camp after two days and nights on herd, lay down on their saddle blankets in the rain and sleep like dead men. They got up laughing and joking about some good time they had in Ogallala or Dodge City.

Although most cowboys "rode for the brand," sometimes they refused to do so. In March 1883 twenty-four hands from three large

ranches in the Texas Panhandle—the LX, LIT, and LS ranches—
went on strike. They signed a strike notice saying:

> We, the undersigned cowboys of Canadian River, do by these
> presents agree to bind ourselves into the following obliga-
> tions, viz:
>
> First: That we will not work for less than $50. per mo. and
> we farther [sic] more agree no one shall work for less than $50.
> per mo. after 31st of Mch.
>
> Second: Good cooks shall also receive $50. per mo.
>
> Third: Any one running an outfit shall not work for less than
> $75. per mo.
>
> Anyone violating the above obligations shall suffer the con-
> sequences. Those not having funds to pay board after March
> 31 will be provided for for 30 days at Tascosa.

The original group quickly grew to about two hundred, amid rumors of range burning and fence cutting. Current wages for hands
on the three ranches were twenty-five a month. The LIT offered
thirty-five, but the cowboys held firm. On March 29 *The Caldwell Commercial* had this comment:

> The strike of the cowboys in the Panhandle seems to be more
> serious than was first thought. The boys threaten to prevent
> [other] men taking their place. It is thought a compromise
> will be effected. Cowboys have some knowledge of the im-
> mense profits cattle owners are making, and it should not be
> at all surprising if they asked fair wages for what is the hard-
> est kind of work.

The strike didn't last long, mainly because the cowboys quickly
gambled, guzzled, and danced away their savings in the saloons of
Tascosa, Texas. At the time the town was full of drifters willing to work
for the standard thirty-dollars-a-month wage. Soon the striking cowboys gave in and returned to their old jobs.

Three years later, in Colfax, New Mexico, eighty cowboys and
small ranchers formed an association called the Northern New Mex-

ico Small Cattlemen and Cowboys' Union, and issued a statement of purpose:

> No cattle owners who employ more than two men are to be received into the union.
>
> We, the cowboys, pledge ourselves to look after the interests of small cattlemen, who are members, and the small cattlemen pledge themselves to do all in their power for the interest of the cowboys.

Their timing was off, and the union fell victim to two years of blizzards.

The last day of 1885 had dawned mild and clear in the northern prairies, but by noon a cold drizzle began to fall, and temperatures began to drop. By nightfall the rain had turned to a fine white, powdery snow swept along by increasingly violent winds. The snow began clinging to everything—weed, bush, tree, man, and animal. The wind blinded cattle, men, and horses, and soon the whole eastern portion of the range country was in the grip of the worst blizzard in the history of the West, from the Dakotas to Texas.

That first night eighteen inches of snow fell, and temperatures plunged to twenty degrees below zero. The storm lasted three days and three nights. Writing in a livestock industry magazine, an anonymous cattleman described the blizzard:

> The sun was hidden behind a leaden sheet of cloud that dipped below the entire circle of the horizon but was thicker and darker in the north and northwest. There was a strange feeling in the quiet, colder-growing air. The silence of the range became deeper and more oppressive. The cattle stop feeding, raise their heads and look uneasily toward the north. . . .
>
> Then, with a sweeping rush, the blizzard itself whirls down upon them. Horizon, hills, draws, and all the rest vanish from sight in an instant in the whirl and swirl of sleet and fine snow that sting and smart all living flesh they strike. . . .

More than a hundred people died in Kansas alone, more than three hundred over the whole West, many of them cowboys and settlers trapped in huts so shabby the men froze to death. Many ranchers lost between fifty and eighty-five percent of their stock. One outfit alone lost every one of its 7,000 cattle. Another, which had 6,000 cattle when the blizzard struck, could round up only 150 the following spring. A Kansas rancher who'd been offered twenty-five thousand dollars for his herd a few days before the storm hit managed to get only five hundred dollars for what he had left after the storm. A Texan who counted 2,300 head of cattle before the blizzard had only 50 when it was all over.

Climatologist Robert DeCourcy Ward suggests that the word *blizzard* may have derived from the German word *blitzartig*, meaning "lightninglike." The *Oxford Universal Dictionary*, however, suggests that it's an American word and came into existence around 1870. Wherever the word came from, the storm of 1886 generated amazing tales.

A group of train travelers trapped by hugh drifts in the town of Kinsley, Kansas, near Dodge City, invented a bit of folklore while they waited for rescuers to reach them. They printed a four-column, four-page newspaper with a bold masthead: "*The B-B-lizzard, Vol. One, Number One.*" They introduced the lead story:

TERRORS OF THE PRAIRIES!!!
Locked in the Embrace of the Grim Frost King
Terrible Sufferings of a Snowbound Raymond
Excursion Party. Hope Not Yet Wholly Abandoned.

In exaggerated phrases the travelers told of how the tops of the train's Pullman cars were twelve feet below the surface of the snow; how the marooned travelers had consumed all of their crackers and cheese, and drunk all of the spiritous liquors that they'd carried with them for medicinal purposes; and how they were reduced to subsisting on polar berries and mosses dug out from the snow. Some brave souls, they claimed, had tried to go for assistance in a sledge drawn by reindeer but had failed. They claimed that the wind blew so hard that passenger cars rocked as though they would be tipped off the track.

Another story has two cowboys caught in the blizzard. It's so cold that when they shout at each other, their words freeze in midair.

Weeks later, when the thaw comes, travelers are frightened by sudden outbursts of profanity coming from empty air.

So many exaggerated tales were told, and so many of them made their way into eastern newspapers, that in February 1886, the editor of the *Estelline Bell* in Dakota Territory had to put out an edition headlined *Blizzard Lies*.

Reality was enough. The spring of 1886 saw the plains covered with dead and bloated cattle, and only the skinners, who took the hides and later gathered the bones, made a profit from cattle that year. Cattlemen had overstocked the range and failed to take adequate steps to protect their cattle.

Wyoming, Colorado, Montana, and the western Dakotas escaped the blizzard of 1885–86, but their turn came. Summer of 1886 was unusually dry and hot. Rancher Lincoln Lang noted that

> like a huge, sullen, glowing ball, the sun arose each morning through a cloud of haze that seemed to have settled upon the country. . . . Temperatures ranging up to 120 in the shade were common.

Seven and a half million hungry cattle were competing for grass in the northern prairie. Meanwhile, cattle prices began to drop. The business of raising cattle had been virtually risk free; now it was in trouble.

Prairie fires hit and cowboys worked almost continuously to stamp them out. A haze of smoke hung in the air, as dust, ashes, and cinders floated through the prairies, covering everything and everyone. "There was hardly an evening in the last week," the *Rocky Mountain Husbandman* reported in August, "that the red glare of the fire demon has not lit up our mountain ridges, while our exchanges bring news of disastrous fires in all parts of the territory."

And then fall and winter storms hit. It began snowing on November 13, 1886, and didn't stop for a month. "In November we had several snowstorms," Teddy Blue Abbot remembered, "and I saw the first white owls I have ever seen. The Indians said they were a bad sign, 'heap snow coming, very cold.' . . . It got colder and colder. It was hell without the heat."

In late December, temperatures registered thirty-four degrees—even forty-four degrees—below zero; January 1887 was the coldest month on the northern plains that anybody could remember. Early that month a blizzard hit that was even worse than that of the year before. Sixteen inches of snow fell in sixteen hours. The snow fell so hard during one seventy-two-hour period that a survivor wrote, "It seemed as if all the world's ice from Time's beginnings had come on a wind which howled and screamed with the fury of demons."

Rancher Hermann Hagedorn, a neighbor of Teddy Roosevelt in the Dakotas, wrote that "the snow was like the finest powder, driving through every crack and nail hole, and piling snowdrifts within the houses as well as without."

Storm followed storm; privation followed privation, and cattle wandered over the windswept landscape searching for food until they died of cold or starvation. Some were too weak to stand and were blown over by the wind. Others had their feet frozen into the ice and died like statues. Came late January, a warm southern wind partly melted the snow. Then another blizzard hit. Teddy Blue Abbott was in Montana that year and described the way cowboys struggled to save the cattle:

> The cattle drifted down on all the rivers. . . . On the Missouri we lost I don't know how many that way. They would walk out on the ice and the ones behind would push the front ones in. The cowpunchers worked like slaves to move them back in the hills, but as all the outfits cut their forces down every winter, they were shorthanded. No one knows how they worked but themselves. They saved thousands of cattle. Think of riding all day in a blinding snow storm, the temperature fifty and sixty below zero, and no dinner. You'd get one bunch of cattle up the hill and another one would be coming down behind you, and it was all so slow, plunging after them through the deep snow that way!
>
> It was the same all over Wyoming, Montana and Colorado, western Nebraska and western Kansas.

To survive the cold, Abbott remembered, cowboys wore "two suits of heavy underwear, two pairs of wool socks, wool pants, two woolen shirts, overalls, leather chaps, wool gloves under leather mittens, blanket-lined overcoats and fur caps." Still, it was so bad that riders died frozen in their saddles as they tried to rescue stranded cattle.

When the spring thaw came, ranchers looked about and were appalled at what they saw. Everywhere were dead animals by the thousands—sprawled across the hillsides and along fence lines, heaped up where they'd been trapped in coulees, floating in rivers swollen by melting snow. Teddy Blue found that

> the coulees in some places were piled deep with cattle where they had sought shelter and died, and the ones that were left were nothing but skin and bone and so weak they could scarcely stand. That was the story behind [artist and writer] Charlie Russell's picture, "The Last of Five Thousand." A friend of his wrote and asked him that spring how his cattle were doing. For an answer Charlie painted that picture of a dying cow and sent it to him. . . .
>
> [In the spring] there was an old fellow working with us who had some cattle on the range; I don't remember his name. But I'll never forget the way he stopped, with sweat pouring off his face, looked up at the sun, sober as a judge, and asked, "Where the hell was you last January?"

Between a million and a million and a half head of cattle, sheep, horses, and mules died in the blizzard of 1887. Cattlemen remembered it as the "Great Die-up." Ranchers by the handsful were wiped out. Many eastern investors withdrew their funds from western ranches, and foreign landowners packed up and went home.

A St. Louis shoe company earlier had bought a ranch in the area for more than a quarter of a million dollars. The blizzards of 1886 and '87 destroyed the company's cattle and the company sold out what was left to a cowboy for his year's wages.

Theodore Roosevelt was in Europe on his honeymoon when he learned about the blizzard. He hurried back to see how bad the damage was. "The losses," the future president said, "are crippling." Ranchers who did survive learned a lesson from the blizzards: In the future they had to have some means of sheltering and feeding cattle in an emergency.

Charlie Siringo probably was the first real cowboy to write a book about his experiences, a cowboy by nature, only by chance a writer. Siringo admitted that "My excuse for writing . . . is money—and lots of it." Unlike most other writers then and now, Siringo truly got it, lots of money. He sold nearly a million copies of *A Texas Cow-boy; or, Fifteen Years on the Hurricane Deck* of a Spanish Pony.*

Siringo's version of a cowboy's life may not have been so much myth after all. Owen Wister changed the way the world viewed the myth. Wister was born in Rhode Island, graduated from Harvard University (a classmate of Teddy Roosevelt), and was a Philadelphia lawyer when he first visited the West in 1885—like many others he went west to improve his health—the same year Charlie Siringo published *A Texas Cow-boy.* Wister stayed at a ranch in Buffalo, Wyoming, and returned to the region several other times. Undoubtedly he met a few real cowboys, but for the most part he associated with wealthy ranch owners and cattle barons.

Wister published his first short story, "Hank's Woman," in 1891, a collection of stories *(Red Men and White)* in 1896, and two novels *(Lin McLean* in 1896 and *Jimmyjohn Boss* in 1900), but it was in 1902 that his best novel (in fact, many consider it the classic cowboy story of all time) was published: *The Virginian,* based in part on the Powder River War in Wyoming, part on the Johnson County War. The main character was a soft-spoken knight on horseback. "The Virginian's pistol came out," Wister wrote

and his hand lay on the table holding it unaimed. And with a voice as gentle as ever, the voice sounded almost like a caress, but drawling a very little more than usual, so that there was almost a space between each word, he issued his order to the man from Tranpas: "When you call me that, smile."

---

*The "hurricane deck" was the name sometimes given to the saddle of a bucking horse and aptly describes the circumstances.

The Virginian was the basis of a television series of the same name. "When you call me that, smile." Indeed. *The Virginian* sold over one and a half million copies and that was enough to make a man smile, certainly enough for Owen Wister. After that he never published another novel.

Cowboy Andy Adams was born in Whitley County, Indiana, northwest of Fort Wayne, in 1858 and moved west when he was eighteen. He drove cattle and horses and became a merchant in Rockport, Texas. Later, he took up gold mining in Cripple Creek, Colorado, before settling down in Colorado Springs. He went on to write five novels, all more or less autobiographical. His writings, as did those by Teddy Blue Abbott *(We Pointed Them North)* and Siringo and Wister, blended realism, wit, and folklore.

Most cowboy novels—indeed, most cowboy movies and TV shows—used four standard locations and scenarios: a bar, a stagecoach, a holdup, and a chase. But, that wasn't the life of your usual real-life cowboy. Real cowboys seldom saw a stagecoach and only occasionally stopped off at a saloon; the chances of witnessing a holdup were remote and the only things they chased were mustangs and bad-tempered steers.

Under the pseudonym "Rawhide Rawlins," artist and writer Charlie Russell asked, "Ma, do cowboys eat grass?" "No," the child's mother replies, "they're partly human."

Likely as not they were uneducated, yet cowboys "set themselves away up above other people who, the chances are, were no more common and uneducated than themselves," cowboy-turned-author Teddy Blue Abbott claimed.

A rancher named Frank Hasting noted that

> cowboys are ultra sensitive, diffident, and superstitious about anything that they do not understand. . . . They possess a quality that is not necessarily courage, but rather the absence of fear.

The "waddy," as a cowboy was sometimes called,* led a strange life,

---

*Apparently the word comes from *wad*, something used to fill in. *Waddy* was especially used in referring to cowboys who drifted from ranch to ranch.

sometimes exciting, sometimes boring, and often dangerous. "No harder life is lived by any workingman," Andy Adams declared. "Our comfort," he added, "was nothing; men were cheap, but cattle cost money."

Just as colorful as the people of the Wild West was the language spoken there. For instance, if you were "barkin' at a knot" you were wasting your time. If you lost out in a gun battle, chances are you weren't just dead, you were as "dead as a can of corned beef." You might win a poker hand and be "grinnin' like a possum eatin' a yellowjacket," but if your opponent got away, you'd likely be "mad enough to swallow a horn toad backwards," which is to say as "mad as a peeled rattler."

You had little chance of striking "pay dirt." Or "pay gravel" or "pay ore," "pay rock," "pay shoot," "pay streak," or "pay vein"—dirt, earth, or gravel bearing heavy quantities of minerals, especially gold. If you did, you had, at least momentarily, "struck it rich" (discovered a rich vein of ore).

You might "cinch up" (saddle up) your old cayuse (or your grulla, which is a horse of a different color) and head to town and the nearest "parlor house" (a bawdy house so high class because it even had a parlor), to engage in a bit of "galling" (courting) with your favorite "crib girl" (a prostitute). You could indulge in too much "popskull," "tarantula juice," "red-eye," or "rotgut" (whiskey) at the local "dog hole" (saloon), and get in trouble with some other "galoot" (a local character). If you weren't "all horns and rattles" (very angry) at each other, you might take in the next event at the local "rat pit" (a pit or crib, usually in the cellar of a bar, where gamblers bet on fights between dogs and rats—how many rats a certain dog could kill in a given amount of time; if a dog was set against a woodchuck or raccoon, it was known as the "chuck game"). You could, of course, wind up in the "calaboose" (the local jail, the name taken from the Spanish *calabozo*, which has the same meaning).

Summer in the Wild West would be "hot enough to wither a fence post" or "colder'n a witch's tit," a descriptive phrase that lingers today. You drank "black water," "bellywash," "black jack," "brown gargle," "coffin varnish," and "jamoka"—coffee likely as not strong and black, boiled with sugar in the pot or even in a frying pan, thick as sin. As the saying goes, It don't take as much water as you think it does.

Likely as not your coffee came from brothers John and Charles Arbuckle. In 1869, they patented a roasting method by which they sealed in the coffee's flavor by coating beans with a mixture of sugar and egg white. It was a success, helped along, no doubt, by the fact that the brothers Arbuckle packed, with each one-pound bag, a peppermint stick. Fights broke out when the cook called out, Who wants the candy tonight? The winner had the privilege of cranking the coffee grinder.

Arbuckle's Ariosa coffee was so common in the West that it became a generic term for coffee, much as *Levi*'s was for jeans, *Winchester* for rifles, and *Stetson* for hats. Before the Arbuckle brothers found a way to roast and preserve coffee beans, ranchers usually bought green beans and roasted them themselves. Out on the range a cowboy frequently used the metal plate on the butt of his Winchester to crack roasted coffee beans before boiling them over an open fire. In 1878 brothers-in-law Caleb Chase and James Sanborn began selling canned ground coffee, and twenty years later vacuum cans were introduced to the West.

To clear the brew of grounds, some cooks tossed crushed eggshells into the pot. Others used a washed-and-dried fish skin they'd cut into pieces. When not in the coffeepot, the cook kept the fish skins in boxes or paper bags.

The cowboy's habit of drinking coffee transferred to Native Americans. Navajos, like cowboys themselves, insisted on Arbuckle's Ariosa coffee. They'd buy it from the Indian agent, where they'd ask for it as "Hosteen Cohay," literally translated from the Navajo language as "Mr. Coffee."

CHAPTER THREE

Trails West:
Head 'Em Up and Move 'Em Out

"The Marshal will preserve strict order," said the judge. "Any person caught throwing turnips, cigar stumps, beets, or old quds of tobacco at this court will be immediately arranged before this bar of Justice."
Dodge City Times, August 11, 1877

The typical cowboy, according to the . . . correspondents of Eastern papers, is a cross between a bear and wild cat, a sort of man-eating son of a seacook, who isn't comfortable until he has been permitted to chew somebody's ear off.
Denver Times, February 7, 1885

Christopher Columbus introduced cattle to the New World, but it wasn't until later a man named Don Gregorio de Villalobos took six heifers and a young Andalusian bull to Vera Cruz, Mexico. They were the ancestors of just about every cow and bull and, for that matter, hamburger and steak, that we see today.

Accustomed to tropical weather and tropical insects, when the cattle set hoof on the more temperate coastal grasslands of Mexico, they soon grew fat and sassy. Sharp horned and as fast as wild deer, they were wiry and not at all like today's cattle. The first trail driver was that erstwhile discoverer of the Grand Canyon and enemy of the Pueblo Indians, Francisco Vásquez de Coronado. He took a herd of about five hundred cattle along on his unsuccessful search for the Seven Cities of Gold. Just as pigs had escaped Spanish wanderers in the East, out West a few cattle escaped into the wilds and Indians drove off a few others. Within a matter of years the mutated progeny of Coronado's herd had spread out over the southern plains.

By 1842, Texans were driving cattle into Shreveport and New Orleans, Louisiana. A few years more, and hard-bitten Texas cowboys were driving equally hard-bitten Texas cattle to markets as far away as Ohio. By the time Texas won its independence from Mexico, there was a ratio of six head of cattle for every human Texan. There was not, however, much of a market for the wiry beef, so Texas cattlemen invented one—hides, horns, hooves, and tallow. The carcasses generally were considered worthless and were left to the vultures and coyotes.

When America's Civil War took young Texans off to Virginia and Tennessee to fight for the Confederacy, young cattle took to roaming wild. When Civil War veterans returned home, they often found their ranches in ruin, their families living in poverty, and their cattle living in bramblebushes and canebrakes. The good news was that cattle had done what most other living species do when given half a chance: They had multiplied. Estimates are as high as six million cattle roaming in post–Civil War Texas, more than a million of them untended, unbranded, undriven, and unlikely to take kindly to any of the above.

They went under the name of broadhorn, coaster, sea lion, cactus boomer, horned jackrabbit, Indian cattle, mossy back, Texas cattle, Spanish cattle, twisthorn, and—the most popular name—longhorn. They were hardy, wild, cantankerous, nasty, and able to survive on not much more than cholla,* wild grass, damp air, and neglect; the neglect they got in plenty. In the 1840s an anonymous visitor to the Texas brush country described the longhorn:

> They are invariably of dark-brown color with a slight tinge of dusky yellow on the tip of the nose and on the belly. Their horns are remarkably large and stand out straight from the head. Although these cattle are generally much larger than the domestic cattle, they are more fleet and nimble and when pursued often outstrip horses that easily outrun the buffalo. Unlike the buffalo, they seldom venture far out into the prairies, but are generally found in or near the forests that skirt the streams in that section. Their meat is of an excellent flavor and is preferred by the settlers to the meat of the domestic cattle. It is said

---

*Cholla (pronounced CHOY-yuh) is a type of cactus (Opuntia) that grows in weird, twisty shapes. It has clingy spines known to be meaner than your mother-in-law's tongue.

that their fat is so hard and compact that it will not melt in the hottest days of summer.

One of the largest documented set of horns had a rack nine feet seven inches long from tip to tip. Old-timers "remembered" longhorns with racks up to thirteen feet, but you know how old-timers exaggerate. There are stories that some longhorns starved to death after their horns grew so long the animal could no longer graze. It was not, and is not, unusual to see longhorn racks decorating saloons, stores, and even Texas-trimmed automobiles. The bigger the better, longhorns and cars.

As a bull or steer grew older, little wrinkles would appear at the base of his horns, likely caused by the animal pushing against the horns as he grazed. The older the animal, the more wrinkles in the horns, which gave rise to the term *mossy horn* for old bulls. A full-grown steer might weigh as much as eight hundred or nine hundred pounds, but a big mossy horn could go as high as fifteen hundred pounds.

During the Civil War hundreds of thousands of Americans and immigrant Europeans flocked to the mills and factories of the North. They saw beef as the symbol of the American good life, and they wanted it on their tables. After the war cowboys saw those millions of longhorns wandering around and considered the growing hunger for beef in the North.

On Christmas Day, 1865, a 345-acre tract of land in Chicago where nine railroads converged opened for business as the Union Stockyards. By the following spring rumors had reached Texas that a longhorn steer worth five dollars in worthless Confederate money south of the Red River would bring forty dollars in Chicago. And that would be in good United States currency. Now those hundreds of cowboys who'd looked on longhorns as not much more than breakfast or supper began gathering cattle into herds ranging in numbers upwards of thirty-five hundred to drive to the Kansas railheads, and then on to Chicago and other northern markets.

In Chicago a man who'd made a fortune selling pork to the Union army in the Civil War established a meat packing house. That man, Philip Danforth Armour, went on to make a fortune. One of his less-than-successful products was extract of beef, for which the Armour Company claimed great health benefits.

One of Armour's workmen was an Irish packer named Michael Cudahy, and he went on to open his own plant. Not long afterward a New England Yankee named Gustavus Franklin Swift joined the growing legion of meat packers in Chicago and helped make the city, which had been named after a nearby field of wild onions, the center of Western cattle trade.

One estimate has it that in 1867, 35,000 head of cattle were driven north from Texas. By 1871 the number was up to 350,000, and by 1880 nearly 395,000 cattle streamed north. A depression hit in 1881, and the number dropped to 250,000.

The Wild West was a wonderful, mutually beneficial world while it lasted.

In general settlers moved east to west. Cattle went south to north, in huge drives along well-worn routes. Among them: the Santa Fe Trail, the Oregon Trail, the Chisholm Trail, the Shawnee Trail, and Fletcher's route. The Preston Trail drove northward from Dallas. And then there was the Goodnight-Loving Trail.

Charles Goodnight was born in Macoupin County, Illinois, north of St. Louis, on March 5, 1836. The family moved south when he was nine years old, with young Charlie riding bareback all the way from Illinois to Texas. Once he'd left Illinois, Charlie never again saw a classroom, and from the time he was eleven, he worked full time to support his now-widowed mother. At nineteen he tried ranching for a while with his stepbrother, but marauding Indians put an end to that. By 1860 Charlie was a Texas Ranger serving as a private with the Rangers during the Civil War. He spent most of his time clearing the Comanches from the range.

First he was a cowboy; later he was a cattle dealer. In the Western phrase he *learned cow* and became a clever hand at busting mustangs, whacking bulls, splitting rails, and racing horses. With his stepbrother on the CV Ranch, for pay he was allowed to keep one out of every eight calves that were born. Within four years he owned 180 head.

Like other good cowboys Charlie Goodnight learned to locate water by watching the birds and bees; bees would fly a straight route to flowers, which generally grew around water, and birds, especially if they were swallows, carried in their mouths mud for nest building—backtrack a swallow and you're likely to find a water hole. He learned to recognize which grass was good, which was bad; find good grass and in three years a four-dollar yearling could grow into a twenty-dollar steer or heifer. A single cow would need ten acres of grass a year to graze if the dirt beneath her was good, half again as much if it was dry and scrubby. She'd drink up to thirty gallons of water a day, and water, partner, meant wealth, power, and more wealth. Hold on to a water hole and you hold on to land for ten miles around—as far as a cow can walk to get a drink. Maybe fifteen or twenty miles, counting elbow room. Charlie Goodnight learned all of this and more.

He praised hard work and honesty and once said that "only the weak steal." A photograph of a young Charlie Goodnight shows a threadbare man with straightforward, curious eyes. In his waning years Goodnight was the picture of an aging Texan—bearded, bow-legged, and bullheaded.

He crossbred cattle with buffalo, creating the nonsensational "cattalo," which had as a major drawback the fact that the results were infertile. His efforts, however, did go far in saving the rapidly diminishing buffalo herds. Goodnight apparently believed buffalo fat was good for everything. He made soap out of it and he used it for corns caused by tight cowboy boots. "I am satisfied it will relieve rheumatism," he once said and added, "Try it for tuberculosis; I do believe it will work." He was at least certain it was harmless and believed "it stands a fair chance to become the discovery of this age."

Like many another cowboy who spent hours and weeks in the saddle, Charlie Goodnight developed hemorrhoids. He had a home remedy for the problem, a suppository consisting of salt and buffalo tallow. The cowboy's life was a hard one.

By June 1866 Charles Goodnight had a herd of cattle in Palo Pinto County, Texas—some longhorn, some mixed, about two thousand altogether. At the time cattle sold for four dollars a head in Texas, if you could find a buyer, but it would go for up to forty dollars a head in Colorado, and there were plenty of buyers. Charlie decided to drive the herd to the people who wanted beef on their tables.

His partner in the enterprise was a man who frowned on the dangers and difficulties of the project but who joined him just the same.

"If you let me," Oliver Loving told Charlie, "I will go with you." Together Goodnight and Loving drove the first herd of cattle from around Fort Belknap in west Texas, moved them southwest to Horsehead Crossing, then northwest to Pope's Crossing and then paralleled the Pecos River north up through New Mexico, through Navajo and Apache country to Fort Sumner, Las Vegas, and Ratan Pass. At eight cents a pound for the steers, Charlie Goodnight collected about twelve thousand dollars in gold, packed a mule, and headed back down the trail toward Texas. Oliver Loving then drove the cows and calves north to the Colorado gold mines, where he sold them to a failed goldminer-turned-cattleman, John Wesley Iliff.*

The Goodnight-Loving Trail is better known than the men themselves. It was treacherous, and over the Staked Plains of the Texas panhandle it took from thirty to forty hours to drive ninety-six miles across a waterless stretch.

Oliver Loving was born in 1812 in Hopkins County, Kentucky, south of Evansville, Indiana. He was a real pioneer in the Texas cattle business, getting into it in 1845 or so. Ten years later, he drove a herd to Illinois and a few years later pushed another herd to Colorado, the first man to do so. Loving died in 1867, but Charlie Goodnight drove on, going on to build up an immense ranch on the Colorado range, growing wealthy in doing so. He used some of his wealth to build an opera house in the town of Pueblo, Colorado, south of Colorado Springs.

Equally a part of the Goodnight-Loving Trail story was Mary Ann Dyer Goodnight. As tough and patient as her husband, she'd been born in Hickman, Kentucky. A plain-spoken woman, Mary Ann Goodnight drove a wagon up and down the trail that bore Charlie's name. In an era when women normally didn't ride astride a horse, Mary Ann Goodnight rode sidesaddle on an invention of her husband; eastern sidesaddles just weren't safe enough for the rougher western terrain, so he contrived a safer variety.

The Goodnights had with them "Old Blue," a lead longhorn who plodded in front of nearly a dozen trail drives, leading some ten

*See Chapter Four.

thousand head to Dodge City alone. Old Blue wore a bell around his neck, and at night he wandered freely around camp, settling down the herd and, occasionally, wandering into camp to mooch handouts from the doting cowboys. After his eighth year as Goodnight's lead steer, Old Blue retired to a comfortable pasture, and when he finally died at age twenty, his horns were mounted in the Goodnight ranch office.

Rawboned cowboys drove rawboned cattle from the Rio Grande in Texas over the Red River in Oklahoma and into that cattle town of all cattle towns, Abilene, Kansas. But it wasn't easy.

Trailhands covered an average of fifteen miles a day, sunrise to dark, "can see to can't see," the saying went. "The guards [would] ride in a circle," longtime cowboy Andy Adams remembered in *Log of a Cowboy*, "about four rods outside the sleeping cattle; and by riding in opposite directions made it impossible for any animal to make its escape without being noticed by the riders." Adams wrote that "the guards usually sang or whistled continuously, so that the sleeping herd may know that a friend and not an enemy is keeping vigil over their dreams."

The songs remembered friends and enemies and women: "Cotton-Eyed Joe," "Dinah Had a Wooden Leg," "Saddle Ole Spike," and "Sally Gooden." One of the most beautiful was called simply "The Night Herding Song":

> *Oh, slow up, dogies, quit moving around,*
> *You have wandered and trampled all over the ground;*
> *Oh, graze along, dogies, and feed kinda slow,*
> *And don't forever be on the go.*
> *Move slowly, little dogies, move slow,*
> *Hi-o, hi-o, hi-o.*

The singing cowboy, of course, was greatly aided by the jackalope—a strange animal with the body of a jackrabbit and the antlers of an antelope. This taxidermist's dream and subject of cowboys' tall tales was acclaimed for its sweet singing voice as it crooned through the night to sooth jittery herds. Well, maybe.

The trail drive probably was the most challenging and miserable time in a cowboy's life. Like wars, these drives often were the climactic events in the lives of generations of men and gave them a chance to prove themselves. They were, however, a distinctly unromantic business. Dime novels and Hollywood movies gave cattle drives an aura of glory. Cowboys didn't think so. Only one-third of all cowboys who took part in a long drive were willing to undergo a second low-paying and difficult trek with only a dozen other hard-legs and a couple thousand ornery cattle for company.

A small herd might number only 500 or so head of cattle, while the largest ever to hit the trail numbered more than 15,000. Sometimes it seemed like more. Usually the ratio was one cowboy for every 250 animals. Sometimes it seemed cattle were so thick on the trail that longhorns beat the dirt into knee-deep dust. At one point in 1883, in a single day, twenty-eight herds, each numbering between 1,000 and 3,000 head of cattle, crowded a trail near the North Platte River.

In the twenty years of great drives, upwards of ten million cattle walked from the Texas range to mining towns in New Mexico and Colorado, to reservations and forts, then on to railheads in Kansas and Missouri, with some going on to Wyoming and Canada. Most drives had a brief stopover in the Chicago stockyards on their way to the dinner table. When the Chicago yards closed, Omaha took over as the nation's largest cattle pen. Now, Omaha, too, has seen its stockyards close down; there just isn't any need for giant pens and huge slaughterhouses. They've been replaced by smaller facilities, more convenient to the herds. But in the twenty years while they lasted, the long cattle drives set the standard for the West.

Seldom did a drive go smoothly. Quicksand often mired the cattle; unless it was rescued, a cow might sink inch by inch for a day until its nose went under. Rescuing such mired animals was a risky and difficult job. Sometimes streams contained poisonous gypsum deposits that could kill a steer.

Storms could spook a herd, and off they'd go running who knows where, and God help anyone caught in their path. Cattle could drown in a fast-running river. Balls of electricity called "St. Elmo's Fire" often played around the tips of horses' ears and cattle's horns, leaping from tip to tip, animal to animal, around the herd and the drovers, all the while the cowboys hoping they'd left everything metallic in the chuck wagon. Lightning was among the most common causes of death among cowboys on the trail. In a three-year period four men were killed and three others seriously burned by lightning along the Chisholm Trail alone. A cowboy remembering times on the Salt Fork in Kansas said that lightning "would hit the sides of those hills and gouge out great holes in the earth like a bomb had struck them, and it killed seven or eight cattle in the herd back of us."

Lightning often set herds off on a stampede—one jump to their feet and running and the next jump to hell, the saying went. Cowboys could suddenly be blinded by lightning, the cattle would be off and running, and all a trail hand could do was hold on to the hurricane deck and pray his pony didn't stumble. In more than one instance a cowboy died when his horse tripped during a stampede. After one such death, not knowing that a man had fallen, the other cowboys milled the cattle over the dead man's body. After that the trail boss ordered his men to sing out or yell when running with a stampede to let the others know where they were. Still, cattle normally wouldn't run over a man if they could help it, and more men died when hit by lightning than by stampeding cattle.

Water was always a problem, sometimes too much and sometimes too little. If the land was dry, a trail boss might have to scout thirty or forty miles ahead, sometimes a full day's ride, looking for a water hole. Drovers often used the cattle's own desire and need for water to push them along. "Folks didn't really drive cattle," an old hand explained, "they moved 'em." In the spring of 1871 several large herds got jammed up at a Red River crossing, the stream swollen to a mile wide. At least sixty thousand cattle stood mooing and bellowing at the water's edge and wading across. A cowboy at that cattle jam recalled,

the litter of heavy brush and broken trees sweeping by gave you the feeling that, for hundreds of miles, everything that grew had been plucked out by the roots and sent swirling and bobbing down.

Finally a trail boss ordered the cattle into the choppy, red-brown water, but in midstream the herd began swimming in a circle. The cowboy who wrote about the jam-up added that he stripped off his clothes, swam his horse to the center of the herd, then jumped onto the cattle. "They were so jammed together," he remembered, "that it was like walking on a raft of logs. When I got to the only real big steer in the bush on the yon side, I mounted him and pulled for the shore." The rest of the herd followed. It took 350 men ten days to cut the mixed cattle into the thirty original herds that had been backed up at the river.

Cowboys generally hated the water, and most of them couldn't swim. Luckily their horses could. A good cow pony could cross a rushing river with a cowboy holding to the saddle pommel for dear life. Since the main cattle trails went north to south, this meant cowboys (who usually are pictured as thirsty and covered with alkali dust) had to spend many hours naked—naked in order to save their clothes—and up to their necks in river water as they ushered an unwilling herd of cattle across the stream. Floods were always a problem; when the land is bone dry, and a sudden storm hits, a six-inch-deep river can rise to twenty-five feet in a day's time, a flash flood. A slight wave, a floating tree branch, a slippery spot on the bottom—almost anything spooked the cattle into either charging ahead full steam or refusing to move. Cowboys had to handle both situations, and many drovers lost their lives trying to rescue befuddled longhorns.

Crossing the Red River meant northbound cattle (and the cowboys) were no longer under what little protection the state of Texas could give. Now they were in Indian Territory, present-day eastern Oklahoma. Most drives at one time or another went through land that was home to Native Americans, and often confrontations broke out between cowboys and Indians. One usual solution was for the trail boss to trade a few head of cattle for the right to cross Indian-held land.

Cowboys often ran into white raiders and rustlers—that is, cattle thieves. If they caught such miscreants, sometimes hanging wasn't enough. A story goes that when trail hands caught one rustler, they shot him to death, decapitated the steer he'd stolen, and stuffed the would-be thief into the animal's carcass, leaving only the rustler's head sticking out where the steer's head had been.

"Spanish" or "Texas" fever was a problem, likely carried by ticks infesting the cattle. Longhorn cattle driven north were themselves practically immune to this virulent disease, but it wrought havoc among local herds wherever cowboys drove cattle north. In the summer of 1866, cattlemen in the North imposed a quarantine of sorts on Texas cattle, not allowing them in east Kansas and southwest Missouri. In some cases local vigilante groups gathered to keep infected Texas cattle out of the area. They weren't certain just how the fever was transmitted, but they didn't want any southern cattle tramping over their land.

In a number of instances vigilantes were nothing more than gangs of cattle rustlers who exploited the fever scare and intimidated cattlemen into handing over their herds. Then the rustlers-in-vigilantes'-clothing sold the cattle for their own profit. In an 1869 Colorado case rustlers claiming they were preventing the spread of Texas fever stampeded sixteen longhorns, then made off with the strays. Even the redoubtable Charles Goodnight had trouble with vigilantes. During one confrontation, when raiders tried to blockade his herd, Goodnight tried to reason with the vigilantes, but when that didn't work, he took other action. Pulling out his Winchester, Charlie Goodnight told them, "I've monkeyed as long as I want to with you," and he drove his cattle head-on into the would-be blockaders. In 1885 when a gang of Winchester-toting border guards stopped a herd, the drover told his hands to "bend 'em west, boys. Nothing in Kansas anyhow except the three suns—sunflowers, sunshine, and those sons of bitches."

Baxter Springs, Kansas, once was a growing cattle town, but when fear of Texas fever hit, residents stopped cowboys from driving herds into town. At one point more than a hundred thousand cattle were jammed up around Baxter Springs. Grass died or was burned off by defiant farmers; violent skirmishes broke out, often between former Confederate Texans and former Union Jayhawkers. Some dishonest buyers bought cattle with worthless checks.

The quarantine lasted so long, causing so many drives to turn away, it changed Baxter Springs forever and prevented the town from becoming a major cow town. Today Baxter Springs has a population of about forty-seven hundred and likely is best known as the largest town on Kansas's seven-mile stretch of old Route 66.

Twenty-nine-year-old Chicago stock dealer Joseph McCoy had an idea that eventually put millions of dollars into his bank account and put his name in the dictionary of slang. He learned about the Baxter Springs cattle jam and studied the map. The small town of Junction City, Kansas, he believed, would be just the spot for a stockyard. He tried convincing local merchants such a plan would work, but they turned him down. Solomon City and Selma also said no.

In St. Louis McCoy talked with the presidents of both the Missouri Pacific and the Kansas Pacific Railroads.* Neither was impressed. Finally, he found a town that agreed to go along, "a very small, dead place," he wrote, "consisting of about one dozen log huts, low, small, rude affairs, four-fifths of which were covered with dirt." The town: Abilene.

In 1867 the country around Abilene was settled, watered, and had excellent grass. Now it had Joe McCoy, who bought most of the town of Abilene for the princely sum of $4,250.

Joe McCoy began urging Texas cattlemen to drive their herds from the southern grasslands to his town. He promised to ship the cattle north and west to feedlots to fatten them up for slaughter. McCoy himself bought a herd of cattle and drove it to Abilene, making it the first trail herd to reach that soon bustling cowtown. He offered forty dollars a head for cattle, ten times the going rate. In early summer Col. O. W. Wheeler of California gathered a herd of about twenty-four hundred cattle near San Antonio and, with fifty-four armed cowboys driving them, headed for Indian country and on to Abilene. Soon other cattlemen began arriving in McCoy's town. About the only problem was that McCoy—and Abilene—didn't yet have a railroad.

The Kansas Pacific insisted on waiting until several herds arrived before building a twenty-car spur line into town. Even then, they said they'd probably remove the spur the following spring. Well, Joe McCoy held out for a larger, more permanent line, and he got it, one that would handle a hundred cars at a time.

Pine lumber came from Hannibal, Missouri, hardwood from Lenape, Kansas, and then the work began. Abilene was built in sixty

---

*The Kansas Pacific Railroad later became the southern branch of the Union Pacific.

days—a shipping yard that would hold three thousand cattle, a large set of scales, a barn and office building, and, later on, Joe McCoy's three-story hotel, the Drover's Cottage. Within a year Abilene was a wide-open lawless cattle town.

With the Kansas Pacific line in place McCoy arranged for a train-load of Springfield, Illinois, stockmen to come to Abilene, "to cele-brate by feast, wine, and song, the auspicious event" of the opening of his railroad spur. The following morning, "before the sun had mounted high in the heavens, the iron horse was darting down the Kaw valley with the first trainload of cattle that ever passed over the Kansas Pacific Railroad."

McCoy had bragged that he'd deliver two hundred thousand cat-tle in the first decade of business. He did better. In the first year he shipped over thirty-six thousand cattle, and in four years alone Joe McCoy shipped back East more than two million. Abilene boomed, and in the meantime Joe McCoy's name went down in history, not only as a cattle baron, but, as he liked to say, "the real McCoy."

In Abilene "money and whiskey flowed like water down hill, and youth and beauty and womanhood and manhood were wrecked and damned in that valley of perdition." Abilene took on the nickname the "Devil's Addition."

By 1870 the once small town Joseph McCoy had bought boasted ten boardinghouses, ten saloons, five general stores, and four ho-tels. It also had its share of brothels. Apparently Abilene's first ladies of leisure arrived in town just about the time Joe McCoy's stock-men's expedition pulled in. By the following spring, according to a local resident, the girls came "in swarms, as the weather was warm 4 or 5 girls could Huddle together in a tent very Comfortably." For the next two decades prostitutes remained a fixture in the town's life. Just how many of these "soiled doves"* plied their trade in Abi-lene isn't certain; however, from April to August 1880 the police court docket saw twenty-five resident prostitutes prosecuted. No mention of outside talent.

To cattle town residents cowboys were a peculiar problem. With-out the cowboys and the cattle they drove, towns such as Abilene

*See Chapter Five.

and Dodge City wouldn't have existed. But with the cowboys came violence. Legend has it that they fought and they killed, sometimes almost destroying the towns. "Mobs of mounted cowboys 'took over' by day," frontier historian Ray Allen Billington wrote, "their six-shooters roaring while respectable citizens cowered behind locked doors."

Each trail hand was assigned about six horses; sometimes the cowboy himself owned the horses and if the trail boss gave them to another hand (or even sold them) it could end in a shooting war.

Coyboy Andy Adams wrote about a cattle drive during which, for a three-day period, they had no water:

Holding the herd this third night required all hands. Only a few men at a time were allowed to go into camp and eat, for the herd refused even to lie down. What few cattle attempted to rest were prevented by the more restless ones. By spells they would mill, until riders were sent through the herd at breakneck pace to break up the groups. . . .

Good cloudy weather would have saved us, but in its stead was a sultry morning without a breath of air, which bespoke another day of sizzling heat. We had not been on the trail over two hours before the heat became almost unbearable to man and beast. . . . The cattle turned back several times, wandering aimlessly in any direction, and it was with considerable difficulty that the herd could be held on the trail. The rear overtook the lead, and the cattle lost all semblance of a trail herd.

It took the drovers more than two hours to straighten the herd out into a reasonable trailing line. But less than a mile later the lead cattle once more turned and "congregated into a mass of unmanageable animals, milling and lowing in their fever and thirst." The cowboys tried roping the cattle into moving along and

six-shooters were discharged so close to the leaders' faces as to singe their hair, yet, under a noonday sun, they disregarded this and every other device to turn them, and passed wholly out of our control. In a number of instances wild steers deliberately walked against our horses, and then for the first time a fact dawned on us that chilled the marrow in our bones—the herd was going blind.

Adams added that "the bones of men and animals that lie bleaching along the trails abundantly testify that this was not the first instance in which the plain had baffled the determination of man."

Cowboys on the trail worked eighteen-hour days. Under usual circumstances the herd left the bed ground at daybreak and kept at it until dark. The story goes that when one cowpuncher complained about the lack of sleep, the trail boss told him to wait until winter, then sleep all he wanted. A young cowboy called James Henry Cook once asked trail boss Joel Roberts for a job. Roberts looked Cook over and said, "If you can ride the next four months without a whole night's sleep, and turn your gun loose on any damned Injun that tries to get our horses, well, get ready."

The oldest of the northern trails was the Shawnee Trail and began in San Antonio, Texas. It wound from Waco to Dallas, crossed the Red River at Rock Bluff near Preston, and carried on through the Indian Nations to Baxter Springs, Kansas, or Sedalia, Missouri.

Of all the cattle trails the routes most used were the Western Trail to Dodge City and the Chisholm Trail to Abilene, Kansas. Begun around 1865, the Chisholm Trail got its name from the Scot-Cherokee Indian trader Jesse Chisholm* and likely is the best known. Jesse himself didn't drive cattle. Rather, he blazed this trail while hauling merchandise from San Antonio, Texas, to Wichita, Kansas, and back, hauling goods one way and buffalo hides the other. Later on, cow outfits used the trail, and the name stuck. Unfortunately Jesse

---

*There's some confusion over this. In 1866 a man named Thornton Chisholm was trail boss on a drive from Gonzales northwest to Indian Territory and then into St. Joseph, Missouri, and for a while his route was known as the Chisholm Trail. Another man, John Chisholm of Paris, Texas, is also given credit for the trail, and even John Chisum—different spelling—had a "Chisum Trail" in New Mexico. But the famous Chisholm Trail that went from San Antonio, Texas, to Abilene, Kansas, was named for Jesse Chisholm.

Chisholm died of cholera in 1868, before his name was widely associated with Texas cattle drives.

By 1870 the Chisholm Trail was mentioned in Kansas newspapers as the best route to the trailhead. And within a few years it saw upwards of five thousand cowboys and untold numbers of cattle heading northward to Ellsworth and Abilene, Kansas. Within five years of its opening more than a million head of cattle had mooed and moseyed on up the way.

Like all other trails the Chisholm wasn't a narrow lane. Rather, it was a broad, often unmarked, route with many minor paths joining along the way and others dropping off. The Chisholm Trail has been likened to a tree whose roots were the feeder trails, its trunk the main branch, and its branches extensions to various railheads. In some places the Chisholm Trail was from two hundred to four hundred yards wide, the path cut by erosion, as much as a foot below the level of the plains. Beside it, historian William H. Forbis writes, there were

> bones of cows killed in stampedes and calves shot at birth because they could not keep up with the drives. There were the bones of humans, too, interred in shallow graves—a drowned man pulled down next to a river crossing, or an early-day trail hand or settler cut down by Indians.

Every man who set out on a cattle drive "knew the risks and knew that on the trail he was considered less valuable than the cows he drove."

An estimated thirty-five thousand to fifty-five thousand men rode the trails with cattle and horses, with many African Americans and Mexicans swinging lariats alongside Anglos. More than five thousand African Americans were cowboys. Most of them had been born slaves and when the Civil War ended, they joined outfits and went up the trail.* Few black cowpunchers ever rose to be foremen, because most white southerners wouldn't take orders from them. Other cowboys were Indian or had Indian blood.

* See Chapter Nine.

Whatever their race, trail hands generally were held in low esteem. While in the eyes of modern society, the cowboy evokes a literature and mythology and has become a graphic symbol of our lives, let's face it: it was hard, man, hard.

Take the simple need for salt. If the chuck wagon ran out, cowboys could wind up literally licking horse sweat from their saddles to keep from dying of salt deprivation. Dust, thirst, danger, blisters, cold, and heat—all for wages of about one hundred dollars for the drive, generally, around thirty dollars a month "and found," meaning "with food."

Higher up the hierarchy was the cook, who, except for the trail boss, was the most important man on the drive. He had to feed a dozen or more men three meals a day, regardless of weather, regardless of conditions, regardless of how little time or few provisions he had. "Only a fool argues with a skunk, a mule, or a cook," the saying went. "The space for fifty feet around the cook is holy ground," Bruce Siberts wrote, adding, "The cook is the Almighty." The hands found him essential; the trail boss knew that a good cook, more so than any other man on the drive, could determine the trail-hands' morale and, often, the drive's success.

To feed the hungry hands Charles Goodnight invented the chuck wagon, and soon similar contraptions rolled with other drives across the prairie. Goodnight converted a covered wagon by fitting a chuck box at the rear. Lowering the box cover, the cook would let swing down a hinged support, and it became a worktable.

Chuck wagons held everything the cook needed: tin plates and tin cups, fitted drawers for coffee, spices, and baking powder, mixing bowls and a Dutch oven, flour, potatoes, beans, and sides of pork. Traditionally, the chuck wagon was made from Osage-orange wood, the same wood many Indians used for their bows.

Usually the cook was the first to arise in the morning, awakened about three-thirty, either by the last guard to go out at night or by his own internal clock. Often he was African American or Mexican or Portuguese, frequently nicknamed "Sallie" or "Cookie." Cookie's breakfasts almost always consisted of coffee by the gallon, sourdough biscuits, sowbelly or some other kind of meat, and beans—pinto, red, navy, white, or speckled, whatever he had. Most of this he cooked in

Dutch ovens, deep cast-iron pots with wire handles and cast-iron lids. Once he'd loaded the ovens, Cookie placed them on top of hot coals, then piled more hot coals on top of it. He'd soaked the beans overnight, because one of a cowboy's most hated sounds was undercooked, dried beans rattling around his tin plate.

Cookie's work was never done; while the drovers ate breakfast, he started work on the next meal. He was the last to leave the campsite, and around noon, when the trailhands threw the herd off the trail for a rest, he served up—you guessed it—more coffee, more sourdough biscuits, and more beans. Only after the trail hands had eaten, changed horses, and ridden off did Cookie head the chuck wagon on up the trail. By midafternoon he'd caught up with the herd and pushed on ahead down the line until it was time to fix supper, which by now sounded darn familiar: sourdough biscuits, beans, gravy, and coffee. Occasionally, however, Cookie prepared the range chef's specialty, "son-of-a-bitch stew." The recipe for SOB?

2 pounds lean beef	1 set marrow gut
Half a calf head	salt, pepper
1 ½ pounds sweetbreads	Louisiana hot sauce
1 set brains	

Cut the beef and calf head into one-inch cubes. Slice marrow gut into small rings. Put it all into a Dutch oven or deep casserole and cover it with water. Simmer for two to three hours, then add salt, pepper, and hot sauce. Cut the sweetbreads and brains into small pieces and add to the stew. Simmer another hour. SOB stew; it contained everything edible but the hair, horns, and holler.

A cousin to son-of-a-bitch stew was "son of a bitch in a sack," dough and dried fruit sewn into a sack and steamed. Someone suggested that it got its name because of the difficulty in making it.

Space inside a chuck wagon limited what the cook could carry. To the side of the wagon he attached at least one barrel of water and beneath it, a *cuna* (Spanish for "cradle") or "cooney,"* a cowhide

---

*The *cuna* had several other names: "possum belly," "caboose," "cradle," and even "the bitch."

slung by four corners under the wagon. Into it cowboys and cook tossed firewood (occasionally, dead tree limbs roped by the hands and dragged back to camp) and/or cow and buffalo chips to use as an emergency fuel source. Emigrants heading west also used a *cuna*-like device to store fire-making materials.

Oliver Nelson, in *The Cowman's Southwest,* lists the provisions a trail drive would carry in the chuck wagon.

> I took an inventory of the load: forty pounds Climax Plug [tobacco], twenty pounds Bull Durham, and several caddies and packs of smoking tobacco; a dozen .45 Colt single-action pistols and twenty boxes of cartridges; a roll of half-inch rope; ten gallons of kerosene and a caddy of matches; one hundred pounds of sugar; one 160-pound sack of green coffee, five hundred pounds of salt pork, twenty sacks of flour, two hundred pounds of beans, fifty pounds country dried apples, a box of soda, and a sack of salt. There were bows on the wagon [the *cunas*], a grub box on the rear end, a kerosene can cut in half for sour dough, two sixteen-inch ovens five inches deep, a coffee grinder nailed on the side of the grub box, six bull's-eye lanterns for night herd.

If Cookie was good at his job—and if he wasn't good he didn't last long out on the trail—he carried canned tomatoes and dried fruits. Cowboys were especially fond of desserts, and he frequently made fruit pies or, if the trail hands were really lucky, "bear sign," as doughnuts were called. Occasionally they'd butcher a steer, with the cook using only the best cuts. After all, without refrigeration meat spoiled soon out on the prairie, so don't mess with hamburger.

In the early years cattle drives ran across herds of buffalo, and the boys would kill one and have it for breakfast, lunch, and dinner. But as time went on, buffalo were killed at an alarming rate, almost to extinction. Army colonel Richard Irving Dodge wrote that

> for every single buffalo that roamed the Plains in 1871, there are in 1881 not less than two, and more probably four or five, of the descendants of the long-horned cattle of Texas. The

destroyers of the buffalo are followed by the preservers of the cattle.

Cookie tried to find wild turkeys for the hands, but as the number of cattle drives increased turkeys, like buffalo, disappeared. They frequently saw rabbits along the trail but wouldn't eat them. Cowhands considered them "nester food"—food eaten by farmers— and "anybody that would eat rabbit would talk to hisself, and anybody who talks to hisself tells lies."

A good cook in the Wild West was greatly praised. Tired, lonesome, and hungry trail hands didn't object that he was paid more than the cowboys. And *he* is the correct word. Cooks on major trail drives always were men.

Once in camp, with his horses or mules unhooked for the day, the cook pointed the wagon tongue toward the North Star. In the morning it let the trail boss know which way to aim the herd.

The cook was responsible for loading into the chuck wagon the cowboys' blanket rolls, but only if they were rolled up. It they weren't, he'd leave them behind. He acted as nurse, physician, and barber; he carried bandages, needles and thread, a razor and strop, maybe even a bottle of whiskey for strictly medicinal purposes, of course. He carried "eatin' irons" (knives, forks, and spoons) and the trail hands' "war bags" containing their extra clothing. He loaded the chuck wagon with an ax, a shovel, chains, and the cowboys' guns. During thunderstorms the trail hands didn't like to be caught out on the flat plains with anything metal.

Charlie Goodnight laid down firm regulations:

Before starting on a trail drive, I made it a rule to draw up an article of agreement, setting forth what each man was to do. The main clause stipulated that if one shot another he was to be tried by the outfit and hanged on the spot, if found guilty. I never had a man shot on the trail.

Some trail bosses even ordered that no one (with the possible exception of the cook) was allowed to curse during the drive. Get caught cussing, and you'd be handed your wages and kicked off the drive. Despite this cowboys generally were loyal to the home ranch; "riding for the brand," it was.

The Goodnight-Loving Trail specialized in cattle, but the Santa Fe Trail was a people carrier that began as a trade route used by various bands of Native Americans—the Kansas, Osage, Kiowa, Comanche, Cheyenne, Arapaho, Jacarilla Apache, and Pueblo Indians. At the western edge of the trail the ancient Pueblo Indians built hundreds of apartmentlike adobe buildings; among the most impressive of those still standing are the ruins of the pueblo at Pecos, described in 1540 by the Spanish chronicler Pedro de Castañeda. At the time Castañeda wrote, at least two thousand people lived at Pecos.

Cincuye [the natives' name for the village] is a pueblo of as many as five hundred warriors. It is feared throughout that land. In plan it is square, founded on a rock. In the center is a great patio or plaza with its kivas. The houses are all alike, of four stories. One can walk over the entire pueblo without there being a street to prevent it. . . . The houses have no doors at ground level. To climb . . . inside the pueblo they use ladders which can be drawn up; in this way they have access to the rooms. The people of the pueblo pride themselves that no one has been able to subdue them, while they subdue what pueblos they want.

Castañeda and his men paused at the Acoma pueblo. "As it was at peace," he wrote, "the people entertained us well, giving us provisions and birds." Then, as now, Acoma seemed to sit high in the New Mexico air.

Many soldiers climbed up to the top to see the pueblo. They found it very difficult to climb the steps in the rock, not being used to them. The natives, on the other hand, go up and down so freely that they carry loads of provisions, and the women carry water, and they do not seem to touch the walls with their hands. Our men had to hand their weapons to one another when they tried to make the climb.

In 1625 Spanish padres completed their first church at Pecos, but by 1680 Pueblo Indians all over New Mexico were sore from wearing the Spanish yoke of slavery and revolted, trying to drive the Spanish back to Mexico. Thanks to the military genius of Popé, a member of the Taos pueblo, they momentarily succeeded. In what was called the Pueblo Revolt, the Spanish retreated to a small area around today's El Paso. The winning Pueblo Indians, however, seemed to be almost as despotic as the Spanish had been, trying to tear down every vestige of the Spanish presence in the region. A few years later, when Spain fought back, many natives, while not siding with the Spanish, failed to support Popé and his crowd; the Spanish returned stronger than ever and reconquered the Pueblos.

By the 1770s, thanks in large part to European diseases brought in by the Spanish, many of the pueblos were devastated. In 1838 only twenty Pueblo Indians lived at Pecos. By then American traders controlled Pecos, and they moved these last few souls to the pueblo of Jemez. Today, only ruins—and they are magnificent ruins—remain at Pecos.

In 1804, the same year Lewis and Clark set off on their voyage of discovery into the Louisiana Purchase territory, American merchant William Morrison of Kaskaskia, Illinois, followed the Santa Fe Trail westward. And in 1807 Lt. Zebulon Montgomery Pike arrived in Santa Fe.

Pike made two government-sponsored trips into the Louisiana Territory, first northward, where in Minnesota he found what he mistakenly believed was the source of the Mississippi River, and later to the Southwest.

It was on his second trip that Pike spotted a distant mountain peak in the Colorado foothills of the Rocky Mountains. The "Grand Peak," some called it. Others called it "James's Peak" after Dr. Edwin James, who in 1820 was the leader of the first group to reach the summit of the mountain. Finally, thirty-seven years after Pike discovered the towering mountain, it was renamed Pike's Peak and became a landmark for many settlers heading to the West.

When Zebulon Pike reached Santa Fe, he ran into trouble with the Spanish governor. Of course Zeb wasn't exactly honest with the Spanish. He and his men were well over the line between the United States and Spanish-held territory, but Pike feigned ignorance and said, "What! Is this not the Red River?" He'd planned and even re-hearsed his answer. Earlier he had written General James Wilkinson, who'd sent him on the expedition, that if captured by the Spanish, he was sure he could gain a lot of information about them and even escape without harm by claiming to be "uncertain about the head waters of the rivers." Although the Spanish governor claimed that Pike was a guest, not a prisoner, a military escort forced Pike and his men to go south to Chihuahua, to be questioned by Spanish officials. Finally the authorities released the Americans, and Pike and his men headed home.

To keep the Spanish from finding his maps and notes, Pike hid them in his men's gun barrels. From them he wrote a glowing re-port about the Southwest, but he didn't believe Americans would set-tle there, calling the land uninhabitable and predicting it would be-come "as celebrated as the sandy deserts of Africa." With that some people began to call it the "Great American Desert." In his journal Pike wrote that the vast, treeless prairie would restrict "our popula-tion to some certain limits," adding:

> Our citizens being so prone to rambling and extending them-selves on the frontiers will, through necessity, be constrained to limit their extent on the west to the borders of the Missouri and Mississippi, while they leave the prairies incapable of cultivation to the wandering and uncivilized aborigines of the country.

The Santa Fe Trail became a major caravan route in 1822 after news of Mexico's independence from Spain reached the United States. By the mid-1800s it was a major road of commerce, linking Missouri traders with rich New Mexico markets. It stretched from In-dependence, through Council Grove, Kansas, on to Forts Larned and Dodge. Just west of Dodge the trail's mountain branch headed northwest to Bent's Fort, where "leather-clad mountaineers . . . gam-ble away their hard-earned peltries." English visitor George Ruxton wrote that Bent's Fort was home to "St. Louis Frenchmen and Cana-dian *voyageurs*." Outside the fort, Ruxton wrote, were "Indians too proud to enter without an invitation, lean, wrapped in their buffalo robes, sulky and evidently ill at ease to be so near the whites without a chance of fingering their scalp locks."

Past Bent's Fort, the Santa Fe Trail rejoined the main route—also known as the Cimarron Cutoff—at Fort Union, New Mexico, and then on southwest to Santa Fe. In all, the 750-mile-long Santa Fe Trail followed some of the wildest, most desolate, and most beautiful country in America. Often, trains numbered more than a hundred wagons at a time; handkerchiefs and shawls, pots and pans, wallpaper, and even window glass all heading toward Santa Fe.

Between 1826 and 1835 more than fifteen hundred men accompanied 775 wagons carrying $1,365,000 worth of merchandise over the Santa Fe Trail. For Americans it was a trader's paradise. When wagons arrived from the East with all kinds of hard-to-find goods, crowds enthusiastically greeted the traders.

Santa Fe had been the capital of New Mexico for more then two hundred years when wagon master Josiah Gregg first rolled into the town. "Some distance beyond the Colorado," Gregg wrote in *Commerce of the Prairies*, "a party of about a dozen (which I joined) left the wagons to go ahead to Santa Fe."

Five or six days after our arrival [at Santa Fe] the caravan at last hove in sight, and wagon after wagon was seen pouring down the last declivity at about a miles distance from the city.

To judge from the clamorous rejoicings of the men and the state of agreeable excitement which the muleteers seemed to be laboring under, the spectacle must have been as new to them as it had been to me. It was truly a scene for the artist's pencil to revel in.

The arrival produced a great deal of bustle and excitement among the natives. *"Los Americanos! Los Cargos! La entrada de carvana!"* were to be heard in every direction; and crowds of women and boys flocked around to see the newcomers. . . .

Freighters along the Santa Fe Trail hauled just about everything a settler or cowboy could want. They carried needles and thread, cotton and wool and silk; they hauled nails, axes, and saws. Wagons came loaded with men's pants and women's dresses. They carried scissors, razors, and a thousand other items for the home and farm; they carried calico, groceries, leather goods, canned goods, bottled beer, and *bayeta,* a heavy scarlet cloth New Mexican women used to make petticoats.

To pay for these goods people along the way, and especially in Santa Fe itself, swapped gold and silver coins, gold dust and silver bullion, beaver furs and woven blankets. In 1824 a trader carried thirty thousand dollars' worth of merchandise from Missouri to Santa Fe. He returned home with a profit of $150,000. In 1846 more than 350 wagon trains took to the Santa Fe Trail. There were so many traders, selling so many goods, that Americans took home so many silver pesos that, in the mid-1820s, New Mexico virtually ran out of coins.

By the end of the 1850s more than 1,800 wagons a year lumbered back and forth on the Santa Fe Trail, hauling all of the regular loads, but now they had something new. With the discovery of gold more and more wagons were loaded down with mining equipment.

Over time the area through which the Santa Fe Trail made its way attracted thousands of white settlers. The trail was a primary route for transportation of people, animals, and freight, but in the 1880s the railroad arrived, and it followed much the same route as did the wagon trail. The need for the Santa Fe Trail—as, indeed, for the other east-to-west people trails—no longer existed. Foot and wagon traffic died out. Eventually prairie grass covered the tracks that crisscrossed the wilderness. Today faint marks remain to remind us of the thousands who trod the Santa Fe Trail.

Even today New Mexico has trouble finding its place in the history of the United States. It's not unusual for a visitor from back East to wonder whether New Mexico is part of old Mexico. Today the state's auto license plates carry the notation "New Mexico, USA."

As for Santa Fe itself, it remains the state capital and a draw for sun worshipers and tourists alike. It did not appeal to at least one trader. Its single-story houses, he wrote, look "more like a prairie dog village than a capital."

"Upset our wagon in River & lost Many of our cooking utensils," George Duffield wrote in his journal while herding a bunch of longhorns from Texas to Iowa in 1866, adding, "Was on my Horse the whole night & it raining hard." Duffield drove the herd and kept a diary of his ordeal on the drive:

There was one of our party Drowned to day (Mr. Carr) & Several narrow escaped & I among [them]. . . . Many men in trouble. . . . Awful night . . . not having had a bite to eat for 60 hours. . . . Tired.

Life was far from easy. Out of the cattle drives came a song known as "The Cowboy's Prayer":

Lord, please help me, lend me Thine ear,
The prayer of a troubled cowman to hear,
No doubt my prayer to you may seem strange,
But I want you to bless my cattle range. . . .

As you, O Lord, my fine herds behold,
They represent a sack of pure gold.
I think that at least five cents on the pound
Would be a good price for the beef year round.

CHAPTER FOUR

The Cattle Barons:
Making the Wild West Wild, Part Two

*It takes three long houses to make a city in Kansas, but they begin calling it a city
so soon as they have staked out the lots.*

Horace Greeley

I have always had to pit my brains ... against other men's money.

Theodore Judah

Attorney Samuel A. Maverick was an agitator who helped lead Texas
to independence and became a member of the convention establishing the Republic of Texas. In 1839 Maverick became mayor of
San Antonio. But it wasn't what he did that made his reputation so
much as what he didn't do.

During the Mexican War he took in a stock of four hundred cattle as settlement of a debt—a neighbor owed Colonel Maverick something like twelve hundred dollars—and he had the cattle driven to
a range down in the Matagorda area. He marked them with his MK
brand; however, with the Civil War coming on and all, he didn't have
time to brand the progeny of his original herd, and they multiplied
rapidly. And that's what made him famous. Not branding his cattle
caused his neighbors to refer to any unbranded stock as being "one
of Maverick's."

Finally Maverick sold his MK brand to a man from New Orleans,
a gentleman named A. Toutant de Beauregard, who did what other
cattlemen did. He quickly rounded up any unbranded cattle he
found—there were lots of them—and put the MK mark on them.
By 1857, people in areas south of San Antonio had joined in referring to any unbranded cattle as "Maverick's," but it wasn't until after the Civil War that the term came into widespread use in other
parts of Texas and the rest of the West.

Rounding up mavericks and putting your own brand on them—"jacking mavericks," they called it—was accepted for a while, and unbranded cattle seemed to get divided up evenly over time. Later it became illegal. There were cases in which what you might call freelance cattle roundups led to the maverickers being branded themselves—as thieves.

Sometimes the practice of jacking mavericks led to some unusual stories. Such as the one told by artist-historian Charlie Russell in *Good Medicine*. It seems that a onetime cowpuncher quit punching cattle and went into business for himself. He started his herd with six cows and one bull, but the lot quickly grew. Each cow, it seemed, gave birth to six to eight calves a year. Nobody minded much until the bull started having calves. That's when the onetime cowpuncher quit herding cattle and began making horsehair bridles, which was how cowboys passed the time in jail.

In 1888 the powerful Wyoming Stock Growers' Association pushed through the Maverick Act, making the marking of any unbranded calf by anyone who wasn't a member of the group a felony. This prevented small ranchers from rounding up and branding even their own calves without being charged with a crime. The Association-backed law decreed that all mavericks found during a roundup were to be marked with the Stock Growers' Association's own brand and sold at auction for the benefit of the association treasury.

This led to the Johnson County War, when northern Wyoming homesteaders decided to ignore the law and held an early roundup. The Stock Growers' Association, a group of powerful cattlemen intent on controlling farmers and small cattlemen, heard about the roundup and quickly spread the word.

The January 1887 blizzard hit the northern plains with a fury unknown till then. Cattle barons went broke, and cowboys were left unemployed. Some cowpokes became out-and-out thieves, stealing unbranded calves or reworking brands into different patterns for their own benefit, using what's called a "running iron," a twist of barbed wire, or even a saddle cinch ring heated white hot over a quickly built fire.

Many onetime cowboys threw up small shacks or squatted in deserted line camps. Some even fenced off small plots of land. Homesteaders followed and, like unemployed cowboys, set themselves up on land where thousands of branded cattle had once roamed; soon their sod homes dotted the range from the Big Horn Mountains to the Powder River.

Cattlemen who had survived the blizzards of 1886 and '87 now found that much of the open range in Johnson County was held by farmers. The irony of it all escaped them. A few years earlier cattlemen had pushed Native Americans off land they'd held for generations, and the Indians had fought back. Now farmers were pushing cattlemen off the same range, and it was the cattlemen's turn to fight back. A deep-seated distrust between farmer and cattleman blossomed into armed skirmishes.

Greatly exaggerated reports of rustling circulated among the cattlemen. Oh, it was true; cattle were being stolen. It never amounted to more than three percent of the stock, but with an aggregate of two million head of cattle, the number of stolen beeves totaled about sixty thousand. It wasn't always unemployed cowboys or homesteaders doing the stealing, either, although both cowboys-turned-rustlers and homesteaders-turned–cattle thieves pilfered beeves when game was short and they needed meat. Soon cattle stealing became socially acceptable in Johnson County. At least among some cattle barons, if they were the ones doing the stealing.

In some cases it was the cattleman's own ranch foreman who was rustling cattle from eastern- and foreign-owned herds in order to build up a small operation of his own, but usually it was the farmer who was blamed. The Wyoming Stock Growers' Association soon hired range detectives, such as Frank Canton, who did little detecting but looked hard at anyone they suspected of cattle rustling.

Frank Canton's real name was Joe Horner. Born near Richmond, Virginia, in 1849, as a child he and his family moved to Texas where he became a cowboy, working trail herds from northern Texas to the Kansas railheads. In 1871 Joe Horner began robbing banks and rustling cattle, and on October 10, 1874, at Jacksboro, Texas, he got into a gunfight with some Buffalo Soldiers, killing one cavalryman and wounding another. A few years later Horner was jailed for robbing the Comanche, Texas, bank; he escaped from jail and returned to herding cattle.

In Ogallala, Nebraska, where he'd driven a herd, Joe Horner changed his name to Frank Canton and vowed to give up his evil ways. In 1880, at age thirty-one, he turned up in Wyoming as the owner of a small ranch. A couple of years later the voters of Johnson County elected him sheriff, and he kept the job for two years. He married in 1885, and had two daughters, one of whom died in early childhood. Between then and the blizzard of '87, Canton was at times a small-time rancher near Buffalo and an accused murderer throughout the territory.

He hired on as detective for the Wyoming Stock Growers' Association and was, to say the least, zealous in his job as chief inspector. Canton's usual method of dealing with those he claimed were cattle thieves was to try, convict, and hang the alleged culprit on the spot, Frank being policeman, judge, jury, and hangman. Numerous nesters and cowboys were said to be buried in unmarked graves after running afoul of Frank and his crew.

Under Canton's zealous leadership association inspectors seized some sixteen thousand head of cattle bearing unapproved brands— that is, brands not registered by cattle baron association members. Because Johnson County officials and the association sat on opposite sides of the political fence, only occasionally would Frank hand over to county authorities those he suspected of rustling. Usually homesteader-packed juries acquitted those tried by the county, even if the accused clearly were guilty. Reports indicate that, of two hundred cases brought for cattle- and horse-stealing in Johnson County, only five convictions were secured.

The association and Frank Canton found themselves facing a growing number of well-armed nesters. The Stock Growers' Association raised a fighting fund of one hundred thousand dollars and brought in portly and pompous ex–army officer Maj. Frank Wolcott. Together with Frank Canton he recruited a band of hired guns. Their pay: five dollars a day and expenses, plus a fifty-dollar bonus for every man—meaning every rustler or nester—they killed.

The association's army called themselves "Regulators" and numbered more than fifty men. At 6 P.M. on April 5 the army shipped out of Cheyenne. With them were a physician and two news reporters— Sam Clover of the *Chicago Herald* and Ed Towse of the *Cheyenne Sun*. To get close to the action Clover used the time-honored reporter's claim that "I will see that your side of the story reaches the public." Towse had to give up following the association men when he came down with such a bad case of hemorrhoids that he couldn't sit on a horse.

Each Regulator carried two handguns and a rifle. Each rode a hand-picked horse bearing an unidentifiable brand that would keep others from knowing who really was fighting the Johnson County War.

One of their first victims was Kate Watson, also known as Ella Watson, Kate Averill, Kate Maxwell, and later often referred to as "Cattle Kate." She was born in Canada in 1861 and, with her parents, crossed into the United States when she was a young girl. Her father set up a farm in Smith County, Kansas, near Lebanon, that by the late 1870s was listed as one of the area's most prosperous.

Kate apparently married a man named Maxwell (or at least she began using the name Maxwell), but she left him after learning he'd been frequenting boudoirs other than hers. In 1883 Kate (or Ella) settled in Rawlins County, Wyoming, where she met Jim Averill, the local postmaster, saloon owner, and justice of the peace.

By this time Ella (or Kate) had deteriorated into an uncouth, 170-pound, blowzy prostitute, although she apparently still looked good to some women-starved cowboys. A photograph of her shows a full-bosomed woman, sitting astride a horse, full calico skirts flowing over the saddle, a sunbonnet sitting rakishly on her head. In 1888 she gave birth to Averill's son, or somebody's son. She named the boy Tom.

Out in the sagebrush Kate built a small brothel and stocked it with maverick cattle. Well, not all mavericks. Some cattle she apparently obtained by bartering her large body and equally large favors with local cowhands, which, of course, brings to mind offensive thoughts of buying one cow with another.

Word filtered down from the association that, for their health, Kate and Jim Averill should leave the area and, Oh, yes, leave behind your cattle. The couple refused, the association seized them, took Kate and Jim to Spring Creek Gulch, and hanged them. As a reporter described the grisly scene:

Hanging from the limb of a stunted pine growing on the summit of a cliff fronting the Sweetwater River were the bodies of

James Averill and Ella Watson. Side by side they swung, their faces swollen and discolored almost beyond recognition. Common cowboys' lariats had been used and both had died by strangulation, neither having fallen over two feet. Judging from signs too plain to be mistaken, a desperate struggle had taken place on the cliff, and both man and woman had fought for their lives until the last.

The *Casper Weekly Mail* carried the hanging story under a headline:

JIM AVERILL, AN OLD RESIDENT OF SWEETWATER, HANGED TO A TREE. ELLA WATSON MEETS A SIMILAR FATE. CORONER'S JURY FINDS THAT PROMINENT LAND OWNERS ON SWEETWATER COMMIT THE ATROCIOUS DEED.

The coroner's jury charged six men with the hangings; however, no one was ever indicted. Strangely enough, of four men who'd claimed they witnessed the hangings, one mysteriously died before any indictments could be brought and the other three just as mysteriously disappeared.

Local land-grabber and rancher Albert J. Bothwell was widely believed to have been behind the lynchings; twice he'd tried to buy Kate out, and twice she told him what he could do with his money. No one ever charged Bothwell with the deaths, and there's no real proof that Bothwell was behind the hanging. Still, Kate's property *was* in the middle of a tract of land Bothwell claimed to own, and Bothwell *did* appropriate the cabin Kate had used in her tricks-for-cattle business. He turned it into an icehouse.

To justify the deaths rumors started the legend of rustler queen "Cattle Kate," who had to die "for the good of the country." Now, maybe Kate deserved to die because of other deeds, but in this instance she seems to have been innocent, if not pure as the driven snow.

Behind a façade of opulence the Cheyenne Club was home to the hard-nosed Wyoming Stock Growers' Association. Built in 1880, the verandaed building at 120 East Seventeenth Street in Cheyenne gave the cattle barons the comforts they believed befitted their status in life. It was said to have been the first such building in the United States to be equipped with electric lights and was the Wild West equivalent of a London gentlemen's club. Historian Helena Huntington Smith calls the Cheyenne Club a "wonderful institution" that

> boasted of having the best steward and the best chef of any club in the United States, a wine cellar second to none—though Horace Plunkett [Sir Horace Plunkett, the son of Lord Dunsany, who ran the EK ranch] grumbled that Americans did not know how to serve wine—and servants imported from Ottawa where, under the British flag, men were taught to be servants instead of retorting curtly: "Do it yourself!" when requested to shine a pair of shoes.

Limited by charter to only two hundred hand-picked members, the group was composed of cattle barons and wealthy ranchers, who, when not sitting on the shaded veranda and indulging in imported whiskey, also held dances and even played tennis. Horace Plunkett, for example, often could be found playing on the club's tennis court while yelling out chess moves to opponents on the piazza. The club had reading rooms, billiard rooms, card rooms, and much sought after baths.

According to Cheyenne Club member John Clay it was champagne for breakfast, lunch, and dinner. Members dressed in white tie and tails for gala occasions, inspiring one old Nebraskan to nickname them "Herefords" in honor of the dark-coated, white-chested cattle. Cheyenne Club members dined on caviar, pickled eels, French peas, and Roquefort cheese. After dinner they'd retire to the smoking room for sherry and cigars. "Cow punching, as seen from the veranda of the Cheyenne Club," an English member recalled, "was a most attractive position."

Rules of behavior were strictly enforced and members would be disciplined for profanity or drunkenness; they'd be expelled for an act "so dishonorable in social life as to [render them unfit] for the society of gentlemen." One of the club's founders, the colorful

Charles M. Oelrichs—he often kept a sixteen-passenger rig waiting at one of the club's nineteen hitching posts—was suspended for thirty days after he hit a bartender and kicked the man down the stairs. The Canadian-recruited bartender apparently had picked up some American ways and declined to hold Oelrichs's horse. Oelrichs refused to accept his punishment, and the board of directors revoked his membership. Yet another member, John Coble, was suspended for taking potshots at an oil painting, a pastoral scene he declared a travesty on purebred stock.

John Clay was also president of the Wyoming Stock Growers' Association. In the spring of 1891 he and Maj. Frank Wolcott got to talking about Wolcott's plan to end the antiassociation doings. It startled Clay so much, he claimed, that he "departed for Europe very soon after" talking with Wolcott. According to Clay, the first he heard of what happened came to him when he was en route home from his European holiday. Sure.

Apparently what the major told Clay was that he would take his army, march through northern Wyoming, and exterminate any and everyone they thought was a rustler. His men would round up Johnson County sheriff William H. "Red" Angus as well as dozens of homesteaders. To this purpose Frank Canton carried in his topcoat pocket a "dead" list that featured seventy names—men they wanted to do away with. To give the cattle barons' actions an air of legality, Wolcott and Canton would hang those on the list instead of simply gunning them down. Then they'd take over law enforcement in the county.

With the trainload of association enforcers heading toward Casper, word reached the Regulators that two "rustlers," Nathan Champion and Nick Ray, were living out at the old KC Ranch building. Champion and Ray were said to be among the rustler elite, even having their own "maverick" brand registered with the county. Champion had about two hundred head of cattle, but, yes, by golly, he and Ray were on Canton's dead list. The hired gunmen detoured for a mopping-up operation.

Historian Helena Huntington Smith describes Champion as

> stockily built, with steely blue-gray eyes; a quiet sort, people said; laconic, soft-spoken. He was a lion of a man who feard noth-

ing and would stand up to anybody, and he was lightning with a gun. The cattlemen hated him very greatly. Four of them [tried to kill him] but couldn't . . . even in his bed. It took fifty men to do the job.

In the end both Champion and Ray were killed, but it took some doing. And all during the time the association Regulators were attacking him Nate Champion kept a diary:

Me and Nick were getting breakfast when the attack took place. Two men here with us—Bill Jones and another man. The old man went out after water and didn't come back His friend went out to see what was the matter and he didn't come back. Nick started out and I told him to look out, that I thought there was someone in the stable and would not let him come back. Nick is shot, but not dead yet. He is awful sick. I must go and wait on him.

It is now about two hours since the first shot. Nick is still alive. . . .

They are still shooting and are all around the house. Boys, there is bullets coming in like hail. The fellows is in such shape I can't get at them. They are shooting from stable and river and back of the house.

Nick is dead. He died about 9 o'clock. I see smoke down in the stable. I think they have fired it. I don't think they intend to let me get away this time.

It is now about noon. There is someone at the stable yet; they are throwing a rope out at the door and drawing it back. I guess it is to draw me out. I wish that duck would get out further so I could get a shot at him.

Rancher and sometime rustler Black Jack Flagg, who owned the nearby Hat outfit, happened to ride by during the attack and saw what was happening. The Regulators shot at him, but Flagg got away and rushed on to the town of Buffalo, fifty miles away, to raise the alarm.

This mopping-up operation is taking entirely too long, Wolcott thought, and he decided to set fire to Champion's cabin, who all this time continued writing his diary:

Well, they have just got through shelling the house like hell. I heard them splitting wood. I guess they are going to fire the house tonight. I think I will make a break for it when night comes, if alive. It's not night yet. The house is all fired. Good-bye, boys, if I never see you again.

NATHAN D. CHAMPION

Champion put his diary into his vest pocket and rushed out the back of his cabin, a rifle in his hand. The Regulators saw him and opened fire. He shot back but missed and a bullet knocked his rifle away. He tried drawing his revolver, but they shot him again, this time in the chest. Then, third and fourth shots hit him and he died. Later, they would recover twenty-eight bullets from Nate's corpse. The Regulators stood around and looked at the man they had just killed. "By God," Wolcott said to his victim, "if I had fifty men like you, I could whip the whole state of Wyoming!"

One of the killers found Champion's pocket diary and read it aloud. Nate had recognized some of his attackers and written down their names, including that of Frank Canton. Instead of completely destroying the diary they used a knife to cut their names out of it, then tossed the book back onto Champion's corpse.

Someone took a card, wrote "CATTLE THIEVES BEWARE" on it, and pinned it to Champion's vest. They confiscated Champion's guns and gun belt for souvenirs. And with that the Regulators mounted their horses and headed for Buffalo.

Meanwhile Black Jack Flagg had reached Red Angus in Buffalo, and the sheriff swore in a posse of homesteaders. Sheriff Angus also tried to enlist the aid of regular army troops stationed at nearby Fort McKinney, but the army denied his request. The posse rode off without the army.

About the same time, Major Wolcott was preparing to ride north to Buffalo. When he heard about the posse, he fell back onto a deserted ranch, the now-bankrupt TA holdings on Crazy Woman Creek. He had his men throw up log breastworks and prepare for a siege.

By the time Sheriff Angus reached the TA ranch, his posse totaled more than three hundred men. They set to building rifle pits and barricades around the buildings, and by sunup the battle had begun. It lasted two days.

When it became obvious that the posse couldn't dig out the hired guns without a major brawl, one of its members, Arapaho Brown, came up with an idea: Build a gigantic mobile bomb—a wagon chassis, lashed to a barricade of logs and loaded with a large amount of dynamite. It's gone into books under such names as "Go Devil" and "Ark of Safety." The idea was to push it against the side of the ranch building and then set it off with a lighted match, a lucifer.

The posse wheels the contraption into position on the morning of April 13. Arapaho Brown is about to set off the Go Devil, when, as in the best of dime novels and cowboy movies, a bugle sounds. The 6th Cavalry is coming to the rescue, but to whose rescue it's uncertain.

Sheriff Angus wants the hired guns put in his custody, but army colonel J. J. Van Horn decides he'd rather not have fifty lynchings to deal with and keeps the Regulators under his protection, escorting them back to Cheyenne. The sheriff is furious. "I had them in my grasp," Angus fumes, "and they were taken from me."

Both sides in the dispute bellowed and cried against the other, but nothing much happened. A legal wind of sorts swept Wyoming. In the way such things go, Johnson County wound up paying for the Regulators' expenses. Wolcott's army hired their own guards and moved freely about town during the day, only returning to jail at night. The county even had to pay the "jailers." Altogether it cost some eighteen thousand dollars. It cost so much that the county almost went broke.

With that the Johnson County War ended. Except that the predominantly Republican cattle barons lost much of their influence, and predominantly Democratic ranchers gained some, which was what it had all been about in the first place.

In their parlors cattle barons passed around word that Nate Champion had been a thoroughly bad guy with a long criminal record, that, as the saying went, he "needed killing." This "reputation" was backed up by a March 12, 1892, article in what historian Helena Huntington Smith calls the "now forgotten Chicago newspaper, the *Saturday Blade*." The article, she says, was "evidently based on an interview with a Wyoming cattleman passing through Chicago and so wonderfully garbled it appears to have been written by a reporter who lost his notes and then wrote his story while drunk." The *Blade* article claimed Champion was an "unhung scoundrel" who was well known as a cattle thief. Not so, claims Smith. "The bad man story is bunk."

Meanwhile, *Chicago Herald* reporter Sam Clover, who, you may remember, had been a witness to Champion's killing: well, he'd found the dead man's diary, and he now published excerpts from it on the front page of his newspaper. It turned Champion into a short-term hero. A song based on Champion's diary as reported in the *Chicago Herald* was popular for a time:

> It was a little blood-stained book which a bullet had torn in twain.
> It told the fate of Nick and Nate, which is known to all of you;
> He had the nerve to write it down while the bullets fell like rain.
> At your request, I'll do my best to read those lines again. . . .
> The light is out, the curtain drawn, the last sad act is played.
> You know the fate that met poor Nate, and of the run he made.
> And now across the Big Divide, and at the Home Ranch door
> I know he'll meet and warmly greet the boys that went before.

The Johnson County War was over.

At one point the Montana Stock Growers' Association tried emulating their Wyoming brethren's example. At an 1885 meeting in Miles City, members introduced a resolution, to be binding on the association, forbidding them to employ any cowboy who owned cattle. Unlike the Wyoming association most of the Montana members objected, including Granville Stuart, the father-in-law of cowboy Teddy Blue Abbott. According to Teddy, Stuart "made quite a speech to allow . . . cowpunchers to own cattle on the range." Stuart "said that 99 per cent of them were honest men, that if they were allowed to brand mavericks and own cattle it would give them a chance to get ahead and give them an interest in the range, that this would do more than anything else to stop rustling."

If taking part in a trail drive was something of a rite of passage for cowboys, for cattle barons it simply was a means of moving masses of beef to market at a cost of about a penny a mile. A trail drive offered comradeship among the hands, but it offered profit to the owners.

John Wesley Iliff was born in McLuney, Ohio, in 1831, and attended Ohio Wesleyan University. His father offered him a seventy-five-hundred-dollar interest in the family stock-breeding operation, but Iliff turned it down for a five-hundred-dollar stake to go west. He tried his luck mining gold in Cherry Creek, Colorado, but he failed. Then he opened a store and sold goods to other wannabe gold diggers and settlers. Iliff would barter with passing emigrants for their lame and emaciated cattle and oxen, then turn the animals loose on the nearby plains.

They flourished on bunchgrass, a natural hay accessible even in winter; snow in the plains seldom formed a hard icy crust, and pawing cattle could easily reach this natural storehouse of protein and minerals. His once-scrawny cattle fattened up on this free grass, and Iliff sold them as beef.

During the Civil War John Iliff drove a few head of cattle to the South Platte Valley for sale in Denver butcher shops. In 1867 the Union Pacific Railroad gave him a contract to supply beef to its construction crews. When he couldn't fill the demand from his own herd, Iliff rode south to the Apishapa River, where he ordered forty-five thousand dollars' worth from Charlie Goodnight.

John Iliff kept his headquarters at Julesburg, Colorado, but he had so many ranches along the South Platte River that it was said he could sleep at a different one every night of the week. John never wore a gun but by sheer force of his personality made his word law for miles around. He was a stern teetotaler and a devout Christian.

John met his future wife, Elizabeth, when she was a Singer sewing-machine saleswoman, trudging across a country road. If John was a cattle baron, then Elizabeth was the perfect baroness, able to handle whatever crisis arose.

Iliff went on to own 15,000 acres of land along the South Platte, which allowed him to graze cattle across 650,000 acres of public land—"free grazing," it was called. On this land he could graze enough cattle to, according to the homestead theory then at work on the plains, feed four thousand farmers and their families. Iliff became known as the "cattle king of the Plains," controlling the range along 150 miles of the South Platte River. At his death Iliff's herd totaled about fifty thousand head. He was only forty-eight and left a large part of his estate to found the Iliff School of Theology in Denver.

On John's death one of Elizabeth's first thoughts was of the cattle empire her husband had built. She telegraphed their ranch foreman, telling him to double the guard on the herds before rustlers could move in.

The marquis de Mores—complete with curly black hair and waxed mustache points—became the social leader of the Dakota Badlands. He built sheep and cattle ranches near the town he named after his bride, Medora von Hoffman—Medora, North Dakota. He built a twenty-six-room château with a French-English-German library and had twenty servants just to keep it all running smoothly. When he got lonely, he invited his neighbor in to dine— a neighbor named Theodore Roosevelt. The marquis built a 225-mile stage line connecting Medora to Deadwood. He also built a quarter-of-a-million-dollar slaughterhouse; a refrigerator-car company with ice plants at twelve points along the Northern Pacific Railroad; a string of stores in New York City, where he sold the beef he raised, slaughtered, and refrigerated. All this said, he was a disaster as a cattle baron. He went belly up, because each of his enterprises had at least one fatal flaw. The stage line, for instance, couldn't get a vital mail contract. The marquis wound up dead at the hands of an Arab murderer in North Africa.

Abel "Shanghai" Pierce was "as uncouth as the cattle he drove," a neighbor once claimed. An up-from-bronco-busting cowboy, Pierce was known for his flamboyant ways. Shanghai once hired three brothers to round up a bunch of strays, but the boys began rounding them up for themselves as well. He didn't take too kindly to this and when he caught them, Shanghai strung all three up from the nearest cottonwood tree.

Shanghai Pierce was a cattle baron with a lot of gall and very little integrity. At the start of his career he owned only eleven acres of land, but he eventually increased that to more than a million acres and more than fifty thousand head of cattle.

Murdo Mackenzie was a Scot who was in charge of the Prairie Cattle Company, Limited. When the U.S. cattle market went bust in 1911, Mackenzie took over an even bigger outfit in Brazil.

Pierre Wibaux's money came from France; Christopher Columbus Slaughter's father was an English baron; Moreton Frewen failed in India, Australia, and Canada before coming to the United States; and Granville Stuart dug a fortune in gold out of the Montana mountains before turning to cattle. Big names in a growing country. Sometimes, some of them weren't exactly smart. Go back to Moreton Frewen. He once bought the same herd of cattle twice; the less-than-honest seller drove the steers around a hill, then brought them back and claimed it was a different bunch. Moreton paid up.

Cotton had once been king in the American South, but in the American West grass was king; and cattle made it worthwhile for many otherwise occupied. Chicago dry goods owner Marshall Field invested in cattle. As did railroad magnate William K. Vanderbilt. Fortune seekers from England and Scotland and other parts of Europe also invested in grassland cattle. Newspapers routinely proclaimed profits of forty cents on the dollar. "The range in the eighties," cowboy Teddy Blue Abbott recalled, "were as full of [rich men] as a dog's hair of fleas." Some of them, he said, were "good fellows and some were damn fools."

Out on the range cowboys built fences out of poles and logs, rocks and sod—whatever they could find; brush and shakes (logs whipsawed into thirty-inch blocks, then split into thin boards like shingles). But on November 24, 1874, that all changed. The United States Patent Office registered De Kalb, Illinois, farmer Joseph Farwell Glidden's patent on a product that would alter the face of the Great Plains and the West in general. As the plains were cut into small homesteads, larger ranchers needed a way to fence in the range, but in a virtually treeless land wooden fences were hard to come by and expensive.

Glidden solved that; he invented barbed wire, or at least he got the patent on the most popular variety. He first used a coffee grinder and a grindstone to wind short barbs around one of two wires in a strand of fence, bracing the barb with the second wire. For a year or so he did little with his patent, but then he was joined by a twenty-five-dollar-a-week drummer named John Warner Gates. By the 1880s Glidden was in full production with his barbed wire. As Gates put it, "This is the finest fence in the world. Light as air. Stronger than whiskey. Cheaper than dirt." Free range became private pasture and cropland.

To show off the product Joseph Glidden and his Barbed Fence Company built a barbed-wire corral in the main plaza of San Antonio, Texas, and released inside it a bunch of longhorn cattle. The wire not only held the longhorns, it didn't even harm them. That was enough to convince even Texas cattlemen. They bought up every roll of barbed wired that Glidden had and fenced in huge areas of grassland.

Cattle barons fenced in water holes and roads and even whole towns. Glidden's product (and that of his competitor, Jacob Haish) soon restricted free movement across the land; legally and illegally, thousands of miles of winding steel cut up the prairie. The prickly coils of barbed wire redrew the geography of the West.

The XIX spread in Texas used so much barbed wire that the staples used to attach it to posts had to be shipped in by the freight-car load. At one time the King Ranch of Texas had more than fifteen miles of barbed wire fencing in its spread.

That's when war began between cattlemen and sheepmen, between ranchers and cattle thieves, and between cowboys and Indians. As barbed wire closed in more and more open range, small stockmen, nesters, and farmers protested. They formed masked, night-riding bands, which cut down ranchers' wire. In turn ranchers stampeded cattle over the farmers' crops. Violence and murder was everywhere, until 1885, when Congress passed a law forbidding the fencing in of public lands.

Joseph Glidden and one of his salesmen, Henry B. Sanborn, built a ranch in the Texas Panhandle, on Tecoras Creek in Potter County. Their brand was designed to look like a panhandle, but to cowboys it looked like something else, and it became known as the "frying pan" brand.

Glidden's other salesman, J. W. Gates, took advantage of the opportunities he'd helped create and began manufacturing barbed wire on his own, becoming chairman of the board of directors of the powerful American Steel and Wire Company. Later Gates got into the oil business and helped develop the city of Port Arthur, Texas, where he built up the Texas Company, better known today as Texaco.

He was, perhaps, better known to the outside world as "Bet-a-Million" Gates, because he is said to have done just that. True or not, it *is* true that John Warner Gates died a wealthy man in 1911.

CHAPTER FIVE

Westward Ho!*
Beauty Is in the Eye of the Beerholder

Some were young—in their teens. The hair of others was growing gray and their faces hardened in sin. . . .
                                    The *Denver Republican,* May 4,1889

Kitty Le Roy was what a real man would call a starry beauty. Her brown hair was thick and curling; she had five husbands, seven revolvers, a dozen bowie-knives, and always went armed to the teeth, which latter were like pearls set in coral.
                        Admiring newspaper correspondent, Deadwood, South Dakota

Wyoming was the first state to give women the right to vote. Earlier a few women (as well as a few free blacks) *had* voted in local East Coast elections—in New Jersey, for example. Property was a prime requisite for voting, and some women had inherited land from their dead husbands, but in general women were prevented from voting. That is, until December 10, 1869, when women's suffrage became law in the new Wyoming Territory, twenty-one years after Elizabeth Cady Stanton had chaired a meeting at Seneca Falls, New York, calling for the vote for women.

Wyoming had a population of only about nine thousand, and some people thought giving them the vote was a publicity stunt to attract women to the territory. The *Cheyenne Democratic Leader* called it a "shrewd advertising dodge" and "a cunning device." Cunning or shrewd, it stuck, and women were also allowed to own property separate from their husbands', to sit on juries, and to hold public office.

Not long after Wyoming, women in Utah got the vote, then came Colorado and, by 1896, Idaho. Still, women's suffrage was opposed nationally. In 1910 President Grover Cleveland, writing in the *Ladies'*

*From William Shakespeare's *Twelfth Night,* Act III, Sceen 1, line 149.

Home Journal, stated that "sensible and responsible women do not want to vote." It would be ten years later, in 1920, that the Nineteenth Amendment to the Constitution was enacted to give women the right to vote.

Almost every kind of person peopled the American West, from almost every stratum of life, from just about every nation in the world. Some had little or no education; others were college educated. It's not certain how much education the writers of some cemetery epitaphs had or where they came from. What is certain is that in many cases, those epitaphs are both telling and entertaining. Take the inscription left on the Oregon Trail by someone apparently headed for the gold fields:

> To follow you is not my intent
> Unless I know which way you went.

An epitaph in the Black Hills marked the graves of three horse thieves:

> Here lie the bodies of Allen, Curry and Hall,
> Like other thieves they had their rise, decline and fall;
> On yon pine tree they hung till dead,
> And here they found a lonely bed.

And there's a frequently quoted epitaph in an Ouray, Colorado, cemetery:

> Here lies Charlotte,
> She was a harlot.
> For fifteen years she preserved her virginity,
> A damn good record for this vicinity.

Which brings to mind a bawdy song, probably out of the Wild West, but one that lingered in certain circles well into the twentieth century to become a drinking song for World War II Army Air Corps pilots:

> She's Charlotte, the harlot,
> The cowpunchers' whore.
> She'll do it for a dollar,
> Take less or take more.
> She's Charlotte, the harlot,
> The cowpunchers' whore.

When men went west, they left a lot behind. They left behind their past. Often, they even left behind their names, taking instead names such as "Honest Whiskey Joe," "The American Pie-Eater," "Truthful James," and "Johnny Behind the Deuce," whose real name was Michael John O'Rourke, and whose biggest claim to fame (other than his nickname) was that Wyatt Earp once saved him from a lynching.

Most of all they left behind their women. The scarcity of women made for a rougher life. It lowered their sexual morality, and although it now may be sexist to say so, it left them without the gentling influence of mother, sister, wife, or next door neighbor. In their place, the Wild West offered prostitutes.

Prostitutes were given several names, "working girls" perhaps being among the most benign. Often they were called "soiled doves." They were known as "daughters of Eve" or "gay young chicks," "sporting women," "*nymphes du prairie*" (prairie nymphs), "*nymphes du pavé*" (street nymphs), or "*filles de joie*" (young girl). Some were "hurdy-gurdy girls" or simply "hurdies" who danced in hurdy-gurdy houses, where mechanical hand organs provided music. They could be "ladies of the evening," "ladies of the night," or "ladies of easy virtue." "Frail denizens," "ceiling experts," "chippies," "horizontal workers," and "women of evil name and fame." High-classed prostitutes might be called "courtesans," a term left over from seventeenth-century Europe, usually meaning the young lady had a wealthy and often prominent clientele. A "demimondaine," or "demimonde," was a woman who'd lost her reputation due to some improper behavior on her part, and who then became a prostitute. If she was around the trade long, a soiled dove became an "old-timer," in which status she didn't usually last long due to diseases and hard living—drugs and alcohol among the more obvious vices of such an existence.

Left over from before the Civil War was the name "Cyprians." Others were "painted beauties," "frail sisters," "calico queens," "calico cats," and "painted cats." Just as today, a "streetwalker" solicited sex on the street, often in the town's "tenderloin"—an expression that originated in New York—a section of town where vice and police corruption were common. San Francisco's tenderloin section, for instance, is alive, if not well, today, situated between Union Square and the Civic Center. Not far away is the once bawdy Maiden Lane, now perhaps the headiest of San Francisco's high-rent, high-class, high-cost, pinstriped shopping areas, loaded with boutiques and galleries. "Proper" women did not wear makeup, so anyone who did was a "painted lady," a phrase given today to some restored Victorian houses.

A main-line brothel charged customers as much as $100, but a simple soiled dove might get as little as fifty cents per client—"She'll do it for a dollar/Take less or take more. . . ." However, in Helena, Montana, prostitutes in 1880 had an average monthly income of $233, which boggles the mind at fifty cents per client. Bank clerks earned $125 while carpenters, bricklayers, and stonemasons made $90 a month. A popular girl in a popular house, however, charged more and earned as much as $200 a week.

In the Wild West, women generally fell into two categories: "good women"—the marrying kind who included mothers, wives, or sisters—and soiled doves. The two groups seldom mingled. According to their own code cowboys wouldn't even mention a "good" woman's name in a saloon or brothel, and "good women" weren't even supposed to know that soiled doves existed. When wives and daughters of George Armstrong Custer's command were driven through Hayes City, Kansas, during the town's most notorious, trail-town period, the curtains on the women's carriages were strapped down so that the "good women" wouldn't have to see "bad women" or the red light district where they worked.

A miner at Copperfield, Utah, wrote that "there was a regular red-light district, but on paydays, 250 prostitutes came into town and the men gave up their rooms to accommodate them during their stay." The term *red-light district* originated in Dodge City, Kansas, where railroaders hung their red signal lamps outside the bawdy houses to let other railroaders know where they were in case of emergencies. In some cases brothels had blood-red glass in the front door windows.

As a Topeka newspaperman wrote in 1872, "The Texan, with mammoth spurs on his boots . . . and a broad brimmed *sombrero* on his head, is seen dancing by the side of a well-dressed, gentlemanly appearing stranger from some eastern city; both having painted and jeweled courtesans for partners."

The custom in many cheaper establishments allowed that, while a man dallied, he couldn't remove any of his clothing except his hat. Now, since cowboys wouldn't be caught dead without their hats—it was the last thing they took off at night and the first thing they put on in the morning—that meant they dallied fully dressed.

With or without their hats on, men of the Wild West generally were fond of the girls on the brothel line. One Dodge City resident called his favorite whore "Tid Bit" and said, "The only thing anyone could hold against her was her after-dark profession, and by Godfrey, I allow she elevated that considerably." Or, as a Bodie, California, miner once described soiled dove Rosa May, "She was a gal who had a smile you'd go to hell for, and never regret it."

A "procurer" made his living obtaining customers for a prostitute; today, he's called a "pimp." A "mistress" was the illicit ladylove of a married man, but a "madam" or "mother" was one who ran a "parlor house," an elite house of prostitution, a "bagnio," "bordello," or even a "boardinghouse," which is not to be confused, of course, with more legitimate boardinghouses where all customers did was eat and sleep.

In gold mining towns miners seemed to favor cats for pets. When the miners left town or were killed or just disappeared, local prostitutes often took in their cats. Over time so many miners gave so many prostitutes so many cats, brothels came to be known as "cat houses."

The military didn't officially allow prostitution on the posts, which isn't to say prostitutes and soldiers didn't break the rules. Sometimes laundresses hired by the military did more than just wash and starch your shirts. Regulations tried to prevent women with venereal disease from consorting with troops, another regulation ignored early and often. If prostitutes didn't work on army posts, they worked nearby.

The "girls" often worked at "hog ranches," which may have described the soiled doves but had nothing to do with creatures of a more porcine nature. Inside a hog ranch, prostitutes plied their trade (and sometimes lived) in "cribs," small rooms or adjacent houses. There even were "floating hog ranches"—flatboats, keelboats, or whatever—that worked rivers and waterfronts.

Some soiled doves traveled with husbands or sons or brothers. Some set up shop in cowtown cribs. Often prostitutes took up their trade when they were thrown on their own resources and faced desperate economic choices, because most women's work, as it was defined in the Wild West, paid too poorly to provide decent food, clothing, and shelter. Others sought excitement or independence from their families. Some, of course, just plain liked it. Prostitutes sometimes were forced into the trade through "white slavery," the interstate (often international) transportation of young women for illegal and immoral purposes.

They might end up on "skid row," a term that apparently began in Eureka, California, where a trail of greased skids was used to haul logs to the sawmills. Skid row, or "skid road," as it sometimes was called, became that district in any town containing brothels and saloons catering to the wants of loggers and lumbermen. Today, it's a general term used for any down-and-out section of town.

Whenever they had the chance, lonely cowboys lined up outside brothels, which was good for the soiled doves' business, but bad for their health and welfare. Working hours for working girls usually were noon until dawn, with girls getting one day off a week.

Let's face it, the life of a soiled dove was hard. Wild West prostitutes led anything *but* glamorous lives; certainly most weren't high-priced professionals. Mostly they were plain women who wore gaudy clothes. Still, wherever they went—dance hall to bordello to crib— they elicited a great deal of excitement and tended to add a gentling, more civilized flavor to cow and mine towns. A Montana man remembered that "many's the miner who'd never wash his face or comb his hair, if it wasn't for thinkin' of the sportin' girls he might meet in the saloons." In many cases saloons and brothels were the only real homes that some men knew—brightly lit rooms, glittering chandeliers, mirrors, decanters, bottles, and music, paintings on the wall, and the painted ladies themselves—all in contrast to a cowboy's dimly lit bunkhouse or a miner's dismal hovel.

Like their male counterparts, early female arrivals in the Wild West were rugged individualists who just wanted to be left alone to do what they pleased, which sometimes meant earning a living on their backs. Many, of course, went west to escape their past, others to create one. Some saw too many restrictions in eastern society and wanted to create a future in a new land of opportunity. Many had nothing to lose, and all were hoping against hope. If they worked hard and saved their money, soiled doves believed, they could get out of the business, buy new, less gaudy clothing, hop a train for someplace else, and begin a new life in another town as a "respectable widow."

In 1860 a madam called Mary Miller spent three months in jail for "depressing real estate values," but prostitution generally was condoned and even sanctioned in the early West. Many community leaders didn't let it interfere with business. Ellsworth, Kansas, even made a profit on it. According to a local newspaper:

> The city realizes $300 a month from prostitution fines alone. . . . The city authorities consider that as long as mankind is depraved and Texas cattle herders exist, there will be a demand and necessity for prostitutes, and that as long as prostitutes are bound to dwell in Ellsworth it is better for the respectable portion of society to hold prostitutes under the restraint of law.

Cowboys were sentimental about all women, including prostitutes. They gave the girls nicknames such as "Queen," "Irish Queen," and "Spanish Queen." In addition to the "Yellow Rose of Texas," there was just plain "Rose" as well as "Wild Rose," "Prairie Rose," and "Velvet Ass Rose." "Little Gold Dollar" was well known, as were "Contrary Mary," and "Peg-Leg Annie." Calamity Jane once had a partner in Wyoming called "Cotton Tail," who apparently was a natural blonde.

Court records and newspapers of the day record the names of "Little Dot," "Hop Fiend Nell," "Emporia Belle," "Scar-Faced Lillie," "Miss One Fin" (an interesting if bewildering name), "Oglala Shorty," "Jack-Rabbit Sue," "Four-Ace Dora," "Kansas Cow," "Razorback Jennie," "Society Annie," "Sallie Purple," and "Cowboy Annie." "Connie the Cowboy Queen" sported a $250 dress embroidered with the brands of every outfit from the Yellowstone to the Platte River. "Squirrel Tooth Alice" of Dodge City kept a squirrel as a pet. Lusty women all: "Hambone Jane," the "Galloping Cow," "Big Minnie" (six feet tall, 230 pounds of loveliness in pink tights), "Rowdy Kate," and "Big Nose Kate," whose real name was Mary Katherine Haroney.

Mary Katherine was born November 7, 1850, in Budapest, Hungary. In a life filled with romance, tragedy, and spectacular fights, she shaped her life by her own rules.

Not much is known about her early life, and a lot of literature portrays Kate as your basic two-bit whore, a poster child for western prostitutes: poor, uneducated, looking for the perfect man to get her out of the business. Historian Pat Jahns, for instance, recounts a scene in which Kate is

> sprawled out on the bed with a cigarette in one hand and a piece of imported French chocolate in the other, one heel on top of her upraised knee, idly flipping through the latest issue of *Frank Leslie's Illustrated Weekly,* looking every inch a whore— and completely happy.

Jahns's version wasn't true. For various reasons Kate didn't want those around her to know anything about her family or past; she may not have wanted her family, children of Hungarian aristocrats, to know what she'd become. Even some of her friends apparently didn't know her real name.

Not only had she come from an aristocratic family, she was well educated and probably spoke at least English, Hungarian, and Spanish. In 1862 Mexico's emperor Maximilian appointed her father, Dr. Michael Haroney, as his surgeon, and the Haroney family left Hungary for Mexico. The job didn't last long, however; Maximilian's court crumbled three years later, and the Haroney family had to flee Mexico, moving on to Davenport, Iowa. Within a year both Kate's mother and father died, and the children were put in foster homes, where her foster father apparently molested her. So, Kate ran off and stowed away on a steamer headed for St. Louis. The ship's captain—

his name is known only as "Fisher"—discovered the young girl, but instead of leaving her at the next stop, he took her to St. Louis, where Kate assumed his name. As Kate Fisher she enrolled in a convent school.

Later, she claimed, she married a dentist known as Silas Melvin and the couple had one child. Well, maybe. The 1870 census records for St. Louis don't list a Kate Fisher who would match a description of our Kate. No listings, either, under her other known names and pseudonyms—Haroney, Horony, Melvin, Elder, or Michaels. There is, however, a "Kate Fischer," listed in the census as age twenty-three with Baden, Germany, as her birthplace, who told the census taker that she could neither read nor write. Some of this fits Kate, some does not, and the discrepancies could be due to Kate's habit of altering facts about herself. For example, the census report of the woman's age was three years older than our Kate would have been; she'd been seventeen when she arrived in St. Louis but may have wanted to appear older. The Baden birthplace could be explained as a young runaway trying to conceal her identity from her fondling foster father. The same could have been true of the claim of illiteracy, a desire to avoid detection and possibly a return to Iowa.

Whoever "Kate Fischer" was, she apparently didn't attend any convent school, residing instead in a house with eight other nonrelated women, seven of whom listed their occupation as "whore." The eighth woman said she was a whore's "personal servant."

At any rate, according to Kate, both her husband the dentist and their child died of fever. It wasn't long after their deaths that her life began moving in a darker direction. In the summer of 1874, in Wichita, Kansas, a "Kate Elder" paid a fine while working in her chosen profession at Sally and Bessie Earp's bordello. Later that year, a notice appeared in a Wichita newspaper that the postmaster was holding a letter for Kate Fisher, who apparently was now Kate Elder. No longer a teenager on the run, this twenty-four-year-old working girl stood about five eight or nine and had reddish-blond hair.

Wyatt Earp was Bessie's brother-in-law. According to Kate she met Wyatt during her stay later in Fort Griffin, Texas, but once again she may have told something less than the truth. Given her occupation and place of work, it's likely the two met at Bessie's. How much of a relationship, if any, Kate and Wyatt had at the time isn't certain. Later on she professed a strong dislike of the man.

In any event, Kate moved to Dodge City in 1875, the year a twenty-four-year-old Kate Elder, from Iowa, appears on a census as working in a dance hall owned by Tom Sherman. About three years later she turned up in Fort Griffin, Texas, where she met the man who had the greatest impact on her life: dentist John Henry "Doc" Holliday, Wyatt Earp's sidekick and "the answer to an undertaker's prayer."

Doc faced continuous ill health (apparently, tuberculosis or "galloping consumption") and the threat of an even more violent death. Still, he insisted on living a life centered around gambling tables in smoky saloons, which isn't the best way of life for someone chronically ill. Kate's job in Fort Griffin gave her a life where she answered to nobody but herself and apparently enjoyed it: a freelance prostitute.

According to a possibly apocryphal legend, Doc got into trouble at the gambling table. A disagreement with a man named Edward Bailey led to the bowie-knife disembowelment of said Mr. Bailey, which led to Doc being arrested, which led to him being locked up in a hotel room, since the town didn't own a jail, said locking up to continue, pending trial or one of the West's infamous little "necktie parties," whichever came first. It seems that Ed Bailey was a member in good standing of Griffin's community of crooks who thought that a good lynching was in order. The would-be necktie partygoers, however, didn't take into consideration Doc's mistress, Kate, who proceeded to set fire to a shack, which in turn set fire to almost the whole town, which greatly diverted attention from Doc, which gave Kate time to pull a gun on Doc's guards, which allowed the pair to say so long to the guards, the would-be hangmen, and to the town of Fort Griffin, Texas. In fact, they said good-bye to Texas, turning up later in Dodge City, Kansas, where they set up housekeeping at Deacon Cox's Boarding House as Mr. and Mrs. J. H. Holliday, even though there's no evidence of the loving couple ever standing before priest, minister, rabbi, judge, justice of the peace, or ship's captain.

For a while Doc took another shot at dentistry—on June 8, 1878, the *Dodge City Times* announced the availability of Doc's dental services. And Kate? Well, she was now a good little hausfrau. Sure.

This picture of Doc and Kate as a clean-cut Western family lasted, oh, maybe two months. Then Doc went back to gambling and Kate went back to whoring. Doc slipped farther and farther from dentistry and moved into a life of gambling, and he followed the game wherever it went. Kate followed Doc.

Their relationship apparently went through various stages but was always a bumpy one—domestic disputes, fabulous fights, and frequent reconciliations. Both were strong individuals, with Kate often described as a "hot-tempered" person who did exactly what she wanted, when she wanted to.

Doc continued his work as a gambler and Kate went on with her occupation as a ceiling expert, which, among other things, gave her a separate income, something unusual for a nineteenth-century woman. Doc apparently loved Kate and felt indebted to her for getting him out of Fort Griffin, even for nursing him when he was sick; he resented her as well. Both had come from aristocratic families. Doc was the only son of Maj. Henry B. Holliday of Griffin, Georgia— planter, lawyer, and medium-size cog in local politics. Both Doc and Kate were educated, but Doc looked down on her as somewhat inferior, possibly due to her chosen occupation, as if his was much better. Likely he also resented her health, because as time went on, Doc Holliday's health went downhill.

Despite their turbulent relationship Doc and Kate stuck together. Doc's luck as a gambler may have been an incentive to Kate, but apparently they also shared something deeper than four aces.

Doc and Wyatt Earp had met back in Fort Griffin when Wyatt came to town looking for a crook named Dave Rudabaugh and Doc helped track him down. In Dodge, about the time Doc and Kate made it their home, Wyatt was known as the town's marshal. While the three of them were in Dodge, Doc helped get Wyatt out of a jam involving a group of Texas cowboys, and that sealed their friendship.

Doc and Kate moved on to Las Vegas, New Mexico, where he had one last fling at dentistry. Once more his attempt at honesty failed, and Doc bought a saloon. That was in 1879, and all seemed to be going well until Doc and a man named Mike Gordon got to trading lead. Mike lost the trade and Doc once again became a fugitive. He and Kate returned to Dodge, apparently expecting to find Wyatt

Earp still there. He wasn't; by then he was in Tombstone, Arizona Territory. Doc and Kate went looking for him, stopping off in Prescott, where Doc hit a lucky streak. In 1880, his lucky streak having struck out, Doc joined Wyatt and his fellow Earps in Tombstone, without Kate, however. She may have had enough of fighting with Doc or she may have had enough of Wyatt Earp. In a letter to her niece Kate wrote, "I wanted Doc to go with me. The Earps had such power I could not get Doc away from them."

Whatever her reasons for not following Doc at first, Kate soon found herself on the way to Tombstone. Doc had won four thousand dollars gambling, which may have outweighed her concerns about Wyatt Earp.

There's some confusion over this time in their life, whether Mary Katherine Haroney-Fisher-Fischer-Elder-Holliday was somebody else. Somehow, and we can only imagine how, she'd picked up the nickname "Big Nose Kate," and there's been some question over whether she was also known as "Rowdy Kate." Big Nose, however, was Big Nose and Rowdy was Rowdy.* They even operated a brothel together, which of course could have caused the confusion: Who, during a tryst with a hooker, stops to consider whether she's rowdy or has a big nose? At any rate, in the spring of 1881 our Kate left Tombstone for the town of Globe.

On the night of March 15 armed robbers tried to hold up a stage near Contention, Arizona. During the attempt the would-be robbers killed stagecoach driver Bud Philpot and a passenger, Peter Roerig. Well, maybe. Wyatt's and Doc's enemies claimed that Earp and Holliday staged the robbery.

It was about this time that Doc and Kate were having one of their infamous knock-down,-drag-out fights, and Doc had thrown Kate out. Cochise County, Arizona, sheriff John Behan and his deputy, Frank Stillwell, went looking for Kate.

---

*Adding to the confusion is that for a while Big Nose Kate and Rowdy Kate were good friends. Wyatt Earp biographer Stuart Lake even identifies a photograph of Rowdy as Big Nose, but it just ain't so.

Behan was a friend of the Clanton gang and an enemy to Doc Holliday and the Earps. Historian Denis McLoughlin says that the Cochise County sheriff's job "was worth thirty thousand dollars a year, if you happened to be corruptible, and Behan may have been."

Anyway, Behan and Stillwell get Kate drunk, get her signature on an affidavit stating that Doc killed driver Philpot, and Doc gets angry. For once in his life Doc Holliday is innocent.

Kate sobers, realizes what she's done, and repudiates the written statement. With that the judge drops the charges against Doc, and the former dentist gives Kate some money, a stagecoach ticket, and waves good-bye to Kate, who goes to Globe to run a local hotel or something.

One thing about Doc and Kate (as it is in many abusive relationships), they fight and then get back together. Over and over and over. Several times while she's living in Globe, Kate travels to Tombstone to visit Doc. In fact, Big Nose Kate claimed she was with Doc in Tombstone during the famous gunfight at the O.K. Corral.

The business of being a "lady of leisure" was a crowded one. Along Denver's Holladay Street, where many soiled doves roosted, a local resident remembered that "men took their liquor neat and women took what they could get their hands on." Jennie Rogers was one of Denver's most successful madams during the 1880s. Once, she caught her lover Jack Wood in the arms of another woman and shot him. She shot him, Jennie claimed, because she loved him, which apparently was so, because when Jack recovered, she married him.

Mattie Blaylock grew up on an Iowa farm; she had large bones and a fine face. Not long after going west she began work in Dodge City as a dance hall girl. She did okay, but like many girls on the line she wanted to find the right guy and leave that way of life. She met a local police officer and moved in with him, happy to be off the streets. Her live-in lover soon tired of the low pay of police work and became a bartender, gambling on the side. He bought Mattie a mine with his winnings, naming it the "Mattie Blaylock."

They traveled together as man and wife, following the gambling circuit, and for a while it was good. But then things went south in their relationship, and he left her for another woman, never saying good-bye, just leaving town. Mattie tried to make it on her own, but there was little she knew how to do. She went back on the bordello line, and things went downhill from there. Trouble was, Mattie was older now and lacked the appeal of the younger girls. She woke up one morning in a small shack in a one-horse town with a stranger in her bed. That was too much for her. Mattie bought a bottle of laudanum, drank it all down, and went to her final sleep.

At an inquest looking into Mattie's death the coroner in Pinal, Arizona Territory, asked a laborer named T. J. Flannery if he had known the deceased. Yes, Flannery replied. Her name? Well, she called herself "Mattie Earp." The man who'd left Mattie was none other than Wyatt Earp.

Did the deceased ever threaten to take her own life? the coroner asked.

Yes, the witness answered. Mattie had told Flannery that Wyatt Earp had deserted her, wrecking her life. And she didn't want to live without him.

Not only did a whore's life lack glamour, but when she died, most people shunned her. Miners and cowboys may truly have "loved their gals" in life, but they ignored them when soiled doves died, watching as towns laid "their gals" to rest in outcast cemeteries far from the plots of "good women."

By all accounts the woman born Martha Jane Cannary was twice as ugly as sin, with a face that only a grizzly could love. She was, however, convinced that, if not beautiful, she was at least attractive to men. Off and on Martha Jane was a hooker, a lady of the evening, no matter what time of day.

She was also a mule skinner who more often than not wore men's clothing and showed a preference for fringed buckskins; she drank hard liquor, smoked foul cigars, and chewed plug tobacco. By her own claim she married none other than James B. "Wild Bill" Hickok. Martha Jane Cannary (or "Canary") was Calamity Jane.

Born on May 1, 1852—or thereabouts, depending on who's telling the story—on a two-hundred-acre farm in Princeton, Missouri, Marthy, as she called herself in her *Life and Adventures of Calamity Jane by Herself,* was the oldest of three girls and two boys:

As a child I always had a fondness for adventure and outdoor exercise and especial fondness for horses which I began to ride at an early age and continued to do so until I became an expert rider being able to ride the most vicious and stubborn of horses, in fact the greater portion of my life in the early times was spent in this manner.

Her family pulled up stakes in 1865 and headed west for Virginia City, Montana, and the lure of gold. She was a sandy-haired girl who, by 1869, was on her own in Cheyenne, Wyoming. Along the way she gained experience in handling guns, cards, and men, claiming that "in fact I was at all times with the men when there was excitement and adventure to be had." After her parents died, Jane became a camp follower of the Union Pacific crews.

Somewhere near Abilene, Kansas, along about 1870, Calamity Jane and Wild Bill Hickok were married, or at least that's the way some accounts have it. Some fans of Hickok and enemies of Jane claim the fastidious Wild Bill wouldn't have gone near the slovenly Calamity Jane. She may even have given birth to Wild Bill Hickok's child.

Married or not, to Wild Bill or anybody else, Jane wasn't about to settle down. In 1875 she joined the U.S. Army as a scout and mule skinner, later claiming she was George Armstrong Custer's scout at Fort D. A. Russell, which is interesting, since Custer apparently never served there.

Calamity Jane also claimed she helped Generals Nelson Miles, Alfred Terry, and George Crook fight the Nez Percé Indians (she called them the "Nursey Pursey") in 1872, which would have been difficult, since the three generals were never anywhere near each other and the Nez Percé outbreak didn't happen until 1877. But who wants to interrupt a good story with the facts? Jane was a scout with General Crook during the 1876 Sioux campaign. She enlisted in the army as a man, and as soon as the army discovered her true sex—don't ask how; sometimes it's best not to know—they tossed her out on her buckskinned butt.

In 1876 Jane turned up in Deadwood, Dakota Territory, hanging around with Wild Bill Hickok again. It's then, she said, that she gave

Bill a divorce so that he could marry Agnes Lake. That was the year
Wild Bill was killed while in a poker game, holding aces and eights
and a queen kicker. Calamity Jane went on to claim she ran to earth
Bill's killer, Jack McCall. "I at once," she wrote in her autobiography,

> started to look for the assassin and found him at Shurdy's
> butcher shop and grabbed a meat cleaver and made him throw
> up his hands, because through the excitement of hearing of
> Bill's death having left my weapons on the post of my bed. He
> was then taken to a log cabin and locked up. . . .

Well, maybe. As a dime novel of the time put it:

> The great gunfighter knew that he was dying. . . . That drop of
> moisture on his pale cheek was not the rain but a woman's tears.
> . . . Calamity Jane was on her knees beside him. "Don't go away
> from me, Bill," she sobbed. "I love you. . . . Don't you know that?
> I love you." And his last message came to her in a whisper she
> was never going to forget: "My heart has been yours from the
> first."

There's another story that as soon as she heard about Bill's death,
Jane hurried over to the No. 10 saloon and joined in his wake.

Calamity Jane was a prostitute with a heart of gold, as such stories
go. In the best of such tales she found herself in the Black Hills in
the middle of a smallpox epidemic. For a while locals called her the
"Black Hills Florence Nightingale," thanks to her nursing the sick
during an epidemic.

A woman named Dora Dufran wrote in her memoirs about Jane,
saying that "her only medicines were epsom salts and cream of tar-
tar . . . but her good nursing brought five . . . men out of the shadow
of death, and many more later on, before the disease died out." If
ever anybody was sick, Dufran declared, "it was 'send for Jane'; where
calamity was, there was Jane; and so she was christened Calamity
Jane." Another way she may have gotten her name was that many of
the men with whom she consorted became infected with a type of
venereal disease called the "calamity."

In November of the year of the epidemic, Jane wrote to a girl she claimed was her and Wild Bill Hickok's daughter, Jean. In part, the letter says:

I met up with Jesse James not long ago. He is quite a character—you know he was killed in '82. . . . He is passing under the name of Dalton but he couldn't fool me. I knew all the Daltons and he sure ain't one of them. . . . To make it stranger, Jesse sang at his own funeral. Poor devil he can't cod me—not even with his long hair and a billy goat's wad of hair on his chin.

The letter came to light in 1941 when Jean Hickok McCormick applied for welfare, claiming she was Calamity and Wild Bill's daughter, a claim which the welfare department believed. Emory University professor Elizabeth Stevenson also seems to believe the Jane-Bill marriage/parenthood stories. In her 1994 book, *Figures in a Western Landscape*, Stevenson writes of three letters Jean claimed came from her mother, Martha Jane Cannary:

The letters are a document to move the reader. They create a character who is believable and haunting. This is not a cheap or cunning fraud, for the letters have the authenticity of art.

A bordello madam in Deadwood claimed that Jane once invaded her whorehouse and started raising the roof in general mayhem and madness. The madam had the loudly cursing Jane locked up in a closet until she sobered up, saying, "I won't have her using that kind of language in front of my girls." According to Teddy Blue Abbott, some of Jane's friends had taken up a collection and "sent her East to make a lady of her, and now she was back."

I joked her about her trip and asked her: "How'd you like it when they sent you East to get reformed and civilized?"

Her eyes filled with tears. She said: "Blue, why don't the sons of bitches leave me alone and let me go to hell my own route? All I ask is to be allowed to live out the rest of my life with you boys who speak my language. And I hope they lay me beside Bill Hickok when I die."

Outside of Wyoming and the Black Hills you don't hear much about the woman once known as "Ma'am" Shepard. She'd been part of a gang of outlaws in Louisiana but, in the 1870s, built a roadhouse near Raw Hide Butte, between Fort Laramie and Lusk on the Cheyenne–Black Hills stage route. She usually wore red pantalettes she'd tie around her ankles; they fluttered wildly as she rode astraddle her favorite horse. "A feather-legged chicken in a high wind," one cowboy remembered. "Mother Feather Legs," another called her.

Whatever the cowboys and miners and townsfolk called her, Ma'am Shepard operated a profitable business. They say she kept a good supply of whiskey, imported honest gamblers to fleece her customers, maintained a "bank" where she kept money and stolen jewelry for outlaws, and ran one of the best little whorehouses in the northern plains. Her career ended one day in 1879, when she was shot to death by someone who also took more than a thousand dollars from her "bank."

Ella Hill was a raven-haired, dark-eyed beauty whose dance hall–brothel was the largest in the Texas Panhandle. Ella kept a clean house, and would not allow alcoholics or drug users to work for her, and profanity was prohibited. Early on she'd been a prostitute herself who worked hard and saved her money. After a few years she resigned from active duty and opened her own house. First a small house, but as her success grew, Ella Hill opened larger and larger brothels. By the time she moved her business to Amarillo, she was a highly regarded madam, if not a highly respected one. When the town needed a church, Ella donated the money to build one. And since it was the money from her not-too-respectful, if highly successful, business that paid for the church, she thought her soiled doves had a right to attend services. Every Sunday morning Ella Hill and her prostitutes (modestly dressed for the occasion) went to church.

Hers was, she claimed, the finest brothel in town, but finally she decided it was time to retire. She moved to Wichita, Kansas, and opened a laundry in which she employed only former prostitutes, women who'd been scorned by society.

Ella Hill had two daughters, but she had them reared away from her. She often visited them, and it's probable they never learned what she really did for a living; they thought she was a housekeeper for a wealthy rancher. When Ella Hill died, her remains were sent back to Amarillo for burial. By then both of her daughters were grown and had married respectable men and were raising respectable families. It's not certain whether they ever learned the true facts about their mother.

There was one prostitute whose nickname obviously came from her appearance. Eleanore Dumont was a plump, dark girl in her mid-twenties. She spoke English with a French accent and reportedly had an air of modesty about her. Eleanore ran a gambling house in Nevada City, offering free champagne for all, somehow convincing miners it was a privilege to lose gold at her tables.

But such is life. The gold ran out in Nevada City, Eleanore progressed beyond plump, she drank too much, and her beauty faded. That's when she gained her nickname. A shadow of down began growing on her upper lip and Eleanore Dumont became dubbed "Madame Mustache" by a disillusioned miner.

She didn't like her new nickname, but it followed her the rest of her life—city to town, gambling den to brothel. In 1877 Madame Mustache was running a brothel in Eureka, Nevada, but less than two years later the *Sacramento Union* ran an item from Brodie, California: "A woman named Eleanore Dumont was found dead today about one mile out of town, having committed suicide."

Where there were men, dance halls sprang up—entertainment emporiums, which existed primarily to provide female companionship within a socially accepted, if not morally approved, format. Logger Ormand Twiford remembered "Misses Lilly and Maud, two scarlet ladies who stay at our hotel." As Twiford wrote, the ladies "came into my room this evening where I sat reading, and putting on my pistols and belts played 'cowboys.' They looked romantic thus accoutered."

It seemed there were never enough women to go around—good, bad, or indifferent. Often at a barn dance you might see a man wearing a "heifer brand," a handkerchief tied around his arm, signifying that he was prepared to take the role of a woman and accept male dancing partners. Sometimes wearing a heifer brand went beyond the dance floor. It got lonely out there, with nothing more than dogies to wrangle.

Myra Belle Shirley posed for an early photograph wearing a plumed hat—like something out of *The Three Musketeers*—sitting sidesaddle on a black mare named "Venus." She wore a holstered .36-caliber Manhattan revolver belted against her right thigh. A long-faced brunette with pouting lips, she's better known as Belle Starr, the "Bandit Queen" of the West.

Born in Arkansas—she always claimed she'd been born in Carthage, Missouri, and the erroneous location was even given on her tombstone—of a well-to-do Virginia family, Belle and her family soon moved north. When she was eight years old, she enrolled at the Carthage, Missouri, Academy for Young Ladies, and over the years she became proficient in Latin, Greek, and Hebrew. She learned arithmetic and algebra as well. She became noted as a gracious young lady.

The Civil War came along and Belle's brother, Edward "Bud" Shirley, was killed by federal troops. This turned Belle against the North, and soon the budding beauty was cultivated by a member of the Quantrill guerrilla gang, Coleman Younger. She married, however, another Civil War–era guerrilla, James Reed, who had ridden with the infamous Tom "Top" Starr, Myra Belle's brother-in-law. It's from "Top" Starr that Starr took her name.

In 1874 Reed was shot dead by Deputy Sheriff J. T. Morris of Lamar County, Texas. Belle gave her children—there were two by now—to her relatives and sold the livery stable she'd operated while James was on the run from the law. She headed for the glittering gambling halls of Dallas, where she worked as a faro dealer and even rode on cattle-rustling sprees.

By 1877 Belle had moved to the rip-roaring town of Galena, Kansas, where she became the common-law wife of Bruce Younger, Coleman's cousin. For a while Bruce rode with the James-Younger band of outlaws that included Jesse and Frank James. When Belle and Bruce had a daughter, Belle named her "Pearl Younger."

She left Bruce and married another Younger, Coleman's nephew, Sam, and together they settled on a sixty-two-acre homestead on a gooseneck bend of the Canadian River in Indian Territory; they called it "Younger's Bend." Those of the more honest persuasion called it "Robbers' Roost."

By now the former Myra Belle Shirley was a hatched-faced trollop called by some the "Lady Desperado," although she certainly was no lady, and the "Petticoat Terror of the Plains," which may be more fitting. In 1882 a reward was posted, offering ten thousand dollars for "the apprehension dead or alive of Sam and Belle Starr."

Finally they were captured and appeared before legendary "Hanging Judge" Isaac C. Parker. During Parker's twenty-one years as a judge at Fort Smith, Arkansas, he pronounced the death sentence on more than 160 men; although only 79 were actually executed. He gave them relatively light sentences, and by the fall of 1883 Belle and Sam were back at Younger's Bend.

The peace and quiet of Robbers' Roost may have been too much for Belle. She left for the affections of a younger man known only by the alias of "Blue Duck," a man who, if it weren't for his adopted nickname, likely would never have made it into any books about the Wild West. Blue Duck is said to have worn a pencil-line mustache and a vacant expression and may have been part Cherokee Indian.

Like Belle, Blue Duck ran afoul of Hanging Judge Parker. Unlike Sam and Belle's cases, the judge sentenced Blue Duck to death. Belle managed to convince the judge to be lenient, and Blue Duck's sentence was commuted to life in prison. And with that Belle Starr continued her wicked ways—a man here, a man there, a bit of rustling here and a bit of gambling there.

The Wild West seems to have thrived on unusual people. Or maybe it's that unusual people thrived in the Wild West. Take, for example, those mentioned in an 1891 Denver newspaper item:

Deputy Sheriff James Wilson is very anxious to find Minnie Smith, who is also known as "Dirty Alice." Alice is the woman who was recently fined by Justice Palmer for being intoxicated. She promised to bring the money to pay her fine to the court room if she was allowed to go home, and as none of the officers cared to be her escort she was allowed to go. She failed to return, however, and now Mr. Wilson has been deputized to find her, and put her in jail. He is not very joyful over the task.

On December 26, 1853, in Dublin, Ireland, a baby was born who, in just a few years, would make a name for herself in the Wild West. In Dublin she was known as Maggie Hall, the product of an English Protestant father and an Irish Catholic mother. As she grew up, Maggie received a better-than-average education and, as a young lady, was lively and outgoing. She was also considered to be a nonconformist.

By the time Maggie was a teenager, she was five feet six inches tall, and had golden-blond hair and expressive blue eyes. She laughed a lot, and because of her shapely figure, women envied and men desired her. At age twenty Maggie Hall decided Ireland wasn't the place for her. She wanted to go to America. Against her distraught parents' wishes Maggie packed up her clothing and personal possessions and headed for the United States. Like many other immigrants' her first sight of America was New York City.

From 1840 to 1860 nearly four million people immigrated to America from Europe, more than a million and a half of them from Ireland alone. In America the basically Protestant population greeted Irish Catholics with mounting hostility. It was tough enough to be an Irish man in New York City; at best he might find a job as a manual laborer. About all that was open to an Irish woman was to be a "Bridget," the name often given to young Irish girls taken in as maids and housekeepers.

Maggie Hall was well educated but she spoke with a bit of an Irish brogue, don't ya know? Not wanting to become a "Bridget," she took a job as a barmaid in a saloon, where she proved to be a sharp, witty, naturally charming young lady, popular with the men. She was a no-nonsense girl whose strong Catholic upbringing kept her out of trouble. At least for a year.

That's when a handsome, well-dressed young man named Burdan wandered into the bar where Maggie was working. It was love at first sight for Maggie. Something else for Burdan. On his third visit to the bar he proposed to Maggie.

Burdan was the son of a wealthy family and something of a womanizer. Maggie was unsophisticated and he completely won her over. The night Burdan proposed, she agreed, and they were married—not, as Maggie had dreamed, by a Catholic priest, but by a sleepy justice of the peace.

Maggie is now Mrs. Burdan, and her husband begins to call her "Molly," because Maggie is too common, he says. Oh, he adds, we have to keep our marriage a secret, or my parents will cut off my income. They would never approve of my marrying a Catholic, you see.

The perhaps not-so-happy couple moves into Burdan's expensive apartment, and for a few months Maggie (now Molly) lives a life of luxury and ease. Until Burdan's father finds out about his son's marriage to a barmaid. With that, Daddy discontinues Sonny's allowance.

Now closing in on penury, the younger Burdans move from expensive apartment to cheaper apartment to cheapest apartment. Molly wants to go back to work as a barmaid, but Burdan, who never manages to find a job of his own, won't allow it.

Now, he may not have a job, and he may not have any money, and he may not want Molly hanging around bars, but that doesn't slow down young Mr. Burdan. He drinks and gambles and spends money wildly. His takes his friends home with him, and they all like, or at least desire, Molly.

Finally, Burdan comes home with a desperate look on his face. He wants to sell Molly's favors to one of his wealthy friends. But Molly is a good Catholic girl, she is, and refuses the request. His head in her lap, Burdan begs Molly to sleep with this one man, this one time. Shattered, Molly finally agrees.

Well, of course, it's not just one time and not just one man. Burdan peddles Molly's body all over town, as often as he can get a buyer.

Devout young girl that she is, Molly goes to church to confess her sins, which sins of course have been forced on her by her not-so-devout husband. Molly confesses her sins, and goes home, where Burdan once more arranges for a pay-as-you-go lover for his wife. Back goes Molly to the confessional. This time, however, not only does the priest deny her forgiveness, but he also denies her the sanctity of the Church. Molly Hall Burdan is excommunicated.

No longer part of the Catholic Church, her soul damned forever, she believes, Molly has nothing left but the life of a soiled dove. She does, however, dump the man who forced her into such a life. At age twenty-four, Molly divorces Burdan and leaves New York. Like so many before (and after) her, Molly heads west.

She turns up in Chicago, then Virginia City, Nevada. On to the

Dakota Territory and Oregon and San Francisco. She's successful in her new way of life and has money to spread around. In 1884, at about the age of thirty, Molly reads a circular describing a rich gold strike in Coeur d'Alene, and she's on the road again, this time to the Idaho Territory.

When her train reaches Thompson Falls, Montana, Molly and several others get off. She buys a horse and all the accoutrements and joins a caravan headed for Murray, Idaho. It's a long, hard way, through deep snow and freezing temperatures. Along the way Molly notices a young woman carrying a small child. Both mother and child are having a hard go of it, so Molly offers them her horse, her fur coat, and some of her provisions. But mother and daughter are too weak to move, and as the caravan moves out, Molly remains to take care of the young mother and child in a crude shelter by the roadside.

When the caravan arrives in Murray, they carry with them the story of this beautiful young lady who stayed behind. All three, it's believed, will die in the storm.

Obviously, they don't know Molly. The next day she gallops into town. With her on the horse are the now-recovered young mother and her child. The crowd applauds Molly, takes the squalling baby, and huddles around the young mother.

Except for one young man by the name of Phil O'Rourke, who insists on meeting this beautiful young lady who has saved a mother and child. In her thick Irish brogue, she says, "I'm Molly Burdan." O'Rourke, who is Irish himself, somehow misunderstands what she's said and responds, "Well, now. Fur the life o' me. I'd never o' thought it. Molly b'Dam." With that begins the real legend of the woman called Molly b'Dam.

O'Rourke asks Molly if she'll be needing a hotel room. No, she replies, I want Cabin Number One. Now, "Cabin Number One" in the Wild West is where the top red-light-district madam lives. Molly is about to set up a whorehouse.

It's said that Molly b'Dam is kind to her girls, helps needy families, and nurses the sick, another proverbial hooker with a heart of gold. As for gold, Murray, Idaho, is surrounded by mines and miners, and Molly develops a gentle and unusual way of separating the gold miners from their gold. She holds what she calls "big cleanup bath" days. After a big strike miners come to town, and Molly invites them to a place called Paradise Alley, behind Cabin Number One. With a bathtub full of water Molly calls on the boys to dig deep in their pockets and come up with enough gold to cover the bottom of her tub. They do just that, cover the tub with gold, and Molly uncovers herself, hopping into her now-richly-sparkling bath. With chatter and jokes, she entertains the boys. If a miner is lucky, he gets to scrub her back. Nobody, it seems, goes away unhappy.

Pearl Hart made a name for herself as a stagecoach robber. She'd been born Pearl Taylor in Lindsay, Ontario, Canada, in 1878, but changed her name to Hart while away at boarding school at the age of sixteen. That's when she eloped with a ne'er-do-well named William Hart. About the only time William worked was to stave off hunger or thirst. Soon after their marriage Pearl left him and moved to the United States.

By the time she celebrated her twenty-first birthday, Pearl Hart was slinging hash in Mommoth, Arizona. That's were she met miner Joe Boot. He really wasn't much of a miner, and he didn't have much in the way of scruples either. He worked well with Pearl, a woman of doubtful, but interesting, virtue. Pearl would lure would-be lovers into her room, where Joe would hit them over the head and relieve them of any and all cash they might have on them. That failed to bring in much money, since the characters out West were noted for generally being short of cash.

The pair turned to robbing stages. On May 30, 1899, Joe and Pearl flagged down the Benson-Globe stage. To hide her identity Pearl wore men's clothing. Joe carried a scattergun. They got away with $413. More or less got away, that is.

Pearl Hart and Joe Boot lacked something perhaps essential to stage coach bandits: horses. They probably also should have had a compass. As it was, they walked away from the scene and promptly got lost in the surrounding mountains. Finally, three days later, the footsore thieves made it back to their cabin. Trouble was, lawmen were there waiting on their doorstep for them and arrested the pair.

The court convicted Joe and Pearl of robbery and sentenced Joe to thirty-five years in the territorial prison at Yuma; the prison doors clanged shut, and he's gone forever from history. Pearl got a five-year sentence, and was the first female incarcerated there. She finagled her release eighteen months later by claiming she was pregnant. Now, the only men known to have been alone with her in prison were a leading clergyman and the territorial governor, so the warden quietly let her go free. Outside, the public still remembered Pearl, referring to her as the "Arizona Bandit." For about a year Pearl toured local theatres, wearing men's clothing, toting a rifle and a brace of pistols, and telling greatly exaggerated tales of her criminal career.

Perhaps the most famous lady of ill repute in the Wild West was one celebrated in song and legend: Emily Morgan, a twenty-year-old mulatto slave girl, exceptionally beautiful and exceptionally intelligent, and one who, luckily for Texans, was willing to trade on her virtue to aid the cause of Texas independence. Most certainly Emily wasn't the innocent local flower some modern-day, blue-haired Texas ladies would have her be. At best she was an indentured servant; at worst, a slave and prostitute. There are some other claimants, but legend virtually insists that Emily Morgan was the true Yellow Rose of Texas.

Emily began life in New York City, and traveled to Texas as either a slave or servant indentured to Col. James Morgan. Since the legend gives her Colonel Morgan's last name, we can pretty well assume she was a slave, as it was customary for slaves to take their master's name, although that wasn't always true for indentured servants. In any event, Emily lived with Morgan on his plantation at New Washington, near present-day Houston. In spite of her slave/servant status Emily was loyal to the Morgan family and to the cause of Texas freedom.

Whatever the facts—if facts there be—if Emily Morgan was an indentured *servant*, she's now slave to a song. Thanks to television's Mitch Miller in the 1960s, grade-school children grew up singing about her: "There's a yellow rose of Texas."

Unlike songster Miller we shouldn't mince words: Emily Morgan probably seduced Antonio López de Santa Anna, the so-called Napoleon of the West. It was 1836, and Santa Anna was dictator of Mexico. He led the forces that invaded Texas (note that *invaded* is the word Texans would use; Mexicans thought the land was still theirs, so it wouldn't have been an invasion) in order to end a rebellion of Anglo-Celtic settlers. Santa Anna was a man of great daring and intelligence, not the buffoon often portrayed in Hollywood movies and TV shows. He was, however, afflicted with several flaws that would bring about his downfall.

He prided himself on his taste in women and had a reputation for being a ladies' man. A sensual man with extravagant habits, he campaigned in great luxury, taking along with him silk sheets, fine crystal glasses, crystal decanters with gold stoppers, and even a sterling silver chamberpot. He also took along his mistress, with whom he shared an eight-sided, three-room, striped and carpeted tent.

Santa Anna was the undisputed head of a victorious army and the master of his country's rebellious province of Texas. He had wiped out the tenacious defenders of the old Alamo mission in San Antonio, and his troops had captured several hundred more rebelling Texians, holding them under guard at Goliad, where he referred to them not as rebels but as traitors.

Santa Anna had left San Antonio on March 21, riding in his usual elaborate coach drawn by six white mules. Behind him came his pack train and his tent and fine carpeting, his supply of French champagne, an opium kit for when he needed to relax, and crates loaded with his stable of game cocks. Beside him in the coach was his favorite mistress of the moment, seventeen-year-old Melchora Iniega Barrera.

On April 2, his troops reached the Guadalupe River at Gonzales, but the wagon train was too large and the river too swollen to cross. Reluctantly, Santa Anna parted with both his warm coach and his even warmer mistress, sending them back to his headquarters behind the lines.

Near the San Jacinto River, Santa Anna and his escort of lancers rode into Colonel Morgan's village of New Washington. It was deserted except for a straggler or two and members of his fifteen-hundred-man army who were busy confiscating the remainder of Morgan's property.

Down by the river landing Santa Anna found something both Morgan and the stragglers apparently had forgotten: a beautiful mulatto girl. It was Emily Morgan and she was helping some of the colonel's other slaves to pack a boat with what few possessions they'd rescued.

No dummy, Santa Anna; he immediately realized he'd found a replacement for his now-departed mistress, and he took Emily captive.

However, he literally didn't have time to fool around: The Texian army was nearby and threatening Santa Anna's Mexican troops. It would be a couple of days before the general could give full attention to his newest acquisition.

Emily wasn't exactly a shrinking violet and realized what Santa Anna had in mind for her. She might not be able to get away, but she wanted to get word to Texian leader Sam Houston. Emily persuaded a young slave boy to steal a horse, find Sam, and warn him that the Mexicans were coming.

A couple of days after Santa Anna had first captured his mistress replacement, he called a halt to his trooping army. It was time to enjoy the spoils of war. In particular he felt it was time to enjoy Emily. All through the night, in the general's gaudy red-striped tent, champagne and chocolate flowed like . . . well, flowed like champagne and chocolate. By now the slave boy had reached the Texian army, and it was less than a mile away, obscured from the Mexican troops by trees and undergrowth.

For some reason, that night Santa Anna neglected to set pickets around his troops. Comes the morning of April 21, and it's all quiet on the Mexican front; arms are stacked, horses are unsaddled, and the Mexican army—apparently having taken a lesson from their fearless leader—is still in bed after a night of revelry with camp-following women. From the woods the Texians note a beautiful woman taking the general his breakfast. Around noon Santa Anna himself is seen, dressed in a bright silk robe, apparently unaware of the nearby enemy.

About four o'clock that afternoon Sam Houston's army strikes, eight hundred Texians surging forward through the tall prairie grass and low-lying trees. They completely surprise the Mexicans; when the Texians are about twenty paces from the Mexican camp, they open fire. Mexican soldiers scurry in all directions, as the Texians come crashing into the unguarded camp. If Santa Anna had been up and about, he might have been able to stop the aimless scramble of his men. As it was, the so-called Napoleon of the West was nowhere to be seen.

Emily's activities apparently led to Santa Anna's defeat. Thanks either to heady romance, the ways of the flesh, or a daze of opium, the Texian army beat the Mexican army while their leader caroused in bed. It took only twenty minutes for the Mexicans to fall, and then the Texians began to exact revenge for the Mexican atrocities at the Alamo. They slaughtered the bewildered Mexican troops. By sundown only about one-fourth of Santa Anna's army still lived, and Texas had won its independence.

And where was General Antonio López de Santa Anna? Initially no one knew; his body wasn't found and he wasn't among the captives. Texian troops finally captured him the next day. He'd been hiding in the tall grass, wearing clothing that apparently had been discarded by a slave. He carried with him a bundle containing a water bottle and his dirty underwear. General Santa Anna never explained what had happened to his regular clothes. He'd been caught—literally caught—with his pants down and had to grab whatever he could to try to escape.

As for Emily, well, she didn't have much to say, but everybody south of Washington City got the idea of where she'd been and how she'd kept Santa Anna's mind off the war. Colonel Morgan realized what had been going on, and when he got the chance, he purchased at auction the gaudy red-striped tent that Santa Anna had owned. And he granted Emily her freedom.

Today even blue-haired Texas ladies admit privately what their heroine had been up to that April day in 1836. "Oh, sure," says Margaret Sharpe, a member of a group known as the Texas Rose Rustlers:

> Everyone knows Emily Morgan hung out with Santa Anna. If she wasn't the Yellow Rose of Texas, there were plenty of other loose women you can pick. Acadian girls came down from Maine through New York City. There were Cajuns from Louisiana. They filled the brothels and cantinas, drinking beer with Santa Anna.

Now, one line of the song *not* used by chorus master Mitch Miller hailed Emily as the "Maid of Morgan's Point." Earlier versions of the song, however, proclaimed: "She's the sweetest rose of color, this darky [*sic*] every knew." Miller changed that to: "She's the sweetest little rosebud that Texas ever knew."

Shortly after the Battle of San Jacinto "The Yellow Rose of Texas" became a popular minstrel-show song. Sung by blackface actors, it went something like this:

> *There's a yellow rose in Texas*
> *That I am going to see;*
> *No other darky knows her,*
> *No one, only me.*
> *She cryed [sic] so when I left her*
> *It like to broke my heart,*
> *And if I ever find her*
> *We never more will part.*

Chorus:

> *She's the sweetest rose of color*
> *This darky every knew;*
> *Her eyes are bright as diamonds;*
> *They sparkle like the dew.*
> *You may talk about dearest May*
> *And sing of Rosa Lee,*
> *But the yellow rose of Texas*
> *Beats the belles of Tennessee. . . .*

By 1866 Mexico's General Santa Anna had (1) won the Battle of the Alamo, (2) lost the Battle of San Jacinto, (3) lost the Mexican War, and (4) been exiled to Staten Island, New York. He had as his interpreter and secretary a young American named James Adams. The aide noticed that Santa Anna constantly cut slices from an unknown tropical vegetable the former general had shipped to him from Mexico. Santa Anna would then chew on the sliced vegetable. When Adams inquired as to what the vegetable was, Santa Anna replied that it was called "chicle."

Santa Anna left Staten Island in May 1867, but he left behind his supply of chicle. Adams experimented with it by adding different sweetening agents to boost its flavor. And the rest, as they say, is history. James Adams invented chewing gum.

The onetime interpreter founded the Adams Chewing Gum Company, and since that time Americans have been happily, if at times noisily, chewing away. Thanks to the man who'd won the battle at the Alamo but lost the war at Cerro Gordo, lost it to the Yellow Rose of Texas.

Prostitutes were plentiful in the Wild West, but it was a time and place that was predominantly male. Women went west as settlers, missionaries, and even tourists, but on the whole the Wild West was notoriously a male realm. For instance, it's said that in the spring of 1849, there were only fifteen women in all of San Francisco. Of course, there weren't many men in the city by the bay at the time either. They'd all gone east, as it were, to Sutter's Mill looking for gold.

Women were so scarce that tough, bearded, weather-burned men would stand in the streets for hours to get a sight of any nonprostitute who came to town. One young man from New England rode thirty-five miles after a hard week's work in a gold claim just to see a newly arrived woman, "because," he admitted, "I wanted to see a home-like lady; and, father, do you know, she sewed a button on for me, and told me not to gamble and not to drink. It sounded just like mother."

These days many westerners claim to have sprung from stock unstained by rumor. Their grandparents were settlers who walked thousands of miles, cowboys who tipped their hats and said, Howdy, ma'am. They were the good guys, native sons and daughters who forged a nation out of quicksand and the hides of longhorn cattle. Well, maybe.

It's best to remember that most of us have ghosts hanging out in our closets. Or as a poem summed up California's early arrivals:

> The miners came in '49,
> The whores in '51,
> And when they got together
> They produced the native son.

CHAPTER SIX

Settlers and Celestials:
Those Who Toiled, Those Who Wept

There is nothing like the elbow room of a new country.

John Tyler

Our horizon is never quite at our elbows.

Henry David Thoreau, *Walden*, 1854

In July 1845 editor John Louis O'Sullivan wrote in the expansionist-minded magazine *The United States Magazine and Democratic Review* that "our manifest destiny is to overspread the continent allotted by Providence for the free development of our yearly multiplying millions." It was our "obvious" fate that We the People of the United States should take over whatever we wanted, whether in the East or West, North or South.

The term was appropriated by other publications and by politicians, among them Congressman Robert C. Winthrop. On January 5, 1846, Winthrop spoke of "the right of our manifest destiny to spread over the whole continent." The U.S. House of Representatives passed a resolution to end the joint Anglo-American occupation of the Oregon Territory. The American people themselves took to heart O'Sullivan's proclamation and Congress's resolution.

Wells Fargo became more than a stagecoach line. It was the nineteenth century's parcel delivery service. Look, Maude! The Wells Fargo wagon is a-comin' in. You could even buy mail-order trees, which would have been especially welcome in treeless Nebraska, where the state tree apparently is a telephone pole.

Sarah Royce kept a diary about her cross-country trip in 1849. Crossing Nebraska, her party had been "destitute of timber for nearly two hundred miles," she wrote, with the exception of one, solitary tree . . . marked down [on their map] as the 'Lone Tree.'"

> From this time for several days we went on, with nothing special to mark our progress, except passing the "Lone Tree," which I made into an event to myself, by straining my eyes to get the first glimpse of it. . . . It was not a large tree but its branches, covered with foliage, formed a well rounded canopy for two or three. To me it was an impressive way-mark. . . .

An early answer to the lack of wood on the Great Plains was the soddy, or sod house. It was a primitive house or shack built from the turf itself. A settler would strip about half an acre of sod, cut it in three-foot lengths—"Nebraska marble," some called it—and stack them like bricks. Using techniques similar to English turf shelters and Indian earth-covered lodges, a settler could build a twenty-four-foot-long soddy in a week. What soddies had going for them was the price: the basic building materials were free and adding doors and windows would set you back less than ten dollars. Of course, there was Isadore Haumont of Belgium, who built an elegant and magnificent sod "castle" in Nebraska in 1884. Complete with wallpaper and lace curtains, it cost five hundred dollars.

Sod homes were warm in winter and cool in summer and lasted for decades. Of course, the inside always had problems of dripping rain in storms and sifting dust in droughts. Insects and snakes dropped from the ceiling at an alarming rate and soddies generally were dank and damp. Otherwise, they made fine houses. They were still common in Nebraska and Kansas well into the 1930s, and a few remained even into the 1960s.

Nebraska Dr. John Wesley Thompson recalled how one winter he got lost in his buggy while searching for a patient. Stopping to look for landmarks, he found himself surrounded by frightened children, and he heard a man shout, "Get out of here! What do you think you're doing? Get off my house!" Doc Thompson had found his patient; he'd stopped his buggy right on top of the man's sod house. Like many soddies it was part dugout, with one wall dug out of a hill.

From the term *sod house* came another—*sod house claim,* a claim on public land filed by someone who lived in a sod house. You even had "sod fences" where there was no wood or stone and before barbed wire came along.

Water was always a problem for farmers in the Great Plains. Sometimes they had to drill down five hundred feet to get water, and at about twenty cents per foot, that could get costly. In the late 1860s Daniel Halladay of Chicago developed a successful windmill for the West. Selling for about a hundred dollars, it had small blades and a governor to reduce the blades' pitch when winds came whistling down the plains.

Which brings to mind a headline from an 1880 newspaper: REAL ESTATE MOVED CONSIDERABLY THIS WEEK. To prevent soil erosion, settlers sometimes used "dry farming," harrowing fields after every rainfall to create dust mulch, which would stop evaporation and keep the water near plant roots.

In 1841 the first group of thirty-two pioneers set out from Missouri on the two-thousand-mile Oregon Trail to the Pacific Northwest. In 1842 more than a hundred emigrants walked the Oregon Trail, and by 1843 the westward movement was in full swing.

Families gathered at the edge of American society—in St. Joseph, Council Bluffs, Nauvoo, or Nebraska City. They loaded wagons with all their worldly goods (usually too much and some of it they'd have to jettison along the way), waved good-bye to friends and loved ones (some of whom would later make the same journey), and set off to colonize a new land beyond the Mississippi River. Some of them made it.

Like twentieth-century Vietnamese who tried to escape the Communist regime in the 1970s, those who immigrated to America from Europe in the 1840s were called "boat people." Many reached America only to board another kind of boat, a "prairie schooner," a covered wagon given that name because its front and rear panels were slanted and thought to resemble a frigate. Actually, most emigrants walked to the West, with only the very young, very old, and very infirm riding—once again, Hollywood got it wrong. However the vehicle they walked beside—in which they carried their past life and hopes for a new one—was not the Conestoga wagon that became a symbol, but another type referred to as a "mover's wagon."

The Conestoga wagon originated about 1750 in the Pennsylvania town that gave it its name. It flourished for a century with a boat-shaped bed and sloping sides, a cover hanging out over both front and rear, giving it a "swayback," almost romantic, appearance. Nevertheless emigrants seldom used the Conestoga wagon, certainly once they got beyond the Missouri River. Freighters along the Santa Fe Trail used the Conestoga, but they were the exception. For the long pull to Oregon and California, emigrants found the Conestoga wagon too heavy. Earth beneath the high grass was too soft, and Conestogas sank into the rich soil.

The smaller mover's wagon—slab sided and easier to maneuver—replaced the Conestoga in all but mythology, Hollywood, and mid-nineteenth-century romance-school paintings. Its front wheels were smaller than its rear, making it easier to turn. Its white canvas cover lacked the billowing round arch of the Conestoga, but still it kept the traveler dry at night. It was even amphibious, because it had to cross streams and rivers by the hundreds. Many came from a South Bend, Indiana, company that built mover's wagons into the twentieth century, then changed over to automobiles. Finally, in 1966, it failed—the Studebaker Company.

Beneath this prairie schooner, emigrants loaded twigs and buffalo droppings into hammock-like canvas hangings, the same *cuna*-style device used beneath chuck wagons. With few trees along the way, these gleanings were needed for fires.

They were farmers, prospectors, schoolteachers, traders, missionaries, abolitionists, and some who went west to avoid the law. English crofters, German farmers, Irish potato growers, and Scandinavian dairy farmers trekked across the West looking for a better life. During the peak year of migration 55,000 pioneers walked along the Oregon Trail, along with over seven thousand mules, nine thousand wagons, and more than five thousand cows. By 1869, when the transcontinental railroad was completed, 350,000 emigrants had gone to Oregon, with another half million turning off onto the California Trail to hunt for gold.

A California saying has it that "the cowards never started," and it often continues, "only the madman started!" A wagon broke down, a child took sick, an ox died. Still they traveled on, beyond Iowa and Missouri, beyond Nebraska and Kansas.

In 1825 Congressman John Floyd called on Congress to aid emigrants in occupying Oregon with the design of establishing a new nation there, declaring that the Rocky Mountains were the natural western boundary for the United States. There, Floyd contended, "the statue of the fabled [Roman] god Terminus should be raised . . . never to be thrown down." Anything west of that would become a sister republic, allied with the eastern nation (that is, the United States of America) by common ideals against encroachment from the Old World. It didn't work. Once Americans heard about, then saw, the West, nothing was going to stop us from extending the nation across the whole continent.

Take wild-eyed Boston schoolteacher Hall Jackson Kelley. In 1828 he hadn't even seen the West, but he did his best to help push along emigration. Kelley tried to talk the U.S. government into giving him a hundred miles of land along the lower Columbia River, which he called the "grand river Oregon." Kelley vowed that if they would, he'd take three thousand settlers westward. The government said no, which of course didn't stop Kelley. In 1832 he organized the American Society for Encouraging the Settlement of the Oregon Territory. He wanted to "repeat with appropriate variations the history of the Puritan colony of Massachusetts Bay."

> Its physical appearance and productions, its qualities of soil and climate, suggest, not only the practicability of founding a colony in it; but the consequent beneficial results to our Republic. . . .

Like Congressman Floyd, Kelley recognized that such an Oregon settlement might become the nucleus of a separate nation, but he believed all Western colonies should be part of the United States. He advertised in a "General Circular," suggesting that emigrants be regarded as "a Colony, planted, cherished and protected" by the mother country.

Kelley's American Society for Encouraging the Settlement of the Oregon Territory didn't amount to much. However, his promotion of the West stirred up some thoughts.

In 1837 banks closed and wages fell thirty to fifty percent. More than twenty thousand unemployed laborers demonstrated in

Philadelphia. In New York an estimated two hundred thousand people were left jobless, wondering, according to radical historian Sidney Lens,* how they would survive. In February many of them demonstrated against high rents, high prices, and the low availability of fuel, and ransacked flour warehouses; it was one of the first indications of the coming depression.

In 1845 magazine editor John Louis O'Sullivan proclaimed America's "Manifest Destiny," and in 1846 President James K. Polk proclaimed war on Mexico. Most Americans backed Polk; we were, after all, superior to the Mexicans in just about every way—in our heritage, culture, our way of living. Or so many Americans apparently felt. Henry David Thoreau, however, opposed the war, and wrote about civil disobedience. Practicing what he preached, he went to jail rather than pay his Massachusetts poll tax and thus contribute to the war.

At the time nearly half of the U.S. Army's enlisted men were recent immigrants who'd joined the military mainly for the money. When they realized killing Mexicans might not be worth the financial advantages (not to mention the danger to themselves), and when they grew ashamed of their fellow soldiers sacking Mexican towns, raping Mexican women, and killing generally defenseless Mexicans, a total of 9,207 deserted.

Which brings up a Terre Haute, Indiana, newspaper editor named John Babsone Lane Soule, who, in 1851, advised many Americans to do what the army deserters did: Head for the hills. Or the plains. Go west. Four years later, Horace Greeley of the *New York Tribune* picked up the saying, changing it to "If you have no family or friends to aid you, and no prospect opened to you there, turn your face to the great West, and there build up a home and fortune." Greeley's version got shortened to "Go west, young man, and grow up with the country."

---

*The author had the pleasure of studying political science under Mr. Lens for a short time in Chicago. When Mr. Lens made a mistake about Bacon's 1676 rebellion in Virginia, this young and brash student told him he was wrong. "Prove it," Lens demanded. The next time the class met I did, to which Mr. Lens fulsomely replied, "Okay," and went on with his lecture.

The Civil War changed America in many ways, not the least by propelling the predominantly agricultural nation toward more manufacturing. During the "late unpleasantness," Northern factories hired European immigrants by the thousands. For four years those factories grew and prospered, but when the war ended, factories laid off a lot of workers in the usual postwar depression.

Bankrupt farmers in 1817, Hall Jackson's believers in 1832, the 1837 depression's unemployed, Mexican War deserters of 1845, gold miners of '49, Go Westerners of '55, Civil War veterans and former slaves of 1865, and postwar immigrants and unemployed factory workers of '66. Go west, young man, indeed.

The ignorance of some emigrants about just how to go west sometimes was quite startling. Take an instance, an event from 1841, when a group assembled their wagons on the Missouri frontier, all ready to start, when they discovered that not one of them knew where the route was. Despite this, "going west" seemed to many emigrants—Englishmen, Germans, the Scots, and Irish—"as natural as swimming upstream is to a salmon," as historian George R. Stewart writes.

Sometimes, however, the swim wasn't easy. Often it was deadly. In January 1847 the San Francisco *California Star* carried a small paragraph:

> It is not probably generally known to the people that there is now in the California mountains, in a most distressing situation, a party of emigrants from the United States, who were prevented from crossing the mountains by an early and heavy fall of snow. The party consists of 60 persons, men, women and children. . . . We hope our citizens will do something for the relief of these unfortunate people.

The "party of emigrants" was the stranded Donner Party. Here tragedy occurred when a group of California-bound settlers found themselves trapped by heavy snow and circumstances.

The group, headed by several Illinois farmers, started late in the summer of 1846, with California as its goal. Springfield, Illinois, businessman James Reed first organized the party. His wife, Margaret, suffered from "sick headaches," and they hoped going west would improve her health, so, in a way, a headache caused it all. Reed told his neighbors, the aging brothers George and Jacob Donner, about his plans to go west. Nine wagons left Springfield in April, rolling on to Independence, Missouri, their jumping-off point for the West. On May 12 the emigrants elected George Donner as their wagon master. He'd been born in North Carolina, but lived in Kentucky, Indiana, Texas, and Illinois. It is his name, of course, that is irrevocably attached to the party and the disaster.

They were a bit late in getting started, but not much. Neither the emigrants nor George and Jacob Donner were experienced, but that wasn't unusual; the outcome of the trip, of course, was anything *but* usual, thank goodness. After all, the brothers Donner *had* read the *Emigrant's Guide to Oregon and California,* a book written by land speculator Lansford W. Hastings, and that told them everything they needed to know, right?

By the time they reached the Little Sandy River in Wyoming in late July, the Donner Party numbered some sixty wagons and three hundred souls. It was about here that they made their biggest mistake. They decided to take Hastings's advice and abandon the California Trail at Fort Bridger, bearing "west southwest to the Salt Lake; and thence continuing down to the Bay of St. Francisco." The guidebook author modestly called it the "Hastings Cutoff" and claimed it would shave miles off the trek and save the emigrants 120 days. With hindsight a member the Donner Party wrote his eastern kin, "Never take no cut ofs and hury along as fast as you can." Too bad this *was* hindsight. It could have saved dozens of lives.

During the Little Sandy River meeting, mountain men guiding the party argued *against* taking the Hastings Cutoff, but they convinced only part of the group. The wagon train split in two, the majority taking the usual route to Fort Hall, Idaho, and beyond; however, eighty-seven* members of the party, including George Donner, headed for Fort Bridger. Guidebook writer Lansford Hastings himself said he'd

---

*Some sources give it as eighty-six, others at eighty-eight.

meet them at Jim Bridger's fort and lead them along his route. James and Margaret Reed were among those voting to take the cutoff. Party members had to widen the trail to accommodate the couple's oversize wagon.

With the help of Fort Bridger guide Juan Baptiste, the truncated Donner Party rounded the head of Weber Canyon, and passed the southern end of the Great Salt Lake. Here Donner found a note stuck on a stick; it was from Hastings: Wait for him, and he'd lead the party through the Wasatch Range. Eight days later Hastings still hadn't shown up, and George Donner sent a messenger back down the trail looking for him. The messenger returned without Hastings but with the land-speculator-turned-writer's instructions to proceed along *another* new trail. No, thanks, guide Juan Baptiste told the emigrants, and he refused to take any further responsibility for them. Wisely, as it turned out, he returned to Fort Bridger.

According to Hastings the new route would take only a couple of days, but it took the Donner Party more than twice that long. Even then they had to abandon furniture and other valuables they'd carried all the way from Illinois. They also left over three hundred head of cattle and oxen.

Food was low; morale was even lower. A man known only as "Hardcoop" grew so ill they left him beside the trail to die. Somebody murdered a man named Wolfinger.

James Reed got into an argument with John Snyder, a driver for another family, and the two fought with wagon whips. Reed pulled a knife and killed Snyder. As punishment the party banished Reed to the desert—alone, although friends managed to slip him some provisions and a horse.

On September 18 Donner decided to send two men on to Sutter's Fort in California for supplies—Charles Stanton and William McCrutchen. The rest of the party struggled on.

A month after he'd set off for Sutter's Fort, Charles Stanton returned with two Indian guides and a mule train loaded with food. At Truckee Meadows they rested, and it wasn't until October 23 that they again began their snaking trek toward the Sierra Nevada.

At Alder Creek George Donner's wagon broke an axle. The rest of the party—fifteen wagons—went on to Truckee Lake and there, on October 28, they camped in cabins abandoned earlier by settlers who'd gone on to California. In late summer the party had run into an early snowfall in Utah's Great Salt Desert. Now, more snow hit them, and when the emigrants awoke in the morning, the snow was deep and the Truckee Pass was blocked. The Donner Party was snowbound in the High Sierras; time had run out, and their provisions were rapidly doing the same.

On December 1 Irish-born Patrick Breen Sr. wrote:

Still snowing wind W about 5½ or 6 feet deep difficult to get wood. no going from the house Completely housed up looks as likely for snow as when it Commenced, our cattle all Killed but three or four of them, the houses & Stantons mules gone and Cattle suppose lost in the Snow no hopes of finding them alive.

Fourteen days later the first of the party died, Bayless Williams, a man hired along the way by the Reeds. It was clear someone had to go for help, so on December 16 Charles Stanton again volunteered to lead fourteen of the strongest of the survivors—seven men, five women, and the two Indian guides—through the snow. They wore makeshift snowshoes and carried six days' rations. Those who remained behind gave the volunteers the name "Forlorn Hope."

So much for hope. Stanton developed snow blindness and the others left him to freeze to death. On Christmas night a violent storm hit, and four more died. Stranded and starving, the survivors felt they had no choice. They stripped the flesh off their dead comrades' bones, roasted and ate it. What was left, they carefully packed and labeled. The "Forlorn Hope" struggled on. Then, two more died. The two Indians had refused to eat human flesh; so the others shot them, butchered and ate them. Finally, on January 18, 1847, five women and two men stumbled into Johnson's Ranch.

It would be more than a month before a relief party would leave to rescue the Donner Party, on February 19. When rescuers finally reached Truckee Lake, they found half the party dead and the others half crazy. Only twenty-three of the survivors were strong enough to be led out. The rest huddled around stoves, trying to gain strength

on supplies the rescue party had brought them, waiting for additional relief.

Before the second rescue party could reach the pass, another
storm hit, and the would-be saviors were delayed. Once again food
at Donner Lake ran out. Like the "Forlorn Hope," many, if not all,
of the emigrants in the camp turned to cannibalism.

Finally, near the end of February, the main relief party made its
way through the snow-clogged pass. The leader: James Reed, who
had managed to find his way alone out of the desert and on to California. As Reed climbed toward the camp, his wife and two of their
children struggled down the pass. The couple briefly greeted each
other, and James pushed on to find the couple's other two children.

All around him in the camp Reed saw evidence of cannibalism.
"Bones and skulls," he wrote, "filled the kettles." Years later his
daughter, Virginia Reed, who was thirteen years old at the time of
the disaster, claimed that no one in their family—no, not their family!—had resorted to cannibalism. She claimed they'd survived by
eating the family pet, which, if true, must have been a king-size dog.
We ate, she said,

> his head and feet and hide & evry thing about him. We went over
> [the] great mountain . . . in snow up to our knees little James
> walk over the hole way . . . in snow up to his waist. he said every
> step he took he was gitting nigher Pa and something to eat.

Among those still unable to move were George Donner and his
wife, Tamsen, at the separate camp where their wagon had broken
down. Yet another, Lewis Keseberg, later wrote of the disaster:

> At midnight, one cold, bitter night, Mrs. George Donner came
> to my door. It was about two weeks after Reed had gone, and
> my loneliness was beginning to be unendurable. I was most
> happy to hear the sound of a human voice. . . . She was going,
> alone, across the mountains. She was going to start without
> food or guide. She kept saying, "My children! I must see my chil-
> dren!" She feared she would not survive, and told me she had
> some money in her tent. It was too heavy for her to carry. She

said, "Mr. Keseberg, I confide this to your care." She made me promise sacredly that I would get the money and take it to her children in case she perished and I survived. . . . She said she was very hungry, but refused the only food I could offer. She had never eaten the loathsome flesh.

Rumors would circulate that Lewis Keseberg had murdered Tamsen Donner, a point he always denied—"Before my God, I swear this is untrue!"—even though she died in his cabin: "I think the hunger, the mental suffering, and the icy chill of the preceding night [when she came to tell him she was leaving] caused her death." It didn't help his cause when "sometime after Mrs. Donner's death, I thought I had gained sufficient strength to redeem the pledge to her. . . ." That is, he went after the gold and silver she'd told him she'd hidden in her tent. Later that night Keseberg returned to his cabin, wet and cold, falling asleep without even building a fire, he said. When he awoke the next morning:

To my utter astonishment my camp was in the most inexplicable confusion. My trunks were broken open, my cloak, my pistol and ammunition were missing. I supposed Indians had robbed my camp during my absence.

He claimed that he heard voices, "and saw white men coming toward the cabin."

He was "overwhelmed with joy and gratitude at the prospect of my deliverance," he wrote but:

Imagine my astonishment upon their arrival to be greeted, not with a "good morning" or a kind word, but with the gruff, insolent demand, "Where is Donner's money?"

It's uncertain what became of the Donner family money. It's equally uncertain whether Keseberg's version of her death and his claim of visitation by thieves is true. At any rate, he never lived down his cannibalism and the accusation that he'd killed Tamsen Donner for her money.

Finally, after an April thaw, yet another relief party reached the survivors. The remaining emigrants of the ill-fated Donner Party were rescued. The last relief party was under the command of a Captain Fellun, who wrote in his journal:

Entered the cabin, and a horrible scene presented itself—human bodies terribly mutilated, legs, arms, and sculls [sic] scattered in every direction. One body, supposed to be that of a Mrs Eddy, lay near the entrance, the limbs severed off and a frightful gash in the skull. The flesh from the bones nearly all consumed. . . .

Of the members of the Donner Party who set out from Fort Bridger on the Hastings Cutoff, thirty-six died, fourteen of them young children. It's not certain how many of those who were cannibalized died of starvation and how many, like the two Indian guides who went looking for help, were killed and then eaten.

The Donner Party was, thankfully, the exception among emigrants. All of them had one thing in common: They wanted to make a better life for themselves or for someone else.

Among the groups traveling the Oregon Trail were missionaries sent out by the American Board of Commissioners for Foreign Missions, which represented the Presbyterian, Congregational, and Dutch Reformed Churches.

Beginning in 1836, parties of missionaries made the two-thousand-mile trek from Missouri to what would become Washington State. Their goal originally might be Fort Vancouver, but often members of the wagon trains dropped out to set up their own missions or to take up farming.

Proving, if you will, that emigration makes poor bedfellows, take the stories of two sets of missionaries: Henry and Eliza Spalding and Marcus and Narcissa Whitman. Doctor Marcus Whitman had traveled the West before, and in 1815, the first year he was out, he ran across Lucien Fontenelle (who earlier had taken a group of Indians to St. Louis) at Independence, Missouri. Fontenelle and his party were headed west but before they could get very far along, they fell

151

victims to a disease known to some as the "bloddy fluz," that struck many emigrants.

Marcus Whitman was a greenhorn newcomer when he came across an outbreak of cholera in the Lucien Fontenelle party. Marcus himself wasn't feeling well; he had a chronic ache in his side, which, in the best tradition of nineteenth-century medicine, he tried to cure by bleeding himself. That didn't help, of course, and when Fontenelle woke the ailing doctor in the middle of the night, Whitman answered the call of his medical trade. For twelve days Whitman nursed the sick, including Fontenelle himself, who by then had also come down with the bloody flux. Marcus's care seems to have saved the caravan, even though the medicine he administered—calomel—itself was dangerous, its chief ingredient being poisonous mercury.

When Whitman first met up with the Fontenelle caravan, the other emigrants openly resented him and fellow missionary Samuel Parker. Parker was "inclined to self-applause," someone once wrote of him, "requiring his full share of ministerial approbation or respect." By the time the party reached Fort William, Wyoming, however, thanks to Parker and Whitman, hostility between trappers and missionaries had dissolved. It was not, however, a love fest. At the time Whitman was thirty-three years old and described his venture with the Fontenelle caravan as a dreadfully godless experience.

Before he left Fontenelle Whitman took part in a rendezvous in 1835 at Green River, Wyoming. Such gatherings were held several times a year and brought together Indians, trappers, and factors for the American Fur Company, an early competitor of Canada's Hudson's Bay Company. It was during one such rendezvous that Whitman removed an arrowhead from famed mountain man Jim Bridger's back, an arrowhead Bridger had carried around for three years.

Whitman reportedly had a fine mind and an appealing character. He was sincere, honest, and above all, according to historian Robert Utley, "tenacious in pursuing any purpose he set for himself."

Whitman never considered himself among the converted, but he did work as a "missionary-physician" and even married into the religious calling, his bride the beautiful if racist Narcissa Prentiss.

According to a young emigrant girl named Catherine Sager who met the missionary in Washington, Narcissa was "fair complexioned, with beautiful auburn hair, nose rather large, and large grey eyes." When Catherine and Narcissa first met, the blue-eyed older woman "had on a dark calico dress and gingham sunbonnet; and we thought as we shyly looked at her that she was the prettiest woman we had ever seen." Narcissa later adopted Catherine after the girl's father died of "camp fever" and her mother passed on a while later.

Emigrants and traders alike remembered Narcissa. Trapper Joe Meek, who'd been a mountain man at age eighteen and later became a judge in Oregon, went out of his way to see Narcissa Prentiss, such a beauty she was.

Seemingly unlike Narcissa in many ways, Eliza Gray was tall and naturally thin, and travel and illness made her emaciated. She was dark-haired and had a sallow complexion, by turns frightened and appalled by the uproar around her.

Narcissa Prentiss and Eliza Gray were the first white women to see Scotts Bluff, Nebraska. And to be seen by local Indians, who made quite a fuss over them.

The Reverend Henry Harmon "Hart" Spalding was from upstate New York. He'd been born out of wedlock to a woman who neglected him and a father who refused to acknowledge him. Perhaps because of this, Spalding became a rigid, embittered man. He married Eliza Gray. She was not, however, Henry's first choice. Earlier, he'd proposed to Narcissa Prentiss, but she'd turned him down. That's when he married Eliza. Soon, Henry and Eliza were part of the missionaries-across-America movement trekking to the West.

In that same wagon train was another young couple. You guessed it, Narcissa Prentiss and her new husband, Dr. Marcus Whitman.

It was an arduous journey made even more difficult by Spalding's nursing a grievance against the woman who had spurned him. To make the trip even more onerous, the two couples shared a tent, which must have made for some lively conversations during the midnight hours.

Narcissa sometimes rode (sidesaddle, of course) alongside their wagon. At other times she drove the wagon team herself. Eliza, apparently, had trouble with the sidesaddle and usually just sat in the wagon.

With the Whitmans and Spaldings were two young Nez Percé boys who drove a herd of cattle. Every day they milked the four cows, giving the party milk and cream. One of the boys, Richard Tackitonitis, was so taken with Narcissa that he called her "Mother."

The wagon train arrived at Fort Vancouver on September 13, where they met with John Ball, who had opened the first school in the present state of Washington. Narcissa quickly went to work and taught the children to sing "Rock of Ages." Then she and Marcus moved on to live among the Cayuse band at Walla Walla, which, as it turned out, was not good for either Indians or missionaries. Narcissa once noted that

> some [of the Indians] feel almost to blame for us telling about eternal realities.... One said it was good when they knew nothing but to hunt, eat, drink and sleep; now it was bad. [Still,] we long to have them know of a Savior's pardoning love.

One thing that rankled the local Indians, the Cayuse, who were close relatives of the Nez Percé, was that Narcissa and Marcus refused to pay for the land they took from them for their mission. The Whitmans also declined to offer the Indians gifts, a practice customary to the Indians.

On March 14, 1837, Narcissa gave birth to a daughter, Alice Clarissa, the first American white child born west of the Continental Divide. The curious Cayuse wanted to see the child. The Whitmans, however, barred the Indians from their parlor, saying "they would make it so dirty and full of fleas that we could not live in it."

Meanwhile, the man who carried a torch for Narcissa was doing a bit better than the Whitmans, missionary-wise. Henry and Eliza settled among the Nez Percé Indians at Waiilatpu, the "place of rye grass," and began their missionary work. Three years after arriving in Washington, Spalding officiated at the baptism of his first two converts. Both were local chiefs. One was Tamason, whom Spalding called Timothy, and the other was Tuekakas, renamed Joseph. The following year, 1839, Tuekakas-Joseph had a son and named him Hin-mah-too-yah-lat-kekht, Thunder Rolling from the Mountains. Spalding baptized the child and called him Ephraim. The name never really stuck. Hin-mah-too-yah-lat-kekht or Thunder Rolling from the Mountains or Ephraim came to be known throughout the Wild West as Chief Joseph.

In 1877 Chief Joseph tried to flee from the Nez Percé reservation in Idaho to Canada with a band of about seven hundred, most of them women and children. He almost made it. After a fourteen-hundred-mile flight, they were captured.

Back with Narcissa Prentiss and Marcus Whitman. The couple greatly confused the local Cayuse when the Presbyterian missionaries took to arguing with a neighboring group of Catholic missionaries over who had the true religion. To the Indians, after all, Catholicism and Presbyterianism seemed close to the same and pretty far from the old Cayuse religion. Which may be why, in their first five years among the Indians, the Whitmans failed to convert a single Indian to Christianity. Oh, they converted a Scottish visitor, and a French-Canadian Catholic, and even a group of Hawaiian laborers who were working for them. But not a single Indian, a fact that rankled Narcissa. Narcissa didn't like much about her life and considered herself something of a martyr. "Never," she wrote,

was I more keenly sensible to the self denials of a missionary life. Even now while I am writing, the drum and the savage yell are sounding in my ears, every sound of which is as far as the east is from the west from vibrating in unison with my feelings. . . . Dear friends will you not sometime think of me almost alone in the midst of savage darkness.

The Cayuse may not have taken to the Whitmans' missionary attempts, but apparently they liked to hear Narcissa sing. Her voice, it was said, was "as sweet and musical as the chime of bells."

By late 1847 the Whitmans' mission community numbered seventy-four persons, excluding Indians. Daughter Alice Clarissa was not among that number, having drowned when she was just two years old.

After a while the Whitmans abandoned their work with the Cayuse, whom Narcissa believed were irredeemably "insolent, proud, domineering, [and] arrogant." The Whitmans much preferred ministering to other—that is, white—residents of the area. "It does not concern me so much," Narcissa wrote, "what is to become of any particular set of Indians." Marcus agreed and wrote their church superiors back in Boston, "I have no doubt our greatest work is to be to aid the white settlement of this country and help to found its religious institutions."

The Whitmans considered the land on which the mission was built to be their own, even though it previously had been the home of the Cayuse. On it Marcus and Narcissa built a house, corncribs, henhouses, a smokehouse, a blacksmith shop, a sawmill, and a gristmill. They had an apple orchard and thirty acres of wheat and corn, along with sizable herds of cattle and sheep and hogs. Back East the American board was "glad to hear of your prosperity in secular matters," but told the Whitmans that "the work of guiding men to Christ is a better one and coincides better with the vocation of a missionary laborer."

All over the West settlers came and did what settlers do; storekeepers built stores and went to work; farmers marked off farms and farmed.

Those who farmed the land did more than just till the soil; they literally overturned land that was the Great Plains, and beneath the tall grass they discovered some of the richest soil in the world. Often, when settlers reached the Great Plains, they commented on how rich and fertile the land was, without ever thinking about what made it that way. In many cases credit was due to beavers. The bucktoothed, flat-tailed animals have an almost insatiable craving to build dams; they'll build a dam, someone will come along and tear it down, and the beavers will do it all over again. So insatiable is this craving, and so pervasive are beavers, that even in the late 1990s they were discovered trying to cut down trees and build dams in some of our major cities.

Back in the 1800s, before much of their population was trapped and converted into hides and hats, beavers built dams over much of the plains. Weeds had grown in ponds, then died and sunk to the bottom, where they decomposed. Along came a beaver colony that built its dam, cutting off part of the pond. The pond dried up, and the decomposed weeds that once covered the lake bottom became rich, fertile soil. Out of this grew crops that, even today, thrive beyond all earlier dreams.

Crops, of course, needed field hands, and so migrant workers roamed the West, traveling from range to range, farm to farm, digging out weeds, cultivating new fields. Usually they were boys, seldom much older, who traveled with their trusty hoes, and they became known as hoe-boys. Hobos. Only later did the name take on today's definition.

When immigrants from eastern Europe came to America, they frequently ran into problems with officials regarding names. People whose families had been here awhile often were less than understanding with what, to them, were overly long, perhaps complex, names. For instance, an immigrant whose name was Moskovitz might end up simply as "Mosko," a perfectly good name but not the one—equally good, maybe even better—the immigrant started life with. The German Mölichs might end up Malicks. For some wanting to trace their genealogy today, this is a problem, not to mention a source of anger, at the willy-nilly way in which immigration officials trimmed, pruned, and shortened family trees.

That's just what happened to George Mölichs, whose family came from Germany. By the time he married Abigail Jackson in Pennsylvania, the name had become Malicks. At any rate, Abigail and George married, against her father's wishes. In 1836 the couple—now a sextet, thanks to their four children—bundled up their belongings and headed west in a wagon with no springs and "only a canvas to keep out the rain." From Sunbury, Pennsylvania, they headed to Tazewell County, Illinois, where they lived a dozen years. About 1848 the Malickses set out for Oregon. They weren't alone.

In 1822 explorers and trappers found a high mountain basin in what is now the state of Wyoming. They also found the soon-to-be-famous South Pass through the Wind River Range in the southwestern part of the state, a twenty-mile pass cut through the Continental Divide. Likely the trappers didn't know what they'd found, which was perhaps the best—certainly about the easiest—route between the Great Plains and California and the Southwest. It ran from the Missouri River west to the Platte, northwest along the North Platte, west across Wyoming to the valley of the Snake River to Idaho. From there the Snake led to the Columbia River, on to Oregon, the Willamette Valley, and the Pacific Ocean.

In time it became a major part of the Oregon Trail, the two-thousand-mile-long road that ran from Independence, Missouri, to the Pacific. If all went well, it took four to six months to travel the entire length. Every day on the Oregon Trail was long and lonesome and hard. A "good day" saw emigrants make twenty miles.

Animal traffic numbered even more, and in time the Oregon Trail became a road for cattle. During the gold rush, animal traffic may have numbered twice that of humans. In 1852 the ratio was roughly four to one. And by 1853 it was more like eleven to one. As one pioneer put it, "It seemed as if Missouri would be totally drained of cattle."

In 1842 hunter and mountain man Christopher "Kit" Carson guided another soon-to-be-famous individual over the Oregon Trail, John Charles Frémont. Soon, because of his explorations (the account of which his wife would write up under John C.'s name), Frémont would be known as the "Pathfinder."

Almost as soon as they reached the eastern shores, many immigrants to America quickly found themselves boarding boats or trains to do it all over again, once more heading westward. Often they were joined by those whose families had been Americans for generations. Farmers of the Mississippi Valley and the plains states began to feel crowded—"people were sitting right under [my] nose" one Missourian said, and he pulled up stakes and headed for the West.

Many took to the Ohio River as the easiest and fastest first step westward. From its origin in Pennsylvania the Ohio flows to the southern border of Illinois, at Cairo (in Illinois it's pronounced "Kay-roh" or "Care-oh"), where it joins the Mississippi. Even before the United States won its freedom from Great Britain, nearly fifty thousand Americans were living along the Ohio and its tributaries.

Emigrants often rode the Ohio River in flatboats, ponderous rectangular craft that ranged from thirty to forty feet long, and were about twelve feet wide. The bottom was fastened together with wooden pins and caulked to prevent leaking. Chest-high sides were added, and in some cases a covering of sorts was provided to keep the rain out and serve as a pen for horses, oxen, cattle, chickens, and pigs. In Kentucky, covered flatboats were known as "broad horns," because it always seemed that someone onboard carried a tin horn to announce the boat's arrival and in case of fog.

Flatboats generally had a pair of barely manageable oars—one at the bow, the other near the stern—which served to steer the unwieldy craft.* They were cheap (about thirty-five dollars each) and easy to build, and many were constructed of the lumber settlers hoped to use for cabins at their destinations.**

Going downstream, a flatboat was a pretty simple and effective mode of transportation. The problem was, it couldn't be handled against the current. When they got downstream as far as they wanted to go (or as far as they could go), settlers either broke the flatboats up and used the wood for building or, if they didn't use and couldn't sell them, simply set them on fire and let the river reclaim its own.

Unlike flatboats, keelboats could be used to move upstream. Varying from fifty to seventy-five feet long, and from twelve to twenty feet wide, a typical keelboat was pointed at both ends like a canoe and covered by a roof. Unlike a flatboat a keelboat carried a mast and sail. Fully loaded, a keelboat would carry from twenty to forty tons of freight and generally took a crew of from six to ten men plus the captain, who also acted as steersman.

If the current was slow, the crew used long poles to push the boat upstream. Sometimes keelboat crewmen tied towlines or ropes upwards of a thousand feet long to the mast, swam ashore, and then pulled the boat along behind them. If the current was faster, they'd edge the keelboat close to shore and the crew pulled it along by

---

*Boats sailed by early Vikings sometimes had a steering oar on, as you face forward, the right side. This became known as the "steer board," which led to that side of the boat being called "starboard."

**There's a story that automaker Henry Ford used the same idea to order parts for his early model cars. He had them shipped in boxes exactly so long by so wide and with screw holes in just the exact positions. Ford's workers would carefully empty the boxes, then use them for the Model A's floorboards.

grabbing onto low-hanging tree branches. The practice became known as "bushwhacking," a term that took on another and more ominous meaning at the beginning of America's Civil War, where it denoted someone who made a surprise attack from a concealed position behind a tree or bush. A variation on bushwhacking was known as "ambushing," and had about the same definition then as it does today.

Brothers Micajah and Wiley Harpe had been Loyalist sympathizers from North Carolina during the Revolution and were hounded from their homes after the English surrender at Yorktown in 1781. They wandered to the Illinois-Indiana border and into a life of crime. Along the Ohio River they lured travelers ashore, then attacked, robbed, and sometimes killed their victims. They used what's known as "Cave-in-Rock" for their hideout and continued their personal reign of thievery and murder until they themselves were killed.

In the 1820s about three thousand flatboats traveled the Ohio annually. Because it wasn't unusual to have river bandits waiting to ambush settlers traveling on keelboats and flatboats, boat owners often traveled in large groups for protection. It was the same convoy technique emigrants later used in traveling across the prairie and cargo ships used in World War II to cross the Atlantic Ocean.

They emigrated from Virginia and Indiana, Ohio and Illinois, Michigan and Kentucky. They wanted to live their (and their ancestors') dream of land of their own, cheap land if possible. They walked and rode to Nebraska and Wyoming and Oregon. They hunted deer and antelope, fought off boredom and Indians. They baked johnnycake over buffalo-chip fires, nursed newborn infants, and tended ailing loved ones. They buried husbands and wives, brothers and sisters, children and strangers. The trails west are covered with graves of those who never made it beyond last night's glorious sunset or this morning's snowstorm.

Often, the emigrants' enthusiasm bubbled over: What say, Maw. It's God's country, and off they'd go. First, build or buy a wagon, "of the simplest possible construction," Capt. Randolph B. Marcy wrote in 1859, in his famous handbook, *The Prairie Traveler*. A wagon, along with teams of horses or oxen, were the emigrant's most expensive items, costing as much as four hundred dollars. A loaded wagon carried as much as of twenty-five hundred pounds and required at least four and possibly six yoke of oxen to pull it across country. Captain Marcy preferred mules to horses or oxen. "They travel faster, and endure the heat of summer much better," he believed. Others felt just as strongly in favor of oxen, and generally, wagons *were* pulled by oxen. Horses were seldom used because they were more sensitive to heat, thirst, and disease. Besides, they cost more.

A two-mule team, called a "span," cost from two to four hundred dollars in the 1840s. A pair of oxen, called a "yoke," cost a good deal less, from twenty to thirty dollars. Oxen were strong, dull, and a bit slow; they traveled only about fifteen or twenty miles in a day; however, a yoke of oxen had one decided advantage: If things went really bad, you could eat your oxen, just like the cattle they were. In dire straits, of course, you *could* eat your horse or mule, but there was something about eating a horse that never did sit right with most people. On the other hand, Indians were said to be particularly fond of mule meat.

Wagon tongues broke, axles cracked, wheels split. Spare parts were carried slung under the wagon beds along with *cunas* for buffalo chips and the occasional twig. Water barrels and grease buckets, heavy rope. And more spare parts. Wagon bows and covers to replace those ripped and torn by the wind and rain.

The 1845 *Emigrant's Guide to Oregon and California* provided a list of items families heading west would need. That and Captain Marcy's *The Prairie Traveler* were bibles to many American pioneers. They'd need

200 pounds of flour for each emigrant, packed in double canvas sacks, well sewed, 100 pounds each sack.

150 pounds bacon, well cured, packed in strong sacks "or, in very hot climates, put in boxes and surrounded with bran, which in a great measure prevents the fat from melting away."

10 pounds coffee.

20 pounds sugar, "secured in India rubber or gutta-percha sacks (thin, waterproof material made from the juice of a Malayan tree), or so placed in the wagon as not to risk getting wet."

10 pounds salt, dried vegetables (Captain Marcy gives a source for desiccated or dried vegetables: "Chollet and Co., 46 Rue Richer, Paris").

By the time of the great push to the West, the need for vitamin C was known and documented to prevent scurvy—British ships carried limes, and thus English sailors came to be called "limeys." Marcy advised "all persons who travel for any considerable time through a country where they can procure no vegetables to carry with them some antiscorbutics." Citric acid, he says, "answers a good purpose, and is very portable."

When mixed with sugar and water, with a few drops of the essence of lemon, it is difficult to distinguish it from lemonade. Wild onions are excellent as antiscorbutics; also wild grapes and greens.

Vinegar, baking soda, chipped beef—they were all needed. Rice, tea, dried beans, pickles, mustard, and tallow. Kettles, frying pans, a coffeepot, tin plates, knives, forks, and cups. Rifles and a supply of powder, lead, and shot or cartridges if your weapon was more modern. Cost? From three hundred to six hundred dollars for provisions, bringing the grand total to upwards of a thousand dollars at a time when you could buy a good meal in a medium-size town for twenty-five cents.

Emigrants starting out east of the Mississippi River had the added expense of just getting to the usual jumping-off point. Add to this, cash needed for unexpected expenses—fees for ferries over rivers and replacements for items that broke or were lost along the way. A hint from Captain Marcy: "The accidents most liable to happen to wagons on the plains arise from the great dryness of the atmosphere and the constant shrinkage and contraction of the woodwork in the wheels, tires working loose, and the wheels . . . often times falling down and breaking all the spokes where they enter the hub."

Settlers would need cash to buy food to last though the first winter in the new land. Money to buy seed. It all mounted up, and most of those who would go west, young man, go west, were far from wealthy. They saved and scrimped back home and liquidated their property—home, farm, household goods—to have enough money. Sometimes it took years to save the money. Sometimes would-be settlers were never able to scrape together enough and had to borrow from friends or family.

Between 1841 and 1848 about 20,000 emigrants moved westward. In the gold rush between 1849 and 1852 as many as 185,000 people made the trip. "One could look back for miles on a line of wagons," an overlander wrote in 1852, adding that "the sinuous line [resembled] a serpent crawling and wriggling up the valley." Over the next six years another 90,000 made the trip—men, women, and children plodding along. The number of pilgrims heading west in the 1850s nearly equaled the populations of all of Wisconsin or West Virginia or Arkansas and Florida combined.

Settlers by the thousands headed west on the Santa Fe Trail, and even more walked and rode on the Oregon Trail. Others identified it as the California Trail, or the Platte Trail, and still others called it the Mormon Trail. Native Americans had two other names for this great trail: the Great Medicine Road of the Whites and, because of the number of wagons on the trail, the White-Topped Wagon Road. From Independence or St. Joseph, Missouri, across the Wakarusa, the Kansas, and the Big Blue Rivers, then on into "Nebrasky." The valley of the Platte River became a thoroughfare for thousands who went to California looking for gold, to Oregon looking for land, and others who went looking for heathen fields where they could plant Christ's word. They crossed the Rockies by way of South Pass, or if they were headed for the California gold fields, they turned left at either Fort Bridger or Fort Hall. They spent weeks on the trail, fought foul weather and thieving Indians, and many of those who left the East never lived to see the West they'd dreamed of and prayed over.

Many wagon trains began the long journey firmly adhering to Sabbath observances, but that didn't last long. When they stopped for Sunday rests, they felt increasingly vulnerable to Indian attacks. The later the season got—moving rapidly from midsummer to August to early fall—the less often they stopped, afraid not only of Indians but the weather. Getting caught by early snowstorms could easily lead to a repetition of the Donner Party's tragedy. Soon the only observance of Sunday was a quick reading from the Bible.

Mornings came early on wagon trains, with bullwhackers or mule skinners hitching up their teams before dawn, trying to get a good start on the trail while the air was still cool. Around 10:00 A.M. the wagon master called a halt to rest the animals and so the men could have breakfast. It was the biggest meal of the day. While they were stopped, men might go hunting for some kind of meat for the pot. Or they might repair anything that was broken. Or they might just catch up on their sleep. By two in the afternoon the teams were re-hitched and the wagon train was on its way again. After another three or four hours they stopped for the night. Or if it was extremely hot—as it often is in the Southwest—they'd travel more at night and less during the daytime heat.

Charlotte and Bynon Pengra set out for Oregon with their three-year-old daughter, Stella. When Charlotte came down with dysentery, he made her a bed in the wagon and they rode on. When Bynon also was hit by dysentery, Charlotte took over as the teamster. "I have suffered great pain which resulted in the Dysentery," she wrote.

I have suffered much pain and feel a good deal reduced but all are sick and I must keep up to the last. . . .

I took my turn and drove until I was quite outdone. . . . I am all used up. dark times for we folks.

Later, when they ran out of meat and sugar, Charlotte added, "I am Somewhat discouraged, and shall be glad when this journey is ended." Again: "I feel lonely and almost disheartened. I feel very tired and lonely."

In 1871, at the age of seventeen, Illinois-born Charles William Post borrowed a thousand dollars from his mother and, in partnership with Charles Moody, opened a hardware store in Kansas. Within two years Post had doubled his investment and returned to Illinois to work, first as a salesman, then as manager, for a farm machinery company. Later, with a friend, A. L. Ide, Post perfected a seed planter and they were granted a patent on it in 1878. Over the next several years he took out patents on three different cultivators, a sulky plow, a harrow, and a hay stacker. In 1885 he organized the Illinois Agricultural Works, with a capital stock of three hundred thousand dollars, a far cry from his borrowed thousand dollars a decade or so earlier. Everything was going well for C. W. Post until he suffered what was then called a nervous breakdown at the age of twenty-seven. In August 1886 he moved to Texas for his health.

While he was there, he drank a mixture of chicory, wheat, and other ground grains Texas housewives often used as a makeshift coffee. In 1890 Post moved again, this time to Battle Creek, Michigan, where he checked into the sanitarium run by John Kellogg. A major part of Kellogg's treatment was his vegetarian diet, which in Post's case didn't do much good.

Kellogg declared Charlie a hopeless case, but Mrs. Post thought differently. She contacted a Christian Science practitioner, and under her care, Charlie recovered. While he was recuperating, Post remembered the Texas ersatz coffee and began experimenting on a brew of his own, one that tasted like coffee but didn't have the effects of caffeine. Finally he developed a mixture of wheat, bran, and molasses and brewed up a pot for the editor of the *Grand Rapids Evening Press*. The editor liked it, convinced his staff to try it, and then the newspaper carried a highly favorable story about the coffee substitute. Sales took off for the beverage its inventor named "Postum food coffee."

With his ersatz coffee launched C. W. Post introduced a breakfast cereal he called "Grape-Nuts." He advertised heavily, made money hand over fist, and by 1895, his sales grew from $5,000 to $840,000 in 1898.

The Wild West was a whole new world, and to live in it emigrants used a whole new language—part English, part Spanish, Chinese, Polish, Yiddish, and German, with some Russian thrown in. Sometimes they just made up words and phrases and meanings. *Cayuse* was a horse, especially a wild horse of the northwest; the word came from the Cayuse band of Indians of Oregon; later it came to mean a cold wind from the east. Taken from the Chinook Indians, *chinook* is a warm, dry wind originating on the leeward slopes of mountains, coming in suddenly and raising the air temperature sharply. Chinook is also a variety of salmon. *Chinook talk* is a bastardized language made up of Chinook, French, and English words. Traders used it extensively in the Northwest.

A month after President Zachary Taylor died, San Franciscans honored him with an elaborate funeral procession—a symbolic hearse beside which marched politicians and clergymen; behind them came a group from the Sons of Temperance and, strangely enough, members of the more jovial International Order of Odd Fellows and an even more convivial group from the Davy Crockett lodge. Whole contingents of foreign consular officials marched, including a mounted unit of Britons. Perhaps most distinctive of them all, however, was a hundred-strong group of blue-coated, pigtailed Chinese holding a sign identifying them as "China Boys."

Earlier that year eight Chinese immigrants had arrived in San Francisco, the first trickle of a coming wave. By the fall, as a visitor from Pittsburgh, Bill Johnson, put it, there were "many Chinese mechanics" in town. In 1850 probably two to three thousand Chinese entered California, but soon the trickle of these new emigrants from the East turned into a downpour.

Most Chinese emigrants were farmers from the Pearl River Delta near Canton in southeastern China. During the 1840s that area suffered repeated crop failures and high unemployment. With flyers describing California as Gum San, the "Gold Mountain," shipping agents in Canton and Hong Kong lured peasant farmers to America. Passage cost as little as forty dollars. When rebellion broke out in China in 1850, brokers even advanced passage money on the understanding it would be repaid out of the emigrants' profit from the Gold Mountain. The brokers' "generosity" left many of the new workers deeply in debt.

Forty-five shiploads of Chinese workers sailed for California in 1850, and two years later a total of 20,026 Chinese emigrants passed through San Francisco's customhouse. More than two thousand came ashore in a single forty-eight-hour period. A reporter, watching a shipload of Chinese miners debark, noted that they carried "long bamboo poles across their shoulders" and wore "new cotton blouses and baggy breeches . . . slippers or shoes with heavy wooden soles [and] broad-brimmed hats of split bamboo."

No one knows just how many Chinese workers emigrated to America during the gold rush. It's estimated, however, that at least 200,000 came between 1876 and 1890.

Called "Celestials," from the old name for China, the Celestial Empire, the *California Alta* wrote, "The Celestials are very useful, quiet, good citizens and are deserving the respect of all." Another newspaper, the *Sacramento Placer Times,* called Chinese miners honest, efficient, and orderly. Local merchants provided newcomers with supplies and transportation to the gold diggings around Sutter's Mill.

One of the first gold-seekers at Sutter's Mill was a young Cantonese named Chun Ming. He struck it rich and wrote home about his good fortune.

At first other miners regarded the Chinese as somewhat comical but otherwise harmless and admirable. That changed. Without doubt the greatest racial hatred in California's gold rush days was for the Chinese. Not only did they look different from whites, not only did they speak a different language, they also were industrious; many non-Chinese miners hated them for that fact alone. They were tough, disciplined, and more accustomed to backbreaking work than were many American prospectors, often laboring from dawn to dusk. White miners permitted the Chinese to mine only tailings, played-out claims long abandoned by whites as unprofitable. More often than not they made a profit of them.

Usually they worked in self-contained bands of fifty or more. They provided their own entertainment—gambling and, often, opium. Most Chinese immigrants-turned-gold-miners later returned home to their families in the Celestial Empire. In America they spent little, and when they returned home, they took most of their profits with them. That itself brought criticism: They took gold out of America's mountains but left nothing in return.

There were, however, ways to stop that. Californians harassed them with taxes. Mexican bandits stole their gold. And even the group always at the bottom of the Wild West's pecking order, the Indians, took advantage of the Chinese. There's the story of a band of Indians on the Merced River who couldn't decide whether the Chinese were white or Indians, so they devised a test: If they were Indians, they could swim; if they were whites, they would drown. So

167

they seized two Chinese and tossed them into the river. The test "proved" they were white.

Americans had once welcomed the Chinese, but soon they began attacking them. "The manners and habits of the Chinese are repugnant to Americans in California," said a San Francisco newspaper, adding:

Of different language, blood, religion, and character, and inferior in most mental and bodily qualities, the Chinaman is looked upon by some as only a little superior to the Negro, and by others as somewhat inferior. . . .

From the word *China* came the derogatory term *Chink,* and that slur was among the least of the indignities in their American lives.* At times anti-Chinese sentiment turned violent. Their homes were looted and their men routinely beaten, flogged, and harassed; sometimes they were murdered. To white miners out on a drunken spree it was great fun to cut off a Chinese worker's pigtail. When competition for jobs worsened, it was easy to blame all of the workers' problems on a glut of inexpensive Chinese labor, sometimes referred to as "slave labor," even though it wasn't. Organizations such as the California Workingman's Party wanted to pack up all the Chinese and ship them back to the Celestial Empire. In 1876 the party's campaign slogan was, "Treason is better than to labor beside a Chinese slave."

Some never made it to the Gum San, the Gold Mountain. Instead they remained in San Francisco or Sacramento. One white miner remembered that "the best eating houses in San Francisco are those kept by Celestials and conducted Chinese fashion," adding that "the dishes are mostly curries, hashes and fricassees served up in small dishes and as they are exceedingly palatable I was not curious enough to enquire as to the ingredients." It was, of course, a Chinese immigrant who invented chop suey, not in China but in Amer-

---

*Today, in the western Illinois town of Canton, the local high school calls itself the "Canton Chinks," with their teams' mascot dressed as many believe a Chinese coolie (an unskilled laborer) would.

ica. The Chinese immigrant who came up with the dish wasn't a cook, but rather a dishwasher in Sacramento.

A Chinese man was likely to be called "John Chinaman" in the Wild West, and from that came "Chinaman's chance." In America most Chinese quickly realized it wasn't chance that would lead to success, but rather hard work. That was something they were familiar with.

In 1851 a man named Wah Lee opened San Francisco's first large hand-laundry at the corner of Washington and Grant Streets. Before then some of the town's wealthier citizens were sending their shirts to Hong Kong and Honolulu to have them washed and ironed, at a cost of twelve dollars a dozen. When Wah Lee went into business, he charged just five dollars and got rich doing it.

A number of Chinese girls were forced into prostitution, in some cases amounting to slavery—they were coerced, kidnapped, and sold into the world of soiled doves. In 1873 *Frank Leslie's Illustrated Newspaper* carried the following item:

California—At an auction sale of Chinese girls on the 28th ult., 22 were disposed of, the youngest bringing $450 each, while middle-aged women commanded only $100. . . . The authorities of San Francisco have discovered a Secret society which furnishes and protects houses of prostitution.

Perhaps the biggest Chinese contribution to the Wild West came not in gold mining, or even in restaurants or laundries. Perhaps their biggest contribution came in building the railroad.

CHAPTER SEVEN

The Railroads:
Iron Horse and Pony Express

What do we need with this vast, worthless area? This region of savages and wild beasts, of deserts, shifting sands and whirlwinds of dust, of cactus and prairie dogs? . . . I will never vote one cent from the public treasury [for postal service] to place the Pacific Coast one inch nearer to Boston than it now is.
Daniel Webster, 1838

In the Plains country . . . the railroads preceded the population. There was nothing, comparatively speaking, in the Plains country to support them—practically no population to travel on them, few supplies to be shipped, and, aside from cattle and hides, little produce to send to market.
Walter Prescott Webb

On the morning of June 6, 1816, snow fell in Vermont and much of the rest of the Northeast, and it kept on falling. In places as much as twenty inches of snow hit, leaving drifts two feet high. Killing frosts ruined crops on August 20 and 21. Down South, Charleston, South Carolina, wasn't much warmer than the North; the city's high temperature on July 4, 1816, was just forty-six degrees. Again in July, another snowstorm and another killing frost hit New England. Yet again in September.

For the American East 1816 was a year without summer, apparently due to an event thousands of miles away. The previous spring, between April 7 and 12, 1815, Mount Tambora, near Java, Indonesia, had exploded in the greatest volcanic eruption in recorded history. Twelve thousand people had died in the immediate area of Mount Tambora, and an estimated eighty-two thousand people died later through starvation and disease. The eruption spewed an estimated thirty to one hundred cubic miles of ejecta—fine dust, ash, and debris—into the atmosphere, effectively blocking much of the usual sunshine for several years. By 1816 the dust had worked its way to the American East, and for the next several years it reduced the amount of warming sunlight able to reach the earth's surface, creating the opposite of today's much talked about and dreaded "greenhouse effect."

An American writer back in 1816 called it "the most gloomy and extraordinary weather ever seen." Because of the volcanic dust, snow fell in colors—red and blue and brown—and people all over the world starved.

In France furious mobs rioted over the high price of grain. In England citizens brandished iron spikes and carried banners that read BREAD OF BLOOD. In Switzerland people ate stray cats, and in Ireland an estimated fifty thousand people eventually died as a result of a typhus epidemic brought on by a famine.

There were no riots in the United States, but there was no summer either. The weather was so bad, with so many crops failing in so many areas of the country, that hundreds of farmers went broke.

Coupled with the usual postwar panic and depression—in this case following America's War of 1812 with Britain—many farmers gave up on the East and headed for the West. Eighteen seventeen saw the first major American migration westward.

Between 1810 and 1820 the population of states west of the Appalachians more than doubled. Four new states—Indiana (1816), Mississippi (1817), Illinois (1818), and Alabama (1819)—joined the Union. As historian Paul Johnson put it, "in size and potential power" it was like adding four "new European countries."

Also in 1817, for the first time, a steamboat chugged its way up the Mississippi River to Cincinnati. Within two years sixty light-draft stern-wheelers—remember Mark Twain's years on a steamboat?—regularly plied the waters between New Orleans and Louisville. Freight went south and settlers went north.

In 1817 construction began on the Erie Canal, a seven-million-dollar, 363-mile-long canal that connected New York harbor with Lake Erie, by way of the Mohawk River, and in effect opened up the upper Great Plains to water transportation.

And in 1817 the West began.

In the 1820s the Mexican government hoped to attract settlers to its northern province of Tejas, so it offered large tracts of land for small amounts of money to anyone who would move in. They got much more than they bargained for. Some entrepreneurs, most notably Stephen F. Austin, brought in large contingents of settlers and controlled large tracts of land. As part of the cheap-land agreement the settlers became Mexican citizens and, at least officially, converted to Catholicism. Still, their loyalty was to the United States, not Mexico. Over the years they led small uprisings against the government of Mexico City and encouraged others to do the same. For them the answer was secession from Mexico and annexation by the United States. In 1835 about fifty thousand Americans lived in Texas, and on December 20 they rebelled against the Mexican government to set up the Republic of Texas.

Six years earlier General Antonio López de Santa Anna had made his reputation with a military victory over the Spanish and become emperor of Mexico. On February 26, 1836, he led troops northward to end the rebellion.

When Texians—at the time they preferred that word over *Texans*—declared their independence, they named Sam Houston as the leader of a small army that would fight for independence. Houston, who'd earlier been governor of Tennessee, rallied troops under two men—Lt. Col. William B. Travis, an ambitious South Carolina lawyer, and James Bowie of Georgia, a swashbuckling adventurer and reckless land speculator, who may have invented the knife that still bears his name.* Travis and Bowie bickered over who was in charge but later broke it down: Travis would command volunteers, and Bowie would be in charge of regular troops.

They would defend the heavy-walled Spanish Church of the Mission of San Antonio de Valero, a settlement established on the outskirts of the Presidio of San Antonio de Bexar, present-day San Antonio. Completed in 1757, by 1805 the building was an industrial school for Indians—they were taught weaving, building, and stock raising—and lost its high-sounding title to be referred to simply as the "Alamo." In a story told to every schoolchild in America (certainly told to every *Texas* schoolchild), 187 Texians defended themselves against Santa Anna and his army.

With them was Tennessee legend Davy Crockett, who'd spent three terms in the U.S. House of Representatives and who, when he

---

*More likely it was Jim Bowie's older brother, Rezin, who invented the bowie knife.

lost the August 1835 election by 252 votes, said of his detractors, "They can go to hell. I'm going to Texas." With that Davy and a group of friends took off, going through Little Rock, Arkansas, across the Red River at Lost Prairie, and into Texas. A little short of funds, Davy sold a gold watch he'd been given by a group of Philadelphia Whigs during an eastern campaign tour; he got thirty dollars.

It's not certain whether Davy Crockett went to Texas to get in the fight or just fought while he was there. He had many old friends from Tennessee living in Texas, and got together with several of them in December to go hunting near the falls of the Brazos River. In Nacogdoches, Davy swore allegiance to the days-old Republic of Texas—"to the Provisional Government of Texas or any future *republican* Government that may be hereafter declared." Swearing allegiance may have been preparation to running for a Texas constitutional convention, once, of course, Texas won its freedom from Mexico. "I have but little doubt," he wrote his daughter Margaret on January 9, 1836, "of being elected a member to form a constitution for this province."

Even though a small Mexican force earlier had given up the town of San Antonio de Bexar and retreated south of the Rio Grande, there was no real army in Texas, Mexican or Texian. Nevertheless, Davy Crockett wrote Margaret that he'd joined the army and was headed for the Rio Grande. "Do not be uneasy about me," he wrote. "I am among friends." And on January 13, sometime lawyer, sometime poet Micajah Autry wrote his wife from Nacogdoches that "Colonel Crockett has joined our company."

Davy, along with his nephew and a dozen or so others that were dubbed the "Tennessee Mounted Volunteers," headed for San Antonio, where it looked as if a battle was about to take place. "We go with arms in our hands," volunteer Daniel Cloud of Kentucky wrote, "determined to conquer or die."

Sam Houston had ordered Colonel Travis to abandon the Alamo as hopeless, but the band of desperadoes refused. One reason Houston had ordered the Alamo abandoned was that Travis and Bowie's troops were hopelessly outnumbered and hopelessly untrained. However, "We are all in high spirits," Davy Crockett wrote on February 19, though we are rather short of provisions, for men who have appetites that could digest anything but oppression; but no matter, we have a prospect of soon getting our bellies full of fighting, and that is victual and drink to a true patriot any day.

One night shortly before the final battle of the Alamo, the Texians (and would-be Texians) held a fandango and got drunk. There are some reports claiming Davy Crockett even picked up his fiddle and played a tune or two. On February 23 Crockett noted in his diary that "this morning the enemy came in sight, marching in regular order, and displaying their strength to the greatest advantage, in order to strike us with terror." Davy believed that Santa Anna's army numbered "about sixteen hundred strong," but another version says there were more than five thousand Mexican regulars outside the mission-turned-fortress. Although most of the Alamo's defenders were amateur volunteers, most of Santa Anna's troops were trained, regular army soldiers. When Mexican forces raised the red flag—by tradition that meant they would give no quarter—the battle was on. At the same time, flying above the mission was not the Lone Star flag of the Republic of Texas, but a Mexican flag someone had forgotten to lower.

Inside the fort Jim Bowie was in bed, either ill with pneumonia or typhoid or tuberculosis, or he was wounded or he'd broken his hip in a fall from a builder's scaffold in the fort. Truth is, no one is certain just what was wrong with Jim. Whatever it was, it can be said that Jim Bowie died in bed.

When things got tough and it became obvious anybody remaining in the fort would die, according to Texas history Colonel Travis used his sword to draw a line in the sand and proclaim, "I now want every man who is determined to stay here and die with me to cross this line." The bedridden Bowie supposedly called out, "Boys, I wish some of you would . . . remove my cot over there," and he joined Travis. Well, maybe. There probably was no line drawn in the sand, but it makes for a good story, and better propaganda when you want to attract attention to your cause.

Inside the old and crumbling mission the Texians had twenty-one pieces of artillery of various sizes they'd captured earlier from the Mexicans. They also had a good supply of old British brown-Bess muskets, the kind left over from the American Revolution more than half a century earlier, and sixteen thousand rounds of ammunition left by the Mexicans.

Travis had sent a messenger out of the fort, hoping for aid. In the early morning hours of March 1 thirty-two men arrived from Gonzales. Not many, but it cheered up those in the garrison for a couple of days. On March 4 Crockett told Susannah Dickinson, the wife of Travis's aide, Lt. Almaron Dickinson, "I think we had better march out and die in the open air; I don't like to be hemmed in." When the other women and children left the Alamo under a flag of truce, Susannah and her fifteen-month-old daughter, Angelina, stayed and would live to tell about the coming battle.

In the final moments of the battle Susannah took Angelina, a Mexican nurse, and a young black slave into the sacristy of the Alamo church. Four Mexican soldiers burst in, shot gunner Jacob Walker, who was with them, then took his body outside and hoisted it overhead on their bayonets—it seemed to be a favorite postbattle gesture for Santa Anna's troops. Just then a Mexican officer appeared at the door and asked, "Is Mrs. Dickinson here? Speak out! It's a matter of life and death." Susannah identified herself, and the officer said, "If you want to save your life, follow me." She did and Santa Anna gave her two dollars and a blanket and sent her to Gonzales to spread the word of his victory.

The final Mexican attack began with a spectacular artillery barrage. "Pop, pop, pop!" Davy Crockett wrote on March 5, "Bom [*sic*], bom, bom! throughout the day. No time for memorandums now. Go ahead! Liberty and independence forever!" It was the last entry in his diary. Before dawn the next day, March 6, the Mexican bands played the "Deguello"—an ancient Spanish battle song that, like the red flag, signified "no quarter."

Travis died defending the gate, one of the first Texians to fall. Mexican soldiers killed Bowie as he lay in bed; then they tossed his body into the air and speared it with their bayonets. What happened to Davy Crockett is today being questioned.

Hollywood, in its frequent telling of the tale, has gone by the general patriotic belief that, although women were allowed to ride out of the fort, all of the men—including Travis, Bowie, and Crockett—died defending the Alamo. The picture is often given of Davy, with Mexican dead and dying at his feet and now out of ammunition, going down swinging his trusty musket at anyone who comes near until, finally, he's overwhelmed and killed. Well, maybe.

However, in 1975, along came the purported journal of one Lt. José Enrique de la Peña, *With Santa Anna in Texas: A Personal Narrative of the Revolution*. It clearly contradicted the popular version of Davy at the Alamo:

> Some seven men had survived the general carnage and, under the protection of General Castrillon, they were brought before Santa Anna. Among them was one of great stature, well proportioned, with regular features, in whose face there was the imprint of adversity, but in whom one also noticed a degree of resignation and nobility that did him honor. He was the naturalist David Crockett, well known in North America for his unusual adventures.

Now, here was Davy, alive if not well, *after* the Alamo was lost! De la Peña's version, translated by Carmen Perry and published by Texas A & M University Press, says that Crockett and six others *surrendered,* after which their captors took them to Santa Anna. The infuriated general had them executed. Soldiers then threw Crockett's body onto a funeral pyre with his fellow Alamo defenders.

Needless to say, this version doesn't sit well with those who believe Davy was brave to the end. Davy Crockett? Gave up and was executed? Not a chance. One of the Perry/de la Peña detractors is part-time Alamo historian and full-time New York City Fire Department investigator Bill Groneman. In his book *Defense of a Legend: Crockett and the de la Peña Diary*, Groneman claims there are many forgeries of historical documents in Texas and the purported de la Peña diary is one of them. Groneman says, for instance, that whoever wrote the journal—it's in more than one handwriting, he claims—knew too much, that many of the events de la Peña "saw" weren't known at the time the document was supposed to have been written; in one case it cited another journal that wasn't written until two years *after* the fall of the Alamo.

In favor of the de la Peña version is University of New Mexico history professor Paul Andrew Hutton, who claims the journal wasn't written until several years after the Alamo, while the former army officer rotted in prison "as a result of his bold defense of Federalism against the centrist state that brought such ruin in Mexico." It was then, not day-to-day reminiscence, but "a truly remarkable historical account"—reconstructed "from his diaries and letters, as well as other sources." On the other hand, Groneman believes, the de la Peña journal was written, not shortly after the event, but in the twentieth century.

Remember Susannah Dickinson, who, along with her daughter, survived the battle? She later claimed that she saw Davy Crockett's quite dead body after the battle. "I recognized Col. Crockett," she wrote, "lying dead and mutilated between the church and the two-story barrack building, and even remember seeing his peculiar cap by his side." Apparently, even before the 1950s television series, Davy, Davy Crockett, King of the Wild Frontier, wore a coonskin cap.

However Davy and the other defenders of the Alamo died that March day in 1836, losses to the Mexican army and cause were even greater. At least six hundred Mexican soldiers died that day, many of them shot in the back by their poorly led, poorly aiming comrades who came along behind them. General Santa Anna, however, officially admitted to just seventy deaths among his men. Three weeks later, on Sunday, March 27, three hundred to four hundred Texian troops—really, mostly Americans with only a few Texians—under Col. James Walker Fannin (it was Fannin to whom Travis had appealed for relief) were captured at Coleto Creek by Santa Anna's men. The Mexicans told them they would be paroled to New Orleans and marched the men back to the south Texas town of Goliad, to the Presidio La Bahia. There, Santa Anna ordered his troops to kill the captives. Colonel Fannin, and others too wounded to travel, were carried from their rooms, and the Mexican army butchered more than three hundred men. As at the Alamo they set the bodies ablaze.

This was too much for the Texian-Americans. Thousands ran for the border. Survivors remembered it as the "Runaway Scrape."

On April 21 Sam Houston and his army turned on Santa Anna and annihilated the Mexican army at San Jacinto, outside present-day Houston. "Victory is certain," Houston pronounced, as he pranced in front of his troops on a white stallion called Saracen. "Trust in god and fear not. And remember the Alamo—remember the Alamo!" It not only became the battle cry of the Texas Republic but lingered into World War II, when it became "Remember Pearl Harbor as you did the Alamo!"

Sam led the charge that day at San Jacinto, swinging his saber until Saracen was shot dead with five musket balls in his body. Houston climbed onto another horse, and it, too, was shot from under him. This time Houston was also hit, his right leg splintered by a ball.

And this time the fighting was a one-sided affair with the Texians on the winning side, and they took retribution for the Alamo and Coleto Creek. "I sat there on my horse and shot them until my ammunition ran out," one Texian private remembered. "Then I turned the butt of my musket and started knocking them in the head." Within eighteen minutes the battle was over, though killing fleeing Mexicans continued well into nightfall. A Texian soldier told an officer that "if Jesus Christ were to come down from Heaven and order me to quit shooting Santanistas, I wouldn't do it, sir!" Another recalled the slaughter:

A young Mexican boy (a drummer I suppose) [was] lying on his face. One of the Volunteers . . . pricked the boy with his bayonet. The boy grasped the man around the legs and cried out in Spanish, "Hail Mary, Most Pure! For God's sake, save my life!" I begged the man to spare him, both his legs being broken already. The man looked at me and put his hand on his pistol, so I passed on. Just as I did so, he blew out the boy's brains.

More than six hundred Mexican soldiers were killed that day and over seven hundred of Santa Anna's "Invincibles" were taken prisoner. Only six Texians died at San Jacinto.

The Battle of San Jacinto was fought on property owned by a Mrs. McCormick. After the battle she went to Sam Houston complaining about the dead Mexicans that were littering her place. "Madam," Houston told her, "your land will be famed in history as the classic spot upon which the glorious victory of San Jacinto was gained!" To which Mrs. McCormick replied, "To the devil with your glorious victory. Take off your stinking Mexicans."

Among the Mexican prisoners taken that day: Santa Anna himself, dressed as a slave and trying desperately to pull on his pants.* It didn't help that when the other prisoners saw him, they called out, "El Presidente!"

In 1853 it took four days, nine hours, and thirty minutes for the steamboat *Eclipse* to travel the 1,440 miles from New Orleans to Louisville. A few years later, in a famous race pitting the *Natchez* and the *Robert E. Lee*, the *Lee* made the 1,218-mile New Orleans to St. Louis run in three days, eighteen hours, and fourteen minutes.

The four main eastern rivers—the Mississippi, the Ohio, the Missouri, and the Arkansas—were cleared of snags and sandbars. Snag-caused accidents cost Mississippi steamboats $653,976,000 in 1853.

The nation was on the move, with much of the movement westward. Business boomed. Settlers, miners, mining companies, and mining suppliers got rich, not to mention those who conned, robbed, and bamboozled anyone brave enough to go west. To cash in on this boom, in 1859 the freighting firm of Russell, Majors & Waddell proposed a stage line from Leavenworth, Kansas to Denver, Colorado. It was a chancy business at best, so Alexander Majors and William Waddell quickly dropped out, but John S. Jones joined with William Hepburn Russell in the Pike's Peak Express Company.

The following year, hoping to draw attention to this ambitious venture, Russell, along with Frederick Bee and Senator William Gwin

*See Chapter Five.

of California, dreamed up a dazzling publicity stunt. They posted want ad bulletins:

PONY EXPRESS
ST. JOSEPH, MISSOURI to CALIFORNIA
in 10 days or less.

☞ WANTED ☜
YOUNG, SKINNY, WIRY FELLOWS

not over eighteen. Must be expert riders,
willing to risk death daily.
Orphans preferred.
Wages $25 per week.

APPLY, PONY EXPRESS STABLES
ST. JOSEPH, MISSOURI

Those hired as riders had to memorize and recite aloud—hand held on an open Bible—a pledge to the company:

I do hereby swear, before the Great and Living God, that during my engagement , and while I am in the employ of Russell, Majors & Waddell, I will, under no circumstances, use profane language; that I will drink no intoxicating liquors; that I will not quarrel or fight with any other employe of the firm, and that in every respect I will conduct myself honestly, be faithful to my duties, and so direct all my acts as to win the confidence of my employers. So help me God.

They also had to promise "not to gamble, not to treat animals cruelly, and not to do anything incompatible with the conduct of a gentleman." It is, of course, doubtful whether any rider ever lived up to the pledge or whether any other company ever had a more profane, hard-drinking, and quarrelsome bunch of employees.

On April 3, 1860, the Pony Express began, with riders racing hell bent for leather from station to station, where they changed horses and raced on—from St. Joseph, Missouri, to Sacramento, California. Transcontinental mail service was under way, with the cost of sending a letter more then than it is now, five dollars an ounce, but then the Pony Express guaranteed delivery in ten days. Actually they made it in about eight days.

Among the most famous Pony Express riders were fourteen-year-old William F. Cody and "Pony Bob" Haslam. Cody, of course, went on to become "Buffalo Bill" Cody, bison killer and showman. Haslam once was attacked by Paiute Indians in Nevada, where he was wounded in the face and arm. "Pony Bob" escaped and rode 120 miles in eight hours and ten minutes, using thirteen horses. He rested a few hours, then did the return trip.

Good job with your Pony Express, Messrs. Russell, Bee, and Gwin. Problem was, your promised ten days' mail delivery was way too long, as it turned out. Apparently, you didn't know about two events from back in 1832, and those two events doomed your Pony Express service.

One was the building of the first American railroad. Many more would follow.

The second event was the invention, by a New York professor of painting and sculpture, of the telegraph. Samuel F. B. Morse followed up earlier work done by a man named Charles T. Jackson, but mainly it was Morse who got the job done—a practical, working machine. After much pestering by Morse, Congress gave him a thirty-thousand-dollar federal grant to build an intercity telegraph line between Baltimore and Washington.

On May 24, 1844, Morse sat at a table in Washington, D.C.—using a dots-and-dash system that he'd cadged from others and reworked; it would later bear Morse's name—and sent a message to a friend in that Maryland city. The message: "What hath God Wrought!" which Morse also had cadged, this time from the Holy Bible, Numbers 23:23. Later that spring, operators used the telegraph system to transmit news from the Whig and Democratic conventions, which were meeting in Baltimore, to the capital.

On December 18, 1847, the *St. Louis Republican* reported that "the [telegraph] posts and wires have been put up to the east bank of the [Mississippi] river, and . . . in a few days connections will be made into the city. We are told that the wires work well and have been tested up to this point from Vincennes [Indiana]."

And two days later, the newspaper reported:

DISPATCHES BY THE LIGHTENING LINE FOR THE REPUBLICAN

The lightening commenced operating vigorously yesterday at 1 P.M., and from that time there was a constant flow of communications from all cities along the line until a late hour, and many messages from our neighboring cities, as we may style New York, Philadelphia.

Morse's assistant Ezra Cornell built the first telegraph line from Baltimore to Washington and, just two years after Samuel F. B. had sent his first historic message, formed the private Western Union Telegraph Company. The company did at least two things: (1) It generated enormous profits, part of which Cornell used to found a university in 1868, giving it his name, and (2) it drove the Pony Express out of business.

That left Messrs. Russell, Bee, and Gwin with not much more than debts on their hands, to solve which problem they sold the Pony Express to Wells Fargo.

For several years, even before starting the short-lived Pony Express, Russell, Bee, and Gwin had been taking monetary infusions from Ben Holladay, who called himself the "stagecoach king." Holladay had worked his way up (or down) from liquor salesman to saloon keeper to hotel owner to transportation contractor for the U.S. Army. His contract with the army during the Mexican War left Holladay with enough of a stake that, when the California gold rush came along, he got into the freight business. At this he made something more than just profit; he inflated prices to underprovisioned miners to such an extent that he was able to buy control of the Central Overland California and Pike's Peak Express Company. Why, he made so much money, he paid his general manager an annual salary of ten thousand dollars, quite a handsome sum in the 1860s. And this made the manager both loyal and efficient.

Ben changed the name of his company to the Holladay Overland

Mail and Express company. Eventually he controlled five thousand miles of stagecoach routes.

As time went on, more and more robbers ordered Ben Holladay's stagecoaches to "stand and deliver," as an earlier saying went—Pull up, stop the damn coach, and throw down the box and everything else valuable you've got! Like other coach lines Ben's was robbed several times by the notorious Black Bart. Marauding Indians also hit stagecoaches, but neither robbers nor Indians were Holladay's biggest worry. His biggest worry was the "iron horse," the railroads. As the tracks spread westward, Ben Holladay realized the day of his stagecoaches had come and was going fast. He sold out to the New York enterprise Wells Fargo in 1866. Holladay got one and a half million dollars in cash and three million dollars in Wells Fargo stock, not too shabby a deal for a business that had no place to go but downhill, with robbers and Indians riding after it. As for Wells Fargo, it expanded and went into the banking business.

In 1850 three firms—Butterfield, Wasson, and Company; Livingston and Fargo; and Wells and Company—united to become the American Express Company, with the new Wells, Fargo, and Company being the largest stage line in the firm. In 1918 it merged into the American Railroad Express Company, with only the banking line retaining the Wells Fargo name, and now even that has been altered and probably will be altered again.

Meanwhile, the Pony Express had given way to the telegraph. And an integral part of the communication system, the part that led Ben Holladay to sell out, was growing as the saying of the time went, "like Topsy."*

---

*In 1851 Harriet Beecher Stowe had a friend row her across the Ohio River into Kentucky, where Harriet put in several hours—literally, only hours—researching the South for a novel she was writing. With that background, and with the support of her Bible-toting family, she wrote the highly successful *Uncle Tom's Cabin*. It's not too preposterous to say that Harriet Beecher Stowe's depiction of slavery started the Civil War. In fact, President Abraham Lincoln said just that, calling her "the little lady who started this great war." In Chapter 20 of *Uncle Tom's Cabin* the character Topsy is asked who made her. "I 'spect I growed," she replies. "Don't think nobody never made me." The term t*o grow like Topsy* is still used by newspaper editorial writers.

* * *

In 1876 East and West were virtually two different nations, with the ninety-eighth meridian, west of Omaha, being the arbitrary boundary line where eastern forests ended and western plains and deserts began. To the east: thirty-one states and 42 million people. To the west: all or parts of seven states and only 2 million cowboys, farmers, miners, storekeepers, and their families.

The dream of a transcontinental railroad had excited Americans since 1847, when James Marshall stumbled across gold while building a sawmill for John Sutter along the south bank of the American River in California. It was, after all, a long way from the East to the West, whether gold seekers went by ship (down the Atlantic Ocean to Panama, ride the Panama Railroad across the isthmus, then board another ship for San Francisco), or they walked, rode, and possibly crawled across the Great Plains. Not to mention up and down various mountains.

Besides, once these would-be gold millionaires made their hoped-for strikes, the gold would have to go back east the way the miners had gone west. A railroad could haul gold by the truckload. Boxcar load.

At the beginning of the Civil War the Union had thirty thousand miles of railroad track, by far the largest amount in the world; the South, in contrast, had less than half that. During the four years of war the North added an additional four thousand miles of track. While the war was going on in the East, the vision of laying a railroad to the West started to become reality.

In 1844 John C. Frémont had begun a survey for a Pacific railway, although his idea didn't get far at the time. In 1861 four California merchants—Collis P. Huntington, Charles Crocker, California governor Leland Stanford, and Mark Hopkins—together sank eight and a half million dollars into founding the Central Pacific Railroad. The following year Congress passed the Railroad Act, granting Huntington, Crocker, Stanford, and Hopkins a western charter. And a lot of money: federal loans of sixteen thousand dollars a mile over flat land and forty-eight thousand dollars a mile over the Sierras. Congress also approved federal funds and loans for the Union Pacific Railroad in the East. There's not much doubt that both railroads en-

gaged in rather dubious financial activities to attract money and people—basically, they existed as joint stock companies, empowered to
raise cash by selling stocks and bonds to the public, even though the
companies had little to back them up—but in the end it came to one
point: it worked. By 1866 things were well on their way, with the
Union Pacific already pushing its tracks through Nebraska at an incredible mile-a-day rate.

On a wet January afternoon in 1863 Hopkins, Stanford, and
Crocker—three of the four partners in the Central Pacific Railroad—
gathered in Sacramento for the groundbreaking of their railroad.
Stanford wasn't exactly a spellbinding orator, but he thought he was.
He did have a certain ponderous flair on great occasions, and on this
auspicious day he laid it on heavily. Because of the railroad the streets
of Sacramento, he said, would soon resemble the fabled streets of
the Orient, teeming with "the busy denizens of two hemispheres" as
they passed through town "over the great highway of nations." All
well and good (if flowery), but at the time Sacramento's streets
leaned more to mud, and there weren't all that many people passing through town. Oh, there'd been the gold rush of '49, but that
was over.

Flowery or not, exaggerated or not, Governor Stanford's speech
so moved Charles Crocker that he called for nine cheers. Even the
frail Mark Hopkins joined in the cheers. Collis Huntington wasn't
there; he was getting ready to go back East to raise more money,
something the gang of four desperately needed. The four partners
had paid for the groundbreaking ceremony out of their own bank
accounts.

Stanford coaxed the state legislature into granting the Central Pacific ten thousand dollars for every mile of track laid within the state.
Counties along the way signed up for more than half a million dollars' worth of CP stock, and in April the gang of four asked San Francisco voters to give the railroad six hundred thousand dollars in cash.
The governor sent his brother Philip around to polling places to talk
voters into approving the plan.

To put it simply: They tried to buy the election. Philip Stanford,
it was said in a sworn statement, "used his money profusely, now
throwing it by the handful among the voters, who gathered around

him in crowds; now making bargains with gangs of men to vote in a body for the subscription." Not too surprisingly, the railroad won, but the town's big money managed to tie the funds up in court; they didn't like the idea of a group of storekeepers (plus, of course, Governor Stanford) from bucolic Sacramento building a railroad. Opposition came from, among others, Wells Fargo, which wanted to keep its stagecoach lines going. Even the Sitka (Alaska) Ice Company objected to the railroad; they were afraid that, instead of buying the ice they shipped in from Alaska, merchants would get ice from the Sierra snowfields. There even were accusations of the four CP partners owning a wagon toll road that linked the town of Dutch Flat, California, to the Nevada silver fields. The toll road brought in a good bit of change, but the railroad would meet the road at Dutch Flat, and that sounded too much like a swindle. So that's what opposition-owned newspapers cried: "Swindle!" Don't give the CP funds, the newspaper pleaded, saying, "There are obstacles [to the railroad] which cannot be overcome." In reply the four would-be magnates argued that, yes, indeed, they were going to build their railroad.

About this time there rose the question of where the mountains began. Remember that the federal government would loan the CP $48,000 a mile to build the railroad over the Sierras, but only $16,000 a mile over flat land? Leland Stanford recalled an old geological report that, because of certain soil and rock formations, put the base of the Rocky Mountains at the Mississippi River. Well, what about the Sierras? A California geologist said, yes, indeed, and the report was sent to Washington, where a startled President Lincoln was told the Sierras began to rise twenty-four miles west of where they really did. Let's see: Twenty-four miles times that additional $32,000 a mile meant an additional $768,000. As the late Chicago Cubs' baseball announcer Harry Carey would have said, "Holy Cow!"

Lincoln wanted the railroads to go through, apparently at any cost, even at the expense of fooling Mother Nature. Former Congressman Aaron Sargent was now working for the Central Pacific and presented the geologist's report to the President. As Sargent later remarked, "my pertinacity and Abraham's faith removed mountains." Altogether it netted the CP, not just $768,000, but well over a million dollars in increased loans for laying tracks across the "difficult terrain" of the nearly flat Sacramento Valley.

The gang of four got the money, but that didn't get the CP out of the red. Financially there were at least two problems. One was that the government paid in good ol' American greenbacks, but nobody in the West trusted them; it could cost the railroad up to fifty-seven cents on the dollar to convert the greenbacks to gold, which people in the West *did* trust because they could feel it. The second was wartime inflation. The CP's first locomotive cost $13,688—just a small engine with two pairs of drive wheels—but, as the line's owners soon learned, a much larger engine had earlier sold for just $10,000. The price of rails went up, from $55 a ton before the Civil War to $110 during the conflict. And that was just the cost as the rail sat on a Boston pier; getting it around Cape Horn cost a helluva lot more. Once, the CP couldn't wait for a locomotive to be shipped round the Horn and had it brought in the hard, and expensive, way: down the Atlantic to Panama, across the isthmus on railroad flatcars, then by steamer up to San Francisco. Shipping fees alone totaled $37,000. This whole thing was getting expensive.

Thank God for cheap labor, which is where the Celestials—the Chinese—came in. It was Charles Crocker who suggested hiring the Chinese, who'd come to California a decade earlier to work tailings and played-out gold mines.

James Harvey Strobridge, the CP's construction boss, an ex-forty-niner who walked around with a pickax in his hands—he called it his "persuader"—hated the idea, probably because he hated the Chinese: strange little men with dishpan straw hats, pigtails down to here, floppy blue pajamas, and funny sandals for shoes. Not to mention the outlandish fodder they ate—bamboo shoots, mushrooms, rice, cuttlefish, and seaweed. Why, compared to the "Terrestrials"— his brawny Irish crews, the survivors of the potato famine who'd gone west—the frail Celestials just couldn't match up. "I will not boss Chinese," Strobridge cried.

Which he didn't do until Irish workers threatened to strike, that is, so Strobridge agreed to try fifty Chinese for a month to see if they'd work out. More likely, to prove they wouldn't. Well, they could and did.

Within months more than eleven thousand Chinese were busy, working on the railroads, all the livelong day. According to journalist Charles Nordhoff, who went on to collaborate with Norman Hall to write the classic fictional trilogy of the mutiny on the *Bounty*, "They do not drink or fight or strike, and it is always said of them that they are very cleanly [*sic*] in their habits." Nordhoff added that "it is the custom among them, after they have had their suppers every evening, to bathe with the help of small tubs. I doubt if the white laborers do as much." Why, the Chinese were so regular in their habits, folks believed, that as novelist Pete Dexter once put it, "if you lined up fifty Chinese to take a bath every day for a month, every day the same Chinese would get the water first, the same Chinaman would go second, and so on right through the number fifty." They had, Dexter wrote, "a way to arrange everything, and an order for everything."

Oh, they bickered and quarreled among themselves, but they did it while sober, unlike some others on the crew. And they gambled incessantly, but that was their problem, not the railroad's, and they stayed out of whorehouses, which meant they stayed out of whorehouse fights and avoided whorehouse diseases. So Crocker advertised in China for more.

Just as they had in the gold fields, Chinese railroad laborers worked in teams of their own making; they arrived at the work site "already divided into smoothly efficient work gangs," historian Geoffrey C. Ward writes, "usually from the same province and speaking the same dialect." They formed themselves into small gangs of twelve to twenty men, each with its own cook and headman, usually a Chinese who'd been in California for some time. Unlike other foremen the Chinese headman worked right alongside the others. He also served as interpreter and clerk, collected wages for the others from the railroad, and he deducted monthly assessments for food and the labor contractors.

There was something else about the Chinese laborers: They didn't get sick as often as their white and black coworkers did, although Crocker and Strobridge didn't know exactly why. Every now and then in the 1990s, one food specialist or the other proclaimed tea drinking—it didn't matter, green tea or black—as the answer to nearly every health problem. Well, the tea-drinking Chinese were healthier, but not because of the tea. It was because they boiled water to make the tea. It was the boiling that did it, removing from tainted water a lot of the bacteria that other workers consumed. And got sick from.

And their strange diet that James Strobridge denigrated? Well, by forgoing their daily rations of beef and potatoes, eating bamboo shoots, mushrooms, rice, cuttlefish, and seaweed, they stayed healthier.

These scrawny little guys laid track and punched out mountains. At one point they came up against solid rock that rose at a seventy-five-degree angle for more than three thousand feet above the American River—they called it "Cape Horn"—swung down from sheer cliff walls in wicker baskets to gouge out two-and-a-half-inch-wide holes, then filled them with explosives, set fuses, and signaled for someone to haul them up. They hoped they'd make it out of harm's way before the blast went off.

For centuries the Chinese had been working with explosives, and while working on the railroad they learned to cut their fuses to varying lengths so that an entire round of charges went off at once. It seemed they believed that the louder an explosion, the more likely it was to scare off personal devils and imps. So they set larger and larger explosive charges. When the CP crew was near Donner Lake, a newspaper reporter witnessed "immense volumes of fire and dense cloud of smoke from the mountainside." It was, he wrote,

> as if a mighty volcano was rending it to atoms. Huge masses of rocks and debris were rent and heaved up in the commotion; then . . . came the thunders of explosions like a lightning stroke, reverberating along the hills and canyons, as if the whole artillery of Heaven was in play. Huge masses of rock rolled far down the steep declivity, and pieces weighing two hundred pounds were thrown a distance of miles. Sometimes the people at the hotel, a mile from the scene of destruction, were obliged to retire to avoid . . . the falling fragments.

And the railroad moved ahead.

Let's see, funny food, strange clothing, pigtails, scrawny. Why, they seldom weighed much more than 110 pounds. No wonder Strobridge didn't want to boss them. Simply put, if it hadn't been for Chinese workers, a cross-country railroad likely would have taken years longer, and millions more money, to build.

That rock called Cape Horn? They built a ledge around it without losing a single life.

It wasn't just the Chinese, of course. Railroad work crews were a truly cosmopolitan lot, certainly international in their makeup. They were Civil War veterans—from both sides of the fighting—Irish and Scots, British and French, Germans and Poles and Russians, Mormons and atheists, Native Americans—Shoshones, Paiutes, and Washos—a regular United Nations long before there was a United Nations.

When construction was at its peak, work crews laid two to five miles of track a day. They filled some ravines and dug others. Roustabouts graded roadbeds with horses, mules, scrapers, and dump carts. Shovels, spit, and sweat.

Twenty miles ahead bridge monkeys ran spindly trestles across rivers and valleys and sometimes right through mountains. Behind them came horse-drawn wagons piled high with ties.

A flatcar carried rails to within half a mile of the railhead, and from there they were loaded onto carts and carried forward. "A light car," wrote one witness, "drawn by a single horse, gallops to the front with its load of rails."

Two men seize the end of a rail and start forward, the rest of the gang taking hold by twos until it is clear of the car. They come forward at a run. At the word of command, the rail is dropped in its place, right side up. Less than 30 seconds to a rail for each gang, and so four rails go down to the minute.

Then came men with a notched wooden gauge, spacing each pair of rails precisely four feet, eight and a half inches apart. The spike men swung their mauls. Rail, gauge, spike. Rail, gauge, spike. And on and on and on. A journalist reported, "It's a grand 'Anvil Chorus' playing across the plains."

Back in Missouri, 1,777 miles to the east, the Union Pacific was getting nowhere fast. By 1866 the Union Pacific had laid only 40 miles of track, but then the Casement brothers, Brig. Gen. John Stephen and his younger brother Dan, came along as construction bosses. It was, however, often hard to find them; General John was only five feet four inches tall and Dan was "five foot nothing"; they looked like "twelve-year-old boys, but requiring larger hats." In the work they did, and the work they got out of their crews, they turned out to be giants.

That work, one reporter wrote, was "something to see." By the end of the year the Union Pacific had completed 266 miles of track.

One problem the Union Pacific had that its western cousin didn't was finding an adequate supply of wooden ties. It was an endless aggravation on the barren high plains, where about the only timber was the pulpy cottonwood that fringed the rivers. They made do with "burnettizing" cottonwood logs, a method devised by William Burnett of Scotland. It hardened cottonwood ties by impregnating them with a solution of zinc chloride. The Casement brothers interspersed "burnettized" cottonwood logs with freighted-in cedar and oak ties—four junk cottonwood ties to one good-and-durable.

Behind the builders on the freshly laid track came the work train, often called the "perpetual train," since it never stopped for long. It was pushed, not pulled, by an engine and carried just about everything (and everyone) the crew needed. At the head, closest to construction, came flatcars with tools and a blacksmith shop. Next came three barn-like, triple-tiered, eighty-five-foot-long bunk cars that would house three hundred to four hundred men. If they weren't large enough to house the crews, the overflow slept in tents or used hammocks slung underneath the cars. Next came the dining car, a single table running its full length. One hundred twenty-five men at a time ate fast. Tin plates were nailed to the tables, and after a man ate, dish swabbers came along and more or less cleaned the plates without moving them from the table. The first batch of diners made way for the next group of hungry workers.

Next was a three-partitioned car—kitchen, storeroom, and engineers' office. Hanging outside on spikes were quarters of beef, freshly killed from contractor-supplied herds that grazed along beside the tracks.

"It is half past five," a *New York Evening Post* reporter wrote in the fall of 1867, "and time for the hands to be waked up."

This is done by ringing a bell on the sleeping car until everyone turns out and by giving the fellows under the car a smart kick and by pelting the fellows in the tents on top with bits of clay. In a very few minutes they are out stretching and yawning. Another bell and they crowd in for breakfast. The table is lighted by hanging lamps, for it is yet hardly daylight. At intervals of about a yard are wooden buckets of coffee, great plates of bread and platters of meat. There is no ceremony: every man dips his cup into the buckets of coffee and sticks his own fork into whatever is nearest him. If a man has got enough and is through, he quietly puts one foot on the middle of the table and steps across.

Another adventure in good eating over, crews started work at six-thirty. An hour off for lunch at noon, back to work until sundown.

Makeshift towns grew up around the Union Pacific construction sites—North Platte, Julesburg, Cheyenne, Laramie, and Corrine— known to workers as "hell on wheels." In each there was a big tent where a man could get a drink or three. Other tents were traveling whorehouses. And gamblers and con men and pimps and more whores. "Those women," a *New York Tribune* reporter wrote, "are expensive articles, and come in for a large share of the money wasted [by workmen]."

In broad daylight they may be seen gliding through the dusty streets carrying fancy derringers slung to their waists, with which tools they are dangerously expert. Western chivalry will not allow them to be abused by any man they may have robbed. Mostly everyone seemed bent on debauchery and dissipation.

As a sidelight there's this story about the *Tribune* reporter, Henry M. Stanley, whose real name was John Rowlands. When the Civil War broke out, Rowlands enlisted in the Confederate army but was captured and decided he "liked the other side better." He joined the Union army but apparently didn't like that either. He quit the federal army and joined the federal navy, which still didn't satisfy him, so he deserted and sat out the rest of the war in Canada.

When the Civil War ended, Rowlands came back to the United States, changed his name to "Henry M. Stanley," and became a newspaper reporter, first in Kentucky and then in New York City. It was while he was in New York that the multiple-service deserter went to Africa to look for a presumably lost explorer who himself had gone looking for the head of the Nile River. Now, the explorer knew where he was, even if the rest of the world didn't, so he was more than a little surprised when this reporter turned up at his camp. Rowlands, now known as Stanley, stuck out his hand and declared, "Doctor Livingston, I presume."

Back with the railroads. Workers earned thirty-five dollars a month, plus housing and food. Chinese workers, on the other hand, housed themselves in tents and paid for their own food and had it shipped to them from San Francisco.

James Strobridge wouldn't allow a western version of the UP's hell on wheels, and at first crews worked off steam in the Sierra mining towns, but the farther east they got, the fewer towns there were. When saloon owners tried to peddle booze to his men, Strobridge, who really didn't care about their morals but wanted the men to show up for work, charged booze dealers more to water their horses than they could clear on sales of rotgut. At times this didn't work, and he'd gather a couple of burly track hands and beat the hell out of the dealers.

Charles Crocker once bet the Union Pacific's Thomas Durant ten thousand dollars that his eastbound crew could lay ten miles of track in a single day. Durant took him up on it.

Using a hand-picked crew, on April 29, 1869, Crocker got to work—started at sunup, stopped only briefly for a quick lunch, and quit work at sundown. And they won the bet. Not only did they lay ten miles of track, they laid ten miles *plus* two hundred feet, using 3,520 rails and 55,000 spikes.

One thing neither Strobridge nor the Casement brothers could control was the weather. In warm weather there were thunderstorms. Photographer William Henry Jackson witnessed one such storm that hit CP crews out on the prairie:

> It came raging and howling like a madman. It rocked and shook us and started some of the wagons on their wheels. We had serious apprehensions. . . . The rain came down in steady torrents—the roaring thunder and the flashing lightning were incessant, reverberating through the heavens with an awful majesty. The rain came right through the wagon sheets, but we hauled a buffalo robe over our heads.

The winter of 1866–67 was talked about for years by railroad crews who lived and worked through it. The Missouri River even froze over at Omaha—twelve inches thick—but that was the good news. It allowed supply crews to avoid drifted-over roads: Jack Casement laid tracks over the ice and stockpiled supplies on the west bank of the river.

In the mountains Central Pacific crews faced one of the worst winters in memory. "Snow storms, forty in number, varied in length from a short . . . squall to a two-week gale," one official remembered. "The heaviest storm of the winter began February 18th, at 2 P.M., and snowed steadily until 10 P.M. of the 22nd, during which time six feet fell. . . ." Jim Strobridge's crew was caught at the highest, most exposed and vulnerable point in the Sierras—thirty-eight miles above Dutch Flat. Chinese laborers had to tunnel beneath sixty-foot drifts, but work continued on the railroad, "working by lamplight, breathing through air shafts."

A witness remembered going to "a dance at Donner Lake at a hotel and a sleigh-load of us went up from Truckee." On their return, he added,

> we saw something under a tree by the side of the road, its shape resembling that of a man. We stopped and found a frozen Chinese. As a consequence, we threw him in the sleigh, with the rest of us and took him into town and laid him out by the side of a shed and covered him with a rice mat, the most appropriate thing for the laying out of a Celestial.

With spring came another problem: Indians who had never heard of, much less seen, a railroad and didn't like hundreds of men coming into the land they called home and laying track. Sometimes, the meeting of Indian and iron horse was humorous; sometimes it wasn't.

Spotted Tail, chief of the Lakota Sioux—two years later, in 1868, he would sign the Treaty of Laramie—once took a band of braves to see what Jack Casement and his crew were doing. It happened about 150 miles west of Omaha.

First, the Indians surprised the white workmen with a display of the warriors' skill with bow and arrow. Then the whites challenged Spotted Tail and his braves to race their horses against the iron one. They even convinced Spotted Tail to ride in the engine cab during the race. They're off and running with Indian ponies taking a quick lead, but the locomotive catches up and easily passes the band of braves. And Spotted Tail finds himself gazing back at his defeated tribesmen as smoke and ash fly around them.

In another, not so cordial instance, a war party tried to capture a locomotive. They stretched rawhide lariats across the tracks and attached the ends to their saddles. So, the train arrives, hits the rawhide barrier, which of course is no barrier at all, and the Indians and their ponies are dragged into the train's drive wheels and are dismembered.

And then there was the episode on August 6, 1867. A band of Cheyennes, under a chief called Turkey Leg, were traveling along an ancient trail when they discovered the Union Pacific tracks near Plum Creek, Nebraska. At the time, they were moving south to avoid army troops out looking for them. The Indians made a barricade of loose ties and lashed it to the track with telegraph wires ripped from nearby poles. And they waited for the train to come along.

When the Indians ripped down the wires, telegraph operators at the Plum Creek office realized the line was down. Station master William Thompson, an Englishman with long blond hair, loaded a new spool of wire, repair tools, a half-dozen Spencer rifles, and five section hands onto a hand-pump car and went looking for the break. They reached the Indians' barricade, but because by then it was dark, they didn't see it. Worse, they didn't see Turkey Leg and his waiting warriors. Thompson and his hand pump loaded with men and equipment hit the barricade and the men went flying head over telegraph cable. The Cheyennes pounced and within seconds every member of the crew except Bill Thompson was dead. And then he was clubbed to his knees. Before he could stand, he felt a searing pain and realized his long blond hair was being lifted.

Lying there in pain, Thompson saw the Indians walk away. He also saw his now bloody and separated-from-him scalp fall to the ground, unnoticed. Thompson apparently has only one thing in mind; he crawls over to his hair, picks it up, and crams it into a pocket. And full of hope, he starts crawling away.

Meanwhile Turkey Leg's men are working to improve their barricade. Using Thompson's tools, they unbolt two rails, wrench them up, and, with sheer muscle power, bend the rails back onto themselves. Then lash it all together with more confiscated telegraph wire.

Along comes the night train, pounding in from the East with its oil-fire lamp casting a feeble light ahead. Just as Bill Thompson had done earlier, the engineer sees the barricade too late to stop and goes plowing into it, whistle blowing and brakes screeching. The fireman is catapulted against the open firebox and dies right there. The sudden stop impales the engineer on the throttle. He's not dead yet, and the Indians pull him from the cab and kill him. Back in the caboose the rest of the train crew jumps out and runs off toward Plum Creek; before they get there, they flag down a second train and stop it in time to avoid further tragedy.

Back at the wrecked train. The Indians set about looting and burning, throwing the bodies of the engineer and fireman onto the flames. They discover a barrel of whiskey and settle down for a night of revelry.

By this time William Thompson is back in Plum Creek, still clutching his bloody scalp. The railroad calls in a special train to take him to Omaha, about 250 miles to the east, for surgical care. The physician, Dr. C. P. Moore, realizes Bill's detached scalp—a seven-inch-by-nine-inch section—has been mauled too badly to be reattached, and he doesn't even try.

Henry Stanley, intrepid journalist that he was, visited the scalpless telegraph repairman and wrote:

In a pail of water by his side, was his scalp, somewhat resembling a drowned rat, as it floated, curled up, on the water. At Omaha, people flocked from all parts to view the gory baldness which had come upon him so suddenly.

Thompson survived his sudden attack of baldness, and in grateful recognition for his doctor's help the young Englishman had his scalp tanned and sent to Dr. Moore as a gift. What happened to it then is unknown.

It is known, however, that the incident at Plum Creek—sometimes called the "Plum Creek Massacre"—does a lot to harden the will of railroaders to take the continent. There will be more Indian attacks on the railroad, but because of Plum Creek, more army troops are sent west to protect builders, railroad workers, and the railroads themselves.

On May 10, 1869, the dream many thousands first had had more than twenty years earlier, and for which many more thousands had worked, came true. The eastbound Central Pacific and westbound Union Pacific railroads met—the CP locomotive *Jupiter* and the UP Engine No. 119, dozens of people, some with champagne bottles in hand—the Golden Spike being driven into tracks connecting the two companies' lines.

Four spikes—two gold, one silver, and one a blend of gold, silver, and iron—were readied to be tapped into place. A fifth—ordinary except that it was wired to a telegrapher's key—was to be hammered into the ground. A Chinese crew carried in the last rail of the Central Pacific from the West, and Irishmen from the Union Pacific toted in the rail from the East. An operator stood ready to signal the driving of the final spike, and up and down the line telegraph lines stopped singing:

TO EVERYBODY. KEEP QUIET. WHEN THE LAST SPIKE IS DRIVEN AT PROMONTORY POINT, WE WILL SAY "DONE!" DON'T BREAK THE CIRCUIT, BUT WATCH FOR THE SIGNALS OF THE BLOWS OF THE HAMMER.
Then:
ALMOST READY. HATS OFF PRAYER IS BEING OFFERED.

"O Father, God of our fathers, we desire to acknowledge Thy handiwork in this great work. . . . Amen."

WE HAVE GOT DONE PRAYING; THE SPIKE IS ABOUT TO BE PRESENTED.
THE SIGNAL WILL BE THREE DOTS FOR THE COMMENCEMENT OF THE BLOWS.
DONE!

The East and the West were linked. Crowds cheered in Washington and the cracked Liberty Bell was carefully rung in Philadelphia. A four-mile-long parade kicked off in Chicago. One hundred cannons boomed in Omaha. And in San Francisco celebrants unfurled a huge banner: CALIFORNIA ANNEXES THE UNITED STATES.

Suddenly it was possible to travel the three thousand miles from New York to California in a matter of days, six months less than the time it took by ship. People and goods could go from coast to coast.

And it all came together at Promontory Point, Utah, where today you can have your picture taken at a monument commemorating the event. On the exact spot where it happened, right? Well, maybe.

Where the monument says two railroads met isn't where they really did meet. That actually happened about one mile northeast of the famed Golden Spike memorial, at an unmarked place on the edge of a farmer's field. Some National Park Service historians say so. As does one of the leading authorities on the subject, Adrienne Anderson, an historical archaeologist with the service's Denver center. She says the little-known real point where the two railroads met is more important than the one where they built the monument.

"For me," Anderson says in an interview in the *Salt Lake Tribune*, the actual location in the farmer's field "is the most important site," not the Golden Spike National Historic Site. "You had this incredible rush from East and West by the railroads to try and cover the most land they could and the real point where they met is when the two grades connected." But that's not at the Golden Spike National Historic Site.

Meanwhile, to get to the currently unmarked spot where the two railroads really met, you have to use a rutted dirt road. The National Park Service, however, hopes to do something about it and eventually place signs at the true intersection. Maybe even offer tours.

Now, why didn't they erect the monument at the actual meeting site? Well, both lines were paid by the government on a per-mile basis, remember? So, they kept right on working and built more than a hundred miles of parallel tracks that would never be used. Let's see, 100 miles at—remember the figure?—$16,000 a mile comes to $160,000. Construction crews kept constructing, and gandy dancers—those men who walked the tracks prying at spikes and rails and making certain everything was shipshape or railroad shape, using a long steel rod made by the Gandy Company of Chicago—kept on dancing.

Blame it all on Congress. Back in Washington, D.C., they decreed that the last spike should be driven at the point of highest elevation across the broad Promontory Mountains at the place now known as Promontory Summit. Strangely enough, when the Golden Spike was driven back on May 10, 1869, no one realized the historic significance, not only of the event itself, but the location. Oh, they immediately removed the laurelwood tie and the bronze and gold spikes and replaced them with the standard pine ties and steel spikes. But they forgot about the spot where it all happened. Photographs taken only a few months after the big ceremony showed nothing there to mark the spot. Promontory, Utah, became a bustling rail town and it wasn't until years later that anyone began to think about the actual location.

"When the monument was originally erected," Ms. Anderson says, "there was no real knowledge of where the last spike site truly was." She studied aerial photos taken in the 1930s of the area, but in 1965, when the Park Service acquired the land, "they had a very limited time to buy out the private property owners and do the historical research." So, the location where they hammered in the Golden Spike is an educated guess.

The two railroad companies were granted more than thirty million acres of land, twenty-square-mile parcels laid out in a checkerboard pattern along the route. Eventually they received more than 150 million acres, almost the area of the entire state of Texas, one of the most fantastic giveaways in America's history. Even today the corporations that descended from the Union Pacific and the Central Pacific are among the largest private landowners in the West.

On October 6, 1866, John, Frank, Simeon, and William Reno made history: They led a gang of about a dozen thieves and committed the first train robbery in North America. They got away with sixteen thousand dollars in gold, silver, and paper money. This kicked off an epidemic of train robberies around the country.

The Reno boys previously had confined their illegal activities to saloon holdups and highway robbery. They'd also passed off the work of forger Peter McCartney, whose phony money was said to be almost undetectable.

But on that fateful October day the boys decided to step up in the world, and robbed an Ohio and Mississippi train near Seymour, Indiana. Six months later they began robbing trains in northwestern Missouri. In 1868 they decided to repeat their earlier robbery of an Ohio and Mississippi train, only this time the American Express car was loaded with armed guards instead of money. The guards drove the boys off. Pinkerton agents tracked down several members of the gang and left them dangling from trees alongside the railroad tracks. There was a fifth member of the Reno family who isn't much heard of. He was honest and stayed out of the family business.

The Cumberland Gap, the first opening to the West through the Eastern mountains. Nineteenth century historian Frederick Jackson Turner wrote: "Stand at Cumberland Gap and watch the procession of civilization marching single file—the buffalo following the trail to the salt springs, the Indian, the fur-trader and hunter . . ." Harry Fenn, engraving 1872, author's collection.

Cave In Rocks, Illinois, along the Ohio River. It was often used as headquarters by river bandits and pirates. Author's collection.

Daguerreotype by Brady, Library of Congress.

Kansas State Historical Society.

Dickinson County Historical Society, Abilene, Kansas.

(Above left) Sam Houston. Born in Virginia, he became the premier adopted son of the Lone Star State. After serving in the U.S. Senate, he led Texian troops to victory at San Jacinto in 1836 and later became president of the Republic of Texas. *(Above right)* Early photograph of Wild Bill Hickok. The son of an Abolitionist, Hickok was involved in the Underground Railroad. His nickname originally may have been "Duck Bill" because of a protruding upper lip but later became "Wild Bill." *(Left)* Photographed in the 1860s, Hickok sported checked trousers, a Prince Albert coat, a silk vest, a cape with flowered silk lining, and hand-tooled $60 boots. Hickok was shot in the head while holding "dead man's hand" of Aces and Eights.

Belle Starr. Femme fatale and bandit queen of Indian Territory. Born Myra Belle Shirley in Washington County, Arkansas, in 1848, she took her name from Tom Starr, a sometime member of the Cole Younger band of outlaws. Belle became known as "The Petticoat Terror of the Plains." She was murdered by an irate wife who, perhaps, mistakenly believed Belle was fooling around with her husband.
Courtesy Irene R. Johnson.

Teams of oxen pulling prairie schooners to the West. Generally, they were "movers wagons" such as these, not the heavier eighteenth century-style Conestoga wagons. Library of Congress.

Mormon emigrants' covered wagon train, 1885. Beginning in 1844, thousands of members of the Church of Jesus Christ of Latter-day Saints walked and rode to their hoped-for Zion near the Great Salt Lake in Utah. By 1877, Salt Lake City had a population of 170,000. C. W. Carter photograph, National Archives.

James and Margaret Reed. The Donner Party left the well-traveled California Trail and struck out on a shortcut that ended in disaster. Only 46 of the original 87 emigrants survived. California State Department of Parks and Recreation.

James Butler "Wild Bill" Hickok, second from left, in costume while performing with Buffalo Bill Cody's Wild West Show. Cody is in the center. Kansas State Historical Society.

Sod homes were dark and stuffy during the winter months, and during the summer months they often leaked either dirt or water. While some soddies lasted into the 1960s, others, such as this, needed frequent repair. Nebraska State Historical Society.

Emigrant family poses in front of their sod house built into the side of a Nebraska hill. A team of horses waits on top of the soddie with a wagon-load of sod to be used to repair the house. Solomon D. Butcher Collection/ Nebraska State Historical Library.

A family poses with the wagon in which they lived and traveled to Nebraska in 1886. Emigrants often overloaded their wagons with their worldly possessions and had to dispose of much of it along the way west. National Archives.

Frank E. Webner, Pony Express rider, ca. 1861. The Pony Express had a short (18 months) but spectacular career. Beginning in St. Joseph, Missouri, a series of riders such as Webner carried the mail to Sacramento, California, in under ten days.
National Archives.

Cowboy Nat Love. Born in Tennessee, after the Civil War, at age fifteen, he "struck out for Kansas" where he became a cowboy. In his auto-biography, Love claimed to "carry the marks of fourteen bullet wounds on different parts of my body." William Loren Katz Collection, New York City Library.

Hangtown, California, 1849. First called Dry Diggings, it's now known as Placerville and was the third major gold camp after Sutter's Mill and Mormon Island. Its name, Hangtown, came after several would-be claim jumpers were lynched. Author's Collection.

Panning for gold near Virginia City, Montana Territory. After gold was found near John Sutter's sawmill in California in 1848, men and women from all parts of the world trudged and plodded their way west.
A. J. McDonald photograph, National Archives.

Chinese emigrants to the West Coast. Although they were industrious and willing to work, they were exploited, beaten, and killed while being confined to menial jobs like laundering. In the gold field, they were relegated to digging a meager living from abandoned mines.
Library of Congress.

Sand storm that passed over Midland, Texas February 20, 1894 at 6:00 P.M. Such storms were common in the West. In 1880, a Western newspaper reported that "Real estate moved considerably this week."
National Archives.

Rath and Wright's buffalo hide yard in Dodge City, Kansas, 1878, showing 40,000 buffalo hides. Buffalo, or the American Bison, could be counted in the tens of millions in the early 1800s, but by the 1900s, only small herds remained. As a hunter for the Union Pacific Railroad, William F. Cody killed more than 4,000 buffalo in one year, earning the nickname "Buffalo Bill." National Archives.

Gen. William Tecumseh Sherman. Civil War general who led the Union Army "march to the sea" through Georgia. Sherman was in charge of the 1868 Fort Laramie, Wyoming, peace commission. The government agreed to withdraw troops from the Bozeman Trail. Brady photograph, Library of Congress.

George Armstrong Custer while serving as brevet brigadier general during the Civil War. In 1876, as a lieutenant colonel in the regular army, Custer led his troops to defeat into the disastrous Battle of the Little Big Horn. Photographed by Mathew Brady in Brady's Washington Gallery toward the close of the Civil War.

Library of Congress.

Geronimo. Born Goyahkla (One Who Yawns) c. 1823, he took the Mexican name Geronimo (Jerome). He became famous in the 1880s as the last Apache to surrender to the government. Captured and exiled, he died in Fort Sill, Oklahoma, in 1906 at the age of 80.

National Archives.

A band of Apache Indian prisoners on their way to exile in Florida, at a rest stop beside Southern Pacific Railway, near Neuces River, Texas, September 10, 1886. Natchez is center front and his father, Geronimo, in matching shirts. A. J. McDonald photograph, National Archives.

Big Foot, leader of the Sioux, captured at the battle of Wounded Knee, Dakota Territory, then killed. His frozen snow-covered body lies where he died in 1890. National Archives.

CHAPTER EIGHT

The Native Americans:
Warriors of the West

What treaty that the white man ever made with us have they kept? Not one.
Sitting Bull, Hunkpapa Sioux

What is life? It is the flash of a firefly in the night. It is the breath of a buffalo in the wintertime. It is the little shadow which runs across the grass and loses itself in the sunset.
Crowfoot, Blackfoot, his last words, 1890

In 1827 the Illinois legislature petitioned the U.S. War Department to remove bands of Sac and Fox Indians from prime real estate in Illinois and Wisconsin. In 1830 President Andrew Jackson signed into law the Indian Removal Act, authorizing the removal of Indians in the Southeast to lands west of the Mississippi River. In Illinois, however, nothing was done, so in 1831 Illinois governor John Reynolds took the situation into his own hands. He mobilized volunteers and forced the aging Sac leader, Black Hawk, to sign an agreement to stay west of the Mississippi River. Later that winter, however, Canadian officials and members of other Native American bands assured Black Hawk that they would give the Sac aid to fight any removal order. The aid never came, but in April 1832 Black Hawk and his followers, including women and children, recrossed the Mississippi back into northern Illinois and southern Wisconsin.

That brought on the Black Hawk War, which saw the enlistment into the Illinois militia of Abraham Lincoln. It became the only war in which the future president would fight, if *fight* is the word. The most action Lincoln saw was when he and his detachment came upon a group of soldiers recently killed and scalped by the enemy. President Lincoln later admitted that seeing the scalped soldiers turned him against a military career.

The Black Hawk War was short lived, described by some as "a deadly farce." Except, of course, for those who lost the war. A colonel who fought in it referred to the Black Hawk War as "a tissue of blunders," with which both sides might agree. Chief Black Hawk himself tried three times to surrender but each time whites rejected his peace overtures. In early August 1832, as Black Hawk and hundreds of his people left their ancestral lands to move west of the Mississippi, soldiers and settlers attacked them. The Indians tried to escape across the Mississippi, but near the point where the Bad Axe River empties into the Mississippi (some twenty miles south of Lacrosse, Wisconsin, near the fittingly named present-day towns of Retreat and Victory), the two sides fought what Americans called the "Battle of Bad Axe." Instead of a battle, however, the incident at Bad Axe turned into a massacre, with soldiers and settlers on the high riverbank shooting the escaping Indians down below. Later the state of Wisconsin apologized for the Bad Axe Massacre of 1832. The apology came in 1990.

For much of the nineteenth century Native American Indians were almost wholly untamed, often powerful and warlike. They may have been the greatest fighters the world has ever known. They were also poets and painters. They lived in the midst of their god.

The Arapaho were of the Algonquian family and, early on, lived in the northern woods, in earthen-lodge villages. Rival tribes drove them onto the plains, first along the Minnesota River and later into present-day North Dakota along the Cheyenne River, where they lived as nomadic buffalo hunters. In the early 1800s they drifted south into the central plains just east of the Rockies. Over time they became sworn enemies of the Comanches and Kiowas and frequently clashed with them. To the west lay another enemy, the Utes, and to the east they faced the Pawnee.

Once on the high plains, the Arapaho allied themselves with the Cheyennes and fought alongside the Lakota Sioux. They were fighters and took part in two important U.S. Cavalry–Indian engagements: the Fetterman fight and the Battle of the Little Big Horn.

By 1859 the Southern Cheyenne and Arapaho were diseased, dispirited, and disgruntled, all due in great part to their dealings with whites. A treaty between the Indians and the United States signed in 1851 acknowledged the Cheyenne and Arapaho rights to stalk buffalo grazing east of the Rockies between the Arkansas and North Platte Rivers.

Much of the Arapaho and Cheyenne culture centered around buffalo, but now thousands of white prospectors and settlers were crossing the area, scaring away and killing the animals that Indians always needed and often held sacred. In 1862 a Chicago newspaper carried the following notice:

FOR SALE
10,000 BUFFALO ROBES

Ten thousand were, as it turned out, only a handful of the total number of buffalo slaughtered. Hunters killed them by the hundreds of thousands, even the millions. It's estimated that, in 1830, there were thirty million buffalo in the United States. At the end of the nineteenth century there were only about two thousand left, more living captive in zoos than in the wild. In one day former Pony Express rider Bill Cody killed sixty-nine buffalo. And in eight months, while working for the Kansas-Pacific, he killed 4,280 and that's how he got the nickname "Buffalo Bill."

William Frederick Cody was born in Scott County, Iowa, in 1846, where his father, Isaac, drove stagecoaches between Le Claire and Chicago. In 1850 the family homesteaded in Salt Creek Valley, Kansas, where Isaac Cody established a small sawmill and trading post. Isaac was antislavery, and in an argument with several proslavery traders in 1857, he was stabbed to death. William's mother, Mary, carried on the business, sent Bill to school, and permitted him to spend a lot of his free time with the Kickapoo Indians.

Later, in an effort to help out the family budget, Bill got a job as a messenger with the firm of Russell, Majors, and Waddell, freighters whose wagons fanned out into the far West. At age fifteen, when the company opened up the Pony Express, Bill Cody took up the life of forking a horse and carrying the mail. He once claimed that because other riders along the line had been killed, he racked up a 384-mile journey, the longest Pony Express ride on record. Well, maybe. A lot of stories about Cody came from dime-novel writer Ned Buntline, and many of them were purely fiction. In 1868 the twenty-one-year-old Cody went to work for the Kansas Pacific Railroad, killing buffalo. "They have run over our country," said Chief Bear Tooth.

> They have destroyed the growing wood and green grass; they have set fire to our lands. They have devastated the country and killed my animals, the elk, the deer, the antelope, my buffalo. They do not kill them to eat them; they leave them to rot where they fall. Fathers, if I went into your country to kill your animals, what would you say? Would I not be wrong, and would you not make war on me?

Chief Bear Tooth was right. Thanks to men like Bill Cody and excursions of easterners and foreigners who called themselves "sportsmen," the animals that had once numbered in the tens of millions were being killed at the rate of two million a year by the 1870s, mainly for their hides. White hunters usually killed the buffalo, stripped its hide and sometimes took the big, furry head, but otherwise left the carcass to scavengers. Not only did such slaughter take away the Indians' meat and hide; it deprived them of trade goods. One estimate says hide hunters killed 4,374,000 buffalo in the southern plains between 1872 and 1874. A decade later the American buffalo was nearly extinct.

Indian agent William Bent (known to Indians as "Little White Man") tried to help end the slaughter. He tried to write a letter to the government on the Indians' behalf, but he was hampered by a nearly total inability to write a coherent sentence. "I have bin so long in the Wild Waste," he admitted, that "I have almost forgotten how to spell." Finally Bent managed to get his words on paper and proposed putting the Southern Cheyenne and Arapaho on a reservation. Without this, he managed to say, the Indians would become the victims of a "desperate war of starvation and extinction."

At the time there was much discussion for and against reservations, with whites and Indians on both sides of the issue. One of those in favor was Cheyenne Chief Black Kettle, a former war leader who was then about fifty years old and who firmly believed that peace was the best course of action for his people.

In February 1861, just as the Union was about to go to war with the rebellious South, Chief Black Kettle joined with nine other Cheyenne chiefs in signing a treaty with the whites. Meeting at Fort Wise near William Bent's trading post, the chiefs put their marks to a treaty. It called for the tribes to stop roaming and start planting. For this they were given fifteen annual payments of thirty thousand dollars and were consigned to a small, roughly triangular-shaped reservation bounded on the north by Sandy (or Sand) Creek in present-day Colorado, on the south by the Arkansas River, and on the west by an arbitrary north-south line that lay some distance from the Rocky Mountains. Today towns abound with Wild West names: Kit Carson, Cheyenne Wells, Arapahoe, and Chivington, this last named for an army officer who was either a hero or a hellion.

This wasn't the best of all possible reservations. During droughts water holes and rivers dried up, and almost year round there wasn't enough game for the tribes. The allotted forty acres for every male Indian sounded good, but with the infertile soil in the reservation it wasn't nearly enough. And through this ill-conceived reservation came several trails: the Oregon, the Mormon, and the Smoky Hill Trail.

One group that didn't sign the treaty was the "Dog Soldiers." These were the professional soldiers, so to speak, of the Cheyenne nation. When they went into battle, Dog Soldiers had a piece of rope about ten feet long, tied to their body; on the other end they attached a wooden spike. If the warrior was forced into a defensive position, he was supposed to drive the spike into the ground, giving him a space roughly twenty feet in diameter, where he'd make a last-ditch stand. If a Dog Soldier managed to live into old age and became incapacitated, he could sell his rope to the highest bidder. Dog Soldiers were also noted for their war dance, called, appropriately enough, the Dog Dance.

Dog Soldiers weren't under the command of any tribal council, and because of this they often attacked white settlers with whom the rest of the band had a treaty and with whom they were on peaceful terms. Since many white soldiers never learned the difference between, say, Cheyenne and Ute, peaceful nonhostile Indians often were mistaken for the more militant Dog Soldiers. Not only did the Dog Soldiers not sign the treaty, they looked on the newly opened Smoky Hill Trail to Denver in about the same light as Red Cloud viewed the Bozeman Trail to the north.

William Bent worked for peace between whites and the Cheyenne and generally was successful, even when Confederate agent Albert Pike tried to exploit the situation. Bent persuaded the Southern Cheyenne and the Arapaho to ignore Pike and to stay out of "the white man's fight."

Meanwhile one of the Union's own, Colorado governor John Evans, was counting on war breaking out. He believed that the tribes stood in the way of further settlement. Stood also in the way of his own ambitions—he wanted to be elected U.S. senator once Colorado became a state.

Supporting Evans was a man the troops called the "Fighting Parson," John M. Chivington, a six-foot, seven-inch Irishman who earlier had been a preacher and a blacksmith. He found his way into the Colorado Territory and became an elder in the Methodist Church. In 1864 he took command of the Colorado Volunteer Force's 3d Cavalry.

The unit's members were known as "hundred dazers," because they'd enlisted for one hundred days. At best they were a band of semidisciplined, untrained rabble, many of them recruited from Colorado mining camps. At worst they wanted to avoid being shipped back East to fight Confederate rebels in the growing Civil War, where chances were far greater that they'd be killed. Under the "Fighting Parson" they were eager to put down any "rebellion" among local Indians. As commander of the newly created Military District of Colorado, John Chivington watched tension grow between white settlers and the Indians.

Cheyenne Chief Black Kettle was the most prominent and influential Indian leader in the area. Earlier, he'd gone to Denver on a friendly visit and was well received. Unlike many other Indians Black Kettle apparently believed that the white men's stay on the Indians' traditional home territory would be only a brief stopover. By now most other Indians had realized that whites weren't just passing through their territory on their way to the far West, that they were appropriating the Cheyenne's traditional hunting grounds, plowing up the land, and putting cattle onto grasslands needed by the buffalo. Meanwhile, the Cheyennes were becoming destitute and restive. They were at peace with the whites but continued their time-honored avocation of war against the Utes.

Whenever small bands of Cheyennes and Arapahos passed near white settlers, they frightened the newcomers. They frightened them even more when they returned from battle, yelling and whooping and brandishing Ute scalps. These same small bands occasionally robbed settlers' homes and stole cattle and other provisions.

Back in March 1862 John Chivington had led the 1st Colorado Cavalry Regiment to help beat back a Confederate invasion force in New Mexico at the Battle of Glorieta Pass. At the time Chivington was a major in the regular Union Army but hoped to be Colorado's first congressman when the territory gained statehood; he believed further military exploits—and whom better to exploit than the Indians?—would increase his political chances. Whether Chivington and Evans provoked an Indian war in order to advance their political careers, or whether they believed war was inevitable, the consequences were the same.

In April 1864 settlers reported that bands of Cheyennes were roaming the area, stealing settlers' livestock. The cattle may have stampeded on their own or simply wandered off, but Chivington used the reports as an occasion to attack the Indians. At first he wanted to disarm the Indians; later he raised the stakes. Ultimately, according to one of his field officers, Chivington gave orders to "burn villages and kill Cheyennes whenever and wherever found."

First came a clash on April 12, when Chivington's volunteers intercepted a band of Dog Soldiers along the South Platte River. Never mind that the Dog Soldiers were on a mission, not to harass whites, but to avenge the killing of a northern Cheyenne chief by members of a rival Crow faction.

Lieutenant Clark Dunn tried to disarm the Dog Soldiers and confiscate the herd of mules the Cheyenne had stolen from a nearby white rancher. The Dog Soldiers didn't mind giving up the mules—

they could always get more—but they refused to turn over their weapons, and a skirmish broke out causing minor casualties on both sides.

Three weeks passed, and then came another confrontation; this time the Cheyenne were suspected, only suspected, mind you, of stealing cattle from a settler's ranch. The commander in charge of the army unit was Maj. Jacob Downing, and he attacked the small band of Indians, killing at least twenty-five and destroying their lodges. As Downing put it, "I believe now it is but the commencement of war with this tribe, which must result in exterminating them." John Chivington couldn't have agreed more.

In mid-May Black Kettle and Lean Bear, with about four hundred of their people had spent the winter near Fort Larned, Kansas. Now, they moved north to hunt buffalo, but they ran into Chivington's soldiers near the Smoky Hill River. In an effort to prove his friendly character, Lean Bear rode out to show the troopers papers signed by President Abraham Lincoln when the chief was in Washington. The soldiers didn't care. They shot Lean Bear and his companions as they sat on their ponies and opened fire with howitzers on others who'd stayed behind. The Indians returned the fire until Black Kettle—still hoping for peace—rode up. As one of the warriors recalled, the chief "told us we must not fight with the white people, so we stopped." Twenty-eight Indians lay dead when the soldiers retreated.

Throughout June and July sporadic fighting broke out along the Platte and Arkansas Rivers. Indians raided wagon trains and burned out several ranches. An estimated two hundred whites were killed. In August, fed by exaggerated newspaper accounts of Indian raids, the people of Denver began clamoring for action. Settlers were terrified, including Governor Evans, who informed U.S. Secretary of War Edwin Stanton that "large bodies of Indians are undoubtedly near to Denver, and we are in danger of destruction both from attacks of Indians and starvation."

Meanwhile Evans pushed his campaign for the U.S. Senate, and Chivington pushed his bid for the House of Representatives. The issue of Colorado statehood went to voters on September 13, but, for the moment at least, they rejected the idea.

Five days after the failed statehood vote a large delegation of southern Cheyenne and Arapaho, along with some Sioux (the whites' name for the Lakota), rode into Denver hoping to negotiate a peace treaty. About 500 shouting, well-armed Indians faced 130 scared soldiers. However, as evidence of their good faith, the chiefs had with them four white captives they'd ransomed from other tribes and were returning to their own people.

As for the negotiations, who said what and who promised what isn't certain. The gist of it was that Black Kettle said the Indians had "come with our eyes shut," adding, "like coming through the fire."

"[W]hat shall I do with the Third Colorado Regiment if I make peace?" Governor Evans asked his aides and added, "They have been raised to kill Indians and they must kill Indians." Evans told the Indians that he no longer had the authority to negotiate a peace, that it was now up to the military.

That's when Colonel Chivington stood up and told the Indians that they must go to Fort Lyon "when they are ready," and that their surrender must be complete. Chief Black Kettle spoke for the Indians, and he wanted peace. Major Edward Wynkoop spoke for the soldiers, and he, too, wanted peace. On the other hand, many whites did not, and the *Rocky Mountain News* spoke for them:

We are opposed to anything which looks like a treaty of peace with the Indians. The season is near at hand when they can be chastised, and it should be done with no gentle hand.

Black Kettle met with Governor Evans and made a passionate appeal:

All we ask is that we may have peace with the whites. We want to hold you by the hand. You are our father; we have been traveling through a cloud; the sky has been dark ever since the war began. We want to take good tidings home to our people, that they may sleep in peace. I want you to give all the chiefs of the soldiers here to understand that we are for peace, and that we have made peace, that we may not be mistaken by them for enemies. I have not come here with a little wolf's bark, but have come to talk plain with you.

Evans answered with some earnestness but with many more evasions and recriminations. In truth he had no intention of ending the war frenzy he had helped whip up. He wasn't alone; the day following the council the commander of Fort Leavenworth, Kansas, Maj. Gen. Samuel Curtis, telegraphed Evans, saying, "I want no peace 'till the Indians suffer more," adding, "No peace must be made without my directions."

After hours of deliberations Chivington declared,

My rule of fighting white men Or Indians is to fight them until they lay down their arms and submit to military authority. They are nearer to Major Wynkoop than anyone else, and they can go to him when they get ready to do that.

What that meant to Chivington isn't certain. To Black Kettle it meant the Indians could have peace by surrendering to Major Wynkoop, and in mid-October bands of Arapaho began arriving at Fort Lyon to do just that. Wynkoop issued them army rations. A couple of weeks later Black Kettle and a party of his followers rode in from their camp at Sand Creek, about thirty-five miles northeast of the fort. Major Wynkoop, however, was leaving; he'd been summoned eastward to explain to General Curtis why he'd been feeding hostile Indians.

Wynkoop, called "Tall Chief" by the Indians, was eager to avoid conflict and promised Black Kettle food and other supplies. He promised to protect Black Kettle and his people, and as a show of faith he gave the chief an American flag to fly over his tepee. He told Black Kettle that, for the moment at least, the army lacked sufficient rations to feed so many Indians. He suggested that they go back to Sand Creek and hunt.

Now came a lull in Indian activity. They made peace in order to get government blankets and food. They remained in their villages, sat around campfires, and reminisced about battles fought long ago.

Whenever the Cheyennes stole cattle, the army dispatched troops to punish them. The community of settlers was appalled when, on June 11, 1864, the mutilated bodies of rancher Nathan Hungate, his wife, and their two children were taken to Denver and put on public display. Their deaths horrified and outraged the people. They wanted something done about the "Indian problem."

Governor Evans apparently believed that a general Indian uprising was under way. Evans tried to break what he perceived as a united front by sending messages to the tribes to report to nearby forts, where they would be given food and protected from troops looking for hostile Indians. Both Governor Evans and Colonel Chivington were itching for a decisive victory over the Indians.

Meanwhile a Kiowa chief whites called Santanta, but whom Native Americans referred to as Set-Tain-te, was growing restless. His name meant "White Bear"; frequently he was seen wearing the plumed brass helmet and epauletted jacket of a U.S. Army general's dress uniform. Alternately ingratiating and insolent, Santanta once ran off Fort Dodge's entire mule herd. Another time, when Santanta approached Fort Larned, Kansas, and was refused entry, he shot a sentry and his braves ran off all of the fort's herd of horses. Later, when other Cheyenne and Arapaho chiefs approached the fort carrying white flags, angry soldiers thought they were Santanta's men and fired a cannon at them. Santanta wasn't among the group, but to the soldiers it didn't matter; all Indians looked alike.

The Colorado press continued its abuse of Colonel Chivington, ridiculing his troops as the "Bloodless Third" because of their inactivity. To save his reputation Chivington considered attacking the indisputably hostile Sioux along the Upper Republican River, but he realized that would be too chancy, especially with the enlistment of the "hundred dazers" about to run out.

Black Kettle and his band are back on the reservation, and Colonel Chivington is anxious to revive his military reputation so that when Colorado setters *do* approve statehood, they'll also approve of him as their congressman.

It's November 24. Chivington and 750 men march out of their rendezvous point about fifty miles southeast of Denver. In addition to the 3d Colorado Volunteer Cavalry, Chivington has three companies of the 1st Colorado. With them they carry four howitzers. The troops reach Fort Lyon on the afternoon of the twenty-sixth but leave that evening, hurrying through the night.

Deep snow blankets the plains and ice covers the area around the village at Sand Creek. All seems peaceful until the morning of November 29, when Colonel Chivington and his troops ride to a ridge overlooking the camp. From this vantage point Chivington sees about a hundred Southern Cheyenne tepees and thirty or so lodges of their Arapaho allies.

An early-rising squaw sees the army troops and runs to Black Kettle, crying, "Soldiers!" Now the chief sees the troops coming his way, but he and his warriors make no hostile move toward them. After all, Major Wynkoop had given Black Kettle an American flag and assured the chief it would be honored, that no harm would befall any Indian who sheltered beneath it. To prove his loyalty to the United States the chief displays the flag and reassures his people that they have nothing to fear from the soldiers.

On the way from Fort Lyon to Sand Creek, Colonel Chivington told a junior officer, "I have come to kill Indians, and believe that it is right and honorable to use any means under God's heaven to kill Indians." He ordered his troops to "kill and scalp all, big and little." To emphasize his point that they should also kill the children, Chivington added, "Nits make lice." Now, at Sand Creek, his troops follow orders, and by many accounts, the skirmish becomes an orgy of murder and mutilations.

As the Colorado Volunteers ride up, Black Kettle stands holding a lodgepole from which he's flying the American flag Major Wynkoop had given him. Robert Bent, whose father had married a Cheyenne woman, is with Chivington's troops, commandeered against his will to show the way to the Indian camp. Three of his siblings—Charles, Julia, and George—are staying in the Indian camp. Robert Bent later writes about the attack:

> From down the creek a large body of troops was advancing at a rapid trot. . . . More soldiers could be seen making for the Indian pony herds to the south of the camp; in the camps themselves all was confusion and noise—men, women, and children rushing out of the lodges partly dressed; women and children screaming at the sight of the troops; men running back into the lodges for their arms.

Black Kettle stood, "calling out not to be frightened," Bent wrote, adding "that the camp was under protection and there was no danger." Many of the Indians huddled around Black Kettle's tepee. An estimated six hundred Indians were living in the camp, but according to Bent, "I think there were thirty-five braves and some old men, about sixty in all" there that morning. The rest of the warriors, Bent believed, "were away from camp hunting."

What Chivington and the volunteers did that day, at first—and only briefly—made him a hero. Later he became an American villain, reviled and denounced in U.S. congressional committee meetings.

Once they'd surrounded the Indian camp, Chivington's troops began firing into the tepees and lodges. Howitzers loaded with canister shot were fired directly into the village. Warriors, women, and children ran out of their lodges, trying to escape. They had no chance. A seventy-year-old chief named White Antelope* frantically ran toward the soldiers, waving his arms, shouting, "Stop! Stop!" The soldiers dismounted and raised their rifles, then they shot White Antelope. As the rest of the village scattered for their lives, the wounded White Antelope stood in the center of the village, arms folded, singing his death song:

Nothing lives long,
Except the earth and the mountains.

The soldiers spread out, still firing. The villagers have no chance to organize resistance. For several hours after the opening attack Chivington's men range the village and surrounding country, carrying out the colonel's order to take no prisoners.

Still, the Indians do "all they [can] to defend their families," Maj. Scott J. Anthony, a regular soldier serving with the volunteers, remembers. "I never saw more bravery displayed by any set of people on the face of the earth than by these Indians." Anthony writes that

*White Antelope was the first of his tribe to visit Washington City, where he received a peace medal from the president.

the Indians "would charge on the whole company singly, determined to kill someone before being killed themselves." It does no good, however. The soldiers greatly outnumber the Indians. "We," he added, "took no prisoners."

"After the firing," Robert Bent writes,

> the warriors put the squaws and children together, and surrounded them to protect them. I saw five squaws under a bank for shelter. When the troops came up to them they ran out and showed their persons to let the soldiers know they were squaws and begged for mercy, but the soldiers shot them all. I saw one squaw . . . whose leg had been broken by a shell; a soldier came up to her with a drawn saber; she raised her arm to protect herself, then he struck, breaking her arm; she rolled over and raised her other arm, when he struck, breaking it, and then he left her without killing her. There were some thirty or forty squaws collected in a hole for protection; they sent out a little girl about six years old with a white flag on a stick; she had not proceeded a few steps when she was shot and killed. All the squaws in that hole were afterwards killed. . . .

At the end of the day some two hundred Cheyenne corpses littered the valley of Sand Creek. About two-thirds of them were women and children. "I heard of one instance," Lt. James Conner writes, "of a child a few months old being thrown in the feedbox of a wagon, and after being carried some distance left on the ground to perish." He added, "I also heard of numerous instances in which men had cut out the private parts of females and stretched them over the saddle-bows and wore them over their hats while riding in ranks." One soldier cut off White Antelope's ears and nose; another took his scalp; yet another castrated him and later used the scrotum as a tobacco pouch. White Antelope had been wearing his presidential peace medal, but it was never found or at least never reported.

The slaughter and butchery appalled regular army officers. Back East, Gen. Ulysses S. Grant privately declared it nothing more or less than murder. But in Colorado it was seen as something else. When word of Sand Creek reached Denver, residents there regarded it as a triumph. The *Rocky Mountain News* claimed Colonel Chivington and his men had defeated five hundred warriors. Instead of a slaughter of innocents the *News* proclaimed Sand Creek a "brilliant feat of arms." It claimed "Colorado Soldiers have again covered themselves with glory." Colonel Chivington agreed. The soldiers, he said, "all did nobly." He wrote that it was "unnecessary to report that I captured no prisoners."

Not long after Sand Creek, at the intermission of a concert at the Denver Opera House, one hundred Cheyenne scalps were put on display, strung across the stage. The orchestra then played patriotic airs while the audience applauded the brave men who had taken the scalps.

It's estimated that the army on the northern plains spent a million dollars for each Indian it killed. Many people in Colorado thought it was justified. In July 1865, Wisconsin's Senator James Doolittle went west to argue on behalf of a peaceful solution. Speaking to a packed audience in the Denver Opera House, Doolittle said the choice was to put the Indians on reservations, where they could support themselves, or to exterminate them. The audience knew where it stood. It gave a "shout almost loud enough to raise the roof of the Opera House—Exterminate them! Exterminate them!"

Twenty years after Sand Creek, Colorado pioneers celebrated settling the territory. Chivington once again was their hero and celebration sponsors invited him to attend. He spoke to the gathering, and when he said, "I stand by Sand Creek," the audience applauded wildly.

By then John Chivington had left the territory, and Colorado had become a state. Onetime pioneers invited him to come back to Colorado. He did and got a job as undersheriff. He lived in Denver until 1894, when he died of cancer, never having made it to Congress.

During the four years of the Civil War, President Lincoln concentrated on bringing the rebelling states of the South back into the Union fold. Mostly he left Indian affairs in the hands of Congress and the Indian Bureau. Frankly, the American public didn't much care what happened in the High Plains; they were more concerned with what happened at Richmond and Atlanta, Gettysburg and Antietam. As commissioner of Indian Affairs, William P. Dole promoted traditional policies, that is, to keep the Indians on reservations and "civilize" them. In other words, to Christianize them.

After the Battle of Second Manassas in 1862, Lincoln exiled defeated Gen. John Pope to Minnesota, where he directed the army's operations against the Indians. Pope was pompous, bombastic, quarrelsome, and verbose; however, he did so well against northern Indians that, late in 1864, Gen. Ulysses S. Grant put him in charge of a command that stretched from British Canada to Confederate Texas. According to Pope's reckoning all Indians were hostile Indians.

In November 1864, even as Denver celebrated the volunteer army's "victory" at Sand Creek, Indian survivors of the encounter straggled into other Cheyenne camps. With them they carried war pipes—to the Lakota, the Cheyenne, and the Arapaho. In the early months of 1865, as the war back East wound down, Plains Indians went on a rampage, burning virtually every ranch and stagecoach station on the South Platte. Twice they sacked the town of Julesburg, Colorado. They ripped up miles of telegraph wire. They plundered wagon trains, ran off cattle, halted supply trains and mail delivery, and for a while completely cut off Denver, Salt Lake City, and San Francisco from the East. The stream of white settlers slowed to a trickle and stopped. Then, suddenly, the raids themselves stopped. The chiefs had decided to join their northern brethren, and when army troops went looking in the Indians' old camps, they found they'd all gone away.

Up until now most of the fighting had been done in the southern plains. With the Civil War over, settlers and gold seekers began another major westward trek. This time it was by a route that ran northwest of Fort Laramie, on the North Platte River in Wyoming: the Bozeman Trail. It cut through the center of the Lakota buffalo range, crossed the Powder River at Fort Reno, continued on to the northern part of the Wyoming Territory, over the Tongue River, skirted the Rosebud, and crossed the Big Horn. It went right through the Indians' prime hunting ground.

While the Civil War raged, volunteer troops out West had been aggressive. In early 1865, when it became obvious the life of the Confederacy could be measured in hours, volunteers (and some captured Confederates who'd agreed to join the Union army as long as they didn't have to fight against their old comrades) began drifting away from their western posts. "Whole units melted away in desertion," historian Robert Utley writes.

In March 1865 Congress turned its attention toward the West and enacted a measure that it described as "conquest by kindness." It was a policy made up of both genuine humanitarianism and crass self-interest, with the emphasis being on self-interest.

Colonel John Chivington believed he'd killed Cheyenne peace chief Black Kettle at Sand Creek. Wrong. Black Kettle's wife died in the massacre, but not the chief. He and several other members of his tribe fled. Wanting no part of any further fight with the white man, Black Kettle took the surviving members of his tribe south, as far away as he could get, to a new reservation on the Washita River. In October, still hoping for peace, Black Kettle showed up at a treaty council on the Little Arkansas River. That he was alive surprised many.

Red Cloud, an Oglala Sioux warrior with eighty coups to his name,* was known to Indians as Makhpiya-Luta. He'd built a reputation as a warrior in battles with the Pawnee, Crow, and Shoshone. He wasn't a chief but was known as a "shirt wearer," that is, a head warrior. He commanded respect among his band and was widely influential. Along with the northern Cheyenne and Arapaho, Red Cloud and his people roamed the northern plains, westward from the Black Hills to the Big Horn Mountains. Over a period of a decade or so they took the country away from the Crows.

---

*From a French word meaning a "blow." Although a coup (pronounced "coo") could result in death for the recipient of the blow, counting coup was usually done with a light coup stick on the bare hands. An Indian had merely to touch an enemy. A coup was not credited to an Indian who killed an enemy with a long-range weapon, such as a bow or rifle; if that occurred, the first brave to touch the corpse could "count coup."

For whites the area held something more promising than just open range and buffalo. Prospectors had found gold in them thar Black Hills! Soon men with gold's glitter in their eyes and its fever in their veins ranged over the Bozeman Trail. If these miners and settlers bothered the Indians, then the columns of blue-coated soldiers infuriated them.

The winter of 1865 was especially cold, and when whites put out peace feelers in the spring of 1866, the no longer youthful Red Cloud hoped the Indian Bureau would feed and clothe his people. Red Cloud and others agreed to a council with the whites at Fort Laramie. Some of the chiefs were tired of war; some had never wanted war with the white man in the first place.

By all accounts the peace council was a magnificent spectacle. Tepees stretched for a mile or more on either side of the fort. Indian ponies by the hundreds were corralled, and from a staff in the middle of the parade grounds, the Stars and Stripes flapped in the breeze. Government officials and the leading chiefs of the Cheyenne and Arapaho sat on a raised platform. With them were representatives of the Brulé, Miniconjou, and Oglala subbands of the Teton Sioux. Forty-four-year-old Red Cloud was there. For several years he and his band had attacked parties of whites along the Bozeman Trail.

On June 13, 1866, the council got off to a good start. The government promised the Indians seventy-five thousand dollars a year in aid and assured them that their land never would be taken by force. But then Col. Henry B. Carrington rode into the fort at the head of a long column of men and wagons.

The government, Carrington told the assembled Indians, had decided to maintain the Bozeman Trail. Carrington and seven hundred troops were being sent into the Powder River country. They would open a chain of forts stretching from Wyoming to Montana, deep into Teton Sioux country.

Red Cloud exploded:

Why do you pretend to negotiate for land you intend to take by force? I say you can force us only to fight for the land the Great Spirit has given us.

The Great Father sends us presents and wants us to sell him the road, but White Chief goes with soldiers to steal the road before Indians say Yes or No! I will talk no more! I will go now, and I will fight you! As long as I live I will fight you for the last hunting grounds of my people!

Red Cloud stormed off the platform and out of the conference. Within days he and his warriors were back to harassing the builders of the forts, the miners on the Bozeman Trail, and the soldiers who tried to protect them. The trail was as unsafe as it ever had been. Security was tightened and workmen went back to building new forts. At the fork in the Little Piney River, Carrington pitched camp and began work on what became Fort Phil Kearny. Fort Phil Kearny (pronounced "car-nee") was named after a Union officer who had fought in both the Mexican and Civil Wars. In September 1862, at the Battle of Chantilly, Virginia, then–Major General Kearny had accidentally ridden into the middle of enemy lines. When Confederates called on him to surrender, Kearny tried fighting his way out and was killed, making him a hero to the U.S. Army and worthy of having a fort named after him.

Fort Phil Kearny was situated about eighteen miles north of Clear Creek in the northwestern corner of Wyoming along the Bozeman Trail. It's not to be confused with Fort Kearney, Nebraska, near the present-day town of Kearney, which was on the Oregon Trail.

"The fort proper is six hundred feet by eight hundred," Colonel Carrington's wife wrote, "situated upon a natural plateau. . . . The stockade is made of heavy pine trunks, eleven feet long, hewn to a touching surface of four inches so as to join closely, being pointed and loop-holed."

One cold day just before Christmas 1866, aging mountain man Jim Bridger stood beside Colonel Carrington, watching workmen building Fort Phil Kearny. It was 11:00 A.M., late in the Moon of Popping Trees, as the Indians reckoned time. The hills on all sides of the fort prevented anyone inside from seeing what was happening in the area. The nearest wood usable for camp activities was more than five miles away. Because of this, and other reasons, Jim Bridger had argued against building the fort on the site, but Colonel Carrington overruled him. At the same time soldiers were working on another fort, Fort C. F. Smith, on the Big Horn River.

Over the next several months Red Cloud's warriors continually ambushed, raided, and sniped at Carrington's soldiers. There was a steady attrition of both men and morale. By August soldiers at Fort Phil Kearny were being scalped and wounded at the rate of one a day. One was shot as he sat in the latrine. Reporter Ridgeway Glover of the popular *Frank Leslie's Illustrated Paper* wandered away from the post. Glover was later found, naked, with his back cleaved open by a tomahawk. In the first five weeks Carrington reported that thirty-three travelers were killed on the Bozeman Trail.

Red Cloud was on the move. With him was a young warrior named Crazy Horse, Tashunca-Uitco, celebrated for his ferocity in battle and recognized among his own people as a visionary leader committed to preserving the traditions and values of the Lakota way of life. Red Cloud looked on Crazy Horse as a troublemaker and tried to prevent him from gaining influence among the Lakota. Even as a young man Crazy Horse was a legendary warrior. Before he was thirteen he stole horses from the Crow Indians, and led his first war party before turning twenty.

It wasn't just Crazy Horse's skill and daring in battle that earned him his reputation among the Lakota but also his determination to preserve his people's traditional way of life. For example, he refused to allow any photographs to be taken of him. He fought to keep Americans out of Lakota lands following the Fort Laramie Treaty of 1868. When George Armstrong Custer sent a surveying party into the Black Hills in 1873, Crazy Horse led the attack against him.

Army captain John G. Bourke described Crazy Horse as about

> five feet eight inches high, lithe and sinewy, with a scar in the face. The expression of his countenance was one of quiet dignity, but morose, dogged, tenacious, and melancholy. He behaved with stolidity, like a man who realized that he had to give in to Fate, but would do so as sullenly as possible.

He was born near Rapid Creek, Dakota Territory, the son of an Oglala holy man and a woman from the Brulé division of the Sioux nation. Oglala Sioux chief He Dog was born in the same year as Crazy Horse. More than half a century after the Battle of the Little Big Horn he spoke through an interpreter, Thomas White Crow Killer and told Crazy Horse's story. He Dog was ninety-two at the time of the interview in 1930, "so you can figure out in what year he was born by your calendar."* The two "grew up together in the same band," He Dog said, "played together, courted the girls together, and fought together."

He had three names at different times of his life. His name until he was about ten years old was Curly Hair. Later, from the time he was ten until the time he was about eighteen years of age, he was called His-Horse-On-Sight, but this name did not stick to him. When he was about eighteen years old there was a fight with the Arapahos who were up on a high hill covered with big rocks and near a river. Although he was just a boy, he charged them several times alone and came back wounded but with two Arapaho scalps. His father, whose name was Crazy Horse, made a feast and gave his son his own name. After that, the father was no longer called by the name he had given away, but was called by a nickname, Worm.

On December 21 General Carrington was supervising workmen, when a message came in from lookouts on Pilot Hill, a few hundred yards east of the fort. A woodcutting detail outside the fort was being attacked by "many Indians." Carrington immediately organized a relief force of eighty men and placed brevet Lt. Col. William Judd Fetterman in command. Carrington's exact orders were: "Support the wood train, relieve it, and report to me. Do not engage or pursue the Indians at its expense. Under no circumstances pursue over Lodge Trail Ridge."

Fetterman acknowledged the order; he did not, however, obey it. He was an ambitious, fire-eating young officer, a greenhorn who had joined the garrison only a month earlier. He considered his uniformed men more than a match for warpainted Indians, no matter

---

*This would indicate that He Dog and Crazy Horse were born in 1838, but other sources say it was in 1842.

the number. Why, with eighty men, he claimed, he could "ride through the whole Sioux nation." He didn't know it, but at the time, in a five-mile area of Fort Kearny, there were several hundreds of Chief Red Cloud's Oglala Sioux mixed with bands of Arapaho.

Red Cloud had won the allegiance of several bands of Cheyenne and Arapaho. Leading his warriors up along the Tongue River and Prairie Dog Creek, he spread them among the foothills near the fort. Then he attacked the woodcutting party.

When Lieutenant Colonel Fetterman and his men arrived, the raiding party skittered away. The frustrated young officer thought his arrival had scared off the Indians. Wrong. It was a classic decoy action; a small detachment of Sioux led by Crazy Horse broke cover and headed for Lodge Trail Ridge. A little before noon Fetterman led his mixed command of cavalry and infantry in hot pursuit. He and Lt. H. S. Bingham raced across the Big Piney River, hoping to intercept the attackers. At least once Crazy Horse dismounted within rifle range to stop and admire the view of pursuing soldiers. And, of course, to tempt the soldiers.

From the fort Colonel Carrington watched the action through binoculars. While the colonel watched, Crazy Horse's braves ran their ponies before the soldiers and waved red blankets in front of the blue-coated American troops, much as a toreador waves his cape in front of a bull. It had the same effect. The trap worked perfectly. Suddenly the Indians wheeled their ponies about to face the soldiers.

"A few shots were heard," Mrs. Frances Grummond, the wife of army lieutenant George W. Grummond, remembered, "followed up by increasing rapidity. A desperate fight was going on in the valley below the ridge . . . , the very place where the command was forbidden to go."

The Indians surrounded Fetterman and his command; between fifteen hundred and two thousand warriors appeared, seemingly from nowhere, as they sprang from cover. Their war cries filled the chill air: "Hoka hey, hoka hey!" Two civilian Civil War veterans had accompanied the Fetterman party, and they used downed horses as a defensive breastwork. Firing sixteen-shot Henry rifles, they managed to slow the attack, but it wasn't enough. They were overwhelmed. Bugler Adolph Metzger was among the last soldiers alive. He used his bugle to beat off attackers until the instrument was a shapeless mass.

"Then followed a few quick volleys," Mrs. Grummond remembered, "then scattered shots, and then, dead silence." Arrowheads had thudded into bodies and war clubs had smashed into heads, wiping out Fetterman's command to the last man. One of the cavalrymen had taken along his pet dog. The dog came running out of the rocks, an arrow through its neck.

Back at the fort Colonel Carrington organized a relief column under Capt. Tenedore Ten Eyck to go to the aid of Fetterman's relief column, but when Eyck reached the crest of Lodge Trail Ridge, he saw there was little his men could do; the valley was swarming with hostiles. They had to wait until the Indians left the valley. As the soldiers watched helplessly, a few Indians searched the battlefield, salvaging some of the forty thousand arrows that had been fired.

Then the nervous search party eased over the ridge. Fetterman and his second-in-command, Capt. Fred Brown, lay close together, each shot in the temple at close range. They had killed one another rather than fall into Indian hands. Above Eyck's party a few Sioux and Cheyenne opened fire, and the cavalry slipped and scrabbled over ice trying to get to the top of the ridge to chase the Indians away. Gradually the braves began moving off toward the west.

None of Fetterman's command survived. Among those whose job it became to gather up the dead was young Private Guthrie:

[We found] the Fetterman boys huddled together on the small hill. . . . We packed them . . . on top of [the ammunition boxes in the wagons]. Terrible cuts left by Indians. Could not tell Cavalry from the Infantry. All dead bodies stripped naked, crushed skulls, with war clubs. Ears, nose and legs had been cut off, scalps torn away and the bodies pierced with bullets and arrows. Wrists, feet and ankles leaving each attached by a tendon.

For the army the Fetterman Massacre was a shocking debacle, and for two decades Washington suppressed Colonel Carrington's report. In it he spared no gory detail: "Eyes torn out and laid on rocks; noses cut off; ears cut out; chins hewn off; teeth chopped out." All had been scalped, except for two, whose heads had been placed in buffalo-skin bags as a signal dishonor reserved by the Sioux for cowardly enemies.

The Fetterman Massacre, as it was soon called, so reduced the garrison that Colonel Carrington was afraid his entire command might be destroyed. Despite a raging blizzard a miner—John "Portugee" Philips—who was staying at the fort, volunteered to ride the 235 miles to Fort Laramie to get reinforcements.

Within hours of the message reaching Fort Laramie, fresh troops rode toward Fort Kearny. It didn't stop the Sioux, however, and for a while travel along the Bozeman Trail was virtually halted. The *Montana Post* offered a solution: "If Indians continue their barbarities, wipe them out." General William Tecumseh Sherman, fresh from the Civil War back East, exploded. "We must act with vindictive earnestness against the Sioux," he said, "even to their extermination—men, women, and children."

The Fetterman Massacre of 1866 stunned the army almost as much as the Sand Creek Massacre of 1864 had pleased it.

In the summer of 1867 Red Cloud and a thousand Sioux warriors wearing their white and green warpaint attacked a thirty-six-man detail under Capt. James Powell near Fort Phil Kearny. Almost instantly four of the detail were killed, but the remainder made it to safety behind the wagons and used the wagon boxes to set up barricades. For nearly four hours Red Cloud's braves made charge after charge, running into almost continuous fire from the troopers, and charge after charge the Indians died in droves.

What they ran up against, what Red Cloud didn't know Powell's men had, were the new breech-loading Springfield rifles. No longer did the soldiers fire the slower muzzle-loaders. As Sgt. Samuel Gibson recalled, "Instead of drawing ramrods and thus losing precious time, we simply threw open the breech-locks of our new rifles to eject the empty shell and slapped in fresh ones." In the Civil War, Confederate soldiers had been slaughtered by the new weapon; now it was the Indians on the wrong side of the rifles. Thanks to the new Springfield rifles, and the fact that soldiers crouched behind wagon boxes, Powell's men managed to hold off Red Cloud's warriors until reinforcements arrived. Years later Red Cloud said he lost the flower of his fighting men in the Wagon Box Fight.

Red Cloud believed he'd suffered a fatal defeat. The government in Washington felt *it* had been defeated. General William T. Sherman, however, didn't agree with Washington. He proposed that hostile Indians "be punished with vindictive earnestness until at least 10 Indians are killed for each white life lost." Congress worried that further clashes with Indians in the northern plains would slow down, maybe even stop, westward expansion. In early 1868 the U.S. government sent a commission, including General Sherman and several other army generals, to Wyoming to draw up a treaty.

Some Sioux showed up to receive presents and sign the treaty, but mainly they were the same old bunch who had signed other agreements and who now sat around army forts looking for handouts. Red Cloud, however, sent a message that was both unmistakable and humiliating to the Great Father's emissaries: "We are on the mountains looking down on the soldiers and the forts. When we see the soldiers moving away and the forts abandoned, then I will come down and talk." Other Sioux—mainly the Hunkpapa and the Blackfoot from around the Powder, Upper Yellowstone, and Missouri Rivers—were equally unyielding.

A low-ranking chief named Gall signed the treaty, but most other Sioux ignored the document to which he'd affixed his signature. Crazy Horse wanted nothing to do with the treaty, and he gave his support to an alliance now coming under the command of Sitting Bull.

Finally, after much haggling over details and irrelevancies, the two sides reached agreement at Fort Laramie. Then, on November 4, to the surprise of some, Red Cloud came riding out of the hills with 125 war chiefs and headmen of the Oglalas, Hunkpapas, Miniconjou, and the Sans Arcs divisions of the Sioux. Sensing an advantage, Red Cloud had agreed to sign the treaty but demanded the army abandon its forts in Sioux country.

The terms of the Fort Laramie Treaty of 1868 covered six pages of fine print and were not easily understood by the Indian chiefs, who relied on interpreters. The treaty ceded back to the Indians all of South Dakota west of the Missouri River, including the Black Hills, an area to be called the Great Sioux Reservation. It returned to the Indians land between the Black Hills and the Big Horn Mountains in Wyoming and Montana. It gave Indians "absolute and undisturbed occupation" of the land until all the buffalo were gone. Whites were forbidden to enter the land.

Not only would the Indians not make war on the whites, they would not disturb the Union Pacific Railroad builders. On the Great Sioux Reservation they would take up farming and send their children to the white man's schools. They agreed to give up their buffalo ways and take up "civilization."

Little of the land was prime hunting ground, and that meant the Indians would have to rely on government-issue rations. Hunkpapa chief Sitting Bull had warned them what would happen, saying that those who signed the treaty were selling themselves short. He told his tribesmen, "You are fools to make yourselves slaves to a piece of some fat bacon, some hardtack, and a little sugar and coffee."

The United States had gone through four years of civil war, even more years of war with the Plains Indians. Now the nation seemed tired, so it agreed to terms. In the summer of 1868 the army abandoned Forts C. F. Smith, Phil Kearny, and Reno. As soldiers marched away from Fort Phil Kearny, they looked back and saw a band of Indians under Little Wolf setting fire to the buildings.

The Fort Laramie Treaty of 1868 carried a pious hope: "From this day forward, all wars between the parties to this agreement shall forever cease." "Forever," it seems, didn't last long in the Wild West. In this case forever lasted only a few months.

Like all other treaties between the United States government and Native Americans, this one was soon broken. In fact, it's still being broken today; Native Americans still insist that they should control the Black Hills.

Almost four years to the day after the 1864 Sand Creek Massacre, Chief Black Kettle again faced the U.S. Army. This time the bluecoats were led by a brash young officer who, when he was barely out of his teens during the Civil War, had been breveted to general: George Armstrong Custer.

George Armstrong Custer was born in New Rumley, Harrison County, Ohio, the child of Emanuel H. and Maria Ward Kirkpatrick Custer. Emanuel's great-great-grandfather, Paulus Kuster (or Kuester), apparently was the first of his lineage to settle in America. By the 1750s the family had settled in Maryland and changed their name to "Custer." Later they moved to Ohio, where, in 1828, Emanuel married twenty-four-year-old Matilda Viers. When Matilda died, Emanuel didn't wait long—not waiting long was the custom at the time—and soon married Maria Ward Kirkpatrick, the daughter of the town's tavern keeper. Like Emanuel, Maria had been married once before, and like Emanuel, her spouse had died in 1835. Both Emanuel and Maria had children from their first marriages. Emanuel was known around New Rumley as a Jacksonian Democrat, one of the area's starchiest supporters of "Old Hickory," Andrew Jackson. Around this time Emanuel owned a blacksmith forge and, thanks to his Democratic politicking, was elected as the local justice of the peace.

Three weeks before Christmas, on December 5, 1839, Maria gave birth to the couple's third child, a curly-haired, blue-eyed, healthy baby boy they named George Armstrong. They called him Armstrong, but in the first years of his life, as things go, he garbled his own name, and it came out sounding like "Autie." From them on, to family and close friends, he was known as Autie.

At the age of six Autie began attending a one-room log school in New Rumley. "He was," the teacher's son later claimed, "rather a bad boy in school, but one thing would be said of him: He *always* had his lessons, yet he was not considered an unusually bright lad." It seems George Armstrong "Autie" Custer *was* bright, but he hated homework and seldom completed his lessons beforehand. After learning to read he smuggled dime novels into class and, instead of his textbooks, read fictionalized versions of the real world.

When he was about sixteen, Autie did what most young men of his and any other age did: He turned his attention to girls, with whom, a cousin remembered, he was "quite a favorite." Briefly interrupting his own education, Custer took a job as a teacher, earning twenty-eight dollars a month at the Beech Point School in

Athens Township, Ohio. Apparently, he was popular. One of his students later wrote, "What a pretty girl he would have made." After a run-in with some of the larger male students, in the spring of 1856, Autie Custer quit teaching and returned to school himself, living in the home of the superintendent of an infirmary, Alexander Holland.

The Hollands had a teenaged daughter, named Mary Jane, or Mollie, and Autie fell passionately in love with her. He wrote her poems:

> I've seen and kissed that crimson lip
> With honied smiles o'erflowing
> Enchanted watched the opening rose
> Upon thy soft cheek flowing.
> Dear Mary, thy eyes may prove less blue,
> Thy beauty fade tomorrow,
> But oh, my heart can ne'er forget
> Thy parting look of sorrow.

Clearly seventeen-year-old George Armstrong Custer was in love. Just as clearly he was no great shakes of a poet.

Autie and Mollie talked about marriage, but it never came about. The two youngsters posed for separate daguerreotypes that they shared with each other—his shows Autie holding Mary Jane's picture in his hands. According to some Custer biographers Autie and Mary Jane also shared a bed. There's even speculation that, by the time he was twenty, Autie had shared the beds of at least two other women as well. At any rate, Alexander Holland believed there was more than bad poetry going on between Autie and his daughter, and he booted the boy out of his home.

Within a few months Custer tried for an appointment to the United States Military Academy at West Point. Not that a military career was what he hand in mind. He wrote a friend saying that he'd heard a graduate of West Point could earn a good living as a civilian. Why, one West Point graduate, Custer declared, was said to be worth two hundred thousand dollars.

One problem, however, was that Congressman John A. Bingham, to whom young Custer had to apply to get into West Point, was a Republican—the Republican Party was only two years old at the time.

"Of course [Autie] was a Democrat," Emanuel Custer said. "My boys all were Democrats." That August, Autie participated in a Democratic rally for presidential candidate James Buchanan, and six weeks later, at a Republican rally, Autie joined several other young men in marching against the Republican candidate, John C. Frémont. This didn't sit well with Congressman Bingham.

It was about then that Alexander Holland, who happened to be a staunch Republican, heard rumors about Autie and Mary Jane. Realizing that a West Point cadet could not be married, he recommended to Congressman Bingham that young Mr. Custer be given the West Point appointment. It was in this way that newly appointed U.S. secretary of war Jefferson Davis (the same Jefferson Davis who would become president of the rebellious Confederate States of America) notified George Armstrong Custer of his appointment to the academy. And early in June of that year Cadet Custer reported to the adjutant's office at what some call their "rockbound highland home" along the Hudson River. He and sixty-seven fellow plebes were admitted to the academy's Class of 1862. He would make it through, but not in the class of '62.

But neither did any of his classmates. By 1861 not only had almost half of those with whom Autie had begun studying at West Point dropped out or been kicked out, but by then the United States was at war. In addition to the regular class of '61, because of the Union army need for officers West Point graduated a second class. And on June 24, 1861, George Armstrong Custer graduated—thirty-fourth in his class of thirty-four.

In his career at West Point Custer compiled 726 demerits, the most in his class. His best subject his final year was artillery tactics. His worst was calvalry tactics. The army did then what it's noted for, appointed him to his least favorite subject: George became a lieutenant in the cavalry. Fellow Civil War officer Theodore Lyman wrote that Custer "looks like a circus rider gone mad!"

He wears a huzzar jacket and tight trousers of faded black felt trimmed with tarnished gold lace. . . . [The] General's coiffure [consists of] short, dry, flaxen ringlets! . . . [He] has a very merry blue eye, and a devil-may-care style.

* * *

With the Civil War over George Armstrong Custer was back to being a lieutenant colonel, though many of his 7th Cavalry troops still called him "general." On the morning of November 27, 1868, "Autie" Custer led his troops out of Fort Cobb, headed for Black Kettle's camp on the Washita River. As they marched out, Custer's band played "Garyowen" (or "Gary Owen," or "Gary Owens"), Custer's favorite battle song.* Black Kettle's village consisted of about forty-nine lodges and sat on the south side of the Washita River, about fourteen miles northwest of the present-day town of Cheyenne in Roger Mills County, western Oklahoma. The area is now part of the Black Kettle National Grasslands.

Other Indians had been raiding settlers' ranches, but Black Kettle had not. Never mind, Custer might have said, he was an Indian.

As dawn broke, Custer's band again played "Garyowen," or tried to. It was so cold, their instruments froze up within seconds. Then a rifle shot rang out. The bugler sounded "Charge!" and men cheered and rushed into the camp, jolting Black Kettle awake. He and his new wife together jumped on a pony and galloped for safety as the cavalrymen charged the village. Pistols fired, sabers slashed, and carbines blasted away. As Black Kettle and his wife reached the Washita, a bullet slammed into the chief's back. Another struck his wife, and together they fell dead into the icy stream.

"There was never a more complete surprise," Custer later reported. Still, the Cheyenne fought back as best they could, but it did little good. When "recall" was sounded about ten o'clock, the bodies of 103 Cheyenne men, women, and children lay dead after what became known as the Washita Massacre. One of the dead was Chief Little Rock. After the battle Custer took the buffalo skin and feather shield that Little Rock had worn in battle; later Custer presented it to a nature society in Michigan. He also gave them Little Rock's scalp.

---

*The title doesn't refer to an individual. Rather, it's a place. The phrase "Gary Owens" is a somewhat loosely Americanized pronunciation of the Gaelic for "Owen's Gardens." In Gaelic *garden* is *garrai*. The Irish troops turned the words around and "Owen's Gardens" became "Gary Owen." During the Civil War much of the 7th Cavalry was recruited from Irish immigrants, and they took the song with them.

Chief Little Rock had a daughter, about twenty years old, Me-o-tzi or Mo-nah-se-tah, as the whites called her. Her name meant "Young Grass That Shoots in Spring." For a month or two Custer took her along as an interpreter. Accounts describe her as a physically striking woman, with raven hair and "bright, laughing eyes." Custer's wife, Libbie, met the young woman and said she was "the acknowledged belle among all other Indian maidens." Custer himself called her "an enchanting comely squaw." He may also have called her to his bed.

When the cavalry returned to Fort Hays, Me-o-tzi joined other captured Indians in the stockade. In January 1869 she gave birth to a child. At the end of the year she gave birth to another child, a son. Me-o-tzi apparently was Custer's mistress, which means that when Custer gave Little Rock's scalp to that Michigan museum, he was giving away the hairlock of his child's grandfather.

Near the end of the Battle of the Washita, Maj. Joel Elliott saw a group of dismounted Indians trying to escape down the valley. He called for volunteers to join him in running down the Indians. The regimental sergeant major and eighteen others responded. As he turned to ride off, Elliott waved his hat and cried, "Here goes—for a brevet or a coffin." He got the latter.

Custer took control of the village and gathered prisoners while his men began an almost systematic destruction of all Indian property, including every one of the tribe's ponies, more than eight hundred animals. Outside the village, Indians from other villages appeared on the surrounding bluffs.

Custer sent a party under Capt. Edward Myers downriver looking for Major Elliott, but when the troops returned, the captain said they'd seen no signs of the missing personnel. Custer felt the twenty men were either lost or had escaped the Indians and still might return to the fort.

At any rate he had the safety of the entire regiment to consider, not just Elliott and his men. Custer abandoned the search for Elliott. The troop prepared its wounded and the band once more struck up "Garyowen." With guidons streaming Custer and his men rode off.

Captain Frederick W. Benteen of the 7th, never a friend to Custer, later charged that Autie had abandoned Major Elliott and his men.

Custer, of course, disagreed. Fred Benteen and George Custer continued their disagreement—jealousy is a more accurate word—until the Battle of the Little Big Horn.

More than a quarter of a century after the discovery at California's Sutter's Mill, gold fever spread into the Badlands of South Dakota. It's an area not nearly so oppressive as the name would have you believe, but it's bad enough.

Due west of the Badlands lies a growth of juniper and pine, a dark contrast to the bleached plains of the east. The Sioux call the area "Paha Sapa," literally "Hills Black."* Lakotas say a man followed the buffalo from Paha Sapa onto the northern plains, and there began their tribe. The Black Hills were sacred to both the Cheyenne and the Lakota Sioux. When this sacredness mixed with the white man's hunger for gold, the result was a long and bitter series of battles.

To the white man the Black Hills weren't sacred, but they were certainly mysterious. There, beyond the Platte River, life seemed to change dramatically. Suddenly one of civilization's bugaboos disappeared: there was no more cholera. It probably was due to the higher altitude, less congestion, and a ready availability of fresh water, but whatever the cause, it bewildered settlers.

In truth the Lakota themselves were relative newcomers to the Black Hills; they had been there for only a century or so. Still, the treaty of 1868 gave them the Black Hills.

In July 1874 more than a thousand soldiers, along with hundreds of wagons, dozens of Indian scouts, and even a trio of newspapermen, marched out of Fort Abraham Lincoln, near Bismarck, North Dakota, on the Missouri River. General Sherman, commander of the U.S. Army's Division of the Missouri, was sending a reconnaissance expedition into the hills under the command of Lt. Col. George Armstrong Custer. Custer's orders were to confirm or deny a rumor that the Black Hills were rich with gold. Well, of course the rumor

---

*Sometimes this is written "Pa Sapa," but that's an incorrect rendering. To the Lakota Sioux *pa* means "head," so *Pa Sapa* becomes "Head Black," or black head, something entirely different.

was true. The editor of the *Bismarck (North Dakota) Times* noted that the area of the Black Hills "bids fair to become the new El Dorado of America."

George Custer, who could never be described as self-effacing, wrote about his adventures for the *New York World,* claiming he had blazed a trail west, shooting deer and pronghorn antelope along the way. And, yes, he added, his men had found gold. Custer also wrote his wife, Libbie, saying, "We have discovered a rich and beautiful country," adding that "I have been Commanding Officer and everything else, especially guide."

Soon thousands of gold-hungry men and women followed the path that Custer and his men had laid out. But remember, the Fort Laramie Treaty of 1868 had given the Black Hills to Native Americans, specifying that whites would stay out.

Fast Bear, of the Oglala Sioux, called Custer's trail the "Thieves' Road." George Armstrong Custer was the "chief of the thieves."

The road to the Black Hills became worn deep and soon by fortune hunters. By the dozens mining camps sprang up: Lead City, Blacktail, Golden Gate, Deadwood, and of course, Custer City. While Fast Bear called it "Thieves' Road," whites called it the "Freedom Trail."

Before the Civil War America's economy primarily was rural and agricultural—cotton and tobacco in the South, dairy farms, produce farms, and timber in the North. Wheat was coming into importance in the West.

As the war progressed—perhaps *regressed* is a more appropriate word for any war—both North and South grew more industrial, especially the Union. Industries directly and indirectly related to the war were born, grew, and expanded. Europeans saw opportunities in America, and immigrants sailed off to New York, Boston, and other industrial cities. America was soon transformed from a nation of small farms to one of small but expanding factories.

Large steam engines ran whole factories. Land-grant railroads spanned the nation. Banks, newspapers, factories—they all expanded, and when expansion slowed down in the East, they began looking westward. It was the Gilded Age. The group we call the "robber barons"—J. Pierpont Morgan, Andrew Carnegie, the Vanderbilts, and the Rockefellers, ruthless and driven men all—amassed enormous wealth by monopolizing entire industries. There were Morgan's banks, Carnegie's steel, Vanderbilt's railroads, and Rockefeller's oil.

They were, says historian Paul Johnson, "ruthless, greedy, and selfish men who exploited the large-scale system of industrial capitalism, and the hapless millions employed in it, to enrich themselves and squander their wealth in 'conspicuous consumption.'" The robber barons lived in unparalleled luxury, while their workers lived in squalid company towns. Money was what they lived for, what they craved, what the robber barons virtually prayed to. "God gave me my money," John D. Rockefeller said: "I believe the power to make money is a gift from God." He added that he believed "it is my duty to make money and still more money and to use the money I make for the good of my fellowman according to the dictates of my conscience."*

The Gilded Age saw unprecedented acts of money making, money grabbing, and the theft of money. Not just in the industrialized East either. Many of the "new plutocracy," as critics called it, "were those who serviced the farming community." Charles H. and John Deere mass-produced modern plows, making lots of money for themselves as they did. Hog packers Edward Wells and Philip Danforth Armour and Philip's brother, Herman Ossian Armour. The Pillsburys of Minneapolis–St. Paul. Frederick Weyerhauser, whose mills provided quantities of lumber for western farmers. San Francisco grain dealer Henry Pierce and farm-machinery pioneer L. L. Baker, not to mention Cyrus McCormick himself. They made their fortunes in a highly competitive world, and it's sometimes asked, Who were the robber barons robbing? Well, perhaps their workers. Were they insensitive to their workers' problems? Well, in the words of William Vanderbilt, "The public be damned!"

The West offered untapped resources, and robber and would-be robber barons set out to tap them. That's when the Black Hills be-

---

*As if in answer to Rockefeller, Finley Peter Dunne, in *Mr. Dooley Says,* wrote, "He's kind iv a society f'r the previntion of croolty to money. If he finds a man misusing his money he takes it away fr'm him an' adopts it."

came important. In the twenty-five years since gold had been found at Sutter's Mill, California, each time a new source of revenue was discovered, hoards of people rushed in after it.

In April 1875 President Ulysses S. Grant bluntly laid down the law to a delegation of Sioux and Cheyenne summoned to Washington. "White people," he told them, "outnumber the Indians at least two hundred to one." If the Indians were so foolish as to resort to hostilities, Grant added, the American government would withhold reservation Indians' meat rations, which were, Grant said, simple gratuities to the Indians and "could be taken from them at any time."

Grant's words threatened the lives of thirty thousand Lakota, Arapaho, and northern Cheyenne, who lived on government reservations. Another thirty-five hundred Indians, however, had chosen not to take government handouts and ranged over hunting grounds to the West. To many whites these were "nontreaties," Indians who did not abide by treaties with whites. They had leaders with names such as Black Moon, Black Eagle, Rain-in-the-Face, and Crazy Horse.

The same Crazy Horse who had gained fame at the Fetterman Massacre back in 1866. The same Crazy Horse who had first counted coup at age fourteen during a raid on the Crow. No one had earned a greater reputation for bravery than had Crazy Horse. Once, during a battle with soldiers guarding a railroad crew along the Yellowstone River, Crazy Horse walked calmly between the lines and sat down. Bullets whizzed around him, but Crazy Horse filled his pipe, smoked it slowly, then passed it back and forth to his companions until the bowl was empty. Finally, he stood and walked away from the raging fight.

On September 17, 1875, a U.S. Senate commission rewrote the Black Hills Treaty. Over seven thousand Indians gathered at the council, and most of them were hostile. Many, including the warrior known as Little Big Man, expressed their scorn. On horseback he led a group of more than three hundred Indians into the council. They were painted for battle and chanted their song:

Black Hills is my land and I love it,
And whoever interferes
Will hear this gun.

* * *

"I will kill the first chief who speaks for selling the Black Hills," Little Big Man said, then he wheeled his horse and led his band away.

This may have stunned the senators, but it didn't stop them. "Gold is useless to you," the chairman said to the Indians, "and there will be fighting unless you give it up." He warned the assembled chiefs, "You should bow to the wishes of the Government which supports you." Another threat to cut off the food the government had coerced the reservation Indians into living on.

For three days Red Cloud and others told the senators their demands:

I want seven generations ahead to be fed. . . . These hills out there to the northwest we look upon as the head chief of the land. My intention was that my children should depend on these hills for the future. I hoped that we should live that way always.

For seven generations to come I want our Great Father to give us Texas steers for our meat. I want the Government to issue for me hereafter, flour and coffee, and sugar and tea, and bacon, the very best kind, and cracked corn and beans and rice and dried apples . . . and tobacco, and soap and salt and pepper for the old people. . . .

Then, he added: "Maybe you white people think that I ask too much . . . but I think those hills extend clear to the sky—maybe they go above the sky, and that is the reason I ask so much." Red Cloud realized that the white man was taking the Black Hills and all the gold it held. Now he was bargaining for the price.

After the Civil War America's only army was the Army of the Great Plains—underpaid, ill equipped, and overstretched. It was this army that Americans in the age of Manifest Destiny depended on to overcome Native Americans. The Indians were hardy, warlike, elusive, capable, and sometimes nomadic.

Some individuals, both military and civilian, thought the government in Washington City didn't go far enough toward exterminating Native Americans. The government's policy was to contain the Indians, and in 1866 the secretary of the interior wrote that "it has been the settled policy of the government to establish the various tribes upon suitable reservations and there protect and subsist them until they can be taught to cultivate the soil and sustain themselves." Lakota Sioux reservations in South Dakota and Montana totaled more land than did France or Spain, but the Lakota didn't want a France or a Spain. They wanted their traditional Great Plains hunting grounds, half a million square miles, nearly one sixth of the United States.

The southern Cheyennes knew of George Armstrong Custer, but only a few had actually seen him. The Lakotas had had a few run-ins with Custer before his expedition into the Black Hills. In fact, both Sitting Bull and Crazy Horse had fought Custer earlier. It happened on August 4, 1873, when Custer was far ahead of his military escort along the Yellowstone River. A large force of Indians attacked him. Their leaders: Sitting Bull and Crazy Horse. Custer and his 7th Cavalry got out of the jam thanks to the impetuousness of the attacking young warriors. The two Indian leaders didn't know their opponent was the man whose fame was growing as "Long Hair." In fact, even at the Battle of the Little Big Horn, Sitting Bull and Crazy Horse didn't know their attacker was Custer, and Custer wasn't sure who they were.

At approximately 12:15 on the afternoon of June 25, 1876, Custer led his troopers hot on the trail of a traveling band of Lakotas and Cheyennes. Custer was full of energy that day, conferring with his officers one minute, his scouts the next, then riding among his troops.

His men had ridden through the darkness the night before, not stopping to sleep, halting only at dawn to make coffee. During the night Arikara and Crow scouts saw them and talked among themselves about how foolish the blue coats were in preparing to attack a village as large as theirs.

Custer's military intelligence was so bad, he didn't know just how large the village was. About 2:15 that afternoon Custer's men discovered a lone tepee and, inside it, a dead Lakota warrior named Old She Bear, who'd been mortally wounded a few days earlier in a battle with Gen. George A. Crook. One Indian and he was dead; there didn't seem anything to worry about. Custer ordered Maj. Marcus A. Reno to get ready for a charge.

Earlier that day one of Custer's Indian scouts, a Crow named Half Yellow Face, said to Long Hair, "You and I are both going home today by a road we do not know." Another scout, Bloody Knife, made a sign to the sun and said, "I shall not see you go down behind the hills tonight." Both men had seen the massive herd of horses and the smoke from thousands of lodges not far off and knew they didn't have a chance. Custer called the scouts cowards.

And so Autie Custer rode off into the hills around the Little Big Horn. In truth the Indians on the other side of the hill weren't prepared for an attack by Custer and his 7th Cavalry, but Custer was even less prepared for them. The battle probably began shortly after five that afternoon. "It was done very quickly," remembered the widow of Spotted Horn Bull.

That charming young lieutenant colonel called "Autie" by his friends, "Long Hair" by his enemies, and "general" by many of his men, was only thirty-seven years old. Soon he was surrounded by a small group of his men on top of a rise now known as Custer Hill. Some reports say Custer also had a dog with him when they rode out of the fort—either a greyhound or a bulldog, it's not certain. He and his men generally had dogs along with them. This time, in the quiet of night before the attack, he'd ordered that all of the dogs be killed to prevent their alarming the Indians. Custer's horse, a sorrel named Vic, either ran off during the battle or Custer killed him and used Vic for breastworks.

Over the years Americans have pictured George Armstrong Custer in several, often revisionist, ways. At first he was a hero:

MASSACRED
GEN. CUSTER AND 261 MEN
THE VICTIMS.

NO OFFICER OR MAN OF 5
COMPANIES LEFT TO
TELL THE TALE

Later some saw his last stand as retribution for all crimes ever committed by whites against Indians. From best-selling books to wildly popular movies, we've pictured Custer in just about every way possible. The 1942 epic *They Died With Their Boots On* saw daredevil Errol Flynn do just what the title says. And more. In this telling of the tale George Armstrong Custer was out to stop the evil developers of the Black Hills, when, in truth, Custer himself started the Black Hills gold rush.

Actually, *They Died With Their Boots On* wasn't shot anywhere near the actual battle scene, but rather only a few miles outside Los Angeles—close enough for government work, as the old saying goes. As for the movie Indians, director Raoul Walsh used only sixteen Indians. Over and over and over.

In a final scene the script has Custer's wife, Libbie, visit Gen. Phil Sheridan to read a letter from her late husband. George, she reads, demanded the government make good its promise to Chief Crazy Horse; the Indians must be protected in their right to live in their own country. To which the movie Sheridan replies that he has the promise of the Grant administration—"from the president himself"—that Custer's wish will be carried out. It was, of course, the real President Grant who ordered the Indians out of the Black Hills. "Come, my dear," the movie Sheridan says to the movie Libbie Custer, "your soldier won his last fight after all." (Music up full: "Garyowen." They walk off together.)

The 1942 movie portrays Crazy Horse (actor Anthony Quinn in a ridiculous wig) as goofy looking and goofy talking. In real life Crazy Horse is one of Native Americans' most revered heroes.

Later portrayals of Custer weren't quite so nice as Errol Flynn's version, and some virtually come out and say Custer had it coming. Far different from the 1942 version of Long Hair, the 1970 hit movie *Little Big Man* has Custer reeling insanely around the Little Big Horn battlefield, shouting incoherent insults at the Indians close on his heels.

Outnumbered seven thousand (about two thousand of them warriors) to six hundred or so (more than two hundred at his side), George Armstrong Custer may have been backing up near the end, perhaps retreating, perhaps trying to find a more advantageous spot where he could await reinforcements. Up until Little Big Horn, George had won every clash he'd had with Indians, and this may have led him to believe that he could beat any Indian force of any size. Retreating? Never, defenders believe. Waiting for reinforcements? Don't bet your scalp on it. Indians survived by withdrawing, and Custer likely felt that if he waited for reinforcements, the enemy would get away; so, Charge! How did Custer know the Indians would stand and attack? It may be that what had been termed "Custer's luck" simply ran out at the Battle of the Little Big Horn.

At any rate, there Custer stood on Custer Hill, with forty or so of his men around him, blazing away at the oncoming Indians with his two self-cocking Bulldog pistols and his octagonal-barreled Remington Sporting Rifle. The only known survivor from the army's side was a horse named Comanche, belonging to Capt. Miles Keogh. It suffered at least seven wounds and was in pretty bad shape when relief squads found it. Still, Comanche was better off than the soldiers.

George Armstrong Custer, his brother Tom Ward Custer, and the entire command died. It had taken no more time than it took for the sun to travel the width of a lodgepole, as the Indians reckoned it. Fifteen minutes, as whites would say.

Whatever really happened in the battle, and it's likely we'll never really know for certain, Custer's death was not as romance poets and painters would have it, but then most deaths aren't. Just before leaving Fort Abraham Lincoln in North Dakota, Autie Custer had his hair cut short; long hair, he realized, got dirty quickly and it was impossible to keep groomed out in the field. "Long Hair" died without the flowing locks of his pictured youth. By the time of the Battle of the Little Big Horn, George Armstrong Custer was growing bald. In fact, he had so little hair, the Indians apparently didn't think his scalp was worth taking.

"Oh, how white they look!" Capt. Thomas Weir of the burial detail exclaimed. That probably was an exaggeration, because the bodies of Custer's last command would have been grimy with dust and gunpowder, bruised and battered and bloodied. After the battle young Indian boys had ridden among the soldiers, shooting arrows at any who still moved. Then the women came along with hatchets and knives and hammers. One soldier, the Indians said, had been playing dead, but when the old women stripped his clothes off and began cutting at him, he jumped up, began fighting with them, and tried to run off. A funny sight, an Indian reported, a naked white man fighting with two fat old women. Another woman stabbed him dead. Later two young girls ran into the Indian camp, swinging the severed head of an Indian. It was Bloody Knife, Custer's Arikara scout. As he had foretold, he did not see the sun set that day.

In the Southwest, the "land of little rain," as it's called, a band of Native Americans known to themselves as "N'de" or "Dine" (in English it means "people") ruthlessly drove out other Indians who'd long been in the region, the Comanche and the Zuni. This new tribe was known by the Zuni word for enemy, *apachu,* the Apache.

Even the steel-helmeted Spanish and their black-robed priests could not conquer the Apache. They were, historian Dee Brown puts it, "unrepentant and exceedingly skillful sinners." U.S. Army captain John Pope referred to them as sneak thieves who were never known to attack more than ten men at a time. Fighting and running, Pope claimed, were the Apache's way of making war.

For years the Mimbres Apache's greatest chief was Mangas Coloradas (Red Sleeves)—tall, muscular, gifted with uncommon intellect, and dynamic. His band ranged over southwest New Mexico, raiding others in the densely forested mountains around the head of the Gila River and across deserts studded with barren mountain peaks and dry salt lakes.

To the west, in what would soon become the Arizona Territory, Chiricahua Apaches occupied a rocky mountain chain. Their leader: Cochise.

The Mimbres and Chiricahua Apaches watched but apparently did little harm to settlers on the road between the Rio Grande and Tucson. When the Butterfield stagecoaches appeared on the scene, the Indians offered no opposition, and Cochise even supplied firewood to the stage station at Apache Pass.

Once they'd run off their Indian competitors, the Apaches were at peace. That all changed in 1861. A band of Pinal Apaches kidnapped a young boy, and the army blamed Cochise. Cochise had nothing to do with it, so when a 7th Cavalry unit, under Lt. George N. Bascom, camped near Apache Pass, Cochise willingly went to the lieutenant's tent for a talk. Bascom had other ideas, and his men tried to arrest Cochise. The chief fought back and, using his knife, cut his way through Bascom's tent, fighting his way to freedom. However, soldiers seized Cochise's companions as hostages—five of the chief's relatives who'd been outside the tent waiting for him. In turn Cochise captured a Butterfield station attendant and two travelers on the road through Apache Pass and tried to exchange them for his relatives. Bascom refused, and Cochise massacred the drovers of a small freight train making its way through the pass, waylaid but failed to stop a stagecoach, then attacked a group of soldiers watering stock. For two weeks the two sides threatened each other but took no action, then Cochise and his band took off for Mexico. Behind him he left the mutilated bodies of the white hostages. In retaliation the army hanged from a scrub oak tree three of the Indian hostages.

This all served to set Cochise against whites for the rest of his life. "I was at peace with the whites," he said, "until they tried to kill me for what other Indians did; now I live to die at war with them."

In the summer of 1862 Cochise and Mangas Coloradas gathered their warriors along Apache Pass, hoping to ambush a party of soldiers. But the soldiers saw them and wheeled out their big guns, opening fire on the Indians, stopping the attack before it could really get going. The next day the Indians tried again to attack, but again army troops opened fire and drove off the Indians.

During the fight Mangas Coloradas was shot and his followers took him down the mountain to Janos, Chihuahua, in Mexico, where they forced a doctor to dig the bullet out of the chief's chest. By the following January, Mangas Coloradas was back leading his men, this time against a group of Pinos Altos miners.

Under a white flag army troops lured the Apache chief to a parley, but the soldiers seized the Indian and held him prisoner. That night, as he slept next to a campfire, the guards heated bayonets and touched them to his feet. When Mangas Coloradas jumped up in protest, he was shot down—killed, his captors said, while attempting to escape. Now, the fight fell to Cochise.

He took no side during the Civil War, raiding both Union and Confederate forces. But with the Union Army's attention focused elsewhere, the Apaches robbed, killed, and harassed white citizens until the interlopers abandoned their homes and huddled together in the towns of Tucson and Tubac. The Chiricahua Apaches attacked stagecoaches, miners, and soldiers. They emptied entire towns of frightened settlers.

Only once did the settlers really fight back, and in that instance they killed 128 unarmed Indians. Before it was all over more than 4,000 people—Indians and whites—died in the continuing war.

In 1871 Cochise met with Gen. Gordon Granger at the Indian agency at Canada Alamosa. After nervously smoking a pipe of peace with the Indian, General Granger said that his government wanted to live in peace with the Apaches. They would, Granger said, give Cochise mountains and valleys in Tularosa in the Mogollon Mountains as a reservation; it would be their home forever. But the Apaches must remain at peace, steal no stock, raid no settlements, and—oh, yes—let white settlers take over the rest of the country.

After retiring with his followers to talk it over Cochise returned and told the general:

When I was young I wandered all over this country, east and west, and saw no other people than the Apaches. After many summers I walked again, and found another race of people had come to take it. How is it? I will not lie to you; do not lie to me. I want to live in these mountains. I do not want to go to Tularosa. That is a long way off. The flies on those mountains eat out the eyes of the horses. The bad spirits live there. I have drunk of these waters and they have cooled me; I do not want to leave here.

When other Chiricahua Apaches were removed to Tularosa Valley, Cochise and his warriors returned to their home in southern Arizona. There, a tall, red-bearded man named Tom Jeffords won Cochise's trust. They mingled blood, and Jeffords talked him into ending his antiwhite campaign.

In 1872 the U.S. Army's one-armed "praying general," Oliver Otis Howard, rode boldly into Cochise's stronghold in the Dragoon Mountains. In sessions of tense negotiations Howard made peace with the Apache leader. For the first time since Lieutenant Bascom's blunder eleven years earlier, in 1861, Cochise and his warriors posed no danger to settlers in the Southwest.

The friendship between Cochise and Tom Jeffords lasted until 1876, and the last time they met was while Cochise lay on his deathbed. The old Indian was worried and wondered if they would ever meet again. Jeffords said he didn't know. "My thoughts on this thing are not clear," Cochise replied. "I have this feeling, a feeling that fills my heart, that somewhere up there"—and he pointed to the smokehole of his wickiup and to the sky above—"we will meet again, my friend."

Within two hours Cochise died, apparently in peace. He was sixty-three.

At Cochise's instance Tom Jeffords had become the government's agent for the reservation, but by January 1877 the military had taken over administration of the Chiricahua lands and began a policy of allowing ranchers and prospectors to invade the territory. Jeffords resigned in anger and refused any other form of government employment until 1886, when he briefly acted as an army scout. After that he couldn't settle down to a regular job. Finally he became a caretaker at a mine, and he lived in a nearby shack, surrounded by a cactus-dotted wilderness, until 1914, when he died. He's buried in a Tucson cemetery, his grave and marker erected in 1964 by the Daughters of the American Colonists.

It likely wasn't until the Spanish arrived, more likely not even until after the English stepped ashore, that Native Americans began using firearms. As soon as they could, Indians traded for or stole muskets, sometimes taking them as spoils of war. Like the settlers themselves this new weapon went from east to west. Still, firearms and ammunition were scarce to Indians in the Wild West.

Well into the late nineteenth century Plains Indians continued using bows and arrows, especially in hunting buffalo and other game, where they were the Indians' weapon of choice. For many Indians they were not only weapons to be used against the enemy or to hunt game but were sacred gifts from the Creator. Traditional Indian healers incorporated arrows into their rituals, and their medicine was believed to be especially powerful. For example, "arrow shamans" were medicine men who could cure arrow wounds with "arrow medicine."

Even though Comanches had firearms from about the middle of the 1700s, they continued to use iron-tipped arrows. A warrior could use a silent bow and arrow from ambush, without revealing his hiding place. A silent attack was also good in hunting animals; just as with human targets, several animals might be brought down before others in the herd realized what was going on.

Not only were arrows powerful religious symbols and powerful medicine, not only could a hunter or warrior fire them in silence, they were a renewable resource. Native Americans might not be able to manufacture bullets, but they had no trouble making arrowheads: from chipped stone (flint or obsidian), deer and elk antlers, oyster- and clamshells, bones, metal, and even some varieties of hardwood. A good arrowhead maker could chip one out of flint in less than ten minutes.

Occasionally, Indians followed the practice of some tribesmen in South America and Africa and dipped arrowheads into snake venom. Or they used plant poisons and even putrid animal matter. They didn't know about microbes and germs and such, but they knew someone shot with a contaminated arrow got sicker than the victim of a nondipped arrow.

Army doctors carried special surgical instruments they used to extract arrowheads: a wire loop inserted into the wound and a surgical knife with a special blade. Surgeons even used an unusual, but apparently effective, method of removing arrows: They'd place a heavy pile of books on the patient's chest, forcing the ribs apart, allowing the surgeon to get a better grip on the arrow.

At least once, when a man was shot in the head with an arrow, surgeons sawed nearly all the way through the victim's skull, finally reaching the arrowhead, then removed it. Four days later the soldier returned to duty.

Of course not all such unusual methods worked so well. Take the case of Salvador Martínez, a civilian working with the army. An arrow entered his chest between the fifth and six ribs. Physician J. H. Bill removed the arrow and gave Martínez an enema. The patient died.

In 1877 the government opened to white settlement a portion of the Nez Percé Reservation in Idaho. The tribe rebelled, and fighting broke out. Chief Joseph, however, tried to flee to Canada with a band of about seven hundred—all but two hundred of them women, children, and old men. He almost made it. They'd been ready to move onto the reservation when a small band of frustrated young warriors attacked local settlers, killing at least eighteen whites. Knowing the U.S. Army would retaliate, Chief Joseph led his band across the mountains.

Three columns of troops pursued them. For fifteen hundred miles Joseph and his fellow chiefs—primarily Looking Glass and Joseph's younger brother Ollokot, who likely were even greater commanders than Joseph—outmaneuvered, outsmarted, and outshot the army. Captain David Perry and the Mount Idaho Volunteers were sent to stop the renegade band. Perry wired his superiors, "Think we will make short work of it." When the Volunteers approached the Nez Percé camp at White Bird Canyon on the Salmon River, Chief Joseph sent out a party under a flag of truce, hoping to avoid bloodshed. The Volunteers opened fire, a mistake if there ever was one. With that, as Joseph's follower Yellow Wolf recalled, "it was just like two bulldogs meeting." Thirty-three soldiers died in the fight, while just three members of Chief Joseph's band were killed. Meanwhile, the Nez Percé captured sixty-three rifles and stores of ammunition. "I have been in lots of scrapes," one army scout remembered, but "I never went up against anything like the Nez Percés in my life."

After that Chief Joseph dodged when he could, fought when he was cornered. And troops of the U.S. Army relentlessly followed him. Finally, cold, hunger, and Gen. Nelson Miles (who took over Custer's command after the Battle of the Little Big Horn) ended the march in the Bear Paw Mountains, thirty miles short of the Canadian border. In a five-day battle both Looking Glass and Ollokot were killed. On October 5, under snowy skies, Chief Joseph surrendered.

Through an interpreter Joseph told Gen. Oliver Otis Howard:

It is cold, and we have no blankets. The little children are freezing to death. My people, some of them, have run away to the hills, and have no blankets, no food. No one knows where they are—perhaps freezing to death. I want to have time to look for my children, and see how many of them I can find. Maybe I shall find them among the dead. Hear me, my chiefs! I am tired. My heart is sick and sad. From where the sun now stands I will fight no more, forever.

CHAPTER NINE

America's Black West:
Buffalo Soldiers and Maroons

It has been an honor which I am proud to claim to have been at one time a member of that intrepid organization of the Army which has always added glory to the military history of America—the 10th Cavalry.
General John J. "Black Jack" Pershing

I went riding over the ground where we had fought the first soldiers during [the Battle of the Little Big Horn]. I saw by the river, on the west side, a dead black man. He was a big man. All his clothing was gone when I saw him. Some Sioux told me he belonged to their people but was with the soldiers.
Unidentified Indian speaking about Isaiah Dorman, part Sioux, part African American, a scout with Custer's 7th Cavalry

For years many Americans used an herbal medicine that grew wild in areas of the East. The root was made into a tonic that its proponents claimed increased their energy and kept them mentally alert. As settlers moved west, they overpicked the root, and soon it was almost extinct in the United States. Until the 1990s, that is. Now it's grown in several parts of America. Today it's even more popular than when America was trekking westward: ginseng.

Immigrants by the millions came to the United States, and here we resort to figures to illustrate how much our demographics changed over the years. In pre–Civil War America, the largest number of immigrants came in 1854: 427,833 individuals. In 1870 that figure dropped to 387,203; however, in 1873 immigration increased, as 459,803 souls entered America's gates. Eighteen eighty-two saw a new record: 788,992. Then things really got busy. Seven times between 1883 and 1903 the number of immigrants totaled one million or more. In a single year! In 1892 East Coast immigration centered at New York's Ellis Island, where, in 1907, an all-time high of 1,285,349 souls came knocking at America's door.

Between 1860 and 1900 more than thirteen and a half million immigrants cleared Ellis Island. Between 1900 and 1930 another thirteen million arrived. In a seventy-year period more immigrants entered the United States than lived in the country at the time of Abraham Lincoln's first election.

Faces and accents and economic status, they all changed as migrants from throughout the world arrived in America. In 1860 thirteen percent of America's population was foreign born. By 1910 that figure was up to fifteen percent.

Many European- and Asian-born immigrants had been peasants in highly stratified societies. In America, a newcomer from Norway boasted, "even a tramp can enjoy a chicken dinner once in a while." Another seemed amazed that "my cap [is not] worn out from lifting it in the presence of gentlemen."

Although there might have been more economic equity inside America, *who* immigrated to the United States remained *un*equal. Europeans flocked to America, but the United States firmly shut its door to the Chinese with the Exclusion Act of 1882. When the government stopped immigrants coming from China, that presented a problem for California farms and mines: where to get cheap labor? The answer: Japan. America's closed-door policy for the Chinese cut off "yellow" farmworkers from China, and the Japanese took up the slack.

All too soon those who had come to America last month began to hate those who came last week. "A while ago it was the Irish," author Robert Louis Stevenson wrote in 1892, "now it is the Chinese that must go."

It seems, after all, that no country is bound to submit to immigration any more than to invasion. . . . Yet we may regret the free tradition of the republic, which loved to depict herself with open arms, welcoming all unfortunates. And certainly, as a man who believes that he loves freedom, I may be excused some bitterness when I find her sacred name misused in the connection.

America, however, was returning to an almost pre-Revolution outlook. It became obvious that the only difference between a seventeenth-century "colonist" and a nineteenth-century "immigrant" was one of timing. Yet, whether looked on by "immigrant" or "colonist," two groups always seemed to be excluded, Native Americans and African Americans. One group had their homes stolen, and the other was stolen itself.

Pedro Alonzo Niño was in Christopher Columbus's crew that arrived in 1492. He was said to be black. Other Africans sailed with Columbus on later voyages, and still more came to the New World with other European explorers.

The Spanish saw them as useful and dangerous at the same time. In 1501 a royal ordinance gave official sanction to importing African slaves to Hispaniola. When some of those slaves slipped away, the Spanish gave them the name "maroons," after a word for runaway. In 1503 Governor Ovando of Hispaniola complained to King Ferdinand that maroons living among the natives had taught the Indians some bad customs. "They never would," he said, "be captured."

When the Conquistadors went exploring, blacks went with them, and in 1513 Balboa's men included thirty Africans, who hacked their way through the lush vegetation of Panama to reach the Pacific Ocean. By 1600 more than ninety thousand blacks had been stolen, bought and sold, and shipped to Latin America. In 1619 the first boatload of blacks were sold as indentured servants at the new English colony at Jamestown. When Indians massacred the Virginia colony in 1622, they "murdered every white [they could] but saved the Negroes." To the dismay of slaveholders blacks and Indians had begun to unite as allies and families.

One African whose name went down in New World history early on was born in Morocco and became the servant of one Andres Dorantes. He was known as Stephen or Estevanico or Estéban Dorantes. He arrived in the New World in 1527, explored Florida, and later looked for Cíbola, the "Seven Cities of Gold" that so enthralled the Spanish in the Southwest. He was the first non-Indian, non-European to explore Arizona and New Mexico, and legends of his journey stimulated the explorations of Coronado and de Soto.

Jean Baptiste Pointe du Sable was Paris educated but became known for his skill as a fur trapper in America. For sixteen years du Sable lived at the mouth of the Chicago River, where he built a business and took to his crude log cabin a Potawatomi Indian woman named Catherine. They were married in 1788 after the couple had a son and a daughter. Du Sable claimed eight hundred acres of land near the present Peoria, Illinois, but considered Chicago his home. There he built a forty-by-twenty-two-foot log house, a bakehouse and dairy, a smokehouse and chicken yard. He was a miller, a cooper, and whatever else was needed around his settlement.

Du Sable hoped to become chief of a neighboring Indian tribe, but failed. In 1800, perhaps because of his defeat, he sold his Chicago property for twelve hundred dollars. Two things he hoped not to do: become a public charge and be buried in a Catholic cemetery. As an old man du Sable finally had to ask for public relief, but when he died, he was buried, not in a Catholic cemetery, but in St. Charles Borromeo Protestant Cemetery.

York was a black slave who traveled with his white master, William Clark, in the Lewis and Clark exploration of the vast Louisiana Purchase. While among the Mandans of South Dakota, Clark "ordered my black Servant to Dance which amused the crowd very much, and Somewhat astonished them, that So large a man"—York was over six feet tall and weighed more than two hundred pounds—"should be active."

Native Americans were aware of the white man; after all, they'd seen mountain men for years. But a man with black skin? This startled the Indians. On March 8, 1705, Le Borgne, the grand chief of the Minnetaree Indians, came to visit the Corps of Discovery at the Mandan village where they were wintering. "The Chief," Meriwether Lewis recorded in his journal, "observed that some foolish young men of his nation had told him there was a person among us who was quite black, and he wished to know if it could be true." York appeared and Le Borgne was dumbfounded; he examined the black man closely, "spit on his [own] finger and rubbed [York's] skin in order to wash off the paint." When York uncovered his head, the Indian chief was astounded by the man's short curly hair. Still, Le Borgne didn't believe what he saw; York, he felt, was simply a painted white man.

Over the years of the expedition York "participated largely" in sexual encounters with Indian women. When Arikara women and children gathered around York, the slave had fun with them, often claiming that he'd been a wild animal William Clark had caught and tamed. Then York let out a roar, scaring the children but apparently fascinating the women.

Meriwether Lewis believed that York's color "seemed to procure him additional advantages from the [Indian women], who desired to preserve them some memorial of this wonderful stranger." Reportedly, York did just that and sired a number of mixed-blood offspring during the three-year expedition.

After the long journey from St. Louis to the Columbia River and back, Clark freed York. According to legend York immediately headed back out West, where he became chief of an Indian tribe, finding freedom in the wilderness he helped explore.

In the wake of the Civil War, with war-created jobs in the North drying up and poverty and oppression staring them in the face in the post-Reconstruction South, many African Americans became convinced that there was no place for them in the East. They believed the West offered them multiple opportunities. The 1870s and '80s saw thousands of blacks go west.

The first popular movement out of the South was headed by a man who believed that he'd been appointed by God to rescue his people, Benjamin "Pap" Singleton. He'd been a slave in Tennessee but ran away and was caught a dozen times before finally making his way to Canada on the underground railroad.

His followers called themselves "Exodusters"; like the Old Testament Hebrews they believed that their salvation lay in reaching a promised land. For many this "promised land" was Kansas, and there they set up farms, businesses, and other professions. They sent home hopeful letters to be read aloud in black churches.

The movement west was aided when a rumor raced through African-American communities: The federal government had set aside all of Kansas for former slaves, and every black family who reached there would be given free land and five hundred dollars. The rumor—and it was only that—got its start in 1877, when former slave L. W. Ballard wrote Mississippi lawmaker Blanche K. Bruce, saying, "We are not Africans now, but Colored Americans, and are entitled to American citizenship." Another correspondent told Senator Bruce that, if blacks could not enjoy citizenship "among the white people," then the government should set aside "one of the States or Territories" for their settlement.

That solution might, of course, have relegated African Americans to a condition not unlike that which Indians fought *against*: confinement to reservations. It didn't much matter, however, because Congress took no action on the idea.

In the late 1870s African Americans took up the cry of internal emigration. A group of Mississippi freedmen proposed moving en masse to New Mexico or Arizona. Another group circulated pamphlets describing land available in Nebraska under the Homestead Act.

In 1860 Abraham Lincoln had campaigned on a platform of providing homesteads out West. Two years after his election the act marched through Congress. It offered settlers 160 acres of already surveyed public land, virtually free at a dollar fifty an acre for anyone living on the property for six months, and totally free if the settler lived there for five years or more. As a result of the Homestead Act the West developed more rapidly than it would have without free land. Kansas became a state in 1861, Nevada in 1864, and Nebraska in 1867. Meanwhile the Dakotas and Colorado were officially developed as territories and, by 1870, Arizona, Idaho, Montana, and Wyoming were on their way to statehood.

Not all African American leaders approved of black emigration to the West. Frederick Douglass opposed it, saying that doing so would tacitly be abandoning the struggle for citizenship rights in the South. "Pap" Singleton, however, set up a real estate company and circulated lithographs depicting black farmers surrounded by livestock and abundant crops and showed them lassoing buffalo on the open range. Singleton claimed that he'd been responsible for the "Exodus of 1879." "I am the whole cause of the Kansas migration!" he claimed, and many believed him. Singleton's Exodus caused violence in the South, resentment in the North, and led Congress to launch an investigation. After seventeen hundred pages of testimony the Senate declared that it wasn't a Republican conspiracy that was making blacks leave the South, but white oppression and the dream of owning land in Kansas.

Later, however, Singleton and other black leaders advised those leaving the South not to head toward Kansas. Many settlers were poor, and Kansas's relief facilities were already strained, but Kansas residents collected more than a hundred thousand dollars to aid the newcomers. Much of those funds came in the form of Staffordshire pottery donated for sale. Meat packer Philip Armour toured Wyandotte, Kansas, near Kansas City, and collected twelve hundred dollars in donations from Chicago industrialists; he sent that and beef from his plant to the Exodusters.

By 1880 more than fifteen thousand African Americans had migrated to Kansas. However, since most lacked either the funds or the experience to take up farming on the plains, they wound up working menial jobs in small towns—Juniper Town, Dunlap, and Rattlebone Hollow. About the only black settlement from the Exodus of 1879 that remains today is the town of Nicodemus, and its early days were tough. Settlers spent their first winter there in dugouts, unable to build homes until the following spring. They were hit by repeated crop failures, and as if that weren't enough, searing winds whipped across the town, blowing away much of what few crops remained in Nicodemus. The rest of Kansas was untouched. As one minister active in the movement west put it, "We had to suffer and be free."

Suffer they did in other areas as well. A crowd of whites drove 150 ex-Mississippi blacks out of Lincoln, Nebraska. In Denver, Exodusters found that "the owners of houses would not rent to them."

Like their men, black women made their mark on the American frontier. "The mountains were free and we loved them," recalled Dr. Ruth Flowers of Boulder, Colorado. "Black women," she said, "were the backbone of the church, the backbone of the family, they were the backbone of the social life, everything." Mothers sought to rescue themselves and their children from areas where they were denied education and which restricted their lives while ignoring white terrorism. Testifying before a congressional committee in 1879, Louisiana state senator John Burch, who was black himself, said, "The women have had more to do with [the Exodus] than all the politics and the men."

By 1910 the black population of the West had nearly doubled in some states, and in Washington, Oregon, and California it had increased to five times what it had been in 1870. Just as white settlers had, African American pioneers learned the frontier was no El Dorado. They went looking for land opportunity and equality, but in the end they often found neither.

As more towns were built in the West, more laws were enacted, and—perhaps especially—more white women arrived, racial barriers were hoisted and segregation reentered black lives. As an example, black cowboys who'd been able to drink at bars side by side with their white saddle-mates now had to gather at one end of the bar. The racial patterns of the East had traveled across bumpy roads to the open prairies, and discrimination and segregation became, as one author puts it, "as commonplace as the Sears Roebuck catalog."

The first man shot in Dodge City was a black cowboy named Tex, an innocent bystander to a fight between two whites. A black cowboy had the dubious honor of being the first to be housed in Abilene's new stone jail. Trouble was, he was innocent, and when the rest of his trail crew found out he'd been hauled in, they shot up the town. Therefore, the first man jailed in the new facility became the first to break out of it when the trail hands set him free.

Historian Kenneth Wiggins Porter says that black cowboys probably suffered less from discrimination than did African Americans in any other job open equally to blacks and whites. Still, African-American cowboys were almost invariably referred to by such names as "Nigger John" and frequently faced social discrimination. In 1878, for example, a trail crew driving a herd from Texas to Kansas hired a black cowboy. A white cowboy named Poll Allen objected to the new man and wouldn't let him eat or sleep with the rest of the hands. Finally, the obviously racist Allen fired shots at the black man and drove him off.

Although they were discriminated against, black cowboys usually worked it out just the same as white cowboys did—they relied on a combination of good humor, fists, and six-guns. Historian William Loren Katz says that "oddly enough, clashes between the black and white cowboys themselves were rare."

Longtime trail boss Charles Goodnight praised Bose Ikard, who for years was a top hand:

> His behavior was very good in a fight, and [he] was probably the most devoted man to me that I ever had. I have trusted him farther than any living man. He was my detective, banker, and everything else in Colorado, New Mexico, and any other wild country I was in.

There obviously *was* prejudice, even if Goodnight didn't recognize it. "When we carried money," he said, "I gave it to Bose, for a thief would never think of robbing him—never think of looking in a Negro's bed for money."

Just as in other areas of the country in the nineteenth century, the West offered blacks little chance for upward social mobility. Cowboy Jim Perry worked for twenty years at the giant XIT—the Ten in Texas outfit.* At one point the XIT included seven divisions or ranges, each requiring a foreman. "If it weren't for my damned old black face," the African-American Perry claimed, "I'd have been boss of one of these divisions long ago." As it was, Jim Perry ended his days on the ranch as a cook.

African-American Bill Pickett came out of Taylor, Texas, and may have invented "bulldogging," as the art of jumping off a running horse and wrestling a steer to the ground is called. In 1880, when he was only thirteen years old, Pickett hired on to the 101 Ranch in Oklahoma. It was there, about seven years later, while touring with the Miller and Lux 101 Wild West Show, that Pickett bulldogged his first steer. As Zake Miller of the 101 Ranch told it, Pickett "slid off a horse, hooked a steer with both hands on the horns, twisted its neck, and then sunk his teeth into the steer's nostrils to bring him down." Bill said he'd seen bulldogs do the same, and that's why he gave it the name "bulldogging." The technique, incidentally, no longer is allowed on the rodeo circuit as being too dangerous. For the steers.

---

*Owned by the Capitol Freehold Land and Investment Company, or the Capital Syndicate, it was the Ten in Texas ranch because it supposedly covered ten Texas counties, but in truth, it was only nine.

For a while Pickett traveled with movie star Tom Mix and humorist Will Rogers as the show went around the country. Several times Bill took his act out of the country, appearing in England and Mexico. In Mexico Pickett took on a bullfighting bull. And won. In 1932, however, he was kicked by an unbroken horse and died eleven days later.

Perhaps the most famous African American cowboy in the Wild West was Nat Love. Born a slave in 1854 in a cabin in Tennessee, several years after the Civil War, Love, as he said, "struck out for Kansas." At the time he was just fifteen years old. He became a cowboy and remained one until 1890. Nat Love told how he got into the game outside Dodge City:

Approaching a party who were eating their breakfast, I got to speak with them. They asked me to have some breakfast with them, which invitation I gladly accepted. They proved to be a Texas outfit who had just come up with a herd of cattle and having delivered them, were preparing to return. There were several colored cowboys among them, and good ones too. After breakfast I asked the camp boss for a job as a cowboy. He asked if I could ride a wild horse. I said, "Yes, sir." He said, "If you can, I will give you a job."

So he spoke to one of the colored cowboys called Bronko Jim, and told him to go out and rope old Good Eye, saddle him and put me on his back. Bronko Jim gave me a few pointers and told me to look out, for the horse was especially bad at pitching. I told Jim I was a good rider and not afraid of him; I thought I had rode pitching horses before, but from the moment I mounted Good Eye I knew I had not learned what pitching was. This proved the worst horse to ride I had ever mounted in my life, but I stayed with him and the cowboys were the most surprised outfit you ever saw, as they had taken me for a tenderfoot, pure and simple.

Love got the job and was paid thirty dollars a month. The trail boss asked him his name, but when he answered, "Nat Love," the boss said to the other cowboys, "We'll call him Red River Dick." The name stuck with Love for the better part of a generation, during which he took part in drives guiding Texas beef northward.

In 1876, when the outfit arrived in Deadwood, South Dakota, at the end of the drive, the hands joined in a rodeo. Nat Love won several roping and shooting contests. "Right there," Love wrote in his autobiography, *Life and Adventures,* "the assembled crowd named me 'Deadwood Dick'* and proclaimed me champion roper of the Western cattle country."

Nat Love obviously wasn't just your run-of-the-mill serious cowpoke. He once tried to rope and steal an army cannon, and it took his good friend Bat Masterson to get him out of that scrape. In his autobiography, which sometimes reads like a Deadwood Dick dime novel, Love told how he rode into a Mexican saloon one day and ordered two drinks, one for him and one for his horse. He admitted to losing "all courage" in his first fight with Indians but claimed that after a few shots, he "lost all fear and fought like a veteran." Even considering that the longer his story went, the more boastful he got, Nat Love's story is still fascinating. "I carry the marks of fourteen bullet wounds on different parts of my body," he bragged, "most any one of which would be sufficient to kill an ordinary man, but I am not even crippled." He had horses shot from under him and "men killed around me, but I always escaped with a trifling wound at the worst."

Nat Love claimed many things: That he was adopted by a tribe of Indians, that he rode a hundred miles in twelve hours (on an unsaddled horse, at that), and that he knew Billy the Kid and Billy's killer, Pat Garrett. Well, maybe.

What is true is that he was just one of many black cowboys who rode, roped, whored, and sang right along with all the rest. It's also

---

*Nat Love claimed that he was the "real" Deadwood Dick, but it's not likely. There were several other men with that nickname, including Richard Clarke, who claimed to be the model for dime novels of the day. In 1860 the publishing house of Beadle and Adams began printing dime novels—the first, *Set Jones,* or *The Captives of the Frontier,* sold more than half a million copies—featuring a Wild West background. The company's "Deadwood Dick Library" included thirty-three Deadwood Dick books and ninety-seven others about Deadwood Dick Jr. There were so many Deadwood Dick books sold that the reading audience assumed there had to be a real hero of the West.

true that age and the iron horse caught up with Nat Love. Coast-to-coast railroads made long cattle drives unnecessary, which made long-drive cowboys unnecessary. Locomotives could move more cattle a helluva lot faster than cowpokes could.

In 1890 Nat Love left the range and took a job with the competition. It was, in fact, one of the few jobs available to black men at the time, but certainly a long way from galloping across the western prairie. He was a Pullman porter and died in 1907 at the age of fifty-three, the same year his autobiography appeared on bookshelves.

In 1866 Congress organized four regiments of African-American infantry and mounted troops to help pacify Native Americans in the West: the 9th and 10th Cavalry and the 24th and 25th Infantry. In an age that viewed blacks as either comic or dangerous, the army sent black regiments to control conflicts between mainly white settlers and Indians, conflicts created by the government's own Indian policies. Together the 9th and 10th Regiments comprised twenty percent of the U.S. Cavalry in the West, a fact usually overlooked by Hollywood and television.

Long before John J. Pershing commanded American forces in World War I, he was a young lieutenant in the Wild West, serving with the all-black 10th Cavalry. He won the respect of those who served under him, but because of the color of his troops he became known to his fellow white officers as "Black Jack" Pershing. Many white officers virtually refused assignment to black regiments. Among those who wouldn't serve with them was George Armstrong Custer. However, the 9th and 10th had, among others, white scouts Kit Carson and Wild Bill Hickok.

Members of the 9th and 10th also earned the respect of those they fought, including the Indians of Montana, who called them "Buffalo Soldiers" and compared the troops' short, curly hair with that of the animal they considered sacred. They called the infantry "Walk-A-Heaps," because of the long distances the regiments marched. White soldiers, however, called them all "Brunettes."

Buffalo Soldiers and Walk-A-Heaps carried the white man's law to the West during a time when antiblack violence was growing in both the East *and* the West. Meanwhile, eleven black soldiers earned the Congressional Medal of Honor while fighting Indians out West.

They kept order among civilians and fought Indians, ran down rustlers and guarded stagecoaches; they built roads and protected survey parties and kept peace during railroad and mine strikes. And they did it under a handicap, often working with secondhand gear and worn-out horses, frequently being issued wagons and animals cast off by the favored all-white 7th Cavalry of George Custer. Even the 10th's regimental banner was homemade of wool, unlike the standard silk-embroidered flags supplied to white regiments.

Historian William H. Leckie, in his 1967 *Buffalo Soldiers*, claims that the army high command dealt more harshly with the Buffalo Soldiers than with whites. Although punishment meted out to black troopers was harsher than accorded white soldiers, Leckie writes, black cavalrymen had fewer courts-martial for drunkenness and boasted the lowest desertion rate on the frontier. "Their stations were among the most lonely and isolated to be found anywhere in the country" . . .

and mere service at such posts would seem to have called for honorable mention. Discipline was severe, food usually poor, recreation difficult, and violent death always near at hand. Prejudice robbed them of recognition and often of simple justice.

A ballad written by a Buffalo Soldier describes one encounter with Indians:

The Ninth marched out with splendid cheer,
The Bad Lands to explore,
With Colonel Henry at their head
They never fear the foe.

So on they rode from Christmas eve;
'Till dawn of Christmas day;
The Red Skins heard the Ninth was near
And fled in great dismay.

As well as fight and keep peace, members of the 25th Infantry did something a lot more unusual. For a while they rode bicycles.

A few years earlier, in 1874, H. J. Lawson had invented the chain-driven "safety" bicycle, and in 1888 John Boyd Dunlop developed the pneumatic tire. Cycling for pleasure and transport became popular and fairly commonplace. In Europe several armies formed bicycle units for reconnaissance and courier services. But ride a bike out West?

Historian Jeanne Cannella Schmitzer tells how, in 1896, the U.S. Army began experimenting with bicycles. They gave the job to eight 25th Regiment African-American enlisted men and one white officer, Lt. James A. Moss.

For a five-hundred-mile experiment each man had to carry a ten-pound blanket roll that included a shelter half (half a tent), an extra set of underwear, two pairs of socks, a handkerchief, toothbrush, and powder. And food: bacon, bread, canned beef, baked beans, coffee, and sugar—all packed in hard leather cases and attached to the bicycle frame. In addition, each man toted his ten-pound Krag-Jorgensen rifle and a fifty-round cartridge belt. Fully loaded, each man's kit would weigh about fifty-nine pounds.

That August the unit pedaled out of Fort Missoula, Montana, and ten days later they reached Yellowstone National Park. Sometimes over less-than-perfect roads, sometimes with no roads at all, they'd averaged about six miles per hour over even the steepest part of the route, more than twice the speed infantrymen would have made over the same terrain. This was not a weekend outing!

The following year they made an even longer trip—to St. Louis. The first day the bicyclists traveled fifty-four miles. Four days after leaving Missoula they crossed the Continental Divide, lashed by freezing rain and sleet, buffeted by blowing snow. And then they had to go downhill.

On the evening of June 25 the bikers reached the site where, exactly twenty years earlier, George Custer had fought and lost the Battle of the Little Big Horn. From there the cycling Walk-a-Heaps pedaled through Wyoming, South Dakota, and Nebraska. The temperature was boiling hot and water quickly became a critical problem. They took their supply from railroad tanks, but sometimes that wasn't enough. Near Moorcroft, Wyoming, an axle broke, the water supply was too critical and the men couldn't stop. The soldier pushed his bike into town.

Once, when the unit's water supply ran out, Lieutenant Moss drank alkali-tainted water. He fell ill near Alliance, Nebraska, and the corps waited four days until he recovered. Back on the road, the "road" became the Nebraska Sand Hills, with eight- and ten-inch-deep, 170-mile-long dunes. West of St. Louis newspaper reporter Henry Lucas joined the bicycle corpsmen and sent word back to his paper:

> It is no uncommon sight for residents of this city to see a company of wheelmen . . . but in today's visitors there is a distinctiveness which will make then at once as different from other riders. . . . All belong to the African race except the Lieutenant.

Finally, on July 24, they reached the outskirts of St. Louis, and hundreds of other cyclists rode out to meet the regiment. With this escort the 25th Infantry Bicycle Corps rode into town.

This experiment in the military use of bicycles lasted forty days, thirty-four of them in travel, with only six days taken off for rest and repairs. The corps had hoped to average about fifty miles per day. In the end they were making sixty miles a day. They rode and pushed their bikes a total of some nineteen hundred miles—numbing pain and rough roads. And hunger. The rations the men carried were intended to last for two days, but really amounted to only four meals. To lessen the pain of not-so-smooth roadways, Lieutenant Moss recommended equipping the bikes with shock absorbers.

All in all the bicycle experiment seemed a success. They were faster than the infantry, even faster than the cavalry, all things considered. A bicycle was cheap, Moss reported, and didn't need much care, "it is noiseless and raises but little dust, and it is impossible to determine [a bicycle's] direction from its tracks."

The problem was, of course, there weren't many good roads in the West; in fact, there weren't many good roads in the whole United States in 1897. So the army rejected the idea of a permanent bicycle corps. To return to Montana the 25th Infantry Bicycle Corps took to the rails.

A typical army patrol consisted of detachments of either one or two companies, each with from fifty to a hundred mounted troopers. Each soldier carried supplies to last him several days. It wasn't an easy load for cavalry horses: rifle, pistol, extra ammunition, canteen, tin cup, knife, shelter half, haversack, saddlebags, poncho, and—for the poor horse that had to carry it all—a feed bag. Out on the trail each trooper carried his own rations—bacon, hardtack, and coffee. In his pockets the soldier might carry a few pennies from his monthly pay of thirteen dollars.

CHAPTER TEN

Gold Fever:
When the World Rushed In

A miner's life is one of hardships, toil and exposure. There is no easy way for him to obtain the precious metal.
William McKnight, July 11, 1852

The great Rush from San Francisco arrived at the fort, all my friends and acquaintances filled up the houses and the whole fort....
John Augustus Sutter, diary, May 19, 1848

For much of the eighteenth century, military dress uniforms often included bicorn hats, kind of two-pointed, fore-and-aft versions of the seventeenth century's tricorn hats. The military being the military, the higher the officer's rank, the fancier the hat. They took on the French name *chapeau de bras*, and now we not only give their hats this name, we apply it to the officers themselves: brass hats.

Of course, it wasn't brass that preoccupied the last half of the century, but another metal, one far more precious.

In 1839 John Augustus Sutter landed at Monterey, California, and within a year applied to the Mexican government for a grant for nearly fifty thousand acres of land in two parcels. One parcel of land he applied for was the present site of Sacramento. Sutter called it New Helvetia, after the town in Switzerland. Later he wrote that

agriculture increased until I had several hundred men working in the harvest fields, and to feed them I had to kill four or sometimes five oxen daily. I could raise 40,000 bushels of wheat without trouble, reap the crops with sickles, thrash it with bones, and winnow it in the wind.

John Sutter was a native of Switzerland, born in 1803. Growing up he dreamed of an important military role for himself. It was, however, a dream unfulfilled. Instead he became an autocratic landowner who ruled his enclave in feudal splendor. Three years after Sutter began work on New Helvetia, the town that came to be called Fort Sutter, Swedish scientist G. M. Sandels visited the settlement and said it had "more the appearance of a citadel than an agricultural establishment." New Helvetia, he said, was "protected by an uncompleted wall, ten feet high, made of adobes . . . also having a turret with embrasures and loopholes."

When the Russians (who had holdings along the northern California coast) pulled out of Fort Ross near modern-day Eureka, Sutter bought their fort and equipment for thirty thousand dollars. He agreed to pay the Russians in wheat at two dollars per *fanega,* a Spanish measurement equal to about a bushel or a bushel and a half. In 1847 John Sutter began building a new flour mill at Natoma, about five miles from his fort. To provide building material for his flour mill Sutter hired a sometime carpenter named James W. Marshall to supervise construction of a waterwheel-powered sawmill at Sutter's second parcel of land.

On January 24, 1848, James Marshall walked along the race, inspecting the flow of water. Later he recalled the moment. "My eye was caught," he said, "with the glimpse of something shining in the bottom of the ditch." As he reached down and picked it up, "it made my heart thump, for I was certain it was gold." It was about half the size of a pea. "Then I saw another." Marshall fully appreciated what he had discovered: "After taking it out I sat down and began to think right hard."

James Marshall had been born on October 8, 1810, in New Jersey, the great-grandson of a signer of the Declaration of Independence. As a youngster James learned carpentry and worked for a while as a wheelwright. After twice being rejected by young women Marshall—he never did marry—wandered west, first into the Ohio Valley, then to California. In 1846, still feeling restless, James Marshall joined the Bear Flag Rebellion to free California and served under John C. Frémont in the Mexican-American War. By 1847 he'd been discharged and returned to civilian life as an employee of John Sutter.

As water rushed through the Sutter's millrace along the American River, gold that had been buried for centuries was freed and separated from the rocks and gravel and sand. "Boys," Marshall remembered telling his construction crew, "I believe I have found a gold mine." At first they didn't believe him, and several went down to the race to look for themselves. Marshall showed the workers what he had found. One bit into the metal; it bent but didn't break. Another tried crushing it between two stones; once again it flattened out but didn't crack. That was good, if nonscientific, proof that what Marshall found was gold.

Each day he and his men found more gold. Four days after Marshall had first sighted the glittering particles, he rode over to Fort Sutter. "Marshall arrived in the evening," Sutter wrote, "it was raining heavy, but he told me he came on important business." *Important* may not have been a strong enough word:

[H]e showed me the first Specimen of Gold, that is he was not certain if it was Gold or not, but he thought it might be; immediately I made the proof and found that it was Gold. I told him even that most of all is 23 Carat Gold.

Marshall was excited. Sutter was cautious. But over the next week the construction workers found more and more gold, and finally John Sutter became as excited as James Marshall. He boasted, "I have made a discovery of a gold mine which, according to the experiments we have made, is extremely rich."

Marshall and Sutter tried to keep secret their discovery. It didn't work, of course. All of the workers abandoned their duties and began their own search for gold. "Very soon," Sutter wrote, "all followed and left me only the sick and lame behind. At this time I could say that every body left me from the Clerk to the Cook."

Sutter's flour mill stood unfinished, his fields were untended, and hides rotted in his warehouse at Sutter's Fort. Mormon workers at the gristmill noted the similarity of the riverbed and gravel bars at the sawmill. Scratching and digging around, they found more gold, and this second location became famous as Mormon Island.

By March word had leaked out, and a few outsiders from San Francisco and nearby valleys came, looked around, and they, too, found gold. On the fifteenth the four-page *San Francisco Californian* carried a one-paragraph, page-four article with the almost self-effacing, apologetic tone:

> GOLD MINE FOUND. In the newly made raceway of the Saw Mill recently erected by Captain Sutter, on the American Fork, gold has been found in considerable quantities. One person brought thirty dollars worth to New Helvetia, gathered there in a short time. California, no doubt, is rich in mineral wealth; great chances here for scientific capitalists. Gold has been found in almost every part of the country.

Meanwhile, local Mormon leader Sam Brannan was preparing a special edition of the *California Star,* California's first newspaper, extolling the virtues of the area. By the time news of the Sutter's Mill discovery reached San Francisco and filtered down to the *California Star*'s staff, the paper was nearly completed; only a couple of blank inches remained on an inside sheet. Rather than redo the entire paper—remember, the type had to be hand-set—Brannan added a brief paragraph:

> We saw a few days ago a beautiful specimen of gold from the mine newly discovered on the American Fork. From all accounts the mine is immensely rich and already, we learn, the gold from it is collected at random and without any trouble, has become an article of trade in the upper settlements.

At the time San Francisco had a population of just 850, and at first they didn't seem interested. After all, they'd heard it before: talk of gold and other minerals. Ol' John Sutter was at it again, they thought, trying to entice more trade to his outpost.

Still thinking it nothing more than a California booster edition, Brannan printed two thousand copies of the *Star* and sent it overland by an express rider—an unpretentious-looking man, stoop shouldered, freckled, and taciturn in the manner of other mountain men—Kit Carson. He headed first to Santa Fe, then on to St. Joseph, Missouri, where he arrived around the end of July. From there Carson went to St. Louis, and local newspapers reprinted portions of Brannan's boosterism issue. They didn't catch the gold part of the story, and Carson continued on until he reached Washington, D.C., a three-month-long trip from California.

Slowly visitors made their way to Sutter's Mill to check out the alleged discovery. One of those was nineteen-year-old Edward Kemble, the young editor of Sam Brannan's *California Star.* He wanted to "ruralize among the rustics" for a few weeks, he said. When Kemble asked James Marshall and his men about the discovery, they responded with gruff and evasive replies.

Kemble tried panning for gold, but came up with nothing. That night a group of local Yalesumni Indians walked up to the visitor's campfire. An old man spoke to him through an interpreter: The gold was a bad medicine and belonged to a demon who lived in a lake. The demon had even seized a tribe member who was hunting the elusive metal.

Well, this confirmed Kemble's suspicions that this talk of gold was all a chimera, a delusion. He saw no one prospecting, saw no sign of gold. In his diary Kemble wrote:

> Humbug! Great country—fine climate.... Visit this Great Valley, we would advise all who have not yet done so. See it now. Full flowing streams, mighty timber, large crops, luxuriant clover, fragrant flowers, gold and silver. Great country this.

Thirty-seven years later Kemble laughed at his mistake.

Meanwhile, about three miles downstream from where Ed Kemble had looked and seen nothing, Henry Bigler and his fellow Mormons were successfully digging gold by the handful. According to his journal: On April 14 he made $11; on the fifteenth the take was $22; on the eighteenth (the day Ed Kemble was declaring it all "humbug" a few miles away), Bigler dug out $11. The twenty-first saw him collect $30 in gold; on the twenty-second, he found another $25. He was making almost as much in one day as a worker back East received in a month, when a dollar a day was considered good wages; in 1848, for example, a soldier was paid seven dollars a month. U.S. congressmen, for another example, received eight dollars a day.

It got better, much better, and in one fifteen-day period Bigler panned and dug out $1,600 in gold. In his journal Bigler wrote on March 23, "A lot of Gentiles came into our camp to look for gold." He added, they "found nothing." The *California Star*, however, reported that "we have seen several specimens to the amount of eight or ten ounces of pure, virgin gold."

On May 4 Sam Brannan himself rode out to Sutter's Fort, and the next day he went to Mormon Island, where he selected a site for a store and collected tithes from the Mormon miners—after all, there was that $1,600 in gold they'd found—to give to the Church of Jesus Christ of Latter-day Saints. Then Brannan moved on to Coloma, the town outside Sutter's Mill, where he laid out another store location.

Back at Fort Sutter, Brannan found everything in a frenzy. All of John Sutter's employees had quit work, abandoned their tools, and hastily loaded up wagons and pack horses. There was gold in them thar hills, and everybody wanted part of it.

So, too, did Sam Brannan, and through his many contacts he began gathering gold dust. When he returned to San Francisco, he had with him a bottle that had formerly held quinine. Now it held twenty pounds of gold dust worth about $5,120. "Gold! Gold!" he shouted. "Gold from the American River!" The gold he carried was the tithes he'd extracted from his spiritual wards on Mormon Island.

When copies of the *California Star* that Kit Carson carried east reached New York, the small gold-announcing paragraph was finally understood for what it was: This wasn't just boosterism for the territory, but something real and exciting. On August 19, 1848, the *New York Herald* headlined: GOLD DISCOVERED IN CALIFORNIA.

Colonel Richard B. Mason, military governor of California, decided to see what the excitement was all about at Sutter's Mill, and he wasn't disappointed. Arriving in July 1848, he noted a small ravine that had already yielded $12,000 in gold. He saw another spot where two men had found $17,000 in gold in just seven days. "No capital is required to obtain this gold," he wrote, "as the laboring man wants nothing but his pick and shovel and tin pan with which to dig and wash the gravel. . . ." Raw gold was valued at $16 per ounce, and in those two sites miners had found nearly a ton of the yellow mineral.

Back East, lame-duck president James Knox Polk was preparing his final message to Congress. Polk was ill and hadn't received his party's nomination for a second term in the White House. Instead the Democrats nominated Senator Lewis Cass of Michigan, who later lost the election to Mexican War–hero Zachary Taylor.

Governor Mason sent Polk a report outlining the gold discovery. Midway through his speech Polk hit on the subject that would mean more than anything else:

It was known that mines of the precious metals existed to a considerable extent in California at the time of its acquisition. . . . Recent discoveries render it probable that these mines are more extensive and valuable than was anticipated. The accounts of the abundance of gold in that territory are of such an extraordinary character as would scarcely command belief were they not corroborated by the authentic reports of officers in the public service.

With that, gold fever struck. On May 12, 1848, approximately six hundred men lived in San Francisco. On May 15 only two hundred could be counted. On the fourteenth, an armada of launches, packed to the gunwales with feverish, noisy gold hunters, set sail across San Francisco Bay, through narrow Carquinez Strait, the mosquito-clouded Sacramento delta, then up the Sacramento River. On their way upriver they met a boat heading downriver with a large cargo of gold. Couldn't get a launch, other men went by wagon. No wagon, they went by horse. No horse? Well, they walked.

On May 29 the *San Francisco Californian* claimed: "The whole country resounds with the sordid cry of gold! Gold!! GOLD!!" Then the *Californian* shut down and everyone went to Sutter's Mill. Two weeks later the *Star* added its voice: "We have done. Let our word of parting be, *Hasta luego*." And the *Star* shut down its presses. And where was Ed Kemble, who'd declared it all "humbug"? He went hunting for gold like everyone else. So many sailors left so many ships, never to return to them, San Francisco harbor became awash in rotting hulks. Years later the city would burn the hulks, fill in that part of the harbor, and it became some of the city's most expensive waterfront property.

Within six months of the strike at Sutter's Mill, four thousand miners swarmed over the foothills of the Sierra Nevada. Within a year San Francisco was a tent city of twenty thousand rough, tough, and transient would-be prospectors. It was a city without homes but with a helluva lot of tents, a boom town of men, auction houses, hotels, bathhouses, groggeries, billiard rooms, boardinghouses, eating and drinking houses, two- and four-story office buildings.* "Dens of lewd women," crowded and steep and filthy streets. What a town! Living there wasn't cheap, either, but no one cared. A small room on the second floor of the Parker House Hotel rented for eighteen hundred dollars a month; two other rooms on the same floor went for twenty-four hundred a month.

In tents outside gambling went on round the clock: monte, roulette, and rouge et noir. Throw a plank across two barrels and you had a bar; find a piano and piano player, put up a couple of paintings of naked ladies, not to mention a couple painted ladies, and you had yourself a going enterprise. Next to the Palmer House stood a canvas tent fifteen by twenty-five feet, called El Dorado. It rented to gamblers for forty thousand dollars a year. And again nobody cared. The California gold rush was on.

In 1849 shipping and railroad magnate Cornelius Vanderbilt—he'd first gotten rich after borrowing a hundred dollars from his mother to open a small ferry across New York harbor—decided to get in on the gold rush. Not by going out and panning himself, however—he mined his gold in a different way by founding a steamship line that ran from the East Coast to California. He cut the usual fare in half and saved travelers time by instituting a land crossing at Nicaragua, rather than at Panama, which even before building the

---

*In the San Francisco earthquake of 1906 several buildings lost their top floors. Some truncated buildings remain as reminders.

Panama Canal, was the usual land route. Vanderbilt's route was six hundred miles shorter. He earned over a million dollars in profit in the first year.

In 1853, for some reason, he sold a large block of his stock in the steamship line to a group known as the Nicaragua Transit Company. The new company, however, refused to pay Vanderbilt for the stock.

"Gentlemen," he reportedly said, "you have undertaken to cheat me. I won't sue you, for the law is too slow." Instead Vanderbilt decided to ruin the company. And he did. He established a new line to compete with the Nicaragua Transit Company, and in two years he'd run his enemies out of business. Still, he made a profit: In nine years of running ships from the East Coast to California, Cornelius Vanderbilt racked up an estimated ten million dollars in profits.

The year 1681 saw the first use of oil lamps on the streets of London. It was also the year matches were invented by Englishman Robert Boyle. He dipped a wooden stick into sulfur and drew it through coarse, phosphorus-coated paper, which ignited the stick. A "match" originally was a fuse used to fire a cannon or musket, hence the name "matchlock." It would be another fifty years or so before a friction match was invented, probably by the Frenchman François Derosne. Because of the sulfur first used in making matches, the lit device gave off a pungent odor, making them known in much of the English-speaking world as "lucifers."

Lucifers sometimes came in blocks, with the sticks partially sawed out but left attached to one another like teeth on a comb; you'd simply break off one match at a time if you wanted to. Or maybe not. An old trick of horsemen being chased by Indians was to keep the block intact, light one match, then toss the whole block into thick dry grass along the trail, hoping the grass would catch fire and give them a chance to get away. In some cases it actually worked.

Thanks to a man named Levi Strauss, cowboys and emigrants and miners even had a convenient place to strike their lucifers—the rear of their jeans. However, it wasn't Strauss who invented the product that today more or less bears his name.

Back in 1872 in Reno, Nevada, tailor Jacob W. Davis began making a new kind of trousers that used rivets to strengthen and secure the pockets and seams. Davis wanted to patent his idea, but he couldn't because his wife said he'd already spent too much money on another invention he'd worked on, a steam-powered canal boat.

As a tailor Davis had been getting his cloth from a San Francisco supplier, Levi Strauss, who at the time ran a store rather than a pants factory. In a letter to Strauss, Davis (who was literate in his native Yiddish but not so in English) dictated to a Reno pharmacist:

> I also send you by Express 2 ps. Overall as you will see one Blue and one made of the 10 oz Duck which I have bought in great many Peces of you, and have made it up in to Pents, such as the sample.
>
> The secratt of them Pants is the Rivits that I put in those Pockets and I found the demand so large that I cannot make them fast enough. I charge for the Duck $3.00 and the Blue $2.50. My nabors are getting yealouse of these success and unless I secure it by Patent Papers it will soon become a general thing. Everybody will make them up and there will be no money in it.
>
> Therefore Gentlemen, I wish to make you a Proposition that you should take out the Latters Patent in my name as I am the inventor of it, the expense of it will be about $68, all complit and for these $68 will give you half the right to sell all such clothing Revited according to the Patent, for all the Pacific States and Teroterious, the balince of the United States and half of the Pacific Coast I resarve for myself.

Levi Strauss took a chance and began manufacturing Davis's riv-etted pants. He had some canvas he'd intended to sell for tents, but he noticed that the hard-working miners frequently, and quickly, wore through ordinary cotton pants, which at the least could be embarrassing. So Levi used Davis's idea of riveted bibless overall trousers, but in canvas cloth, and began selling them. The process was patented in 1873. As for Davis, he moved his family to San Francisco and began managing pants production for Levi Strauss.

The Davis–Levi Strauss canvas pants lasted longer than regular work clothes and gave folks a convenient place to strike a match.

There was, however, one problem. Early versions of Levi's pants used a rivet affixed at the crotch seam. The company discarded that particular stress-preventing rivet after cowboys* sitting around campfires claimed the brass got too hot too fast in too personal a location.

Levi Strauss soon switched from canvas to another fabric, cotton that originally was loomed in Nîmes, France, called *serge de Nîmes*. It came in a special indigo-blue color, which, when they were new, assured unvarying color. This *serge de Nîmes* came to be called "denim" from *"de Nîmes."*

A similar fabric was used for pants worn by Genoese sailors, which led to the name "jeans" being attached to Levi Strauss's once canvas, now denim, pants complete with brass rivets. A fashion statement was about to be made, but it would take more than a century. At first Levi's pants were popular with farmers, cowboys, miners, railroad workers, and lumberjacks. By the 1990s they were so acceptable that Americans ended up wearing them just about everywhere, every time. In England, Ireland, and Europe *used* Levi's were being sold for outrageous prices. So high, you had to be rich to afford them, which takes us right back to miners and gold.

The Sutter/Marshall strike attracted thousands of gold seekers. In 1848 about six thousand miners worked at the diggings. By December 1849 there were at least forty thousand miners in the area. Another forty thousand men (and a few women) got their gear together, preparing to head for the hills and try their luck at digging, mining, and panning. Towns sprang up called Volcano and Murphy's and Angel's Camp** and Sonora. At its height the village of Coloma, the nearest town to Sutter's Mill, itself had a population of several thousand. Now it's back to being a sleepy hamlet beset by tourists. South of Coloma there's Placerville, which today boasts the nation's only city-owned gold mine. At the height of the gold rush it was known as "Hangtown," so called in testament to its violent vigilante ways. It's been years since they've hanged anyone there.

---

*Some say it was a company vice president.
**Named after miner George Angel, it was often hit by roving gangs of outlaws. It was the site of Mark Twain's famous story "The Celebrated Jumping Frog of Calaveras County."

CHAPTER ELEVEN

Heroes, Heroines, and Myths: The Stuff of Dreams

A hero is more than just a sandwich.

Anonymous

I had supper, the first course being whiskey, the second whiskey, and the third whiskey.

Oscar Wilde, while on a lecture tour
in Leadville, Colorado, 1882

The German word *Dudenkopf* almost literally means "a lazy fellow." In America it took on the denotation of an affected or foppish person, one unlikely to be skilled or experienced. We shortened it to *dude,* and in the Wild West it assumed the added meaning of one who was ultrafastidious, a tenderfoot, someone from the East who vacationed in the West. The *Oxford Universal Dictionary* offers the female version of *dude* as *dudine.* Other versions have it as *dudess.* Maybe *dudettes.*

Whichever, the individual has a quality of "dudeness" and likely lives in "dudedom," which is any place in the world *outside* of the West. Or maybe in Texas. Libbie Custer, George Armstrong Custer's widow, said in 1888 that, "if the term *dude* had been invented [in 1866] it would have been applied to Texas horsemen."

The first "dude ranch" in America was owned by Howard Eaton in the Dakota Territory. The story is that he once counted up the number of free meals he'd given to visitors in one year and came up with the figure twenty-two hundred. With that he decided to start making money on dudes who came his way. He charged them ten dollars a week for bed, board, and a chance to wear their not-quite-authentic clothes they'd bought back East.

When a combination of the blizzards of 1886–87 and the economic disaster of 1893 wiped out a lot of other ranchers, Howard

275

Eaton held on. Thanks to all those dudes and dudettes. Soon magazines back East extolled ranch vacations. Women especially benefited from dude ranches. Eastern mores condemned them to polite society and social chitchat. In the West dudettes could ride and hike and fish right alongside dudes. By the 1940s dude ranches had blossomed all over the West, and nondudes sometimes took offense. An old-timer told of two newcomers out West: "One wore lavender angora chaps, the other bright orange, and each sported a tremendous sombrero and wore a gaudy scarf knotted jauntily about his throat."

In some cases things went beyond "dude." A longtime striptease artist and dancer had her own version, known as "Sally Rand's Nude Ranch."

Howard Eaton wouldn't have cared. He made such a profit on dude ranching that he soon moved his operation to the Big Horn Mountains of Wyoming, where he led pack trips into Yellowstone National Park when it was established in 1872. Four years later business was interrupted by a battle featuring Custer and Sitting Bull.

When exploits of western pioneers are told, one of the first names heard is that of Jedediah Smith, an outstanding trapper and mountain man. In a time and place when such men were rough and ready and profane, Jedediah Smith was noted for his abstinence from the use of tobacco and profanity; he even is said to have taken regular baths and carried a bar of soap with him wherever he went. Unusual among the buckskinned brethren, Smith reportedly did not make a habit of hauling off to the woods any and all Indian maidens he took a fancy to.

On March 13, 1822, the *Missouri Gazette* carried a message from U.S. Army general William H. Ashley and Maj. Andrew Henry. It was addressed to "Enterprising Young Men" and called for a hundred volunteers to join an expedition to the sources of the Missouri River. Jedediah Smith volunteered, and among his companions were three names that would carry through the history of the West: Mike Fink, David E. Jackson, and James Bridger. Fink, who insisted on spelling his name "Phinck," was a legendary keelboatman from the Ohio and Mississippi, and it's likely that from him comes the term *a real fink*. It's said that, if he asked you to place an apple on top of your head as a target, don't. He'd intentionally shoot your head instead of the apple. He once set his mistress's clothes on fire, forcing her to jump overboard.

Jackson was thirty-four at the time of the Ashley expedition, a veteran of the War of 1812 who had migrated to Missouri, failed to prosper in any known trade, then gambled along with other Enterprising Young Men on the way west.

And Jim Bridger, who was hardly out of adolescence at the time, got a fast start on adventure and grew into a character of epic proportions. "A very companionable man," they said of Bridger, "over six feet tall, spare, straight as an arrow, agile, rawboned, and powerful of frame . . . hospitable and generous, and always trusted and respected." Jim, however, was illiterate and had to have someone read Colonel Henry's newspaper ad to him.

Jedediah Strong Smith was unique among the mountain men with whom he traveled. Not long after the Ashley Party set out, a large band of Arikara Indians attacked them near the mouth of the Grand River, killing many in the expedition. Jed survived and became a trapper for Ashley's Rocky Mountain Fur Company. Once he was mauled by a grizzly while trapping in the Big Horn country. It left him with a permanently mutilated ear; he hid it by letting his hair grow long.

Trapping was his means of fulfilling his interests in exploration, and it's said that no man ever knew more about the American West than did Jedediah Smith. Traveling throughout the Rockies, to California and Oregon, he "drew" a mental map of the West and kept extensive records he hoped to share with others. Regrettably, he didn't live long enough to pass on his knowledge.

In 1831 he led a party of around eighty men out of St. Louis into the Southwest along the Santa Fe Trail. In an arid stretch somewhere between the Arkansas and Cimarron Rivers, the party ran out of water, and Jed volunteered to go in search of a water hole. Jedediah Smith was only thirty-one at the time, and it was the last time he was seen, disappearing somewhere in what is now Meade or Haskell Counties in southwestern Kansas. He may have died of thirst or injury or fallen victim to Comanche lances. His body was never recovered.

Hugh Glass may have been a hero. Truly, however, the only life he ever saved, perhaps the only person to benefit from him, was Hugh Glass himself. As with so many others who made the West wild, Hugh Glass came from "elsewhere." He may have been a mariner before he was a mountain man, and if so, he likely could also have been a pirate. He spent time with the Pawnees, where he apparently learned his wilderness skills. In any event he spent the most important time of his life as a mountain man. As one who trapped with him put it:

> In point of adventures dangers & narrow escapes & capacity for endurance, & the sufferings which befel him, this man was pre-eminent—He was bold, daring, reckless & eccentric to a high degree; but was nevertheless a man of great talents & intellectual as well as bodily power—But his bravery was conspicuous beyond all his other qualities for the perilous life he led.

In the spring of 1823 Hugh Glass joined Maj. Andrew Henry's expedition to the Upper Missouri. More or less, he joined. Glass was so defiantly independent that he generally traveled apart from the rest of the expedition. While the party was exploring and trapping in the vicinity of Grand River, South Dakota, Glass and another mountain man named Moses "Black" Harris were off by themselves. Glass surprised a decidedly unfriendly grizzly bear sow and her cubs. This, of course, brings into question just how good a woodsman Hugh Glass was, stumbling into a thicket to be surprised by a mother bear and her babies.

The bear roared and reared up on her hind feet, then attacked Glass. Hugh apparently was fast on the trigger but not so fast as the bear. He got off a shot, critically wounding the bear. Hugh tried climbing a tree to get away from the raging animal, but the wounded and angry sow pulled him back, threw him to the ground, and tore at him with steel-sharp claws. Finally Hugh's shot took effect, and the bear sprawled dead across the wounded mountain man.

Glass's partner, Black Harris, meanwhile had been off chasing down one of the bear cubs. By the time he'd killed the little bear and located Glass, Hugh was in bad shape—scalp, face, chest, back, shoulder, arm, hand, and thigh deeply gashed. When Hugh tried to talk, blood bubbled from a puncture in his throat.

Major Henry and the rest of the expedition found Glass just after Harris had pulled the grizzly's carcass off the nearly dead mountain man. It didn't look good. Another member of the Henry party saw Hugh and said the trapper had been "tore nearly to peases." He should have been dead and looked close to it.

The men bandaged his wounds, but couldn't do much more. They waited overnight to see if Hugh would live or die. He was still alive the next morning, but Henry decided they couldn't wait any longer; at any moment a band of Arikara Indians might stumble onto them just as Hugh had stumbled onto the grizzly. They fashioned a crude litter and hoisted Glass onto their shoulders, resuming their march.

Progress was slow, and Hugh seemed to be getting worse. After several days Major Henry decided he could no longer risk the entire party for a man he believed certainly would soon die. He offered to pay a sizable sum to anyone who'd volunteer to stay behind with Hugh until the trapper died, then bury him. John S. Fitzgerald and nineteen-year-old Jim Bridger took the major up on the offer.

In later years Bridger became possibly the most famous mountain man of all and built his own trading post on the Green River of Wyoming, Bridger's Fort. He was friendly with the local Indians, especially with a Shoshone woman whom he married and with whom he had four children. Jim eventually got into trouble with Mormons by selling arms to the Indians, and in 1854 Brigham Young's "Avenging Angels" swept down on Bridger's Fort and burned it to the ground. Bridger was one of the last survivors of the generation of mountain men and died on his Missouri farm in 1881, at the age of seventy-seven.

But that was many years after his encounter with Hugh Glass. Now, Hugh lay unconscious along the north bank of the South River. While waiting for the mountain man they called "Old Glass" to die, Fitzgerald and Bridger dug a grave for Hugh. But Glass declined to oblige, and after waiting several hours by the unconscious hunter, the two paid volunteers decided they'd had enough. Fitzgerald and Bridger appropriated Hugh's rifle and other equipment, left Glass to die on his own, and hurried to catch up with Major Henry and the gang. They reached what became known as Henry's Fort at the mouth of the Yellowstone River, not long after the major and the main part of the party had arrived. Yes, they reported in, poor old Hugh had passed on to that great mountain range in the sky. Yes, they lied, they'd buried him honorably, and he lay safely under the South Dakota sod.

Hugh Glass, however, was alive. Barely. Feverish and prostrated, but still alive. In fact, as he lay there in a semiconscious state, he'd even heard Fitzgerald and Bridger discussing what they'd do with his belongings. Now he was awake, and he swore he'd take revenge on the two deadbeats who'd left him with only a knife.

Those thoughts, along with a diet of wild berries and a critter caught now and then (including at least one rattlesnake, who, after dining on a bird or some other small animal, was so torpid Hugh managed to smash it to death with a stone), sustained Hugh Glass over the coming days. He chanced upon a dead buffalo with marrow still rich enough to sustain him. He dug edible roots and drank from the Grand River. Most of all, he crawled toward the nearest fort.

He crawled until he was able to walk, then he walked until he was able to run. And finally, six weeks after his battle with the grizzly, Hugh Glass reached Fort Kiowa, some 150 miles to the southeast of where he'd been left to die. It was an amazing demonstration of strength, determination, and luck, mixed with the desire for revenge. At Fort Kiowa he recovered.

Major Henry had abandoned his earlier outpost and begun building a new one at the mouth of the Big Horn River, and it was here that Hugh Glass caught up with him. Needless to say, Hugh's appearance stunned Andrew Henry, who'd had it on good report that the mountain man was dead and buried.

As for revenge, Hugh Glass confronted Jim Bridger, but the rage had left the older man. Fighting off death and crawling 150 miles had taken it out of Glass, and he merely lectured Bridger on the scruples of life in the mountains. Then he tracked down John Fitzgerald at Fort Atkinson in northwestern Iowa, but there was little Hugh could do about him. John was now in the U.S. Army, and garrison commander Col. Henry Leavenworth refused to let Glass murder one of his soldiers.

Instead, he ordered Fitzgerald to return Hugh Glass's rifle and other possessions. Then he equipped Glass to return to the mountains.

From there Hugh got on with his life, living another ten years or so. He'd had "a hundred escapes and warnings," a friend remembered. At least four times in Hugh's life bands of Indian warriors captured him and even tried to take his scalp. The last time he was seen was in 1833, when he walked out the gate of Fort Cass on the south bank of the North Platte River, along the Oregon Trail. It was winter, and the factor in charge of the American Fur Company at Fort Cass dispatched Hugh as a courier to Fort Union. Two others joined Glass, a mulatto named Edward Rose and a third, unidentified, man. It was then that Hugh's luck seems to have run out. As the three crossed the frozen Yellowstone River south of the fort, a band of Arikara Indians bore down on them and charged. They killed the three men, scalped them, and stripped them of their possessions.

Perhaps. That's one version of his story. But who knows? Hugh Glass may have survived again and walked on to the Pacific. For a man who'd once been given up for dead, who crawled 150 miles through hostile territory to deliver a lecture on ethics among mountain men, nothing would have been impossible.

Men greatly outnumbered women in the Wild West. Take the time at Fort Vancouver, Oregon Territory. Just before Christmas 1850 the officers held a ball, but as one young man complained, there were only seven women present, and five of them were wives. It got worse. "After supper," he wrote,

> one lady left; at ten, two left. At one o'clock one left, leaving but three. At two, another left, leaving but two ladies in the hall. Misses Melleck stopped at three, [and] all hands returned home.

On March 15, 1836, farmer and missionary Jason Lee wrote the Methodist Church board back East, "A greater favour could not be bestowed upon this country, than to send to it pious, industrious, intelligent females." The church fathers understood, and that same winter they sent three single women to Columbia, Washington Territory. Jason Lee quickly married one of them in a ceremony in a grove of fir trees.

He wasn't the only lonely man in the West. According to *Frank Leslie's Illustrated Newspaper* in 1864:

> Three-fifths of the adult white population of California are men without wives. Four out of every five white men are bachelors, and from necessity; for where there are 183,856 men in the state there are only 48,149 women.

Mail-order brides were the answer for many lonely men out West. Sometimes men turned to newspapers for help. Reading about a woman, a man might correspond with her and, if he was lucky, might even get a photograph—picture brides, they were called and were especially popular among Asian and Greek men who wanted to marry someone from their own culture. Others might hear about an unmarried woman—somebody's sister or cousin—and strike up a correspondence.

An 1875 newspaper advertisement in the *Yuma (Arizona) Sentinel* read:

> WANTED: A nice, plump, healthy good-natured, good-looking domestic and affectionate lady to correspond with. Object—matrimony. She must be between 22 and 35 years of age. She must not be a gadabout or given to scandal, but must be one who will be a help-mate and companion, and who will endeavor to make home happy. Such a lady can find a correspondent by addressing the editor of this paper. Photographs exchanged!
>
> If anybody don't like our way of going about this interesting business, we don't care. It's none of their funeral.

The writer apparently was the newspaper editor himself, William J. Berry. No word whether he succeeded.

There was help out there for the poor western bachelor. Or the eastern spinster. In 1849 Eliza W. Farnham organized the California Association of American Women, hoping to encourage women from the East to head out West, meet men, and marry them. Farnham's efforts, however, met with only limited success; she convinced only two women to join her in California. Another organizer, Asa Mercer, was more successful and arranged for two groups of women, each numbering about a hundred, to emigrate to Washington to become brides. Mercer apparently was so successful that he even married a woman who'd accompanied him west.

Not every bridegroom was especially romantic. Take Elkanah Walker, a graduate of the Bangor (Maine) Theological Seminary. He almost went to Africa as a missionary but instead wound up on the Oregon Trail. He met Mary Richardson after a member of the missionary board that would send Elkanah out West decided that Walker needed a wife and that Mary would make him a good one.

Elkanah came up to her one day and said,

> I am going to surprise you. I may as well do my errand first as last. As I have no one engaged to go [west] with me, I have come with the intention of offering myself to you. You have been recommended to me by Mr. Armstrong (of the missionary board). . . .

Who says Westerners weren't romantic? Mary, however, was satisfied and said yes.

She'd previously been courted by Joshua Goodwin, who wasn't too happy about Elkanah as competition. "I would rather," Joshua told Mary, "have seen you pass on a bier than in a chase [*sic*] [carriage] with W[alker]." Mary and Elkanah were engaged to be married, and Mary's future husband immediately returned to the seminary. They were married a year later. The missionary board informed Elkanah that he wouldn't be going to Africa after all—tribal war had broken out in the area where he and his new wife were to be sent. Instead, they'd be sent to Oregon.

When told that they'd have to keep their baggage to a minimum, Elkanah Walker wrote reassuringly:

> A change of clothes is all we want. Buckskin drawers are the best for riding on horse back—our ladies should also have drawers to prevent being chafted [*sic*] in riding.

* * *

Elkanah Walker graduated the seminary, was ordained to the gospel ministry (Mary couldn't make the ceremony); they packed up (drawers and all), and headed for the Oregon Trail. Along the way Elkanah Walker and Mary Richardson were married.

Marriage ceremonies were causes for celebration in the West. "Us women folks was busy cooking up chickens and nice things for starting out on," Rebecca Nutting Woodson remembered one wedding. "Oh we was going to have just a happy time."

Once married, a now supposedly happy couple would retire for the night at an inn, a hotel, or even their own home. Before they could settle in for the night, however, they could expect friends to pay them a visit, clanging bells, banging drums or pans, and in general making a helluva lot of noise: a shivaree, it was called. An adaptation of the medieval charivari, the tradition of raucous noisemaking after a wedding was a particular frontier favorite.

A woman might be called madame, ma'am, señorita, or squaw, but whatever she was called, it took guts to live in the Wild West. There was no room for the "weaker sex." Women lived among savage men, brutal climates, and indescribable conditions along with the occasional plague. Despite all this—or just as likely, because of it—the Wild West attracted thousands of nonconforming women. Like men, western women were mavericks, loners, eccentrics, and adventurers. Through it all, historian Bob Boze Bell writes, they kept their sense of humor. "I've got 350 head of cattle and one son," he quotes a widowed ranchwoman as saying. "Don't know which was harder to raise."

Emigrants to the West usually were cut off from family, friends, their native culture, and the strictures of eastern and European society, and some were crushed by the experience. Others survived, with more than a few thriving under the stress and strain and dangers.

Of course many women already called the Wild West their homes—Native Americans living in pueblos, in wigwams, hogans, and tepees—from the canyons of the Southwest to the Great Plains, from Sonora to Sonoma, the Badlands of the Dakotas to the California Baja. Like emigrant white women, Indian women counted among themselves feisty individuals unafraid of man or beast or Mother Nature.

Take for instance an Apache woman named Dilchthe, not a woman warrior, a middle-aged grandmother who was captured in the mid-1860s by Sonoran mercenaries at Esqueda, Mexico, south of present-day Douglas, Arizona. As photographer and historian Bell tells it, the mercenaries quickly executed the Apache men in her party. Their captors then herded Dilchthe and several other women southwest to the Gulf of California and sold them into slavery, shipping them across the gulf to a penal colony on the Baja Peninsula where many died in the camp. Dilchthe, however, hung on tenaciously, only to be sold again along with several other women and put to work on a nearby hacienda. Despite her age Dilchthe worked hard and soon earned the trust of her owners.

They treated her fairly, but Dilchthe wanted her freedom. She hid food and planned to make a break for freedom, determined somehow, some way, to get back to her family. Finally, she freed several other women and together they escaped. Traveling only at night, Dilchthe led them from the hacienda to the gulf, then followed the coastline north. They evaded mounted search parties sent out to track them down: an Apache grandmother and a group of women slaves, making monkeys out of a bunch of hard-bitten vaqueros sent out to take the women back.

The women conserved their supplies as best they could, but eventually their provisions ran out, and they ate insects and desert plants. Still, they trudged north for nearly three hundred miles. Near the mouth of the gulf they almost met their match in the biggest obstacle yet—the Colorado River. None of them could swim, not even Dilchthe, but she insisted they would find a way. She made friends with an old Mexican who told her where they could safely ford the wide river. Once again the women pushed northward, to the spot the old man had described, the confluence of the Colorado and Gila Rivers, later the site of the Yuma Territorial Prison.

Carefully, Dilchthe waded into the cold water. Just when it looked as if she would be swept away, Dilchthe found a sandbar and quickly crossed to the other side. Her followers plunged in after her, all of them making it across.

They were now about halfway home, but the second part of their trip would be as hard as the first had been. Near the Yuma Valley they found barren terrain and sweltering heat. Some wanted to leave the lowlands and climb into the cooler mountains to the north, but Dilchthe knew those mountains were home to their enemies. Follow the Gila, she said, and it would eventually lead them home.

Three nights after they crossed the Colorado, a band of Yuma (or Mojave) raiders ambushed them. The raiders captured one woman and killed all of the rest except for Dilchthe and another who had fled into the brush.

Again they were hunted, but again Dilchthe proved too wily for their pursuers. For several days more the two Apache women walked, over the hot, mostly dry river bottom, past the Gila Bend, past present-day Phoenix (Maricopa Wells), and around the Pima and Papago camps and villages.

Almost crazed from grief and hunger, too weak to travel faster than a slow walk, the two women scrambled along for another hundred miles before finally collapsing northeast of present-day Safford, Arizona. Slowly pulling herself up, Dilchthe managed to make a signal fire.

Incredibly enough, one man who saw the fire was her son-in-law. Dilchthe and her friend were saved. She'd escaped her captors, outwitted and outmaneuvered all of her pursuers, carried no map, no weapons, and almost no provisions. She'd walked more than a thousand miles and finally was reunited with her family and welcomed back into her tribe as a hero.

Women of the West generally were tamers, not the shoot-'em-up wild variety. Some were wives, some were unmarried schoolteachers. Some were missionaries and some were prostitutes. Some were ex-slaves, such as Mary Fields, who drove a U.S. mail coach. Very few were the kind we see in movies, sunbonnet tipped back, riding in a covered wagon. Most worked their way west. Sometimes on horseback; more often than not, walking.

When it comes to famous women of the Wild West, one of the most famous wasn't from the West at all, unless you count Darke

County, Ohio, as the West. That's where Phoebe Ann Moses—she often spelled it Mozee—was born on August 13, 1860.*

Her father died in 1870, leaving his wife, Susan Mozee (or Moses), and six children to fend for themselves: Phoebe, sisters Elizabeth, Lydia, Hulda, and Sarah, and brother John. It fell to ten-year-old Phoebe to provide meat for the family table. Over the next few years she developed a skill with firearms, and it's said there always was "something for the pot."

The news of Phoebe's skill with a rifle spread, and in 1879 she was persuaded to compete against professional sharpshooter Frank Butler at Cincinnati's Coliseum Theater. When the match was finished, the embarrassed Butler handed Phoebe the prize of one hundred dollars. Not content with defeating Frank that one time, Phoebe followed him around from town to town, more often than not beating Butler at his own game.

In 1880 Frank Butler got around his competition: He married her, and for the next four years the pair toured theaters and music halls around the country. After that Frank retired from the business to manage his wife's career. In 1885 the Darke County native hit the big time: "Buffalo Bill's Wild West Show."** Throughout the United States, Canada, England, and Europe the little Ohio girl became a household name, idolized by audiences for her ability to split playing cards from thirty paces and, once, using a .22 rifle, breaking 943 out of 1,000 glass balls thrown into the air. No longer Phoebe Mozee, she was known as "Annie Oakley."

Another member of Buffalo Bill's traveling show, Sitting Bull, adopted her into the Sioux nation and gave her yet another name: Watanya Cicilia, "Little Miss Sure Shot." She proved to be as good as her name. Queen Victoria *was* amused, and at her request Annie shot a cigarette from the imperial lips of Crown Prince Wilhelm of Germany.

*Said by some to be 1864, others as 1866; 1860 is most likely the correct year.
**William F. "Buffalo Bill" Cody at first disliked the term *show*, saying it lacked dignity. When he first opened at the Omaha Fair Grounds on May 19, 1883, he called it "The Wild West, Hon. W. F. Cody and Dr. W. F. Carver's Mountain and Prairie Exhibition."

* * *

One of the West's most famous myths wasn't a myth at all. Johnny Appleseed was real, born John Chapman in Massachusetts in 1774. Not much is known about his early life, but sometime in his twenties Johnny took off from Philadelphia for the Ohio Valley with a supply of apple seeds. Wherever he went, he planted seeds, apparently as part of his belief in the teachings of Emanuel Swedenborg, a scientist who claimed that God talked to him about plants and such.

In any event, an anonymous letter written to the Swedenborg Society tells of Johnny, "a very extraordinary missionary of the New Jerusalem." According to the letter Johnny

> goes barefooted, can sleep anywhere, in house or out of house, and live upon the coarsest and most scanty fare. He has actually thawed the ice with his bare feet. . . .
>
> This man for years past has been in the employment of bringing into cultivation, in numberless places in the wilderness, small patches (two or three acres) of ground, and then sowing apple seeds and rearing nurseries. These become valuable as the settlements approximate, and the profits of the whole are intended for the purpose of enabling him to print all the Writings of Emanual Swedenborg, and distribute them through the western settlements of the United States.

Before his death (apparently in 1840), Johnny Appleseed talked with a farmer named Harding. "I shall never forget," Amos Harding said,

> how pleased [Johnny Appleseed] appeared to be when we came up to him in the wilderness, four miles from a living soul but Indians, among bears, wolves, catamounts, serpents, owls and porcupines, yet apparently contented and happy. Here Johnny had some poles put on crotches, covered with elm bark. Some five or six rods from this were logs cut for a cabin and some clapboards for a roof.

This, Johnny said, "is the way I live."

The meeting was near Amos Harding's farm near Blooming Grove, Ohio. Amos Harding? He was president Warren Harding's great-grandfather.

And there's the story of Pecos Bill, who was not, they said, "a man of flesh and blood." They say. Anyway, Bill spoke his first words the moment he was born; "Gimme a drink," he said to his mother.

Pecos Bill was born with a full set of teeth, a full head of red hair, and seven bristly hairs on his chest. Started chawin' 'baccer three days after he was born.

On Bill's third birthday his mammy and pappy set out to stake a claim in the Texas Panhandle. Hitched up a team of oxen to their prairie schooner, tied a milch cow and a horse on the rear end, and stowed a cage of a dozen or so chickens and a barrel of whiskey in the wagon. They put their nineteen children inside—some of them were quintuplets, with Bill the youngest—and headed out. They'd just crossed the Pecos River when the left front wheel hit a big rock and Bill got jolted clear out of the wagon. There were so many youngsters left in the wagon, nobody realized Bill was gone until that night when they counted heads and were one head short.

That's how Pecos Bill got his name. His folks weren't worried much. After all, he was all of three years old and near on to six feet tall. "Old 'nuff to fend for hisself," Pappy said. "Wall, iff'n you say so," Bill's mammy said.

Back at the Pecos, Bill crawled off into the chaparral, where he found hisself face to face with an ol' coyote name of Methuselah, on account he was old an' smart.

"Here, little doggie, nice little doggie," Bill says.

"Doggie, hell," Methuselah says. "I ain't no damn dog. I'm a coyote, boy, and you look like a lost calf without his mammy. I reckon I'll just have to take care of you," which Methuselah did, and showed Bill a lady coyote sucklin' two pups. "That's your chuck wagon," Methuselah says. "Thar's nipples enough for one more."

So Pecos Bill was raised by this pack of coyotes, which called him "No Tail" for obvious reasons.

* * *

We won't go into Bigfoot or Sasquash or the Abominable Snow-man, and you can believe them or not.

Not only the world rushed into the American West. Some may have rushed in from beyond. At least six incidents of flying saucers over the Wild West are recorded.

Twice in 1873 shining objects reportedly roared over military out-posts. Once at Fort Riley, Kansas, whatever the things were, they frightened cavalry horses into a panic. Again that year at Bonham, Texas, an unidentified object reportedly zoomed several times over a group of field-workers. Like the Fort Riley horses the workers pan-icked.

Twice in 1897 there were reports of mysterious aerial objects. Once, over Benton, Texas, an object described as saucer shaped hov-ered and shined a searchlight beneath it. Later that year, in both of the Kansas Cities—Kansas and Missouri—people reported seeing disk-shaped objects bearing brightly colored lights flying through the air.

As the century came to an end in El Paso, residents claimed to have seen an illuminated disk high in the sky. Whatever it was (or wasn't) may have stuck around to visit Prescott, Arizona, where a sim-ilar phenomenon reportedly occurred.

Today those who don't believe in flying saucers claim that many alleged UFO sightings are nothing more than weather balloons, maybe bits of space junk from space rockets. In the 1800s, of course, there were no weather balloons or rockets. We have no idea what the Kansas and Nebraska flying objects were.

Just as the Wild West had its soiled doves and even Emily "Yellow Rose" Morgan, it had their opposite, the "Harvey Girls." Beginning in the 1880s entrepreneur Fred Harvey set up a chain of restaurants along the Santa Fe Railroad in Kansas, Colorado, and New Mexico. Many lasted until the 1950s. Harvey hired thousands of single women to serve hungry travelers. When not working in Harvey-owned restau-rants the Harvey Girls lived in Harvey-owned dormitories. Off duty, however, they could do as they pleased within reason, meaning they could do just about anything that didn't throw a bad light on the restaurant. In 1907 they were remembered in the lyrics of a popular song:

O the pretty Harvey Girl beside my chair,
A fairer maiden I shall never see.
She was winsome, she was neat, she was gloriously sweet,
And she was certainly good to me.

CHAPTER TWELVE

Wyatt Earp and Friends:
Shootouts and Stickups

Agnes, Darling, if such should be that we never meet again, while firing my last shot, I will gently breathe the name of my wife—Agnes—and with wishes even for my enemies I will make the plunge and try to swim to the other shore.
William Butler "Wild Bill" Hickok, written to his wife,
Agnes Lake Hickok, the day before he was killed

Mad, bad, and dangerous to know.
Lady Caroline Lamb, speaking about the poet
Lord Byron, March 1812

Wild Bill Hickok was noted for his steely stare. Some said that he didn't have to shoot anybody, all he had to do was give them a good hard look. Well, maybe.

Historian Joseph Rosa claims that Bill was going blind and blames a condition called trachoma, an eye disease generally limited today to third world countries. The American West of the 1800s *was* a third world country. In the nineteenth century trachoma constituted "so serious a risk of blindness that the immigration authorities no longer allow any case of it to enter the country." Health inspectors at Ellis Island in New York used a button hook to roll back an eyelid to check for inflammation. They didn't always catch it at Ellis Island, of course, and trachoma frequently turned up in schools with large immigrant populations. In New York, for the quarter ending December 31, 1892, out of 24,538 cases of infectious diseases found, 12,647 of them were for trachoma.

It would have been easy for Hickok to have contracted the eye disease from any of the many immigrants he came in contact with in the Wild West.

Of course, there's another possible explanation for Wild Bill's apparent poor eyesight. It seems that, because of the times and his frequent association with soiled doves, Hickok suffered from syphilis, a disease that, if not checked, can lead to blindness.

At any rate, by the time he died in 1876, Wild Bill Hickok was nearly blind. His steely gaze may simply have been a squint to get things in focus.

Two range-weary men walk slowly toward each other as the noonday sun glistens off the star on one man's shirt and beats down on a hot, dusty street. The men stare at each other, anticipating just the right moment, almost daring the other to make his move. Twenty yards apart now. Suddenly! With lightning speed the tall man slaps his holstered gun, and sweat pops out of his opponent's brow—he knows he'll be late and only hopes his aim is better than the marshal's. The lawman's bullet slams into the bad guy's chest. In a last futile gesture the man wanted in four states and three territories squeezes his trigger, and the .45 slug from his Colt Peacemaker clangs off the church bell. He's down now, his black hat with its greasy brim and rattlesnake band rolls beneath the horse tied outside the Long Branch Saloon. The horse rears once at the sound of the first shot, but settles back into his hip-shot stance, tail worrying the flies that worry him.

Twenty yards away the marshal holsters his gun as Doc rushes to check the downed man and red-haired Miss Kitty gently touches Marshal Dillon's arm and says, "Be careful, Matt!" And the director yells, "Cut!"

It's a popular image—a shootout at high noon. The only trouble is there's no evidence of it happening more than once in all the Wild West.

In fact, some historians now say the Wild West wasn't nearly as wild as we've come to believe. Take Billy the Kid, whose real name was Henry McCarty. Legend has him as a psychopathic murderer who had killed twenty-one people by the time he was twenty-one himself. But historian W. Eugene Hollon says that he "can only account for three men he killed for sure, and there were probably no more than three or four." Which, of course, was quite enough.

And William Barclay Masterson, better known as Bat Masterson, a town-tamer whose gun butts were sawtoothed with a score of notches. Nonsense, Hollon claims; "the actual number was only three." Masterson, incidentally, was born in Illinois, lived in Dodge City, Kansas, and wound up life in 1921, as a sportswriter for the *New York Morning Telegraph*.

* * *

James Butler Hickok fairly dazzled Libbie Custer, George's widow. In her 1890 book *Following the Guidon* Libbie Custer wrote:

> Physically, he was a delight to look upon. Tall, lithe, and free in every motion. He rode and walked as if every muscle was perfection, and the careless swing of his body as he moved seemed perfectly in keeping with the man, the country, the time in which he lived. I do not recall anything finer in the way of physical perfection than Wild Bill when he swung himself lightly from his saddle, with graceful step, squarely set shoulders and well poised head, approached our tent for orders.

After reading Libbie Custer's description you wonder why she stayed with poor George. Actually, her husband may have been jealous of Hickok and, in some ways, even patterned himself after him. "Whether on foot or on horseback," George Custer wrote about Hickok, "he was one of the most perfect types of physical manhood I ever saw." Maybe both Libbie and George Custer were in love with Hickok.

Born in Homer (later, Troy Grove), La Salle County, Illinois, on May 27, 1837, Hickok stood six feet two or three—it's not certain—in his custom-made boots, long auburn hair—like his height there's some confusion over Bill's hair color; he may have been a natural blond—tumbling in ringlets to his waist, and he wore a Prince Albert frock coat. His ancestors came from Stratford-upon-Avon, England, neighbors of William Shakespeare; his branch of the family moved to America in 1635 and established themselves in the Connecticut Colony, then spread through New England.

His father died when James was only fifteen and the boy went to work driving a wagon and hunting wolves for bounty money. Three years later, at age eighteen, he got into his first scrap—something like a pushing incident—and thought he'd killed his opponent. He hadn't, but Hickok didn't know this and set off for the West. When he got to Kansas the area was in the middle of one of the bloodiest periods in American history, the pre–Civil War clashes between slaveholders and abolitionists, Quantrill's Raiders and Border Ruffians. "Bleeding Kansas," it was called. Hickok became abolitionist Jim Lane's bodyguard. When he wasn't guarding Lane's body, he was interested in another body, that of an Anglo-Shawnee girl named Mary Jane Owen. Writing home, Bill often mentioned Mary Jane:

> I went to see my girl yesterday and ate blackberries that she picked Saturday. You ought to be there to eat some of her biscuits. She is the only one I ever saw that could beat Mother making biscuits, and I ought to know, for I can eat a few, you know.
>
> Mary cut off a lock of my hair yesterday and said for me to send it to my mother or sisters. If she had not thought a great deal of you all she would not have cut it off, for she thinks a great deal of it. At least she is always combing and curling it, that is, when I am there.

Hickok may have married Mary Jane Owen, although there's no firm evidence one way or the other. Married to or just fooling around with Mary Jane, it got Hickok interested in settling down, and he took up a claim, as it was termed, and began homesteading a dugout home near Monticello Township. In 1858 he was elected the township's constable, his first stint as a peace officer, and it may not have been so peaceful. He later told the highly impressionable Libbie Custer that, while he was constable, a gang of ruffians cornered him in Leavenworth, Kansas, and that he killed five of them. Well, maybe.

Neither his association with Mary Jane nor his job as constable lasted long, and the following year he turned up along the Santa Fe Trail, driving a wagon. His employer: Russell, Majors, and Waddell, who in just a couple of years would open up the short-lived Pony Express.

By then Hickok had dropped the name "James" or "Jim" and become known as "Bill." Toward the end of 1860, while driving through New Mexico's Raton Pass, Bill Hickok tangled with a bear, and it almost cost him his life. Russell, Majors, and Waddell sent the badly mauled Bill to recuperate at their Rock Creek, Nebraska, stagecoach way-station. The man in charge of the station was David McCanles, and he and Bill didn't get along too well. One story is that McCanles took one look at Bill's large, curved nose, short chin, and the way the young man's upper lip protruded over his lower* and called him "Duck Bill" Hickok, and only later did the nickname get changed to "Wild Bill." Well, maybe. Another story is that Bill once talked a would-be necktie party out of hanging one of Bill's pals; as the unofficial jury slunk away, an unidentified woman in the crowd shouted, "Good for you, Wild Bill."

At any rate, McCanles teased Bill about his girlish ways and slim figure and called him a hermaphrodite. Bill resented McCanles's treatment but didn't do anything about it. Dave McCanles, however, had other troubles. He lived with his family in a cabin across the creek from the stagecoach station; he also had a girlfriend, a Miss Sarah Shull, living in a nearby cabin. McCanles warned Bill to stay on his own side of the creek if he wanted to live.

Bill's hormones did get the better of him and Dave McCanles found him in Sarah's cabin. Dave threatened to drag Duck Bill outside, and Wild Bill answered, "There'll be one less son of a bitch when you try that." Dave did try and Bill pulled his gun and shot Dave in the chest. McCanles stumbled outside only to die in the arms of his twelve-year-old son, Monroe. A cousin, James Woods, and another stagecoach employee, James Gordon, were looking on. Woods rushed for the cabin door, and Hickok shot him twice, then turned to fire at Gordon, who was coming in the back way. He missed.

A couple of other station workers, J. W. Brink and Horace Wellman (some say it was Mrs. Wellman), got into the fracas. One took a shotgun to Gordon and the other hacked Woods to death with a garden hoe. It was a fairly bloody mess, but it was even bloodier when the story appeared in the popular *Harper's New Monthly Magazine*, in a story entitled "Wild Bill." The writer, Col. George Ward Nichols, claimed that Hickok was armed with a revolver, a rifle, and a bowie knife when he was attacked by Dave "M'Kandlas" and nine members of his "party of ruffians." Bill reportedly told Nichols, "I was wild and

---

*Because of his protruding upper lip, Wild Bill Hickok later took to trying to conceal the fault under long mustachios.

I struck savage blows, following the devils from one side to the other of the room and into the corners, striking and slashing until I knew that every one was dead." He added:

> As ter killing men, I never thought much about it. The most of the men I have killed it was one or t'other of us, and at sich times you don't stop to think; and what's the use after it's all over? . . . I am a fighting man, you know?

Another account turned up in the *Kansas City Journal,* with reporter J. W. Buel, who was personally acquainted with Hickok, claiming Wild Bill had killed ten outlaws, but that, in return, he suffered four bullet wounds, a skull fracture, numerous knife gashes, and a slash to the head that left Bill's scalp hanging across his eyes. If she'd seen that, it's doubtful Libbie Custer would have been so dazzled by Bill.

And there was a third rendition of the encounter with McCanles, "Wild Bill, the Pistol Deadshot" by dime novelist Colonel Prentis Ingraham. Each time the story was told, things got worse. This time Bill supposedly was shot eleven times while fighting off the McCanles gang.

Some historians claim the real reason behind the Hickok-McCanles shooting was that McCanles was the leader of a band of Southern patriots and that he was going to turn the stage station's horses over to the Confederacy. In steps Bill Hickok, who has already served the abolitionist cause in Kansas, and kills the pro-South station master. An early Hickok biographer, Frank K. Wilsatch, held the theory that McCanles intended to steal the station's horse herd and operate along the Oregon Trail with a band of anti-Union guerrillas. Wilsatch even talked with the then-ninety-three-year-old Sarah Shull. She wouldn't talk about her relationship with McCanles, but when asked if Bill Hickok had shot in self-defense, answered, "Certainly— yes." She backed up the theory that McCanles had gone to the Rock Creek Station to "steal horses for the Confederate cavalry."

Whatever the real story, Bill Hickok and the two men (or maybe one man and a woman) who reportedly did the killing and chopping were arrested by the sheriff of Gage County, taken before the justice of the peace, and pleaded self-defense. Their further contention was that they were defending government property—the wagons, stages, and horses used to carry the United States mail. Justice T. M. Coulter accepted the plea and turned all three loose without a trial. With that Bill left the Rock Creek station* and spent the Civil War years as an army scout and bullwhacker on wagon trains. After the war he showed up in Springfield, Missouri, and it's here that Hickok really earns his Wild Bill nickname and we get our one documented shootout.

In her description of Bill Hickok when he was working as a scout with her husband, Libbie Custer wrote that "he was rather fantastically clad, but all seemed perfectly in keeping with the time and place. He did not make an armory of his waist, but carried two pistols." It was with those pistols—two ivory-hilted, silver-mounted Navy Colt pistols resting in a red sash around his waist—that Bill used in the only documented, man-to-man, quick-draw duel in the West. Which brings us back to Springfield, Missouri, on July 21, 1865.

As biographer Richard O'Connor succinctly puts it: "Enter Dave Tutt, exit Dave Tutt." Bill Hickok was augmenting his salary with frequent gambling, and as any gambler knows, you win a few and you lose a lot. In this case, Bill had been playing cards with a onetime friend, twenty-six-year-old Dave Tutt, and Tutt won.

Earlier, Bill had been a hot item with a young Ozark girl, Susanna Moore; they'd met during the war when Hickok had been in Arkansas on a mission for the army. She was a good-looking blue-eyed brunette, and if the two didn't fall for each other, Susanna at least fell for Bill. But came the end of the mission, Bill rode out of town. Shortly after Hickok arrived in Springfield, Susanna Moore rode into town. She found that although her affections toward Bill were still hot, Hickok's affections toward her had cooled considerably. At the time Bill Hickok and Dave Tutt were friends, but then Susanna fas-

---

*In 1926 the Nebraska Historical Society unearthed a box of moldering documents that told of a preliminary hearing in the case of *The Territory of Nebraska vs. William* [*sic*] *B. Hickok.* They indicated that McCanles's son, Monroe, was called as a witness but for some reason never testified.

tened her attentions on Dave, possibly to make Bill jealous, and the two men's friendship ended.

Bill and Dave get into a poker game at the Lyon House Bar, and Dave wins—Bill says it's twenty-five dollars, Dave claims it's thirty-five. Whatever, Bill gives him his pocket watch to secure the debt, warning Dave not to show it off. Dave, however, isn't impressed by Hickok's warnings and wears the watch openly. Wild Bill Hickok is a proud man, and Dave Tutt, who now is squiring around Bill's former girlfriend, is a boastful one.

Comes the afternoon of the twenty-first. Bill Hickok is standing at the entrance of the Lyon House, and across the square, standing in the doorway of the livery stable, is Dave Tutt. That morning Bill had asked a bystander if Dave was wearing a watch. "If he's wearing it," Bill declares, "there'll be merry hell."

Tutt cuts across the square, and sunlight glistens off Bill's watch hanging from Dave's vest pocket. They're about seventy yards apart, and Bill calls out, "Don't come any closer, Dave." Tutt ignores the warning.

Instead, Dave draws his gun and fires. In a fraction of a second, with his right hand, Bill draws one of his Colts and uses his left hand to steady his shot, not unlike the way modern pistol shooters stand. Aiming carefully—he doesn't want to damage his own watch—Bill Hickok fires. According to one witness, the two shots sound like one.

For a second both men freeze in their tracks, then, stiff as a board, Dave Tutt falls on his face, shot clean through the heart. Hickok wheels around and confronts a group of Tutt's friends standing behind him. "Are you satisfied, gentlemen?" he asks. "Put up your guns or there'll be more dead men here."

Bill Hickok hands his revolver to the sheriff and surrenders. The Greene County Circuit Court's in session, and he doesn't have long to wait for a trial. Some of Tutt's friends are trying to arrange a lynching, but Bill's attorney is a former congressman and wartime governor of Arkansas, John S. Phelps. Hickok had served with an army regiment commanded by Phelps's son, Col. John E. Phelps.

Placed in evidence during the trial is Dave Tutt's gun, with one empty chamber that shows he'd shot at Hickok. With that, and testimony that Tutt looked to be the aggressor, the jury acquits Bill. Hickok goes free and he gets his watch back.

Back with the army as a scout, Bill meets army-deserter-turned-journalist Henry Stanley. Hickok tells the gullible Stanley that he has personally killed over a hundred men.

In 1866 Hickok helped guide Gen. William T. Sherman during the general's tour of the West, and for a couple of years scouted for Gen. Winfield Scott Hancock and Lt. Col. George Armstrong Custer. Off and on from 1867 to 1870 Wild Bill worked as a deputy U.S. marshal. In Hays City, Kansas, on August 23, 1869, he won a special election to complete the unexpired term of the Ellis County sheriff. As sheriff he took to wearing not only his two Colts, but a bowie knife, and carrying a sawed-off shotgun.

Not long after the election Hickok confronted a hell-raiser from St. Joseph, Missouri, Bill Mulvey, who'd gotten drunk at Drum's saloon and begun shooting out lamps and windows. Hickok told him to give up his gun, but instead Mulvey holstered the weapon and then tried to draw on Bill. He never cleared leather, as Bill shot him in the chest. A month later it happened again, and this time at John Bittles's saloon, and ended with Bill shooting Samuel Strawhan* — a "typical frontier desperado," says historian Eugene Cunningham in his 1934 book, *Triggernometry: A Gallery of Gunfighters.* Strawhan and Hickok had had trouble before. A purported witness wrote a Leavenworth, Kansas, newspaper about the shooting:

It seems that there was on the part of this Stranham and some of his associates a bad feeling against certain citizens of this town [Hays], and members of the Vigilance committee. To satisfy their hatred they mobbed together and went on Sunday night, about half-past 11 o'clock to the saloon of Mr. John Bitter [Bittles], with the intent to break up the establishment.

The bunch had been crying, "Beer! beer!" and "the glasses had to be filled up continually. Meanwhile, the men were passing in and

---

*Or Stranham or Strawhim, nobody could spell anything in the Wild West or cared much about it.

out of the saloon," each time carrying out a glass but seldom bringing it back in:

> During all the noise one could hear threats as: "I shall kill some one to-night just for luck," or "some one will have to go up to-night," etc.
>
> Mr. Bitter [Bittles] finally called the policeman, Mr. Wm. Hickok [*sic*], known as "Wild Bill," asking him to go out and fetch the missing glasses back. Wild Bill shortly returned with both hands full of glasses, when Stranham remarked that he would shoot anyone that should try to interfere with his fun. Wild Bill set the glasses on the counter, Stranham took hold of one and took it up in a threatening manner. He had no time to execute his design for a shot fired by Mr. Hickok killed him.

Years later a friend of Hickok's recalled that when Bill carried the glasses back into the saloon, he called out, "Boys, you hadn't ought to treat a poor old man [Bittles] in this way." Stranhan reportedly said that he'd throw the glasses out again. "Do," Wild Bill replied, "and they will carry you out." With that Bill shot first and only later considered the outcome, which was that Sam Stranhan was dead. The killing was ruled justified.

On July 17, 1870, two drunken troopers from the 7th Cavalry attacked Hickok: Two shots from Bill, one dead soldier, one wounded one. Wild Bill Hickok's reputation as a killer, if not as a peacemaker, was growing.

About this time Joe McCoy, the man who virtually built Abilene, Kansas, from the ground up, realized that his town was a lure to pickpockets, crooked gamblers, whores, and confidence men. Cowboys driving herds to town were shooting things up with regularity. So McCoy hired an experienced lawman to be marshal: Thomas James Smith, a husky, Irish, ex–New York policeman and former troubleshooter for the Union Pacific Railroad during riots at Bear River, Wyoming. "Bear River Tom Smith," as he was known, didn't drink, didn't gamble, and didn't cuss.

For the most part he didn't even use a six-shooter to handle recalcitrant cowboys and such. Once, early in his time in Abilene, Smith encountered a cowboy known as Big Hank who had a pistol in his belt, and it was against the law to carry firearms in town. "What are you going to do about the law?" Big Hank asked Sheriff Smith. "I'm going to see it's obeyed," Smith replied. Twice Smith asked for Big Hank's gun and twice the cowboy refused. Suddenly, Smith slammed his fist into Hank's jaw, and the big Texan went down cold. Smith took Big Hank's pistol, and when the cowboy stirred, he ordered him out of town. The next morning the same thing happened with a desperado called Wyoming Frank. Again Smith slugged the bad guy, again the bad guy went down, and again Tom Smith disarmed him. With that others in the saloon offered up their own weapons; Smith said, Check them with the bartender, and he strolled out of the saloon.

Tom had been on the job about five months when he tried to settle a difference of opinion between two homesteaders. One claimed the other's cattle was grazing on his land; the argument got hot, and Andrew McConnell killed John Shea. McConnell pleaded self-defense, but neighbors swore out a murder warrant, and Smith and Deputy James H. McDonald went to bring McConnell in. But McConnell was waiting with a friend at his side and a Winchester in his hand. Smith was barely out of the saddle when McConnell shot him in the chest. Smith and McConnell fought, and McConnell's friend, Moses Miles, slugged Marshal Smith over the head with a gun, then picked up an ax and virtually decapitated the lawman.

All this time Deputy McDonald stood rooted to the spot, offering no help. Finally he turned on his horse and rode back to town to tell everybody what had happened. "There being nobody to dispute him, his story had to go," a witness recalled, "but I can recall the looks that passed between men who had been raised from birth to eat six-shooters." McDonald kept his job as deputy, but no one ever paid him much mind after that. It was obvious the town needed another strong lawman, and on April 15, 1871, the Abilene town council confirmed the appointment of James Butler Hickok, at $150 a month, plus twenty-five percent of all fines he collected and fifty cents for every stray dog he killed. Actually, this was a savings for Abilene. They'd paid Tom Smith $250 a month with the same cut.

For the next nine months Hickok was Abilene town marshal, but unlike Bear River Tom, Wild Bill used his pistols to maintain law and order. Bill didn't strictly enforce the town's no-guns rule, but not too many cared to go up against him, even in September when he closed down Abilene's saloons and gambling establishments. Some of the townsfolk, however, thought Wild Bill spent too much time at the poker table and not enough time enforcing the law.

Remember Susanna Moore? Wild Bill Hickok's onetime Ozark in-amorata who'd followed him to Springfield, Missouri, only to set off an argument between Bill and Dave Tutt? Well, seeing Bill firmly en-sconced in a new job, she followed him to Abilene. Together they shared a cottage for a while, until Bill went wild with some ladies from the local bordello. Susanna said, Oh, no, and cried for Bill as she de-parted town, never again to grace his history.

Joe McCoy was one of Hickok's advocates, especially when Wild Bill carried out McCoy's request to bring a derelict councilman to a meeting; Bill picked up the man and slung him over his shoulders like a sack of corn. McCoy considered Bill "the squarest man I ever saw."

Well-known Texas outlaw John Wesley Hardin claimed he'd once tricked Hickok with a gun spin during the summer of 1871. The story was that Hardin had been doing a bit of roistering in a local saloon. Hickok came in and ordered John Wesley to hand over his guns. Hardin offered them, butts forward. When Wild Bill reached for them, Hardin performed the road-agents spin. Just how the trick works isn't certain now, if it was certain at the time, but Hardin claimed that

I said all right and pulled them [his guns] out of the scabbard [holster], but while [Wild Bill] was reaching for them, I re-versed them and whirled them over on him with the muzzles in his face, springing back at the same time. I told him to put his pistols up, which he did.

Trouble is, there's no evidence it ever happened, only John Wes-ley Hardin's word on it. And, too, note that Bill Hickok was hold-ing his guns on Hardin at the time, and it's difficult to visualize Bill holding his own pistols and reaching out to get John Wesley's at the same time.

Earlier a hardcase known as Ben Thompson had tried to talk Hardin into fighting Hickok. "He's a damn Yankee," Thompson said. "Picks on rebels, especially Texans, to kill."

John Wesley Hardin was having nothing to do with it. "If Wild Bill needs killin'," he replied, "why don't you kill him yourself." Hardin didn't stick around Abilene long after that.

Not long after the purported Hardin–road-agents spin incident, Bill Hickok answered a call to go to the Bull's Head Saloon, where gamblers Phil Coe and Ben Thompson had installed a larger-than-life-size painting of a Texas longhorn bull. The sign may not have been sexually explicit, but it was certainly anatomically correct. Many of Abilene's better sort (maybe its snootier sort) objected to the display and called on Bill to do something about the bull. So Hickok stood by with shotgun in hand while deletions were made to the painted longhorn's anatomy. The thing seemed settled; Thompson left town and Coe sold his interest in the saloon but continued on as the bar's gambler in residence.

Which might have ended it all right there, except that—as happened so often with Wild Bill—a young lady was involved, Jesse Hazel, the proprietor of an expensive bawdy house. Both Coe and Hickok were interested in Jesse. According to some sources, when Bill heard Coe and Jesse were openly consorting (and cavorting) in a local saloon, Hickok barged in and angrily slapped her to the floor. Coe was unarmed at the time and didn't interfere, which likely would have been something akin to public suicide if he had. From then on, Bill Hickok and Phil Coe were sworn enemies.

The trouble came to a head when a bunch of cowboys were in town doing their usual thing—fighting, drinking, carousing, and more drinking. Hickok took a special policeman, Mike Williams, along for assistance. Right in the middle of it all was Phil Coe.

Now, Coe normally doesn't carry a revolver—he considers himself more of a fistfight kind of guy—but this time he does. He and a bunch of Texas friends are headed for the Alamo Saloon, when for some unknown reason a dog tries to bite Coe. Phil takes a shot at him but misses. Bill Hickok appears and demands to know what's going on. Coe tries to explain, but it doesn't satisfy the marshal.

Hickok draws both pistols and shoots Coe twice in the stomach. Phil fires back but misses his target; his bullet rips through Hickok's coat. With Coe lying on the ground mortally wounded, Bill hears footsteps behind him. He turns without looking and fires. It's not one of Coe's pals, but Hickok's deputy, Mike Williams.

Three days later Phil Coe dies of his Hickok-inflicted wounds. Bill pays for Mike Williams's funeral. And the Abilene city fathers tell the Texans there'll be no more cattle drives to their towns, which means there'll be no more hell-raising, which means the town no longer needs Bill's services, which means they fire him as town marshal. It's the last time Bill Hickok serves as a peace officer. From here on out it's gambling, a fling with Col. Sidney Barnett's Wild West Show, and an embarrassing two-day stint in Niagara Falls, New York as an actor—"Fear not, fair maid! By heavens you are safe at last with Wild Bill, who is ever ready to risk his life and die, if need be, in defense of weak and helpless womanhood." Life rapidly goes downhill for Bill. He drinks a lot and forgets these less-than-immortal lines. When he does, he turns to the audience and trades jokes with the paying crowd. Saying he hates performing, the consummate performer quits the stage.

In the spring of 1873 rumors fly that Wild Bill Hickok is dead, that a band of Texans have murdered Bill in Fort Dodge, Kansas. To let everybody know he's still alive, Hickok writes letters to newspapers, including one in which says of dime novelist Ned Buntline, "Ned Buntline has been trying to murder me for years. Having failed to do so, he is trying to have it done by some Texans."

Broke now, Wild Bill accepts Buffalo Bill Cody's offer to tour the East with him. The stint lasts only five months, and Hickok leaves for the West.

Time goes on and there's still some fire left in him, but to some it's obvious that Wild Bill Hickok has become "Weak Eyes" Hickok. He's going on forty, going bald, and wears dark glasses. He marries longtime actress, horsewoman, tightrope walker, dancer, and lion-tamer Agnes Lake, after divorcing Calamity Jane, if that Wild West odd couple really were married. When she first met Bill, one historian writes, Agnes "fell [for him] with a crash, clean through to the basement." She's ten years older than Bill, and they tie the knot in Cheyenne on March 5, 1876, then spend their honeymoon in Cincinnati. A month later Hickok goes off by himself to the western goldfields looking for a grubstake.

The closest he gets to the goldfields is a poker table in Deadwood, South Dakota, and by now he admits, "My eyes are getting real bad. My shooting days are over."

Wild Bill once claimed that "I never allowed a man to get the drop on me," but that would change. Less than five months after marrying Agnes, Bill gets into a poker game at Carl Mann's Saloon No. 10. He holds the now-famous "dead man's hand" of two aces and two eights. A cross-eyed ex–buffalo hunter named Jack McCall slips up behind Bill, pulls a .45-caliber revolver from his coat pocket, and shouts, "Take that!"

Wild Bill Hickok is gone and the Wild West is never the same after that.

Wild Bill Hickok had three passions: poker, women, and baseball. Nearly every Sunday while he was in Kansas City, Bill watched games played by the KC Antelopes on a diamond near Fourteenth and Oak Streets. The game at the time was, like that part of the country, wild and woolly—no grandstand, no scoreboard, no shelter against the sun. If the umpire ruled against the home team in a crucial manner, fans would swarm all over him, sometimes beating the ump with fists or bottles or gun butts.

Which may be the reason the Kansas City Antelopes always won on their home field. Once, however, when they played the Atchison Pomeroys at Atchison, the Pomeroys won. Next time the two teams played in Kansas City the game ended in a riot, with the umpire running for his life. The *Kansas City Times* ran the story under a headline:

THE TOWN IS
DISGRACED

Everybody apologizes, and the teams agree to replay the game the following Saturday. And they have Wild Bill Hickok for an umpire.

Game time, and Bill is behind the plate. No modern-day mask or chest protector, but Hickok has other armaments: his pair of six-shooters. It is, they say, the most decorous game ever played in baseball history, and, in a pitchers' duel, the Antelopes win, 48 to 28.

Robert Leroy Parker was better known as "Butch Cassidy" of the Wild Bunch, sometimes called the "Hole in the Wall Gang." The hole itself was in Wyoming, about fifty miles south of Buffalo, due east of the Powder River.

Butch teamed up with Harry Longbaugh, alias the "Sundance Kid," and together they crisscrossed Wyoming, living off the take of their frequent robbing of banks and railroads. They took especial notice of Union Pacific Railroad express cars, although they weren't always successful. Once the boys used too much of the Kepauno Chemical Company's "Giant" powder to open up a railroad car loaded with a mining camp payroll. The blast scattered more than thirty thousand dollars, worth of bills over the nearby range.

Often Butch and Sundance were accompanied by onetime school-marm Etta Place. She was an extremely attractive and fashionable young lady and apparently shared the love and allegiance of both Butch and Sundance. She and Sundance once posed for a photograph together, and that gives rise to a belief that she and the Kid were more than just friends, but who knows?

Throughout their railroad-robbing career Butch and Sundance were hounded by agents of the detective agency founded by Allan Pinkerton, the man who'd started what came to be the United States Secret Service. After a while the boys decided they'd had enough of the Pinkertons, or at least they had enough loot to last for a while. In 1902 they and Etta Place, along with a valise loaded with thirty thousand dollars in ill-gotten gains, sailed onboard the SS *Soldier Prince* for South America.

There Etta Place kept house with and for the boys. Etta, however, was stricken by what was called "acute appendicitis." It's not certain what the real problem was, certainly not acute appendicitis, which, if untreated, would have killed her in short order. Well into the 1930s the term *acute appendicitis* was used to excuse a woman's absence while she gave birth to an illegitimate child.

Sundance accompanied her back to Denver, where she checked into a hospital, and that's the last heard of Etta Place. She apparently remained in the United States, but the Sundance Kid returned to South America.

Traditionally, gunmen in the early Wild West wore two revolvers and had the ability to use both at once or to shoot with either hand with equal skill. Actually, they almost had to carry two guns, because many grew up carrying flintlock weapons, slow-loading and generally unreliable. To overcome the difficulty of single-shot weapons a number of double-barreled and multishot weapons were developed. Some were unwieldy and consisted of clusters of barrels welded together on a central axle and often called "pepperboxes"—Mark Twain once wrote of seeing a fellow traveler carrying a pepperbox or "Allen" revolver on a western trip in 1861. Some had a number of stationary barrels and a rotating firing pin and others had a cluster of barrels that revolved, not unlike later-designed revolvers. They varied from .22 to .36 caliber and had one thing in common: They all were cumbersome.

In 1807 Alexander Forsyth came up with a firing system using fulminate of mercury, and the percussion cap soon followed, revolutionizing the arms industry. Along came Samuel Colt, who invented a revolver that became the most popular pistol in the West. He patented his invention in 1836—collectors call them "Paterson Colts," because Sam Colt lived in Paterson, New Jersey, at the time—but went broke because nobody bought them. As historian William Foster-Harris says in *The Look of the Old West,* "As usually happens when you first make a better mousetrap—and don't let them tell you otherwise—both the mice and the public [are] suspicious." What was good enough for Grandpa, Foster-Harris writes, seemed good enough for the modern generation of 1836. Sam Colt went down to Texas in 1839 and decided two things: (1) Nobody in Texas had any money to buy his or anybody else's revolvers; and (2) people down there didn't care about his or any other patents and would make their own pistols, using whatever design they chose.

So Colt left Texas, but not before leaving a sample or two in strategic hands. And, in something sounding like a Hollywood script, Capt.

Jack Hayes of the Texas Rangers gets hold of one of Sam's revolvers, likes what he sees, and orders a hundred of them, one for each man then in the force. Paying for them was something else, since Texas money was going rapidly down and finally hit a low of two cents to the American dollar. About that time the Rangers ran into a band of Comanches—the Indians were trying to ambush them at Bandera Pass—who expected the Texans would be getting off only one shot per gun. Ha! They hadn't heard about Sam Colt's Paterson revolvers! The only reason any of the Indians survived was that the Rangers dismounted, which was the wrong thing to do when using revolvers, and a few of the Comanches managed to escape, wondering what in hell they'd run into.

With that, Colt's revolver became the weapon of choice for Texas Rangers. In 1845 Texas joins the Union; in 1846 the Union goes to war with Mexico, and a lot of Texans join Zachary Taylor's army, scarfing up all of the Colt revolvers they can. Zach Taylor sends Capt. Samuel H. Walker of the Texas Rangers after more of Colt's handy-dandy weapons. Between Walker and Colt they cook up the so-called Walker Colt, a he-man-size, 15½-inch-long, 9-inch-barrel revolver, weighing four pounds nine ounces unloaded. Unlike the Paterson the Walker Colt has a trigger guard, a loading lever under the barrel, six chambers in the cylinder—it took on the name "six-shooter" and the name stuck—and could throw a .44-caliber, half-ounce slug from here to there. Little good it did Sam Walker. He died in the fall of 1847, and the Colts bearing his name didn't reach the army until February 1848, near the end of the Mexican War.

Colt called his next weapon the "Dragoon." It was shorter and lighter than the Walker Colt, with a 7½-inch barrel, and was intended for use by the U.S. Army Dragoons, mounted soldiers who rode into battle and dismounted to fight. The Dragoon came with a detachable shoulder stock. Sam Colt eventually designed a shoulder stock that was also a canteen, but that never caught on.

Samuel Colt died in 1862 and didn't see his revolvers—they weren't called "guns," a name then reserved for cannons—come into their own. When they did, the Colt .45-caliber six-shooter known as the "Peacemaker" dominated competitors the way Levi's did jeans and to be a real cowboy you had to wear a Stetson hat.

Custer's men carried Peacemakers into their last battle on the Little Big Horn. Ned Buntline (his real name was Edward Zane Carroll Judson) reportedly gave Bat Masterson one of his new single-action, 12-inch-long barrel revolvers—today they're called the Buntline Special. However, claims that Wyatt Earp used one are false, the story told by his biographer after Earp's death.

The Wild West is full of enigmas—Jesse James, Billy the Kid, and Wild Bill Hickok—but probably the greatest enigma is Wyatt Earp. More than a century after the rest made their marks on the West and then faded in memory, only Wyatt Earp lingers in the shadows, not quite history, not quite legend, and not quite fiction.

Wyatt Berry Stapp Earp was born on March 19, 1848, in Monmouth, Illinois, only about sixty miles from Wild Bill Hickok's birthplace. He was the fourth of seven children, third from the oldest. When Wyatt was only two, the family moved to Pella, Iowa, where he spent most of his boyhood working the family farm under the stern eye of his father, Nicholas. Nick Earp was the town marshal in Pella, and young Wyatt watched his father use his fists to batter troublemakers into submission. "I taught all my boys to fight," Nick Earp once said, "and I'm damned proud of it." In the middle of the Civil War, Nick and Virginia Anne Cooksey Earp moved again, this time joining a wagon train for California.

When Wyatt was eighteen or so, he lost his temper and hit his father. Nick reacted with a kick to Wyatt's groin, then wrestled his son into a horse trough. Wyatt figured enough was enough and left home to join his brother Virgil in driving a freight wagon to Salt Lake City with the Banning Stage Line.

For a while the Earp boys worked as construction laborers on the westbound Union Pacific Railroad, but their contract ran out and Wyatt rejoined his family in Lamar, Missouri. He became the town constable for a couple of years and, in 1870, married Urilla (or Willa) Sutherland. Less than a year later Urilla died either in childbirth or in a typhus epidemic. Wyatt was despondent and, as he would at other times, wandered from city to town, state to territory. Arrested in present-day Oklahoma for horse stealing—his cothief had the now familiar-sounding name of Edward Kennedy—Wyatt paid a five -hundred-dollar fine and bolted town before his trial. Turning to a bit of buffalo hunting, he ran into both Wild Bill Hickok and Bat Masterson. It seemed that, once you were out West, everybody ran into everybody else.

In Wichita, Kansas, Wyatt hired on for sixty dollars a month as a policeman with his brother Virgil. Apparently it's an uneventful interlude, and the only time Wyatt's name shows up in the local newspaper is when the *Wichita Weekly Beacon* describes him as an excellent officer whose "conduct has been unexceptionable." In May 1876 the town council decided not to rehire the brothers Earp, which left them broke and, for the moment, without much of a future. Soon Wyatt and Virgil were charged with vagrancy. A short while later Wyatt showed up in Dodge City, where he hired on as an assistant marshal. It was in Dodge that he met and became friends with John "Doc" Holliday.

Despite television's efforts to show him as "brave, courageous, and bold," Wyatt Earp was interested mainly in gambling, booze, and wild, wild women. He ran poker tables and owned a cathouse; he operated saloons, and like most other tavern owners of the time, he sold cheap rotgut and watered-down booze.

Founded in 1872, just five miles west of Fort Dodge, Dodge City became a center for travelers and buffalo hunters. Over the years it came to be called the "Buffalo Capital of the World," the "Cowboy Capital," "Queen of the Cowtowns," "Wickedest Little City in America," and "Beautiful Bibulous Babylon on the Frontier." Today it's best known as the home of the purely fictitious television folks of *Gunsmoke*—Marshal Dillon, Miss Kitty, Doc, Chester, and Festus.

Again Wyatt lost his job, and again he wandered around—Mobeetie, Texas; Las Vegas; New Mexico—and it was there that, in late 1879, Wyatt married again, this time to Celia Ann "Mattie" Blaylock,* a laudanum addict and small-time hooker.

It's believed Mattie was born in Fairfax, Iowa, in 1850. She left home when she was fifteen or sixteen and met Wyatt as early as 1873

---

*Some reports say Wyatt and Mattie never made their marriage official, only lived together.

when they both were in Dodge City, Kansas. He abandoned her for another woman in 1882, and Mattie drifted to Globe, Arizona, where she spent some time with Big Nose Kate, who had recently been dumped by Doc Holliday. Mattie returned to the life she knew best and worked as a prostitute for several years before committing suicide with an overdose of laudanum in Pinal, Arizona, on July 3, 1888.

By then Wyatt was in Tombstone along with brothers Virgil and James, first as a shotgun guard for Wells Fargo, then as deputy sheriff. Soon, along come brothers Morgan and Warren, along with Doc Holliday.

At the time Tombstone was one of the most turbulent spots in the Wild West. It was overflowing with miners attracted to the pay of four dollars for a ten-hour shift.

Here, in this peaceful setting, the Earps and their assorted wives and/or girlfriends all bought frame houses within a block of each other and settled into lives as registered, civic-minded Republicans who ran for office and founded church organizations, while at the same time continuing gambling, boozing, and whoring—Wyatt, for instance, owned an interest in the Oriental Saloon. Included in their social group were Mayor John P. Clum (who also happened to be editor of the town's newspaper, the *Tombstone Epitaph*), mine magnate E. B. Gage, and youthful Episcopal minister Endicott Peabody, who went on to become White House chaplain for Franklin D. Roosevelt. They were also all Northerners.

N. H. "Old Man" Clanton—it's uncertain what the initials stood for—along with his sons Joseph Isaac "Ike" Clanton, Phineas Clanton (the weakest of the bunch), and William "Billy" Clanton, were non-Republican Southerners. Old Man didn't live to see the big showdown; he was killed a short while earlier. However, just in time to get themselves killed, two brothers, Frank and Tom McLaury, joined the group known variously as the "Clanton Gang" or, simply, the "Cowboys." Every once in a while they'd ride into Tombstone for a spree of whiskey and soiled doves.

Other than the Earp boys, who profited by this drinking and whoring, the Tombstone elite thought it was bad for the town's image and undermined civic efforts to lure investors to the nearby silver mines. At stake were some $25 million in profits from silver that would be dug out of Tombstone between 1879 and 1883. Enough to make the Earps, who also owned a piece of the silver action, want to civilize the Clanton Cowboys.

Comes October 26, 1881, and Billy Clanton and Frank McLaury ride into town to do a bit of shopping before heading for the nearest whiskey bottle. Billy comes out of a store, sees Wyatt Earp pulling a Clanton horse by the bit, and says, "Take your hands off my horse!" To which Wyatt answers, "Keep him off the sidewalks. It's against the city ordinance."

While the two argue, McLaury rides down to the O.K. Corral, where he ties up his horse, then drops into a couple of stores, where he meets up with his brother Tom and Ike Clanton. Tombstone sheriff John Behan is trying to head off what likely will be a lot of trouble and tries to disarm them. Frank, however, refuses to give up his gun, and Ike and Tom claim they're unarmed—Tom had already turned in his gun belt to local saloon keeper Andy Mehan.

Later that afternoon Ike and Billy Clanton, along with Frank and Tom McLaury and Billy Claiborne, are about to leave town. They're near the O.K. Corral when they're met by the Earp brothers and Doc Holliday. "Throw up your hands," Virgil shouts, and Billy Clanton does. "Don't shoot me," he says. "I don't want to fight!" Tom opens his coat to show the Earps that he doesn't have a gun. Morgan Earp fires point-blank at Billy and hits him in the heart. The Gunfight at the O.K. Corral is under way, headed for dime novels, movie and television screens, books, and—every now and then—into real history. It's embedded in our minds for all time.

Within days Wyatt Earp and Doc Holliday were charged with murder, but a justice of the peace ruled that they'd been acting as law officers, and the charges were dismissed. It's been almost 120 years since that thirty-second fight. It was, perhaps, the height of Wyatt Earp's career, and strangely enough it led to a decline in his popularity that wasn't revived until 1931, when the first book was written about his life.

In 1875 residents of the "Town Too Tough to Die" laid out a cemetery—a rocky hill covered with mesquite, cactus, ocotillo, and crucifixion thorn—on a slight rise just northwest of the town of Tombstone, Arizona, calling it simply "Tombstone Cemetery." Soon, however, it came to be known as "Boothill." As Tombstone's population grew, so did the population of Boothill. Narrow piles of rocks mark the final resting places of some of the town's more notorious citizens.

There are stories of epitaphs being burned into odd bits of lumber to give the name, date whoever it is below ceased to be, and, if legend has it correctly, some interesting and often humorous words about the deceased: "Died of lead poisoning," or, for a late and unlamented cattle rustler, "Too many irons in the fire." There's "Johnny Blair. Died of smallpox. Cowboy threw rope over feet and dragged him to his grave." "Margarita, Stabbed by Gold Dollar." And "M. E. Kellogg, 1882, Died a Natural Death." Not many like that in Boothill.

CHAPTER THIRTEEN

Trail's End:
The Sun Slowly Sets

Bury my heart at Wounded Knee.
                    Stephen Vincent Benét, *American Names,* 1927

America, love it or leave it.

                                        Slogan, 1960s

Out West big things were going on in the final quarter of the nineteenth century: Emigrants pushed on, cowboys and cattle barons were kings, gunmen fought and died, as did the buffalo, and Native Americans. Back East big things were also happening. Take, for example, the event of March 10, 1876 in Boston. The immigrant son of a speech teacher spilled acid on his worktable and spoke into a contraption he was working on: "Mr. Watson, come here. I want you." Alexander Graham Bell had invented the telephone. Actually, the U.S. Patent Office granted Bell a patent for his machine three days before it worked, so his accidental call to Mr. Watson maybe wasn't so accidental after all.

Rapidly the telephone (and Bell's AT&T—the American Telephone and Telegraph Company) expanded. Western Union, the telegraph folks, got into the phone-home act, with one of their employees even claiming to have filed a patent on the invention several hours before Alexander Graham Bell did. Western Union sued Bell, but when it became obvious that Bell knew what he was talking about and Western Union's alleged inventor didn't, Western Union dropped the suit.

Interestingly enough, Thomas A. Edison was one of Western Union's brain trust. Among other things, the inventor of the telegraph differed with Bell on how one should answer the phone. Edison thought a simple "Hello" would suffice. Bell preferred "Hoy! Hoy!"

Just as blizzards hit the Wild West in 1887 and 1888, a major snowstorm blasted the East in '88. It felled thousands of newly installed telephone poles and led to a call for underground cables to protect phones and electricity.

On January 25, 1915, thirty-nine years after Bell's original "Mr. Watson, come here. I want you," the two men got to do it all over again, this time in the first cross-country telephone call, Bell in New York and Watson in San Francisco. The second time around Watson ad libbed, "I will [come], but it will take me a week now." This first cross-country phone call became so celebrated, a new phrase was coined: "Operator, get me long distance." And on Broadway that year the hit song was "Hello, Frisco, Hello."

Now, however, gold was found in the Black Hills; all bets were off; and soldiers were headed into the area to protect settlers and prospectors.

At first soldiers tried to keep the land clear for Indians, but it didn't work. One prospector said he'd been captured by the army and evicted from the Black Hills four times. He'd do it again and again, he said. "I guess I can stand it as long as they can." The *Chicago Inter-Ocean* claimed, "We owe the Indians justice and fair play, but we owe it to civilization that such a garden of mineral wealth be brought into occupation and use."

Twice the Indians refused the government's offer of six million dollars for the area. A U.S. Senate commission went west to try to negotiate with tribesmen, but things got off to a bad start when the senators told the Indians they should "bow to the wishes of the Government which supports you." For three days they argued. It became obvious that the Indians would not leave the Black Hills without a fight.

By early 1875 as many as fifteen thousand miners had crowded into the land of the Lakota, searching for gold. On November 3 of that year President Ulysses S. Grant and his wartime friend, Philip Sheridan, sat down in Washington with Grant's secretary of war,

William Worth Belknap, and Secretary of the Interior William E. Chandler. They discussed what had become the near-frantic action of prospectors to enter the Black Hills, treaty or no treaty. According to Sheridan it was at that meeting that the president "decided that while the orders heretofore issued forbidding the occupation of the Black Hills country, by miners, should not be rescinded, still no further resistance by the military should be made to the miners going in." In other words, despite the treaty, despite his own orders that the army clear the Black Hills of prospectors, President Grant secretly told the army to ignore the miners' intrusion.

In the spring of 1876 Sitting Bull of the Hunkpapa band said he'd had a vision: A great dust storm swirled down upon a small white cloud that resembled a Lakota village. Soldiers fell upon the village. The cloud was swallowed up for a time, but in the end it emerged intact. The dust storm disappeared.

Many off-reservation Indians took this as an encouraging sign, and that summer Lakota Sioux, Yankton, Santee, northern Arapaho, and northern Cheyenne gathered in a massive encampment in Montana. The camp stretched more than three miles along the riverbanks, from the site of the railroad station at present-day Garryowen, Montana, to the Minneconjou Ford on the Little Big Horn River. In six separate circles perhaps as many as seven thousand Indians built twelve hundred lodges. A Cheyenne woman named Kate Big Head remembered that "there were more Indians . . . than I ever saw anywhere together."

Sitting Bull's prophecy that the army would fall into their camps was about to come true. President Grant had ordered that all members of the Lakota Sioux must report to reservations or submit to capture or death. To enforce the order he sent black-eyed, brilliant, and profane Civil War veteran Gen. Philip H. Sheridan to lead the army against the Indians. "Little Phil," as he was known—he was only five feet five inches tall—had once stormed Missionary Ridge in the Civil War battle of Chickamauga. From his headquarters in Chicago he now organized a three-pronged campaign. Brigadier General George Crook would move north from Fort Fetterman, which had been named after the loser in an earlier battle with the Indians. Colonel John Gibbons would march east from western Montana.

And George Armstrong Custer would drive west from Fort Abraham Lincoln. "Each column will be able to take care of itself," Sheridan ordered, while they chastised the Indians, should an opportunity for chastising come about. If anyone could crush the Indians, Sheridan believed, Custer could. "If there was any poetry or romance in war, [Custer] could develop it."

Not everyone was as enamored of Custer as was Sheridan, or as was Custer, for that matter. His second in command, Maj. Marcus A. Reno, loathed Long Hair. As did Capt. Frederick W. Benteen, who not only hated Custer, but didn't think too highly of anybody else in the 7th. Except, perhaps, himself.

Historian John Keegan said "George Custer was not a nice man."

> Brave, certainly, bold, dashing, quick in decision, physically attractive, both to men and women, sexually alluring, all that; but nice, no.

Keegan adds that "niceness is not, of course, a prerequisite quality in a successful soldier."

By June 6 thousands of Lakota and Cheyenne and their allies were camped along Rosebud Creek, holding their most sacred ritual, the sun dance. As a sign of sacrifice Sitting Bull slashed his arm a hundred times. And he had another vision: The soldiers were coming, but his people would be ready.

Part of his vision came true on June 17. General Crook and his column had stopped to brew coffee, and he and his officers were playing a leisurely game of whist. Suddenly Crazy Horse and five hundred warriors attacked. Army troops more than doubled Crazy Horse's men, but the battle lasted more than seven hours. Only when the army's Crow and Shoshone allies rode in did Crazy Horse and his men retreat. Crook called it a victory because the Indians withdrew. In reality it was a draw, which meant that the Indians had stopped the first prong of Sheridan's attack.

The second prong, which included Custer's unit, crossed into the valley of the Little Big Horn eight days later. As Custer began his march, Brig. Gen. Alfred Terry called out: "Now, Custer, don't be greedy, but wait for us."

Custer laughed and answered, "No, I will not."

A short while later Custer sighted the Indian camp and ordered his men to charge. Perhaps he remembered the undefended Indian camps at Sand Creek in 1864 and at the Washita River in '68. In those two encounters the Army attack had come at dawn. Now, however, it was afternoon.

Instead of the Indians being taken by surprise it was the soldiers who were shocked. Instead of a small camp they found an estimated two thousand Indians waiting.

It was Sunday, a hot and cloudless day. Through his telescope all Custer could see was a white blur on the valley floor, and he laughed when a Crow scout warned him that there were many Indians in the camp. "I guess," Custer said, "we'll get through them in one day."

With that Custer ordered Captain Benteen and 125 men south to make certain no one was behind him. And then Long Hair hurried toward the Little Big Horn.

A band of about forty warriors appeared but turned and raced back toward their camp. Custer ordered Major Reno and three companies totaling about 140 men to go after them. He, Long Hair promised, would be right behind.

"Where are they going?" asked Lt. Charles Varnum, Custer's chief of scouts.

"To begin the attack," Custer replied, then asked, "What can you see?"

According to Varnum, "The whole valley in front is full of Indians."

As Reno's men crossed the river, the major stopped and allowed his men to water their horses. The files of men and horses became so strung out, it took fifteen minutes to get to the other side of the water. They regrouped in a strip of woods, finally advancing at a trot in three columns. Within minutes they found a group of Lakota and Cheyenne, and Reno's men charged.

The Indians were surprised. They hadn't expected the soldiers to attack until daybreak, just as they had in other encounters.

Sitting Bull's nephew, White Bull, was there and said that "all through that great camp was the confusion of complete surprise." But, as historian Robert Utley puts it, "never before or after were the northern plains tribes better prepared for war." Two thousand warriors—"numerous, united, confident, superbly led, emotionally charged to defend their homeland and freedom," Utley adds.

Reno believed Custer *would* be right behind him, but Autie wasn't. The Indians greatly outnumbered the major and his men; still, they held on until one of the army's scouts, Bloody Knife, was shot in the head. The Arikara Indian's brains splattered over Reno's face, and the major shouted for his men to fall back.

"We heard women and children screaming," Kate Big Head remembered. "Old men were calling the young warriors to battle; young men were singing their war songs." When Reno's men fell back, the warriors followed them. As the soldiers struggled across the river, they kept looking for Custer's men to come to their aid. They never did. Custer had changed his mind. He turned northwest and led his five companies of 210 men toward a ridge that overlooked the Indian encampment.

When Custer got to the top of the ridge, he finally saw the entire Indian village spread out before him. Long Hair, said a Crow scout, "looked whiter than ever." Custer stopped to pencil a note to Benteen, who was behind him with the ammunition train. "Come on," it read, "Big Village. Be Quick. Bring packs. Hurry." A bugler rushed off with the note, and Custer waved his hat at his men and led them down toward the encampment.

Cheyenne warriors led by Lame White Man rode out to meet them. As did the Hunkpapa Lakota under Gall and the Oglala under Crazy Horse—"Come, it is a good day to die, a good day to die."

The "rushing procession of warriors," Kate Big Head remembered, "kept going, going, going. I wanted to go too. . . . I always liked to watch the men fighting."

In less than half an hour the 7th Cavalry was wiped out. White Bull claimed that he played a major part in the battle. "I charged in," he said, and "a tall, well-built soldier with yellow hair and mustache saw me coming and tried to bluff me, aiming his rifle at me." White Bull lashed out with his quirt, "striking the coup," he claimed. The two fought hard, and White Bull said his opponent was desperate: "He hit me with his fists on [my] jaw and shoulders, then grabbed my long braids with both hands, pulled my face close and tried to bite my nose off." The soldier drew his pistol, but the Indian chief "wrenched it out of his hand and struck him with it three or four times on the head." Then, he claimed, he shot the yellow-haired soldier in the head and fired at his heart."

Later White Bull met with a relative, Bad Juice (or Bad Soup), who claimed he knew who White Bull's opponent was: Long Hair himself, George Armstrong Custer. Bad Juice saw Custer lying on the ground and said, "Long Hair thought he was the greatest man in the world. Now he lies there." White Bull looked at the dead soldier: "Well, if that is Long Hair, I am the man who killed him."

Back East, newspapers received word of the battle even before the War Department did. Just after the Fourth of July holiday they reported the defeat, calling the engagement "Custer's Last Stand." "Massacred," the headlines roared. "No Officer or Man of 5 Companies Left to Tell the Tale." There were no survivors, which was patently untrue. Thousands of Plains Indians survived the battle.

At first the army's response was restrained. Sheridan, for instance, believed Custer had badly misjudged his enemy and said the defeat was "due to misapprehension and [a] superabundance of courage." The general, who reputedly said, "The only good Indians I ever saw were dead,"* rejected calls to exterminate Native Americans.

On June 27 Col. John Gibbons's column arrived on the battlefield, slowly advancing up the valley. There, he discovered the carnage. Everywhere, the bodies of dead men and animals. The stench filled the air. To Gibbons's regiment fell the duty of burying their comrades—five companies wiped out; many of them, their bodies mutilated. "It was the most horrible sight my eyes rested on," admitted Lt. Francis Gibson.

Forty-three-year-old reporter Mark Kellogg of the *Bismarck Tribune* had accompanied the soldiers and promised his readers that he would be with Custer at "the death." He kept that promise and, like members of Custer's command, lay dead on the hillside.

---

*After Custer's fight with Cheyenne chief Black Kettle, Comanche chief Turtle Dove (Toch-a-way) was introduced to General Sheridan. The Indian reportedly said: "Me Toch-a-way. Me good Indian." To which Sheridan allegedly answered, "The only good Indians I ever saw were dead." Phil Sheridan vehemently denied making the comment.

General Sheridan now promised that Custer would be avenged, and he sent fresh columns of blue-clad soldiers across the Powder River country. Soon Sitting Bull and Crazy Horse and White Bull and all the others discovered what many before them had learned: Defeating the white man's army in one battle—no matter how large the battle—did not mean the Indians had won. Within a year of the Battle of the Little Big Horn, the Lakotas and Cheyennes, with the exception of Sitting Bull, surrendered.

Within yet another year Crazy Horse was dead. In May 1877 he took his wife, Black Shawl, into the Red Cloud Agency; they were nearly starving, and Black Shawl was suffering from advanced tuberculosis. In September, when Crazy Horse asked to move her to the Spotted Trail Agency, where medical treatment was available, agency officials refused permission. But this was Crazy Horse, and he did what he thought he had to do; he got her safely to the Spotted Trail Agency. While there he was arrested by Indian police and taken to Fort Robinson. Then, in a well-choreographed fight in a guardroom, Crazy Horse was bayoneted to death. Indian police claimed he'd pulled a knife on them.

Crazy Horse's body was removed by his father and secretly buried. The location of the grave remains a mystery.

After the Battle of the Little Big Horn, women from the large Indian encampment ranged over the killing field. They stripped off the soldiers' uniforms, recovered their boots (later, they'd cut off the bottoms, sew them up, and make leather containers of them), and mutilated many of the bodies. They rummaged through the soldiers' pockets and took whatever pleased them, including some of the funny pictured papers the men carried but for which the Indians had no use. They gave them to children to play with.

Custer's mistress, Me-o-tzi, had returned to her people, and by some reports was at the Battle of the Little Big Horn. As Custer lay dying, she prevented his mutilation. Well, maybe.

It's also sometimes reported that Long Hair had "saved the last bullet" for himself and had committed suicide. Well, maybe.

Just as White Bull had claimed, Custer had been shot in the head and near his heart. However, Indians did mutilate Custer's body, which they probably wouldn't have done if he'd committed suicide.

They slashed his left thigh to the bone, severed a finger, and shoved an arrow shaft into his penis. Kate Big Head said they punctured Custer's ear so that in the afterworld he could hear the Indians' pleas.

Captain Frederick Benteen saw Custer's body, and the man who'd been Long Hair's enemy in life continued his hatred for the dead man. He looked at Custer's body and said, "There he is, God damn him, he will never fight anymore."

She Owl, the widow of army scout Bloody Knife, later filed a claim for wages owed her husband up to the time of his death. The government allotted "said widow, She Owl, $91.66." She got the money five years after the battle.

General George Crook (known to his troops as Uncle George and to the Indians as the "Gray Fox") called the Apaches "tigers of the human race," and he considered one of the band's greatest war leaders the most vicious of them all. Called Goyathay by his tribe—it roughly translates as "He Who Yawns"—he became known by his Mexican-given name of Geronimo.

He was born in 1834, into the Mimbreño Apache band, and married into Cochise's Chiricahua Apache tribe. He refused to move to the government-assigned reservation at San Carlos—a hot, barren, terrible place to live—and for more than fifteen years he and a small band of other renegades terrorized both sides of the Mexican-American border from their hideout in the Sierra Madres.

By 1881, with the surrender of Sitting Bull, the wars in the Great Plains came to a close. All of the tribes of the American West had been compelled by military force to go to (or return to) their reservations. All but one: the Chiricahua Apaches.

In September 1882 General Crook arrived in Arizona, determined to clamp military rule on the Chiricahua and to go after Geronimo in Mexico. To do this he recruited five companies of scouts from Geronimo's own tribe, Apache scouts—"the wildest I could get" Crook said—and put them under the army's most energetic young officers. Using mule trains instead of wagons, they rode into Mexico.

Until then the mountains had afforded the Chiricahua Apaches an impregnable fortress—steep ridges, towering peaks, plunging gorges, and canyons. Going high into the mountains where no Mexican troops had dared go, the Indian scouts surprised a band of Chiricahuas under subchief Chato. With their fortress breached and their own people enlisted against them, the renegades slowly began drifting in to talk with the Gray Fox, this strange general who wore a canvas suit instead of a uniform and rode a mule rather than a horse.

The last of the renegades to come in was Geronimo. "We give ourselves up," he announced, "do with us as you please."

It was, however, only a temporary surrender, and Geronimo soon returned to the mountains. His people were accustomed to freedom, and military rule bridled and irked them. So 134 people, including Geronimo and his son, Nachez (or Naiche), escaped the reservation at San Carlos and returned to the Sierra Madres. Once again the army recruited Geronimo's own people to track him down. And once again the renegades grew tired of always being on the run, always afraid of a surprise attack. Geronimo sent word that he wanted to talk.

He met with General Crook at Canyon de los Embudos, twelve miles south of the Mexican border, on March 25, 1886. Seated on either side of a well-shaded ravine, the two men talked as they'd done two years earlier. This time Crook's terms were harsher: Geronimo and his people could return to San Carlos or "I'll keep after you and kill the last one, if it takes fifty years."

Finally Geronimo accepted Crook's terms, and as the general hurried north to telegraph his superiors the good news, the Indians began moving toward the border. Along the way, however, they ran across a whiskey peddler, and in the midst of a drinking bout Geronimo and Nachez had second thoughts. Again they headed north, taking about twenty men and thirteen women.

By now Gen. William Tecumseh Sherman commanded the U.S. Army, and unlike Crook he didn't trust Apache scouts to do the job; he wanted regular army troops to go after the renegades. He issued orders that not only criticized Crook, but required the Gray Fox to break his word to the Indians who hadn't gone with Geronimo. Rather than carry out his orders Crook asked to be relieved of duty. Sherman replaced him with the Gray Fox's longtime rival, Gen. Nelson A. Miles.

Despite making a show of using regular troops, Miles eventually had to follow Crook's example and use Apache scouts to comb the Sierra Madres. Lieutenant Charles B. Gatewood, an officer known to be a friend of the Indians, tried to persuade Geronimo. The Chiricahua must give up; they'd be sent to Florida, Gatewood told Geronimo, to await the president's decision on their fate. Geronimo and Nachez agreed to surrender but insisted they be sent to San Carlos.

You will find none of your kinsmen there, the lieutenant said, only rival tribes. Gatewood said all of the Chiricahuas, even those who had served Crook as scouts, had been deported to Florida. Actually he lied, but Geronimo bit and agreed to give up. But only to General Miles personally. On September 4, 1866, in Skeleton Canyon, just north of the border, Geronimo and General Miles faced each other. Geronimo handed the general his rifle.

The sound of a trainload of Apaches rattling across the southwestern desert signaled the end of armed resistance. The Indian wars were over.

In 1894 the army shipped Geronimo back West, to Fort Sill, Oklahoma. Colorful if pathetic to the last, he sometimes appeared at fairs and exhibitions, posing as the fierce warrior that he'd once been. At the St. Louis Fair he rode in a procession in honor of the inauguration of Theodore Roosevelt. He toured the country with the Pawnee Bill shows, where, for pocket money, he sold photographs of himself and even the buttons from his coat.

Geronimo had always liked his tizwin, a highly intoxicating beverage made by the Apache Indians. Brewed from fermented corn or wheat or even mesquite beans, it's sometimes called the "Apache beer." Now the last Indian renegade spent most of his days in an alcoholic haze. On February 17, 1909, Geronimo died of pneumonia. He was seventy-five.

On New Year's Day, 1889, Wovoka, a Paiute holy man, fell ill. In his delirium he dreamed he visited the Great Spirit in heaven, and there he was told that the time was coming when buffalo would again fill the plains and dead tribesmen would be restored to their families. This would all come about, the Great Spirit told him, if the Indians refrained from violence and if they were virtuous and if they performed the Ghost Dance, a traditional dance in which Indians sang songs and their departed ancestors mingled with the dancers. When Wovoka recovered, he spread the word: Performing the Ghost Dance would hasten the coming of a new world that would cover the old and push the white man back into the sea:

> My brothers, I bring to you the promise of a day in which there will be no white man to lay his hand on the bridle of the Indians' horse; when the red men of the prairie will rule the world. . . . I bring you word from your fathers the ghosts, that they are marching now to join you, led by the Messiah who came once to live on earth with the white man but was killed by them.

Indians in California and Nevada, where the Ghost Dance originated, weren't impressed, but out on the plains, where warfare had devastated the people, it spread like wildfire—among the Sioux, the Cheyenne, Comanche, Arapaho, Assiniboin, and Shoshone. In early 1890 Kicking Bear, a holy man of the Teton Sioux, took the gospel to the Dakota Territory, and that spring the Sioux began Ghost Dancing.

If the dancers dressed in white shirts, painted with special symbols, they could not be harmed by the white man's bullets. This actually wasn't part of Wovoka's teachings, but Kicking Bear thought it was a good touch. They sang:

> *Mother, hand me my sharp knife,*
> *Mother, hand me my sharp knife,*
> *Here come the buffalo returning.*
> *Mother, hand me my sharp knife.*
>
> *Mother, do come back!*
> *Mother, do come back!*
> *My little brother is calling for you.*
> *My father says so!*

By mid-autumn of 1890 the Ghost Dance had reached something of a religious frenzy. Bands moved out of their log cabins and back into tepees, as in the old days. Grown men danced and young children abandoned the white man's school. "That part about the dead returning," one Pine Ridge student said, "was what appealed to me."

Kicking Bear asked Sitting Bull for his opinion of the Ghost Dance. The aging leader didn't believe it would work, but he also didn't believe it would do any harm. So, go ahead, he said. Dance.

Shuffling around in great circles, speeding up until exhausted, dancers reached a state of delirious ecstasy. Thousands danced. And they saw the dead come to life!

The Ghost Dance frightened some white observers, including Daniel Royer, an agent at Pine Ridge, who was so shaken by the Ghost Dance that the Lakota took to calling him "Young Man Afraid of Indians." On November 12 he wired the army for help: "Indians are dancing in the snow now and are wild and crazy. . . . We need protection and we need it now." Five days later Gen. Nelson Miles ordered five thousand troops onto the Sioux reservations, including the all-black 9th Cavalry and the late George Custer's regiment, the 7th Cavalry. By December 3 one-third of all United States armed forces were on the alert, expecting something to happen with the Ghost Dance. Washington also sent west former Pine Ridge reservation agent Valentine McGillycuddy. Unlike Royer the dance didn't worry him. "I should let the dance continue," he wrote his superiors in Washington, but added, "The coming of the troops has frightened the Indians. . . . If the troops remain, trouble is sure to come." He was right, and the Ghost Dancers at the Pine Ridge and Rosebud reservations fled to a remote plateau that nervous white reporters called the "stronghold."

Sitting Bull, a Hunkpapa Sioux, was born in 1831, in what is now southwestern South Dakota. Not much is known of his early life, but it's believed he was a veteran of some thirty-five "winter counts" (which means he was at least that many years old) when he was nominated as the band's leader. Sitting Bull engaged in several skirmishes with bands of Crow Indians, but he never led any attack on the enemy during the climactic Indians versus U.S. Army engagements.

After the Battle of the Little Big Horn, Sitting Bull led his people north to settle in Canada, where he remained for four years. He returned to the United States but was taken prisoner by the army and held at Fort Randall, South Dakota.

In 1885 he became the star attraction in Buffalo Bill's Wild West show, reenacting for paying white audiences the way he had led the fight at the Little Big Horn. Except, he hadn't been there. During the battle Sitting Bull had sat it out, back in the tepee village. While thousands of other Indians fought and hundreds of army troops died, Sitting Bull was back in camp where he said he was too sick to fight.

Now, in mid-December 1890, the army began to believe Sitting Bull might take advantage of the Ghost Dance fervor and lead his people in another war on whites. Lieutenant Henry Bull Head, of the Oglala police, sent Sitting Bull a message, asking him to leave the Standing Rock Agency and come to Pine Ridge "as God was to appear" to the Indians. "I would like to arrest him at once," Bull Head remembered, "before he has the chance of giving [us] the slip. . . ."

Indian agent James McLoughlin, an old enemy of Sitting Bull, acted. He sent forty-three Sioux policemen to surround Sitting Bull's cabin. Two troops of cavalry would follow at a distance. They were to intervene only if the Indian police got into trouble.

Early on the morning of December 15 Henry Bull Head burst into the cabin, awakened Sitting Bull, and grabbed him by the arms. "You are my prisoner," Bull Head said. "You must go to the agency." Sergeant Red Tomahawk walked behind them as they started toward a wagon that would take Sitting Bull to the agency.

At first Sitting Bull agreed to go quietly and sent one of his wives— he had two—back to get his clothes. He asked a policeman to saddle his pony, but Lieutenant Bull Head wanted him in the wagon and they began searching Sitting Bull and the cabin for weapons. By now Sitting Bull's followers were awake, and more than 150 of them crowded around the police. When a policeman shoved Sitting Bull toward the wagon, Catch-the-Bear shouted, "You shall not take our chief!" and raised his rifle and shot Lt. Henry Bull Head. As the lieutenant fell to the ground, he fired his revolver at Sitting Bull, hitting him in the chest. At almost the same time Red Tomahawk, who'd been right behind the chief, shot Sitting Bull through the head.

With that the cavalry came rushing in and more shots were fired. In the end seven members of Sitting Bull's band, including his son Crow Foot, were dead alongside the chief. Sitting Bull was fifty-nine. His body was taken away and buried in a pauper's grave.

After the fight some of Sitting Bull's followers among the Hunkpapa surrendered at Fort Bennett. Some others, half starving and half naked, fled to the Cheyenne River Reservation, where they joined a Miniconjou Sioux band led by a chief named Big Foot.

Big Foot had been an enthusiastic Ghost Dancer, but now he lay ill with pneumonia. Still, the army considered Big Foot another Ghost Dance troublemaker, and they put him under surveillance. Red Cloud and other chiefs asked Big Foot to join them at Pine Ridge to try to find a way to reconcile things with the army. Too much blood had been spilled, and they hoped to find a way to stop it.

When the army surveillance saw Big Foot and his people leave the reservation, three regiments were sent out, including the 7th Cavalry, which was still angry over events at the Little Big Horn. At two o'clock on the afternoon of December 28, the army caught up with Big Foot, who was now so ill he was being carried in a wagon. Too sick to sit up, but still with a white flag over his head as evidence he meant no harm to anyone. He surrendered without protest, and soldiers directed the Indians to a camp at a nearby creek called Wounded Knee. That night about 350 men, women, and children set up camp. About five hundred troopers under the command of Col. James W. Forsyth surrounded them. The soldiers posted four machine-gun-like Hotchkiss guns around them.

Before dawn the next day a bugle sounded and Forsyth called on the Indian men and older boys to stand in a semicircle in front of their tents; there were from 106 to 120 of them, and they squatted on the ground, many still wearing their Ghost Dance shirts. Big Foot was brought out of his tent, and troopers began searching for weapons. The few weapons they found were old and worn out.

Colonel Forsyth demanded that Big Foot hand over the band's Winchester repeating rifles, but Big Foot denied they had any. Troops moved from tent to tent, while "eight or ten Indian boys dressed in the gray school uniforms of that period [were playing] 'bucking horse,' 'leap frog,' and similar games," a reporter noted.

But then a shaman named Yellow Bird jumped up and called, "I have medicine of the white man's ammunition. It is good medicine, and his bullets cannot harm you, as they will not go through your ghost shirts, while your bullets will kill." Forsyth ordered Yellow Bird to sit down, and another officer, James D. Mann, warned his troops, "Be ready; there is going to be trouble."

It's not certain whether the Indians had any guns in their possession, but there's a report that one soldier claimed he spotted a rifle hidden beneath a man named Black Coyote's blanket. The report adds that Forsyth ordered Black Coyote to give up his rifle but that the Indian was deaf and didn't hear the command. A soldier grabbed him and spun him around, and just at that moment a shot was fired. Who fired it isn't known, but Yellow Bird threw a handful of dust into the air, and the soldiers took that as a signal to open fire.

They did so with everything they had. Standing only eight feet or so away, a line of soldiers leveled their carbines at the Indians. A few warriors tried to fight back, but the Hotchkiss guns opened fire, pouring two-pounder fragmentation shells into the village. Indians ran and maddened soldiers ran after them, hounding them out of the rocks and scrub cedar, wherever they tried to hide.

When the fighting ended, 25 soldiers were dead,* some killed accidentally by their own side in the frenzy of firing. Also dead were from 153 to 300 Indians, probably about 250 of the Lakota, some of them found as far as three miles from the creek called Wounded Knee.** Among the dead was Big Foot, left in snow tinted crimson with his blood.

Not until January 3 did the army allow a burial party to return to Wounded Knee, and by that time the bodies were frozen in grotesque positions. In these positions they were thrown into a common grave.

Over the next two weeks fighting stuttered on. Angry warriors set fire to reservation buildings, and Colonel Forsyth led the 7th Cav-

---

* Some reports say 29.
**The official figure for the Indian dead is 64 males, 44 women and girls, and 18 very young children. However, most authorities give the actual number as much higher.

alry in pursuit. He failed to secure the surrounding hills and found himself surrounded by hundreds of angry Lakota, just as Custer and the 7th had fifteen years earlier. This time, however, the outcome was different; the Buffalo Soldiers came riding to their rescue.

By now the Indians were hungry and outnumbered, and they surrendered without additional bloodshed. Gradually the Sioux were coaxed out of the Badlands and back onto the reservation. On January 15, 1891, the last Ghost Dancer—Kicking Bear, who had brought news of the dance to the Lakota agencies—handed his rifle over to General Miles.

The Ghost Dance was over. And so were three hundred years of Indian resistance to the white man.

Until 1973. That's when more than two hundred members of the group called AIM—the American Indian Movement—were arrested while protesting at the site of the Wounded Knee Massacre. U.S. marshals, along with FBI agents and Bureau of Indian Affairs (BIA) police, surrounded the protestors. More than two thousand Indians converged on Pine Ridge to support the protestors' siege. The siege lasted seventy-one days, during which more than three hundred federal agents equipped with guns, armored personnel carriers, and other military weapons faced the protestors. The U.S. Army's 82d Airborne Division was readied for an attack. The siege finally ended with two Indians killed, and 185 others were indicted on charges of arson, theft, assault, and "interfering with federal officers."

Annie Oakley, the woman Sitting Bull called "Little Miss Sure Shot," toured Europe and became the darling of royalty everywhere. In the early hours of October 29, 1901, the special train chartered by Buffalo Bill Cody's Wild West Show howled through the North Carolina darkness. Near Lexington, southwest of Winston-Salem, the passenger train collided with a freight train, and Annie was badly injured. After months of hospitalization she recovered. Because of her injuries she'd been forced to sever her connection with Buffalo Bill, but she continued her career. In the fall of 1902 she was back on the road, playing the lead in a melodrama entitled *The Western Girl.* She still had it, she still was "Little Miss Sure Shot."

In 1912, at the age of fifty-two, Annie Oakley rejoined Buffalo Bill for Cody's farewell tour. After that she worked as a trap-shooting instructor. In 1918, with America at war in Europe, the girl from Ohio gave rifle-shooting demonstrations to U.S. troops. It wasn't until 1922 that Annie retired, and she and her husband, Frank Butler, settled in Leesburg, Florida, northwest of modern-day Orlando.

Four years in the heart of retirement country was too much for the unretiring lady known as Annie Oakley; she wanted to go home, back to Darke County, Ohio. In the spring of 1926, Frank and Annie took up residence in Dayton. Later that year, on November 2, Phoebe Mozee, known throughout the world as Annie Oakley, died. She was sixty-six.

There's a lot of confusion about sometime bullwhacker, sometime prostitute, sometime gambler Calamity Jane. The story of her life comes in "they say" terms: They say this; they say that.

In about 1893 she published a short purported autobiography, "Life and Adventures of Calamity Jane, by Herself." At the least Jane dictated it to a ghostwriter; at worst she had nothing to do with it. In any event it wasn't much of an autobiography, only five and a half pages long as it's reprinted today. The biggest problem is that the "facts" as she wrote them don't match up with the "facts" as they're actually known. For instance, it's believed that Jane met Wild Bill Hickok in 1870 when, according to her own account, she would have been about eighteen years old. That's the same year when, according to her autobiography, she went to work as a scout for George Armstrong Custer—it's this part in her life that had the greatest meaning for her, the time when "I donned the uniform of a soldier."

Other reports have her joining the U.S. Army in 1875, a short-lived military experience that ended when it was discovered that Jane wasn't your average nineteenth-century soldier but, rather, was a woman. Photographs taken of Jane about this time show her in men's clothing, not a raving beauty, but not really masculine looking either.

Her autobiography gives the spring of 1876 as the time when she met Hickok at Fort Laramie, Wyoming. Jane later claimed that she and Wild Bill were married, the wedding being recorded on the fly-leaf of a Bible by the Reverends W. K. Sipes and W. F. Warren near Abilene, Kansas. Jane doesn't mention it in her autobiography, and

Bill's take on this likely will never be known. On August 2, 1876, Jack McCall killed Hickok during a poker game at Nuttall and Mann's gambling parlor in Deadwood.

Whether she married Wild Bill or not, it seems Jane did marry an El Paso cabdriver named Charles Burke. She spelled it "Burk," but nineteenth-century spelling doesn't count for much, since people spelled things any way they wanted.

On October 28, 1887, Calamity Jane gave birth to a little girl, "the very image of its father," Jane wrote, "at least that is what he said, but who has the temper of its mother." Whether the child was fathered by Wild Bill Hickok or Charles Burke isn't certain. Burke claimed the child was his, and you'll notice that the child was born eleven years *after* Wild Bill died. In any event the cabdriver and the bullwhacker divorced in 1895, and Jane moved on to other things and other places.

Whoever the father was, when the child named Jean (or Janey, as Calamity called her) was eight years old, Jane sent her to live at St. Mary's Convent in Sturgis, South Dakota. Later, Jane claimed she'd left the girl with some "swell people," not naming them, however. The next we hear of Jean is in 1941, when the U.S. Department of Public Welfare grants her old-age relief, giving her name as Mrs. Jean Hickok McCormick, listing her in federal records as the daughter of James Butler Hickok and Martha Jane Cannary.

In applying for welfare benefits Jean released three letters she claimed her mother, Calamity Jane, had written her between 1877 and 1903. In part it was these letters that led to her welfare-benefits approval. Jean Hickok McCormick died in Billings, Montana, on February 22, 1951.

Calamity Jane claimed that, in June 1876, she "acted as a pony express rider carrying the U.S. mail between Deadwood and Custer, a distance of fifty miles, over one of the roughest trails in the Black Hills country." This would have been fifteen years after the real Pony Express died and hundreds of miles off the Pony Express route, but, still, Jane hadn't claimed to be a Pony Express rider, only that she "acted as a pony express rider." No capital letters in her claim, so apparently it was a pony-express–*style* delivery system. Note that only historians give a damn about this distinction.

Whatever "they say" history there is about Calamity Jane, it's certain that she was a loudmouthed, foul-mouthed, cigar-smoking, tobacco-chewing harridan. One "they say" story is of a Methodist bishop being stopped cold in his diatribe about how Jane had better change her ways before the Day of Judgment. Jane, the story goes, had known the bishop before he'd gotten religion. "Aw, you go to hell, Hank," she said. "I don't take my preachin' from an old goat I've slept under the same blanket with mor'n a hundred times." Maybe not fact, but probably close enough that you can imagine Jane, imagine the minister, imagine telling of the tale over a bottle of rotgut in a Wild West saloon.

Calamity Jane acted out much of her own legend, touring the Midwest with the Palace Museum show, wearing men's clothes—a not infrequent costume for Wild West women in show business at the time—and telling tall tales about herself. Her act as the "Famous Woman Scout" consisted of telling her version of her life, including, of course, her life with Wild Bill Hickok. She also claimed to have saved Buffalo Bill Cody's life once when he was threatened by a gang of cutthroats. The Palace Museum Show gig didn't last long, however. The management kicked her out, because she'd been drunk and disorderly too often and gave too many free shows at local saloons.

By the turn of the century Jane was living in a bawdy house, sick and aging. After she'd recovered she appeared as a buckskin-wearing cowgirl at the 1901 Pan-American Exposition in Buffalo, New York. Once again, however, she went on a bar-wrecking bender during which she assaulted two policemen. The Exposition fired her. With that Calamity Jane drifted west, from cavalry post to cow town, boomtown to bust.

By the late 1890s Jane had abused herself so thoroughly that a contemporary described her as resembling "a busted bale of hay." In 1902 she showed up in a Billings, Montana, bar. Word got out that Calamity Jane was back in town, and everyone who could rushed to the saloon to see her. In the middle of the street Calamity Jane found herself surrounded by everyone from the town bum, the town harlot, the town storekeeper, to the town sheriff. Jane didn't disappoint them. She pulled out her six-guns and began shooting, making tenderfoot newcomers even more tender of foot. "Dance, you chippie, dance!" she cried out. Local law officers let her shoot as long as by-standers were willing to provide reloading services, then they escorted her out of town.

She drifted to Livingston, where she sold souvenir portraits of herself in her scouting outfits. She panhandled for drinks and food, growing more sottish and bombed every day.

It was in 1902 that a young writer tried to interview her but found her too far gone; she couldn't talk without being primed with liquor. About all she could do then was to parrot mechanically the stilted words of her autobiography. That year, for the first time in her life, Calamity Jane was seriously ill and spent several weeks in the poorhouse.

Next spring, apparently recovered, she hit the road again, taking part in a three-handed brawl—Jane, a sheepherder, and the town sheriff—in Sheridan, Wyoming. The town paid her fare to get out of town. She went to Newcastle, which promptly paid Jane's fare to go to Deadwood, anyplace other than where she was.

Calamity Jane tried once more to return to her occasional profession of prostitute at a brothel known as the Green Front. The madam, however, thought that Jane no longer measured up to the house's professional sexual standards, and she tossed Calamity out into the street.

The girls were rats, Jane cried out, little hussies who'd never seen a bull train or a tie-chopping lumber camp; Damn your hides, pretending you're ladies because you've gone to high school! The girls stood looking out the windows at a woman who'd once had been just like them. More or less, as if anybody could ever be like Calamity Jane.

Later that year Calamity Jane showed up in Terraville (perhaps, Terry; the town's apparently gone away now), South Dakota, not far from Deadwood, where she, literally, caught her death of pneumonia, or maybe it was an "inflammation of the bowels." She lay in a hotel room, sick. Sicker'n all hell's fire. Sicker'n a dog, she groaned, laughing that someone as important as she was had to be fed whiskey with a spoon. Then came delirium and chatter about riding with Wild Bill Hickok, about Janey, the daughter she claimed she'd had by Bill, the daughter who'd been adopted by "swell people" in Virginia City. Or maybe it was Cheyenne, maybe Abilene. Finally her time ran out. It was August 1, 1903.

Her body was taken to the local undertaker's parlor, where photographers snapped her picture, and souvenir seekers clipped off locks of Calamity's hair. Finally an old friend stepped in and put a wire screen over her head.

Many who viewed her remains noted that Calamity Jane looked better in death than she had in life. The same, of course, can be said of her legend.

The record says that, a few hours before she died, Jane said, "Bury me next to Wild Bill." Her friends did, interring her twenty feet from his grave. They even changed the date of her death to August 2, 1903, to coincide with the twenty-seventh anniversary of Hickok's death.

Myra Belle Shirley, aka Belle Starr, was killed by a double blast of a shotgun as she rode from Fort Smith back to Younger's Bend. The blast lifted her out of the same sidesaddle, off the same horse, "Venus," that she'd earlier been photographed riding. Who killed her remains a mystery; she may have been shot by a neighbor woman who mistook Belle for someone who'd been fooling around with her husband. Or, Belle really had been fooling around.

In 1971 A. J. Robinson of Topeka, Kansas, claimed that, sometime before her death, his grandmother, Nana Devena, admitted to killing Belle Starr. Mrs. Devena claimed she'd been waiting for a neighbor with whom she'd been feuding. Belle, she said, was an "innocent bystander" who happened along at the wrong time.

Belle Starr was buried in the yard there at Robbers' Roost—Younger's Bend—the last of the Wild West's big-time lady outlaws. She was only forty-one.

Mormon leader Brigham Young outlived many of his wives and even a few of his children. He died on August 29, 1877, leaving seventeen widows, fifty surviving children, numerous grandchildren, and an estate of over one million dollars.

By late 1847, out in Oregon, members of the Cayuse band of Indians had come to believe that missionaries Narcissa and Marcus

Whitman were sorcerers. Perhaps with good reason. Several Indians mysteriously came down with a strange illness. Strange to them, that is. In truth it was just common, although missionary-induced, dysentery. It seems that the Indians had been stealing the mission's vegetables. When asked to stop, they refused. One of the missionaries, William Gray, injected the melons with a laxative. The missionaries knew about the doctored melons and avoided them; the Indians didn't, and that's where the "mysterious" illness began.

Soon a new batch of emigrants brought a new misery, one not so benign: measles. The disease not only hit the Whitman mission, it hit the Cayuse, and nearly half the tribe died. The Cayuse noticed that, while most of the white children survived the disease, their own children did not. The Indians believed it was another example of sorcery, when in truth it was only that whites were more immune to the disease.

On the afternoon of November 29, 1847, three Cayuse appeared at the Whitmans' door, asking to see a doctor. One, a chief called Tiloukaikt, had earlier considered converting to Christianity, but measles had taken three of his children; that morning he'd buried all three.

Inside the home Tiloukaikt and his companions shot, beat, and hacked Marcus Whitman with a pipe-tomahawk. Narcissa's adopted daughter, Catherine Sager, survived, remembering that "Mother was standing looking out at the window, when a [minié] ball came through the broken pane, entering her right shoulder."

> She clapped her hand to the wound . . . and fell backwards. She now forgot everything but the poor, helpless children depending on her, and . . . poured out her soul in prayer for them: "Lord, save these little ones!" It was her repeated cry.

Marcus was not yet dead, so the Cayuse shot him twice. Then he died. Meanwhile, other Indians carried Narcissa out of the house on a settee and killed her, then lashed her dead face with a riding quirt.

Besides the Whitmans, ten other white men and two children—Catherine Sager's two brothers—were killed. Six-year-old Hannah Sager was ill with the measles at the time of the massacre, and soon she died from lack of medical attention. As did mountain man Joe Meek's half-Indian daughter, Helen Mar. Jim Bridger's daughter Mary Ann was also ill at the mission but survived only to die the following spring.

Most of those that the Cayuse did not kill—eight women, five men, and thirty-four children—the Indians gathered up and took to their own camp to use as hostages when a white posse—there were many whites in Oregon by now—came after them.

Some of the whites at the mission managed to get away and reached the Hudson's Bay fort at Walla Walla. They told authorities about the attack, and militia forces pursued the Indians. Hudson's Bay factor Peter Skene Ogden ransomed the captives for shirts, blankets, ammunition, and tobacco worth about five hundred dollars. Eventually five warriors, including Tiloukaikt, turned themselves in so that the rest of their people would not be hunted down. The militia hanged Tiloukaikt, but before he was executed, someone asked him why he had surrendered. "Did not your missionaries teach us that Christ died to save his people? So we die to save *our* people."

When the militia reached the Whitman mission, they found Narcissa's red-gold hair matted with her own blood, her face welted from blows from the quirt. They buried Narcissa and Marcus in the mission cemetery. Later they returned and found that wolves had dug up her body and eaten the flesh of one of her legs. They buried her again, this time deeper.

For a while, once they'd gone to Bolivia, Butch Cassidy and the Sundance Kid tried to go straight. They earned $150 a month each for tending livestock for the Concordia Tin Mine Company. But by 1909 the lure of robbery was too much, and they took to holding up pack trains loaded with gold. Troops from the Bolivian cavalry tracked them down in San Vincente, and soon the boys were boxed in and under fire. By late evening Butch and Sundance were running out of ammunition.

That's when the Sundance Kid was killed in a volley of fire. Butch was left with only one unexploded cartridge in his Colt .45. The soldiers heard a roar of a handgun, and then all was silent. They found Butch, the man who'd been born Robert Leroy Parker, dead with a bullet wound in his right temple. The days of the Wild Bunch were over.

Or were they? Even today there are claims that Butch and the Kid didn't die in a hail of Bolivian army bullets. Robert Leroy Parker's younger sister, Lula, for instance, claimed that the two men killed in South America were impostors, nothing more or less than two "John Does" who pretended to be the infamous Wild Bunch pair. Butch and Sundance, Lula Parker claimed, returned to the United States under assumed names and lived out their lives as peaceful, solid citizens. Butch Cassidy, she said, died in Spokane, Washington, in 1937. And the man known as the Sundance Kid, Henry Longbaugh, finally passed on in Casper, Wyoming, in 1957. Well, maybe.

After being forced to surrender to the U.S. Army in 1877, Chief Joseph and his people were loaded onto a riverboat and sent down the Missouri River toward Fort Abraham Lincoln in the Dakota Territory. They'd been promised that the tribe could return to their home territory, but General Sherman overruled the settlement. The war with the Nez Percé was "one of the most extraordinary Indian wars of which there is any record," Sherman wrote.

Rather than send them home, Sherman ordered Chief Joseph and 337 others into railroad boxcars and took them to the northeast corner of Indian Territory in Oklahoma. It was, the Nez Percé said, their place of exile, Eeikish Pah, which means "the hot place" or "hell."

Many members of the tribe fell sick and died, sixty-eight in the first year alone. They set aside a cemetery for burying infants, and one hundred were laid to rest there. The army allowed some members of the tribe to go home, but not Joseph.

Chief Joseph continued to plead for his people, and in 1879 he went to Washington, where he met with President Rutherford B. Hayes. He spoke before a gathering of congressmen, cabinet members, and businessmen. "I have shaken hands with a great many friends," Joseph said,

> but there are some things I want to know which no one seems able to explain. I cannot understand how the government sends a man out to fight us, as it did General Miles, and then

breaks his word. Such a government has something wrong with it. . . . If the white man wants to live in peace with the Indian he can live in peace. There need be no trouble. Treat all men alike. Give them the same law. Give them all an even chance to live and grow. All men were made by the same Great Spirit Chief. They are all brothers. The earth is the mother of all people, and all people should have equal rights upon it. . . . Let me be a free man—free to travel, free to stop, free to work, free to trade, where I choose, free to choose my own teachers, free to follow the religion of my fathers, free to think and talk and act for myself—and I will obey every law, or submit to the penalty.

Sympathizers praised Joseph, but nothing changed; the government still refused to allow him to go home. The army sent him to the Colville Reservation in northeastern Washington. He died there in 1904, still a captive far from home.

The young Irish girl born Maggie Hall, but who came to be called Molly b'Dam, had been forced into prostitution by her wellborn, ne'er-do-well husband. Divorcing him, she traveled the Wild West and wound up in Murray, Idaho, where she became the proprietor of the town's best-known whorehouse. She lived happily, if uproariously, in Murray from 1884 until 1887.

That's when a stranger arrived in town burning with fever. He rode up to the first saloon he saw, drank a pint of whiskey, and promptly dropped dead. The stranger had smallpox, and by the dozen, townsfolk came down with the disease. Soon the locals were dying right and left. There was no real doctor in town; of course there was no hospital. Everybody was terrified, and no one knew what to do.

In steps Molly b'Dam, who calls a town meeting. "You don't lick anything by running away from it," she tells the crowd. Don't hide your head under your pillow, don't hole up in your cabin, don't think of leaving town. "There's a dozen sick men up there in my part of town," she says, "and me and my girls are doing what we can for them."

Molly and her girls clean out the town's hotels, forcing paying guests to pay up and get out. Then she fills the rooms with the sick.

She and her girls nurse patients until they can barely drag themselves around. Some of Molly's patients die, but most of them survive.

The ordeal, however, takes a toll on Molly. She grows weary and listless. She develops a fever and hacking cough. She loses weight. By November she's bedridden, and the girls who'd helped Molly care for smallpox victims are now taking care of Molly herself. She apparently has consumption—tuberculosis, a disease which at the time is incurable.

The town's so-called better sort of women once scorned Molly b'Dam, but now they keep a twenty-four-hour vigil at her bedside. It does no good, and on January 17, 1888, Molly b'Dam passes away.

News of her death spreads throughout the area, and a friend asks a Catholic priest to give Molly absolution. He refuses, but a Methodist minister arranges for her funeral. The day Molly is laid to rest, the sluice boxes and drills are silent in nearby gold mines, and thousands turn out to say good-bye.

Molly had realized she was dying and asked that her grave carry a simple wooden marker. That's the way it is:

Sacred
To
The Memory Of
Maggie Hall
Molly-B-Dam
Died
At Murray
Jan. 17, 1888
Age 35 Years

Every August, Murray, Idaho, holds a two-day celebration in honor of their favorite onetime prostitute, and crowds join in singing her song, "The Legend of Molly b'Dam."

For twenty-five years Buffalo Bill rode through the United States and Europe with his Wild West Show, the script virtually unchanging: a Pony Express race, the Deadwood stage attacked by bandits, Custer's Last Stand, and Indians attacking covered wagons. The

pièce de résistance always featured Buffalo Bill himself, a grand figure with snow-white hair and beard riding around the ring on a snow-
white horse.

But Bill wasn't a well man. Toward the end, before each show, a
member of the crew had to help the old man onto his horse. "Ready,
Colonel?" an assistant would ask, and Buffalo Bill Cody would sit tall
in the saddle as he rode into the arena, tipping his white Stetson to
the cheering crowd.

At 12:05 in the afternoon on January 10, 1917, just three weeks
before his seventy-first birthday, Western Union ordered all of its
lines cleared. The world was at war then, but the news went out immediately that the old scout had passed. He always said that he
wanted to be buried on Cedar Mountain, Wyoming, but in the end
it wasn't to be. He was laid to rest atop Mount Lookout high above
Denver.

The blizzards of 1886 and '87 dealt such crushing blows to so
many members of the once-powerful Cheyenne Club that the organization defaulted on its bonds, finally selling out for twenty cents
on the dollar.

In Shoshone (her native tribe), Sacagawea's name means "Boat
Pusher." In Hidatsa (the tribe that kidnapped her), her name is
spelled Tsakawaia and means "Bird Woman." By whatever name,
whatever spelling, she guided and saved the lives of the Lewis and
Clark expedition from North Dakota to the Pacific Ocean and
back.

Her fate after the expedition is uncertain. Her husband, Charbonneau, is known to have traveled the Southwest on fur-hunting
expeditions, and it's likely Sacagawea went along with him. She and
William Clark apparently were reunited on several occasions. After
one, Clark wrote Charbonneau on August 20, 1806, paying tribute
to Sacagawea. He referred to her as "your woman who accompanied
you that long dangerous and fatiguing route to the Pacific Ocian [*sic*]
and back," adding that she "deserved a greater reward for her attention and services on that rout [*sic*] than we had in our power to
give her."

Sometime during 1812 Charbonneau reportedly traveled up the Missouri River and settled at one of fur-trader Manuel Lisa's posts. In the fall of that year Sacagawea reportedly gave birth to a girl whom they named Lisette. After Lisette's birth Sacagawea's health deteriorated.

There are at least three versions of her death. One has her dying of fever in 1812 in St. Louis. Another says that she lived among the Shoshone on the Wind River Reservation of Wyoming. The December 20, 1812, entry in the journal of an employee at Fort Lisa, near Omaha, Nebraska, says that "this evening the Wife of Charbonneau a Snake Squaw, died of a putrid fever she was a good and the best Women [*sic*] in the fort abt 25 years she left a fine infant girl." Her grave supposedly was near Fort Lisa, in what is now northern South Dakota. That report may be the true one. Another, however, has her living to the age of about one hundred. A 1924 Bureau of Indian Affairs (BIA) study claims Sacagawea was also known as Porivo and that she died on April 9, 1884, and was buried in the white cemetery at Fort Washakie, Wyoming. It's unlikely we'll ever know her true fate.

"All in all," Charlie Goodnight wrote, "my years on the trail were the happiest I ever lived."

There were many hardships and dangers, of course, that called on all a man had of endurance and bravery; but when all went well there was no other life so pleasant. Most of the time we were solitary adventurers in a great land as fresh and new as a spring morning, and we were free and full of the zest of darers.

The Charlie Goodnight–Oliver Loving team didn't last long, but it took death to end their relationship. One day in June 1867 Oliver and a cowboy named "One-Armed" Bill Wilson were out on the range, headed for Santa Fe to work a deal selling beef to the army, when a Comanche war party attacked them. For three days Loving and Wilson managed to hold off the Indians, and finally they escaped, hungry, thirsty, and Loving with an arrow wound in the arm. In those prepenicillin days that was as good as a death warrant.

Oliver's arm turned gangrenous and he died September 25, 1867, at Fort Sumner, New Mexico.

But not before he made Charlie Goodnight promise him something. Oliver Loving wanted to be buried in Texas. To keep his word Goodnight had his cowboys make a coffin from oil drums, then, in much like a scene in author Larry MacMurtry's *Lonesome Dove*, Charlie lowered Loving's steel casket into a wagon bed and towed it home along the trail the two men had blazed together. For the rest of his life Charlie kept Loving's photograph on the wall of his home.

After Oliver Loving died, Charlie Goodnight and his wife, Mary Ann, moved back to the Texas Panhandle, a large spread in the Palo Duro Canyon. It was there they built the Old Home Ranch. Several years later Charlie went into partnership with a wealthy Irishman named John Adair, and they operated under the JA brand. By 1884 the JA tallied one hundred thousand head of cattle and two thousand square miles of grazing land. Both the size of the ranch and the herd grew.

Charlie didn't have much luck with partners, and Adair died in 1885. Goodnight struck a deal with Adair's widow and dissolved the partnership, taking about 140,000 acres of land and a fifth of the herd. He called the new outfit the Quitage Ranch, and it was here that he took to crossbreeding cattle and buffalo.

Finally, in 1890, Charlie sold the Quitage Ranch and returned to the Old Home Ranch. In 1926 Mary Ann Goodnight died, leaving Charlie an aging widower. Three years later he had a heart attack and joined Mary Ann. It was December 12, 1929, and Charlie Goodnight was ninety-three years old.

In 1927 fifty-year-old Charles E. Davis quit work, and devoted the next two years of his life to looking for sites along the route the ill-fated Donner Party took. It's unknown how, but Davis knew where to find hundreds of relics from the party, including the grave of John Snyder (who'd been killed by party leader James Reed in an argument) and those of two other men named Hargrove and Harroran. Davis also recovered the remains of five wagons and dozens of oxen skeletons, even household articles and campfire sites long since cold and buried. The puzzle of who Charles E. Davis was, and how he came to know so well the whereabouts of the Donner Party relics, is as deep as the mystery of the party itself.

In 1918 three members of the Donner Party—Patty Reed (James and Margaret's daughter) and Eliza and Frances Donner (George and Tamsen's daughters)—were present when a memorial was dedicated to the party. Isabella Breen was the last surviving member of the Donner Party. She died in 1935, eighty-nine years after the tragedy.

When news of the big gold strike at Sutter's Mill first broke, all of the workmen at the mill ran off to try their luck panning for gold. Even James Marshall quit the job that, if he'd kept at it and managed it properly, could have brought him a fortune in valuable timber. Instead, Marshall joined thousands of others in wandering the Sierras searching for his own "big strike." He never found it. Others grew wealthy, but James Marshall never did. He was a "notional" man, they said, unable to cope with what he called "grabbers." He survived by doing odd jobs. In 1872 the California legislature rewarded Jim Marshall a pension of two hundred dollars a month, but after a few years they let it lapse. Before he died, Marshall got to selling his autograph for money. He died in 1885, in virtual poverty and embittered that the strike that had started it all not only didn't carry his name—the designation "Sutter's Mill" sticks to it—but he benefited little from it. "Yankeedom," the embittered would-be gold miner said, got more than $600,000,000, adding, "Myself Individually $000,000,000."

John Sutter was almost as bad off. As news of the strike at Sutter's Mill broke, all of John's workers left him to try their luck. As gold seekers streamed in, they destroyed his fields and squatted on his land. Finally Sutter went bankrupt, and traveled to Washington, D.C., hoping to be reimbursed for his losses. Senator Daniel W. Vorhees tried to push though Congress a bill that would pay Sutter $50,000, but it was an election year and the lawmakers adjourned for the year without taking action. Vorhees went to Sutter's hotel room to tell him the matter would be taken up next year, but it was too late. John Sutter was already dead. He was seventy-seven.

After the Gunfight at the O.K. Corral, Wyatt Earp wandered the West for a while, becoming, some said, quite a figure in the sporting world with a reputation of "gameness, squareness, and fair play." Out in California he met Josephine "Josie" Sarah Marcus, onetime mistress of anti-Earp Cochise County sheriff John Behan; when her romance with Behan cooled down, another heated up with Wyatt. In 1882 the daughter of a Jewish pioneer merchant from San Francisco became Mrs. Wyatt Earp, either the second or third Mrs. Earp, depending on whether Wyatt and Mattie Blaylock were legally married.

With Josie he went back to wandering, visiting Dodge City a couple of times and spending a year at the Coeur d'Alene gold rush speculating with his brother James in mining claims and saloons. More saloons and more wandering, and in 1890 Wyatt and Josie moved to San Diego to raise Thoroughbred horses. He refereed an 1896 prizefight featuring Bob Fitzsimmons and Tom Sharkey, but Fitzsimmons fans claimed he threw the match to Sharkey.

In 1927 Wyatt got together with western historian Stuart N. Lake, and over a two-year period he told Lake all about his life so far. It wouldn't be published until 1931, and Lake admitted he "put words into Wyatt's mouth because of the inarticulateness and monosyllabic way he had of talking." Talking about the good old bad old days apparently stirred up memories for Wyatt, so he returned to Tombstone for a visit. It wasn't the same. The O.K. Corral was just about gone. Venders sold Coca-Cola and hot dogs at Boothill. Wyatt was just another old tourist.

In Los Angeles Wyatt tried to interest cowboy star William S. Hart in making a movie about his life. Hart turned him down; however, Wyatt Earp did work as a technical consultant on a couple of movies, including some with Tom Mix.

On January 13, 1929, Wyatt Earp died. He was eighty-one.

After Wyatt's death Josie complained about errors in the books and movies about Earp, so in the late thirties she wrote her own: *I Married Wyatt Earp*. Not surprisingly, it covers up many details the aging Josie wanted to leave out. She lived until 1944.

For many years only Josie's family and a few close friends knew the location of Wyatt's grave. But on the night of July 6–7, 1957, possibly because of the popularity of the new *Wyatt Earp* television show, someone stole the 560-pound headstone from the plot where Wyatt was buried at the Hills of Eternity Memorial Park at Colma, California. Overnight the secret grave became packed with tourists.

Big Nose Kate and Doc Holliday were taking in a fiesta in Tucson, Arizona, during the early fall of 1881, when Morgan Earp found them and said Doc was needed back in Tombstone. Moving to Tombstone, Kate settled in Doc's rooms at C. S. Fly's Boarding House.

The next morning she awoke before Doc and heard the news that Ike Clanton was looking for her man. Kate told Doc, and he replied, "If God will let me live long enough, he will see me." It was October 26, 1881.

Doc leaves the room and Kate waits. That afternoon, about two o'clock, she hears shooting nearby and goes to a window, where she and Mrs. Fly watch the gunfight at the O.K. Corral. Actually, it doesn't occur at the O.K. Corral itself, but in a vacant lot behind it. But who wants to change "history"?

During the fight a bullet breaks two windowpanes over Kate's head, but she never ducks or stops watching. Thirty seconds of small-arms fire and a shot or two from Doc Holliday's scattergun. It's Doc and the Earp brothers—Wyatt and Morgan and Virgil—against the Clanton gang—Ike and Billy Clanton, Tom and Frank McLaury, Billy Claiborne, and Wes Fuller. When the ball is over, three men are dead in the dust—Frank and Tom McLaury, and Billy Clanton—and three members of the Earp party are wounded—Morgan with a shoulder wound, Virgil with a shot to the leg, and Doc Holliday, grazed on the left hip. Doc and Wyatt are hauled into jail, but for only a short time. A judge acquits them of murder.

Big Nose Kate returns to Globe, where she continues to manage a hotel. She stays there for several years and, in 1887, receives word that Doc is dying. He'd wandered to Deadwood, Dakota Territory, then on to Leadville, Colorado; now, Kate wants to be with him. His tuberculosis far advanced, Doc enters a sanatorium in Glenwood Springs, Colorado. Six months later Doc Holliday dies, on November 8, 1887.

In 1888, her main man now gone to that great poker game in the sky, Kate marries blacksmith George Cummings. It's not a happy marriage and a year later it's dissolved. When asked why she divorced him, Kate replies, "Cummings was a drinker." Not that Doc drank, you understand.

Kate's story is far from over, however. She keeps Cummings's name, and goes under "Mary K. Cummings." Later in life Big Nose Kate applies to the Arizona Pioneer's Home for the aged, to live out her final days. However, she runs into a problem: The home requires United States citizenship, but that's something Kate has never gotten around to obtaining, since she'd been born in Europe. No problem. Kate changes history just a bit, and the records *now* list her birth as occurring, not in Hungary, but in Davenport, Iowa. In 1931 she enters the home and sets about seeing that everything works just as she wants. She occasionally writes the Arizona governor to complain about the home—her roommates, the food, even her need for a new pair of glasses.

After historian Stuart Lake publishes his biography of Wyatt Earp, Kate realizes her own story might be profitable. The woman who never had much to say about her past now wants to tell it all. For a profit, of course.

Besides, Lake's portrayal of her infuriates Kate. In 1935 she contacts a University of Arizona graduate student, A. W. Bork, and that fall he interviews her. Together they plan to write her memoirs. Unfortunately, it doesn't happen. Not during her lifetime.

Big Nose Kate dies in the Arizona Pioneer's Home. It's November 2, 1940, one week before her ninetieth birthday.

Her onetime inamorato, Doc Holliday, was much younger when he died, only thirty-five years old. We don't know what Kate said in her final minutes. But Doc Holliday? His last words were "I'll be damned."

A severe drought burned the Great Plains in the summer of 1894, and that fall's harvest was the worst in memory for much of the West. By 1895 a lot of the optimism that had carried settlers west had disappeared. Farmers sold horses for twenty-five cents and hay for two dollars a ton. The fall of 1895 brought a near-record harvest, but in a wicked twist the way nature sometimes turns, they saw the surpluses drive prices down. That's when they gave up, and many made the return trip east.

William Allen White was a newspaper editor in Kansas who rose to national prominence as the "Sage of Emporia." That year he wrote about some of the emigrants to the East:

> There came through Emporia yesterday, two old-fashioned mover wagons headed east. The stock in the caravan would invoice four horses, very poor and tired, one mule, more disheartened than the horses, and one sad-eyed dog that had probably been compelled to rustle his own precarious living for many a long and weary day. A few farm implements of the simpler sort were loaded in the two wagons. All the rest of the impedimenta had been left upon the battlefield, and these poor stragglers, defeated but not conquered, were fleeing to another field, to try the fight again. . . . They had such high hopes when they went out there; they are so desolate now. . . . They have come out of the wilderness, back to the land of promise.

Epilogue:
Personal Thoughts on the Wild West

My heroes have always been cowboys. *

Song title, Sharon Vaughn

Most other boys of my era wanted to be either Gene Autry or Roy Rogers. I wanted to be Lash LaRue. Lash—his real name was Albert, so you can see why he used a *nom de movie*—cracked a bullwhip in nearly two dozen low-budget forties and fifties western movies, those Saturday morning flicks perhaps best referred to simply as "cowboy movies." Movies where both the good and bad guys got through an entire popcorn-crunching epic without losing their hats. In the end the good guy always won—battle, horse, and, well, aw shucks, the girl. Cowboy movies were a world where men were men and women only got to look on or were the victims, gazing lovingly up into the hero's eyes, a hero who may have been more interested in his horse than in the heroine. A waste of both women and plotline, but when you're a six-year-old boy, you don't think these adult thoughts. Later, anyway, many cowboy movies were written by women.

In his movies Lash LaRue won by being tougher than anybody else. No songs for him, just whip, crack, and the bad guy was history. Truly, he was badder than the bad guys in *Law of the Lash, Mark of the Lash, King of the Lash,* and other such shoot-'em-ups. Pass the popcorn, brother.

*Copyright, Universal Polygram, Inc.

350

Epilogue

When Saturday-morning cowboy movies became a thing of the past, so did Lash LaRue's career. He fell on hard times, and in 1966 police arrested him for vagrancy in Miami; he had only thirty-five cents in his pocket, an amount that could have gotten him into one of his own movies back in the 1940s but which in the nineties wouldn't buy him a cup of fancy coffee. He later became an evangelist and worked with alcoholics in St. Petersburg, Florida.

Lash LaRue was the classic cowboy who wore boots and Stetson hats and bolo ties until he died in 1998 at the age of seventy-nine, the victim of cigarettes and emphysema. My hero gone, an era ended.

Being city born, the closest I ever came to riding a horse as a child was when an itinerant photographer came around and I had my picture taken sitting atop a woebegone pony. Only later did I learn to ride and, for one short, glorious spring and summer, worked at a local riding stable, taking novices for short walks and canters on horses long past their prime. In truth neither the novices nor the horses needed me to follow the trails, but it was a helluva good time.

The Wild West was more than a time and place. It was a mystery and myth that bewitches us even today when we know that the tales are tall and the facts are few. It remains one of the wildest places in the world and perhaps reminds us all of our childhood as Roy Rogers and Lash LaRue wannabes, of times when playing cowboys-and-Indians was nothing more serious than the child's play we imagined it to be. No political correctness asked, none found.

The "Wild" West today is a place of four-wheel-drive vehicles and cellular phones, "fusion" cuisine and designer jeans. A place where self-styled militia groups gather to "protect" their own rights, while attacking those of others. The American West, after all, is that place in our society where modern-day mountain people share the world with others who, for example, purchase England's London Bridge for $2,460,000, tear it down stone by stone, reerect it near the Mojave Mountains, dredge a channel in the sand to turn a small point of land into an island in a man-made lake, and then build a faux "Merry Olde England" in the middle of the island. Obviously the American West is not an easy thing to understand.

The Wild West never was as wild as dime novels and Hollywood made it. It was, however, decidedly interesting. It was made up of perhaps four separate groups of individuals: (1) mountain men (and a few mountain women) and cowboys (and a few cowgirls), who were the "characters" of fact and fiction—they rode hard, worked hard, played hard, and built and tore down at the same time. (2) miners who believed there was "gold in them, thar hills" and went out to get it. (3) homesteaders, the settlers who would not take no for an answer; they pushed westward into the grasslands of the Great Plains, over the mountains of the Continental Divide, and to the shores of the Pacific Ocean. and (4) Native Americans who, it can be argued, took the land from someone else only to have it taken from them.

Mountain men died out when civilization hemmed them in, and cowboys converted into Jeep-riding herdsmen. Miners panned, dug, and blasted out paydirt until they were supplanted by conglomerates. The settlers including thousands of Mormans, literally walked across the country, stopping off to homestead valleys and prairies, lived in sod houses, and quietly grew sugar beets and corn, wheat, and hops, the same crops they'd grown back in the old country, wherever that was.

Those who remained in the East read dime novels about bad guys Billy the Kid and Doc Holliday, Butch and Sundance, but it was the farmers and storekeepers who became the true Wild West; now, they, too, are an endangered species.

Meanwhile, in the late twentieth century, Native Americans finally found a way to return the favor of the white man's perfidy: They surrounded him with gambling casinos.

In the end we realize that the West is our national myth, and we wouldn't have it any other way.

Gene Autry, Roy Rogers, Lash LaRue, and Clayton Moore—"The Lone Ranger" of 1950s television—they're all gone now, to that Great Range in the Sky. All my heroes are cowboys, and many of them are gone. But, no more heroes? Not so. The Wild West itself is a hero of gigantic proportions.

Bibliography

MODERN WORKS

Abbott, E. C. "Teddy Blue," and Helena Huntington Smith, eds. *We Pointed Them North: Recollections of a Cowpuncher.* New York: Farrar & Rinehart, 1939; reprint, Norman: University of Oklahoma Press, 1955.

Adams, Andy. *Log of a Cowboy.* New York: Farrar & Rinehart, 1939; reprint, New York: MJF Books, 1995.

Aikman, Duncan, ed. *Calamity Jane and the Lady Wildcats: With "Life and Adventures of Calamity Jane by Herself."* Lincoln: University of Nebraska Press, 1927; reprint, 1987.

Ambrose, Stephen E. *Undaunted Courage: Meriwether Lewis, Thomas Jefferson, and the Opening of the American West.* New York: Simon & Schuster, 1996.

Atherton, Lewis. *The Cattle Kings.* Bloomington: Indiana University Press, 1961.

Bakeless, John, ed. *The Journals of Lewis and Clark.* New York: Penguin, 1964.

Barness, Larry. *Heads, Hides and Horns.* Fort Worth: Texas Christian University Press, 1985.

Billington, Ray Allen. *Westward Expansion: A History of the American Frontier,* 4th ed. New York: Macmillan, 1974.

Blevins, Winfred. *Dictionary of the American West.* New York: Facts on File, 1993.

Blum, Ida. *Nauvoo.* Salt Lake City: The Church of Jesus Christ of Latter-day Saints, n.d.

Boatner, Mark M., III. *Encyclopedia of the American Revolution.* New York: David McKay, 1966; reprint, Mechanicsburg, PA: Stackpole Books, 1994.

———. *The Civil War Dictionary.* New York: David McKay, 1959; reprint, Vintage Books, 1986.

Boorstin, Daniel J. *The Americans: The National Experience.* New York: Random House, 1965.

Branch, Edward Douglas. *The Cowboy and His Interpreters.* New York: Appleton, 1926.

Brash, Sarah, ed. *The American Story: Settling the West.* Alexandria, VA: Time-Life Books, 1996.

Brindenbaugh, Carl. *Jamestown: 1544–1699.* New York: Oxford University Press, 1980.

Brown, Dee. *The American West.* New York: Simon & Schuster, 1994.

———. *The Gentle Tamers: Women of the Old West.* New York: Bantam, 1974.

———. *Wondrous Times on the Frontier.* Little Rock: August House, 1991.

Burns, James MacGregor. *The Vineyard of Liberty.* New York: Alfred A. Knopf, 1981.

Camp, Charles L., ed. *George C. Yount and His Chronicles of the West.* Denver: Old West Publishing, 1966.

Cappon, Lester J., ed. *Iron Works at Tuball.* Charlottesville: University of Virginia, 1945.

Carnes, Mark C., gen. ed. *Past Imperfect: History According to the Movies.* New York: Henry Holt, 1965.

Clay, John. *My Life on the Range.* Chicago: privately printed, c. 1924, reprint, Norman: University of Oklahoma Press, 1962.

Colbert, David, ed. *Eyewitness to the American West.* New York: Viking, 1998.

Cook, James Henry. *Longhorn Cowboy.* New York: G. P. Putnam's Sons, 1942.

Crutchfield, James A. *The Santa Fe Trail.* Plano, TX: Republic of Texas Press, 1966.

Cunningham, Eugene. *Triggernometry: A Gallery of Gunfighters.* Caldwell, ID: Caxton, 1934; reprint, New York: Barnes & Noble Books, 1996.

Cusic, Don. *Cowboys and the Wild West: An A–Z Guide from the Chisholm Trail to the Silver Screen.* New York: Facts on File, 1994.

Custer, Elizabeth B. *Following the Guidon.* Norman: University of Oklahoma Press, 1966.

Dary, David. *Entrepreneurs of the Old West.* New York: Alfred A. Knopf, 1986; reprint, Lawrence: University Press of Kansas, 1997.

————. *Red Blood and Black Ink: Journalism in the Old West.* New York: Alfred A. Knopf, 1998; reprint, Lawrence: University Press of Kansas, 1999.

De Voto, Bernard. *Across the Wide Missouri.* New York: American Heritage Books, 1947; reprint, New York: Houghton Mifflin, 1975.

Dexter, Pete. *Deadwood.* New York: Random House, 1986; reprint, New York: Penguin, 1987.

Dodge, Grenville M. *Biographical Sketch of James Bridger, Mountaineer.* New York: Unz, 1905; reprinted as *James Bridger: A Historical Narrative.* Salt Lake City: Shepard Books, 1925.

Drury, Clifford Merrill, and Mina J. Carson, eds. *On to Oregon: The Diaries of Myra Walker and Myra Eels.* Glendale, CA: A. H. Clark, 1963; reprinted as *First White Women Over the Rockies,* vol. 2; reprint, Lincoln: Bison Books, 1998.

Dunbar, Seymour. *A History of Travel in America.* Indianapolis: Bobbs-Merrill, 1915.

Durham, Philip, and Everett L. Jones. *The Negro Cowboys.* Lincoln: University of Nebraska Press, 1965.

Dykstra, Robert R. *The Cattle Towns.* New York: Alfred A. Knopf, 1968; reprint, Lincoln: Bison Books, 1966.

Eaves, Charles D., and C. A. Hutchinson. *Post City, Texas.* Austin: Texas State Historical Association, 1952.

Erdoes, Richard. *Saloons of the Old West.* New York: Alfred A. Knopf, 1979.

Flexner, Doris. *The Optimist's Guide to History.* New York: Avon, 1995.

Flexner, Stuart, and Doris Flexner. *The Pessimist's Guide to History.* New York: Avon, 1992.

Foner, Eric. *Reconstruction: America's Unfinished Revolution: 1863–1877.* New York: Harper & Row, 1988.

Forbis, William H., ed. *The Old West: The Cowboys.* New York: Time-Life Books, 1973.

Foster-Harris, William. *The Look of the Old West.* New York: Bonanza Books, 1960.

Gallutso, John, ed. *Wild West: An Insight Guide.* Boston: Houghton Mifflin, 1997.

Garraty, John A., ed. *1001 Things Everyone Should Know About American History.* New York: Doubleday, 1989.

Gibson, Charles. *Spain in America.* New York: Harper & Row, 1966.

Gras, N. S. B., and Henrietta M. Larson. *Casebook in American Business History.* New York: F. S. Crofts, 1939.

Greene, Jack P. *Pursuits of Happiness: The Social Development of Early Modern British Colonies and the Formation of American Culture.* Chapel Hill: University of North Carolina Press, 1988.

Grinnel, George Bird. *The Fighting Cheyennes,* 2nd ed. Norman: University of Oklahoma Press, 1956.

Hagedorn, Hermann. *Roosevelt in the Badlands.* Boston: Houghton Mifflin, 1921.

Haley, J. Evetts. *Charlie Goodnight: Cowman and Plainsman.* Norman: University of Oklahoma Press, 1967.

Hanighen, Frank C. *Santa Anna.* New York: Coward-McCann, 1934.

Hardin, John Wesley. *The Life of John Wesley Hardin.* Norman: University of Oklahoma Press, 1961.

Hasting, Frank S. *A Ranchman's Recollections: An Autobiography.* Chicago: Breeder's Gazette, 1921.

Heatwole, Henry. *A Guide to Shenandoah National Park.* Luray, Virginia: National History Association, 1978; reprinted 1997.

Holliday, J. S. *The World Rushed In: The California Gold Rush Experience.* New York: Simon & Schuster, 1981; reprint, New York: Touchstone, 1983.

Hollon, W. Eugene. *Frontier Violence: Another Look.* New York: Oxford University Press, 1979.

Holloway, Mark. *Heaven on Earth: Utopian Communities in America, 1680–1880.* London: Turnstile Press, 1951; reprint, New York: Dover Publications, 1966.

Hyslop, Stephen G., ed. *War for the Plains.* New York: Time-Life Books, 1994.

Iowa Mormon Trails. Creston, Ia.: Iowa Mormon Trails Association, 1996.

Jackson, Donald Dale. *Gold Dust.* New York: Alfred A. Knopf, 1980; reprint, Lincoln: University of Nebraska Press, 1982.

Jacobsen, Joel. *Such Men as Billy the Kid: The Lincoln County War Reconsidered.* Lincoln: University of Nebraska Press, 1994.

Johnson, Paul. *A History of the American People.* New York: Harper Collins, 1998.

Jones, Oakah L. *Santa Anna.* New York: Twayne, 1968.

Josephy, Alvin M., Jr. *The Indian Heritage of America.* New York: Alfred A. Knopf, 1968; reprint, New York: Bantam Books, 1969.

————. *The Nez Percé Indians and the Opening of the Northwest.* New Haven: Yale University Press, 1965.

Katz, William Loren. *The Black West.* New York: Touchstone, 1996.

Keegan, John. *Fields of Battle: The Wars for North America.* London: Hodder & Stoughton as *Warpaths: Travels of a Military Historian in North America,* 1995; reprint, New York: Vintage, 1997.

Kuttner, Paul. *History's Trickiest Questions.* New York: Dawnwood Press, 1991; reprint, Buffalo: Owl Books, 1992.

Lang, Lincoln A. *Ranching With Roosevelt.* Boston: J. B. Lippincott, 1926.

Lavender, David. *The Great West.* New York: American Heritage, 1965 as *The American Heritage of the Great West;* revised, Boston: Houghton Mifflin, 1987.

Lederer, John, and William P. Cummings, ed. *The Discoveries of John Lederer.* Charlottesville: University of Virginia Press, 1958.

Lee, Laura. *The Name's Familiar.* Gretna, LA: Pelican Publishing, 1999.

Lens, Sydney. *Radicalism in America.* New York: Crowell, 1969.

Lewis, Jon E. *The Mammoth Book of the West: The Making of the American West.* New York: Carroll and Graf, 1996.

Loomis, Noel M., and Abraham Nasatir. *Pedro Vial and the Roads to Santa Fe.* Norman: University of Oklahoma Press, 1967.

McCrum, Robert, William Cran, and Robert MacNeil. *The Story of English.* New York: Viking, 1986.

McFeely, William S. *Grant: A Biography.* New York: W. W. Norton, 1981.

McHugh, Tom. *The Time of the Buffalo.* New York: Alfred A. Knopf, 1972.

McLoughlin, Denis. *Wild and Wooly: An Encyclopedia of the Old West.* New York: Writers House, 1975; reprint, New York: Barnes & Noble Books, 1996.

Malone, Dumas. *Jefferson the President: First Term, 1801–1805.* Boston: Little, Brown, 1970.

Martin, Charles L. *Sketch of Sam Bass, the Bandit.* Norman: University of Oklahoma Press, 1956.

Maverick, Mary A., and Rena Maverick Green. *Memoirs of Mary A.*

Maverick. San Antonio: Alamo, 1921; reprint, Lincoln: University of Nebraska Press, 1989.

Metz, Leon Claire. *The Shooters.* New York: Mangan Books, 1976; reprint, New York: Berkley Books, 1996.

Miller, Benjamin F., and Claire Brackman Keane. *Encyclopedia and Dictionary of Medicine and Nursing.* Philadelphia: W. B. Saunders, 1972.

Miller, Joseph. *Arizona: The Last Frontier.* New York: Hastings House, 1956.

Miller, Nyle H. *Kansas: A Pictorial History.* Topeka: Kansas State Historical Society, 1961.

Millet, Alan R., and Peter Maslowski. *For the Common Defense: A Military History of the United States.* New York: The Free Press, 1984.

Morison, Samuel Eliot. *The Oxford History of the American People.* New York: Oxford University Press, 1965.

Morton, Richard L. *Colonial Virginia.* Chapel Hill: University of North Carolina Press, 1960.

———, ed. *Hugh Jones: The Present State of Virginia.* Chapel Hill: University of North Carolina Press, 1960.

Moulton, Candy. *Everyday Life in the Wild West: From 1840–1900.* Cincinnati: Writer's Digest Books, 1999.

Myers, John. *Pirate, Pawnee, and Mountain Man: The Saga of Hugh Glass.* Boston: Little, Brown, 1963; reprinted as *The Saga of Hugh Glass: Pirate, Pawnee, and Mountain Man:* Lincoln: Bison Books, 1976.

Niles, Judith. *Native American History.* New York: Ballantine Books, 1959; revised and reprinted, New York: Vintage Books, 1988.

Nye, Edgar Wilson. *Bill Nye's Western Humor.* Lincoln: University of Nebraska Press, 1968.

O'Connor, Richard. *Wild Bill Hickok.* New York: Konecky & Konecky, 1959.

Oxford Universal Dictionary. Oxford: Oxford University Press, 1953; revised 1955.

Richmond, Robert W., and Robert W. Mardock, eds. *A Nation Moving West: Readings in the History of the American Frontier.* Lincoln: Bison Books, 1966.

Richetts, Norma Baldwin. *Mormons and the Discovery of Gold,* 4th ed. Mesa, AZ: Odyssey Press, 1966.

Rittenhouse, Jack D. *A Guide Book to Highway 66.* Los Angeles: Rittenhouse, 1946; reprint, Albuquerque: University of New Mexico, 1989.

Rosa, Joseph G. *The Gunfighter: Man or Myth?* Norman: University of Oklahoma Press, 1999.

———. *Wild Bill Hickok: The Man and His Myth.* Kansas City: University Press of Kansas, 1996.

Rouse, Parke, Jr. *The English Heritage in America.* New York: Hastings House, 1966.

———. *The Great Wagon Road.* Richmond: Dietz Press, 1995.

Royce, Sarah. *A Frontier Lady: Recollections of the Gold Rush and Early California.* New Haven: Yale University Press, 1932; reprint, Lincoln: Bison Books, 1977.

Ruth, Kent. *Landmarks of the West.* Lincoln: University of Nebraska Press; reprint, Lincoln: Bison Books, 1986.

Schlesinger, Arthur M., Jr., ed. *The Almanac of American History.* New York: Brompton Books, 1993.

Schlissel, Lillian. *Women's Diaries of the Westward Journey.* New York: Schocken Books, 1982; revised and reprinted, 1992.

Schlissel, Lillian. Byrd Gibbens, and Elizabeth Hampsten. *Far from Home: Families of the Westward Movement.* New York: Schocken Books, 1989.

Seagraves, Anne. *Soiled Doves: Prostitution in the Early West.* Hayden, ID: Wesanne Publications, 1994.

Seidman, Laurence I. *Once in the Saddle: The Cowboy's Frontier, 1866–1896.* New York: Alfred A. Knopf, 1973; reprint, New York: Facts on File, 1994.

Shenkman, Richard. *I Love Paul Revere, Whether He Rode or Not.* New York: HarperCollins, 1991.

———. *Legends, Lies, and Cherished Myths of American History.* New York: Morrow, 1988.

Shenkman, Richard. and Kurt Reiger. *One-Night Stands with American History.* New York: Morrow, 1980.

Simmons, Marc. *New Mexico: An Interpretive History.* New York: W. W. Norton, 1977; reprint, Albuquerque: University of New Mexico Press, 1988.

Slatta, Richard W. *Cowboys of the Americas.* New Haven: Yale University Press, 1990.

Smith, Helena Huntington. *The War on Powder River: The History of an Insurrection.* New York: McGraw-Hill, 1966; reprint, Lincoln: University of Nebraska Press, 1967.

Stevenson, Elizabeth. *Figures in a Western Landscape: Men and Women of the Northern Rockies.* Baltimore: Johns Hopkins University Press, 1994.

Tindall, George Brian, and David F. Shi. *America: A Narrative History,* 4th ed. New York: W. W. Norton, 1996.

Turner, Martha Anne. *The Yellow Rose of Texas.* El Paso: Southwestern Studies Monograph, University of Texas Press, 1971.

Utley, Robert M. *A Life Wild and Perilous: Mountain Men and the Paths to the Pacific.* New York: Henry Holt, 1997; reprint, Buffalo: Owl Books, 1998.

———. *Frontiersmen in Blue: The United States Army and the Indians: 1848–1865.* New York: Macmillan, 1965.

———. *The Indian Frontier of the American West: 1846–1890.* Albuquerque: University of New Mexico Press, 1984.

Walker, Dale L. *Legends and Lies: Great Mysteries of the American West.* New York: Forge Books, 1997.

Wallis, Michael. *Route 66: The Mother Road.* New York: St. Martin's, 199.

Ward, Geoffrey. *The West: An Illustrated History.* New York: Little, Brown, 1996.

Ward, Robert DeCourcy. *The Climates of the United States.* Boston: Ginn & Company, 1925.

Webb, Walter Prescott. *The Great Plains.* New York: Ginn & Company, 1931; reprint, New York: Grossett & Dunlap, 1957.

Weisberger, Bernard A. *The American Heritage History of the American People.* New York: American Heritage Books, 1970.

Welch, James, and Paul Stekler. *Killing Custer: The Battle of the Little Big Horn and the Fate of the Plains Indians.* New York: W. W. Norton, 1994; reprint, New York: Penguin, 1995.

Wert, Jeffrey D. *Custer: The Controversial Life of George Armstrong Custer.* New York: Simon & Schuster, 1996.

West, Elliot. *The Way West.* Albuquerque: University of New Mexico Press, 1986.

Wheeler, Keith. *The Railroaders.* New York: Time-Life Books, 1973.

Whitcomb, John, and Claire Whitcomb. *Unexpected Anecdotes About American History.* New York: Quill, 1987.

Bibliography

Willison, George F. *Behold Virginia! The Fifth Crown.* New York: Harcourt, Brace, 1951.

Worcester, Don. *The Chisholm Trail: High Road of the Cattle Kingdom.* Omaha: University of Nebraska Press, 1980; reprint, Indian Head Books, 1994.

Wright, Mike. *What They Didn't Teach You About the Civil War.* Novato, CA: Presidio Press, 1996; reprinted 1998.

————.*What They Didn't Teach You About World War II.* Novato, CA: Presidio Press, 1998.

EARLY WORKS

Beadle, J. H. *The Undeveloped West.* Philadelphia: National Publishing Company, 1873.

Custer, Elizabeth. *Tenting on the Plains: Or, General Custer in Kansas and Texas.* New York: Charles L. Webster, 1899.

Dodge, Richard Irving. *Our Wild Indians: Thirty-three Years' Personal Experience Among the Red Men of the Great West.* Hartford: A. D. Worthington, 1886.

Ford, Paul Leicester, ed. *The Writings of Thomas Jefferson.* New York: G. P. Putnam's Sons, 1892–1899.

Greeley, Horace. *An Overland Journey, From New York to San Francisco, In the Summer of 1859.* New York: C. M. Saxton, Baker & Co., 1860.

Leslie, Mrs. Frank. *California: A Pleasure Trip from Gotham to the Golden State.* New York: Frank Leslie, 1877

Lowrie, Walter, and Matthew St. Clair Clarke, eds. *American State Papers: Documents, Legislative and Executive.* Washington, D.C.: U.S. Government Printing Agency, 1832–1861.

Ludlow, Noah M. *Dramatic Life as I Found It.* St. Louis: G. I. Jones & Co., 1880.

Marcy, Captain Randolph B. *The Prairie Traveler.* Washington, D.C.: U.S. War Department, 1859; reprint, New York: Perigee Books, 1994.

Maury, Ann, ed. *Memoirs of a Huguenot Family.* New York: G. P. Putnam's Sons, 1852.

Nelson, Oliver. *The Cowman's Southwest, Being the Reminiscences of Oliver Nelson: Freighter, Camp Cook, Cowboy, Frontiersman in Kansas, Indian Territory, Texas and Oklahoma.* Glendale, CA: Arthur H. Clark Co., 1953.

Pender, Rose. *A Lady's Experience in the Far West in 1883.* London: 1883.

MAGAZINE ARTICLES

Atherton, Lewis. "Cattleman and Cowboy: Fact and Fancy," *Montana, the Magazine of Western History* 11 (October 1961).

Bankes, James. "Wild Bill Hickok," *Wild West* (August 1996).

Barry, Louise, ed. "Albert D. Richardson's Letters on the Pike's Peak Gold Region," *Kansas Historical Quarterly* XII (1943).

Bell, Bob Bose. "Wild Women of the Wild West," *Wild West* (April 1997).

Benenson, Donna Mileti. "Harison's Yellow Rose," *Early American Homes* (April 1994).

Brown, W. L. "Life of an Arkansas Logger," *Arkansas Historical Quarterly* 21 (1962).

"California Gold," *American History* (October 1994).

Dore, Benjamin. "Journal," *California Historical Society* 2, no. 2 (July 1923).

"Dying Miner's Farewell," *American History* (October 1994).

Fleek, Sherman L. "Handcarts Against Fearful Odds," *Wild West* (June 1997).

Gard, Wane. "Retracing the Chisholm Trail," *Southwestern Historical Quarterly* 60 (July 1956).

Hall, Edith Thompson. "The Biography of a Pioneer Nebraska Doctor, John Wesley Thompson," *Nebraska History* 44 (1963).

Harper's New Monthly Magazine (February 1867).

Hatch, Tom. "The Case for David Crockett," *True West* (July 1999).

Hurd, Charles W. "The Fred Harvey System," *California History* 5 (1926).

Kraft, Louis. "After the Washita," *Wild West* (October 1998).

Morrison, John D., ed. "David F. Spain's Diary," *Colorado Magazine* 35, no. 1 (1958.)

Moulton, Candy. "Did Davy Crockett Die Fighting, or Was He Captured and Then Executed at the Alamo?" *Wild West* (February 1999).

Myers, J. Jay. "The Notorious Fight at Sand Creek," *Wild West* (December 1998).

Bibliography

Papinkolas, Helen S. "Life and Labor Among the Immigrants of Brigham Canyon," *Utah History* 33 (1955).

Peterson, Richard H. "James Marshall: California's Gold Discoverer," *Wild West* (December 1997).

Robinson, Olivia. "She Did It Her Way: Doc's Woman," *Colorado Historical Society,* n.d.

Schmitzer, Jeanne Cannella. "The Wheels of War," *American History* (April 1999).

Stewart, George R. "The Prairie Schooner Got Them There," *American Heritage* XII, no. 2 (February 1962).

Stockel, H. Henrietta. "The Arrows That Wounded the West," *Wild West* (October 1997).

"Time Capsule: Where the Rush For Riches Began," *American History* (October 1994).

Traywick, Ben. "Boothill," *Wild West* (October 1997).

Troxel, Kathryn. "Food for the Overland Emigrant," *Oregon Historical Quarterly* (1955).

Wald, Lilian D. "Medical Inspection of Public Schools," *Annals of the American Academy of Political and Social Science* 24 (January–June 1905).

Westermeier, Clifford P. "Cowboy Capers," in *Annals of Wyoming* 22 (July 1950).

NEWSPAPERS

Bismarck (North Dakota) Tribune, July 6, 1876.

Carbon County (Wyoming) Journal, July 27, 1889.

Cheyenne (Wyoming) Daily Leader, June 20, 1876.

Cheyenne (Wyoming) Democratic Leader, April 14 and September 27, 1884.

Chicago (Illinois) Tribune, October 12, 1867; September 29, 1999; June 28, 1999.

Denver (Colorado) Times, January 24, 1891.

Frank Leslie's Illustrated Newspaper, August 20, 1864; August 16, 1873.

Galveston (Texas) News, August 16, 1866.

Laramie (Wyoming Territory) Boomerang, February 28, 1887.

Leavenworth (Kansas) Daily Commercial, 1869.

Nauvoo (Illinois) Times and Seasons, July 1, 1844.

New York (New York) Times, September 10, 1872.
Sacramento (California) Union, September 19, 1879.
St. Louis (Missouri) Republican, December 21, 1847.
San Francisco (California) Alta California, July 14, 1851.
San Francisco (California) Star, April 1, 1848.
Terre Haute (Indiana) Express, 1851.
Topeka (Kansas) Commonwealth, October 17, 1872.
Wichita (Kansas) Eagle, September 14, 1876.

UNPUBLISHED MATERIAL

Allen, R. M., to Governor William Stanley, February 16, 1902; Gov.
   Stanley Correspondence, box 1, folder 10, Kansas State Historical
   Society Archives.
Garrison, Webb. "The Legend of the Yellow Rose," author's collec-
   tion.
Gross, Charles F., to J. B. Edwards, August 23, 1922, in Manuscripts
   Division, Kansas State Historical Society.
Minute Book of the Abilene, Kansas, City Council, 1871, in Kansas
   State Historical Society.

Index

Index

Index